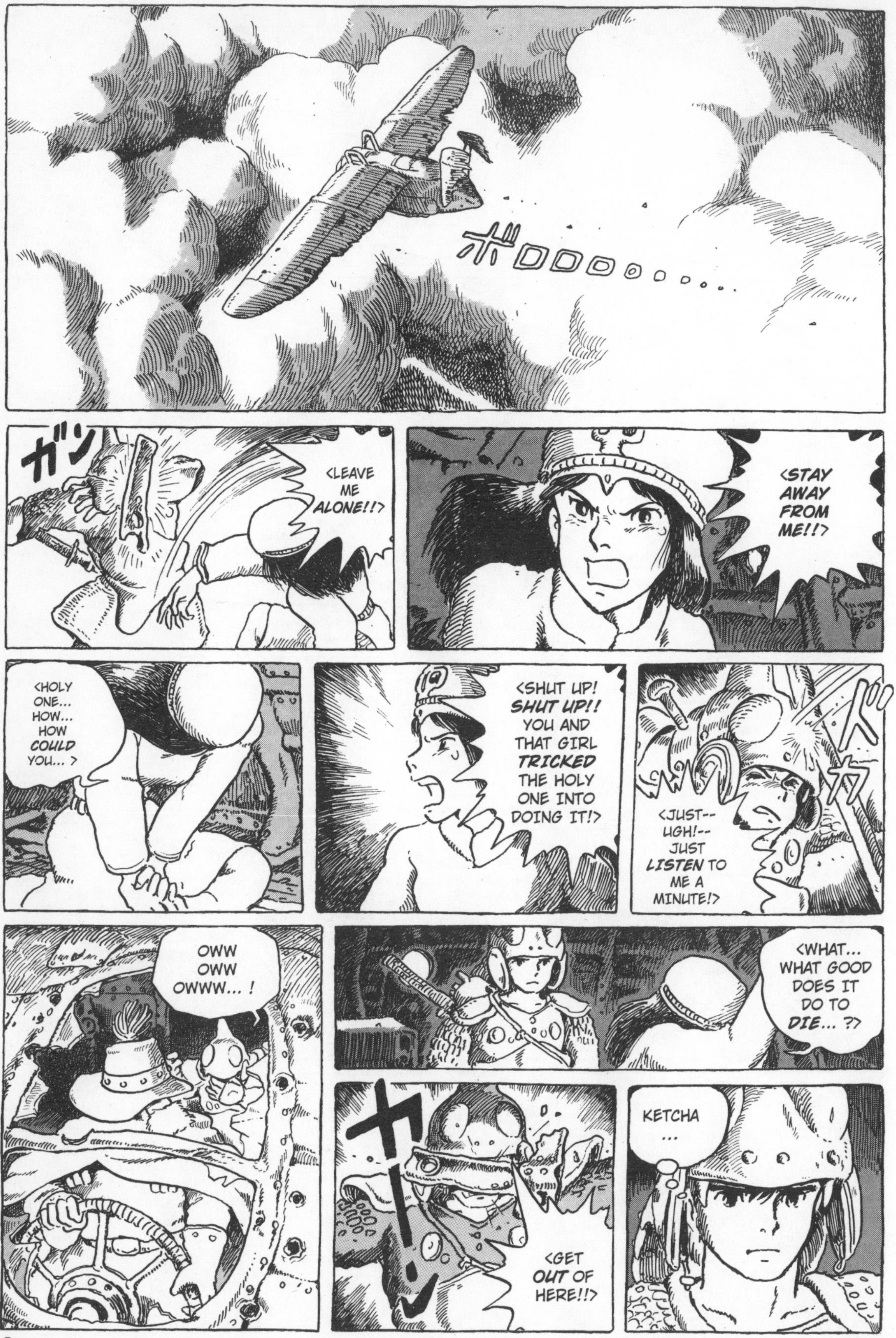
ボDOOOooooo....
<STAY AWAY FROM ME!!>
ガン
<LEAVE ME ALONE!!>
ドカ
<JUST-- UGH!-- JUST LISTEN TO ME A MINUTE!>
<SHUT UP! SHUT UP!! YOU AND THAT GIRL TRICKED THE HOLY ONE INTO DOING IT!>
<HOLY ONE... HOW... HOW COULD YOU... >
<WHAT... WHAT GOOD DOES IT DO TO DIE... ?>
KETCHA ...
ヤ
<GET OUT OF HERE!!>
OWW OWW OWWW... !

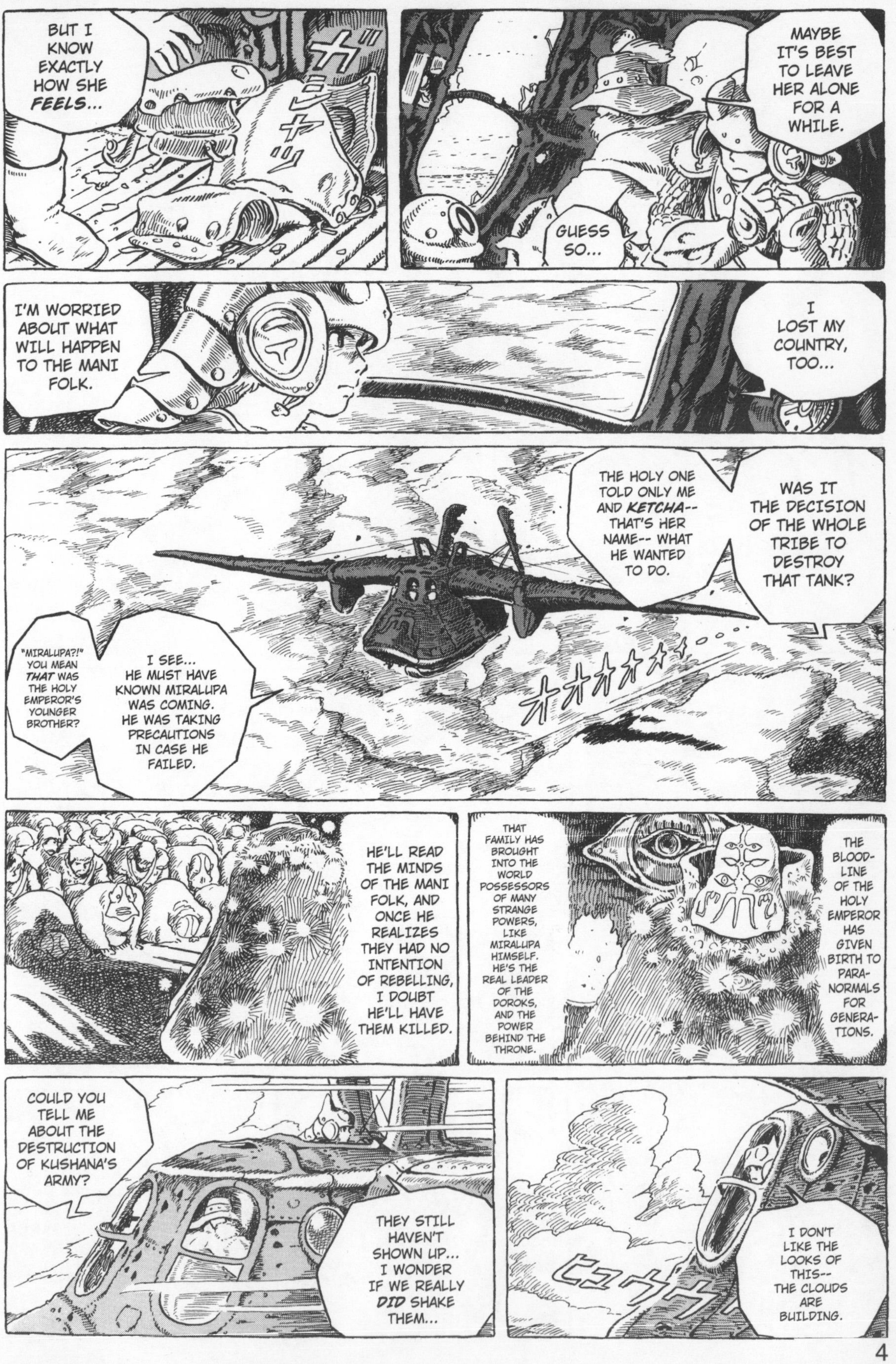

MAYBE IT'S BEST TO LEAVE HER ALONE FOR A WHILE.
GUESS SO...
BUT I KNOW EXACTLY HOW SHE **FEELS**...
I LOST MY COUNTRY, TOO...
I'M WORRIED ABOUT WHAT WILL HAPPEN TO THE MANI FOLK.
WAS IT THE DECISION OF THE WHOLE TRIBE TO DESTROY THAT TANK?
THE HOLY ONE TOLD ONLY ME AND **KETCHA**-- THAT'S HER NAME-- WHAT HE WANTED TO DO.
I SEE... HE MUST HAVE KNOWN MIRALUPA WAS COMING. HE WAS TAKING PRECAUTIONS IN CASE HE FAILED.
"MIRALUPA?!" YOU MEAN **THAT** WAS THE HOLY EMPEROR'S YOUNGER BROTHER?
THE BLOOD-LINE OF THE HOLY EMPEROR HAS GIVEN BIRTH TO PARA-NORMALS FOR GENERA-TIONS.
THAT FAMILY HAS BROUGHT INTO THE WORLD POSSESSORS OF MANY STRANGE POWERS, LIKE MIRALUPA HIMSELF. HE'S THE REAL LEADER OF THE DOROKS, AND THE POWER BEHIND THE THRONE.
HE'LL READ THE MINDS OF THE MANI FOLK, AND ONCE HE REALIZES THEY HAD NO INTENTION OF REBELLING, I DOUBT HE'LL HAVE THEM KILLED.
I DON'T LIKE THE LOOKS OF THIS-- THE CLOUDS ARE BUILDING.
COULD YOU TELL ME ABOUT THE DESTRUCTION OF KUSHANA'S ARMY?
THEY STILL HAVEN'T SHOWN UP... I WONDER IF WE REALLY **DID** SHAKE THEM...

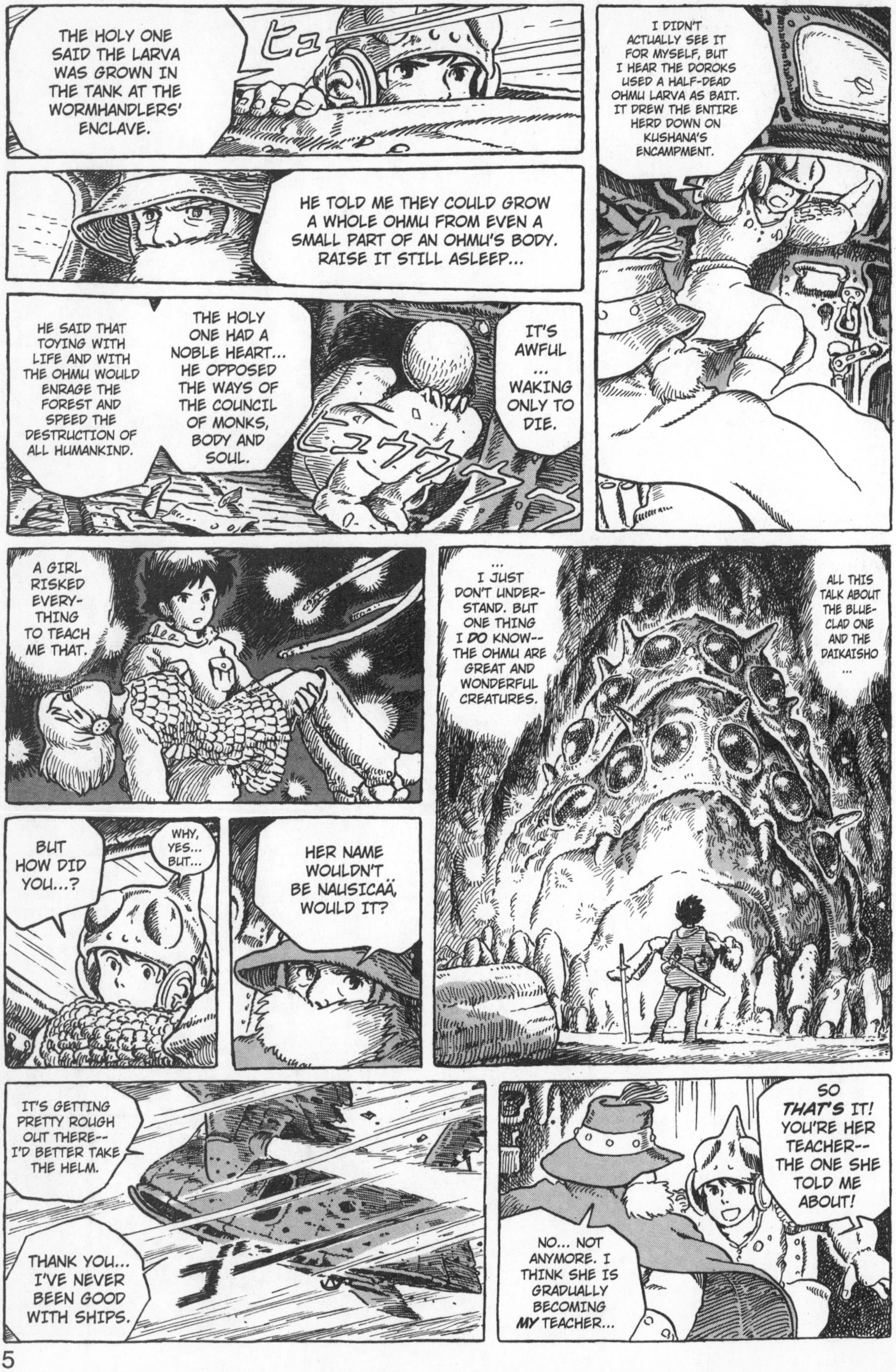
I DIDN'T ACTUALLY SEE IT FOR MYSELF, BUT I HEAR THE DOROKS USED A HALF-DEAD OHMU LARVA AS BAIT. IT DREW THE ENTIRE HERD DOWN ON KUSHANA'S ENCAMPMENT.
ヒュ
THE HOLY ONE SAID THE LARVA WAS GROWN IN THE TANK AT THE WORMHANDLERS' ENCLAVE.
HE TOLD ME THEY COULD GROW A WHOLE OHMU FROM EVEN A SMALL PART OF AN OHMU'S BODY. RAISE IT STILL ASLEEP...
IT'S AWFUL ... WAKING ONLY TO DIE.
ヒュウウ
THE HOLY ONE HAD A NOBLE HEART... HE OPPOSED THE WAYS OF THE COUNCIL OF MONKS, BODY AND SOUL.
HE SAID THAT TOYING WITH LIFE AND WITH THE OHMU WOULD ENRAGE THE FOREST AND SPEED THE DESTRUCTION OF ALL HUMANKIND.
ALL THIS TALK ABOUT THE BLUE-CLAD ONE AND THE DAIKAISHO ...
... I JUST DON'T UNDERSTAND. BUT ONE THING I **DO** KNOW-- THE OHMU ARE GREAT AND WONDERFUL CREATURES.
A GIRL RISKED EVERYTHING TO TEACH ME THAT.
HER NAME WOULDN'T BE NAUSICAÄ, WOULD IT?
WHY, YES... BUT...
BUT HOW DID YOU...?
SO ***THAT'S*** IT! YOU'RE HER TEACHER-- THE ONE SHE TOLD ME ABOUT!
NO... NOT ANYMORE. I THINK SHE IS GRADUALLY BECOMING ***MY*** TEACHER...
IT'S GETTING PRETTY ROUGH OUT THERE-- I'D BETTER TAKE THE HELM.
THANK YOU... I'VE NEVER BEEN GOOD WITH SHIPS.

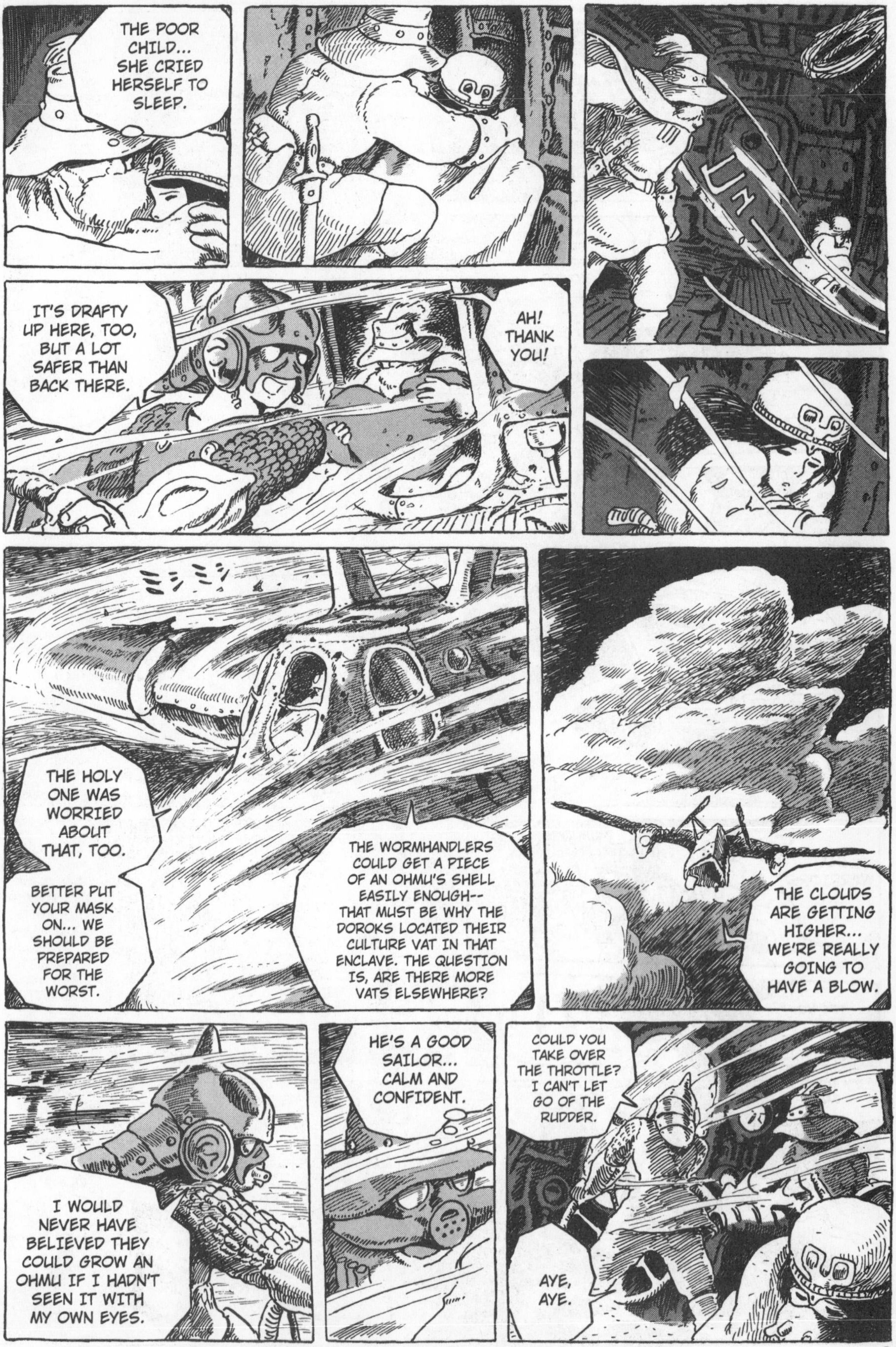
THE POOR CHILD... SHE CRIED HERSELF TO SLEEP.
AH! THANK YOU!
IT'S DRAFTY UP HERE, TOO, BUT A LOT SAFER THAN BACK THERE.
THE CLOUDS ARE GETTING HIGHER... WE'RE REALLY GOING TO HAVE A BLOW.
THE WORMHANDLERS COULD GET A PIECE OF AN OHMU'S SHELL EASILY ENOUGH-- THAT MUST BE WHY THE DOROKS LOCATED THEIR CULTURE VAT IN THAT ENCLAVE. THE QUESTION IS, ARE THERE MORE VATS ELSEWHERE?
THE HOLY ONE WAS WORRIED ABOUT THAT, TOO.
BETTER PUT YOUR MASK ON... WE SHOULD BE PREPARED FOR THE WORST.
COULD YOU TAKE OVER THE THROTTLE? I CAN'T LET GO OF THE RUDDER.
AYE, AYE.
HE'S A GOOD SAILOR... CALM AND CONFIDENT.
I WOULD NEVER HAVE BELIEVED THEY COULD GROW AN OHMU IF I HADN'T SEEN IT WITH MY OWN EYES.

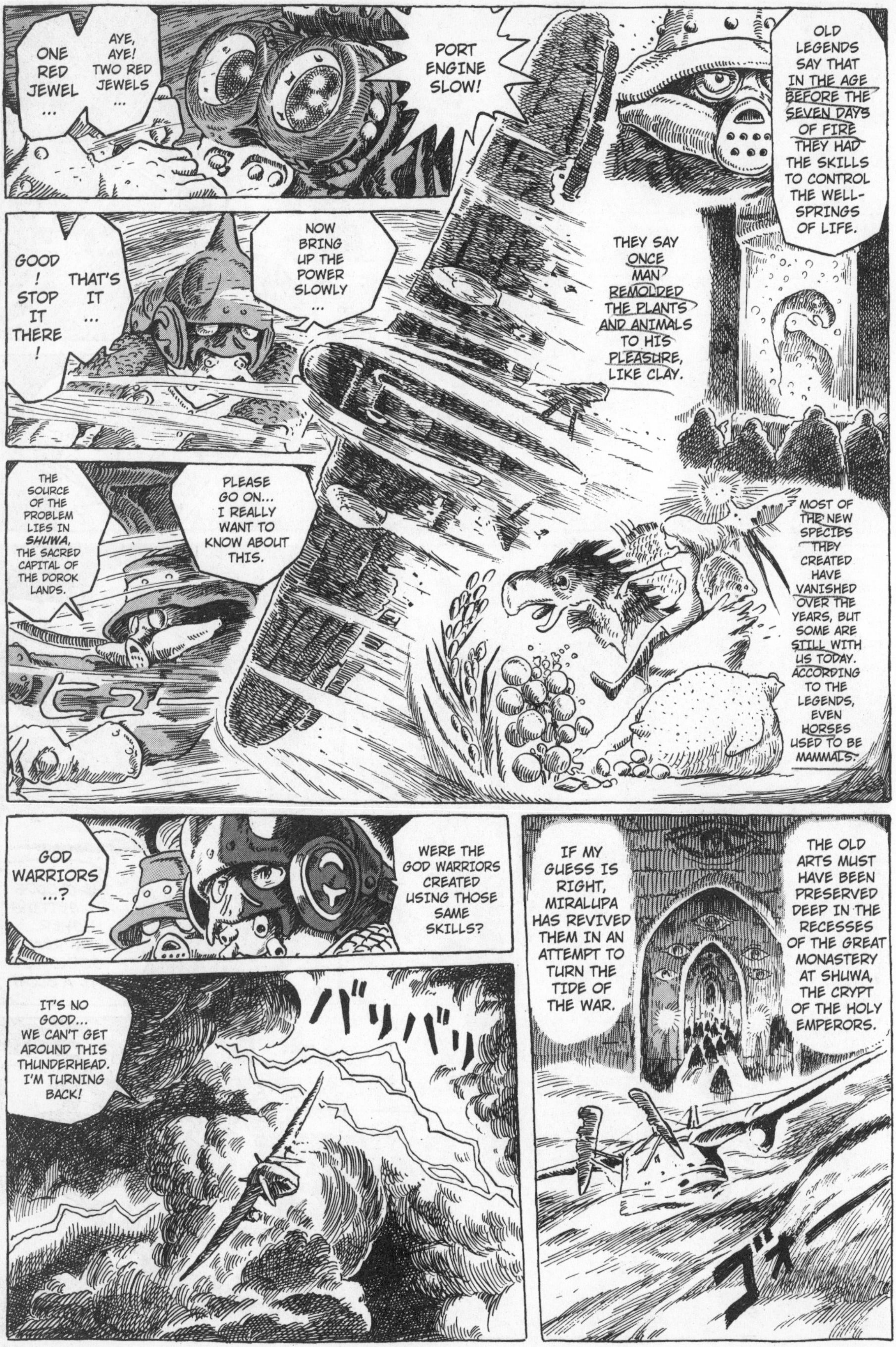
OLD LEGENDS SAY THAT IN THE AGE BEFORE THE SEVEN DAYS OF FIRE THEY HAD THE SKILLS TO CONTROL THE WELL-SPRINGS OF LIFE.
PORT ENGINE SLOW!
AYE, AYE! TWO RED JEWELS ...
ONE RED JEWEL ...
THEY SAY ONCE MAN REMOLDED THE PLANTS AND ANIMALS TO HIS PLEASURE, LIKE CLAY.
NOW BRING UP THE POWER SLOWLY ...
THAT'S IT ...
GOOD! STOP IT THERE!
MOST OF THE NEW SPECIES THEY CREATED HAVE VANISHED OVER THE YEARS, BUT SOME ARE STILL WITH US TODAY. ACCORDING TO THE LEGENDS, EVEN HORSES USED TO BE MAMMALS.
PLEASE GO ON... I REALLY WANT TO KNOW ABOUT THIS.
THE SOURCE OF THE PROBLEM LIES IN SHUWA, THE SACRED CAPITAL OF THE DOROK LANDS.
ヒュー
THE OLD ARTS MUST HAVE BEEN PRESERVED DEEP IN THE RECESSES OF THE GREAT MONASTERY AT SHUWA, THE CRYPT OF THE HOLY EMPERORS.
IF MY GUESS IS RIGHT, MIRALUPA HAS REVIVED THEM IN AN ATTEMPT TO TURN THE TIDE OF THE WAR.
ゴォー
WERE THE GOD WARRIORS CREATED USING THOSE SAME SKILLS?
GOD WARRIORS ...?
IT'S NO GOOD... WE CAN'T GET AROUND THIS THUNDERHEAD. I'M TURNING BACK!
バリバリ

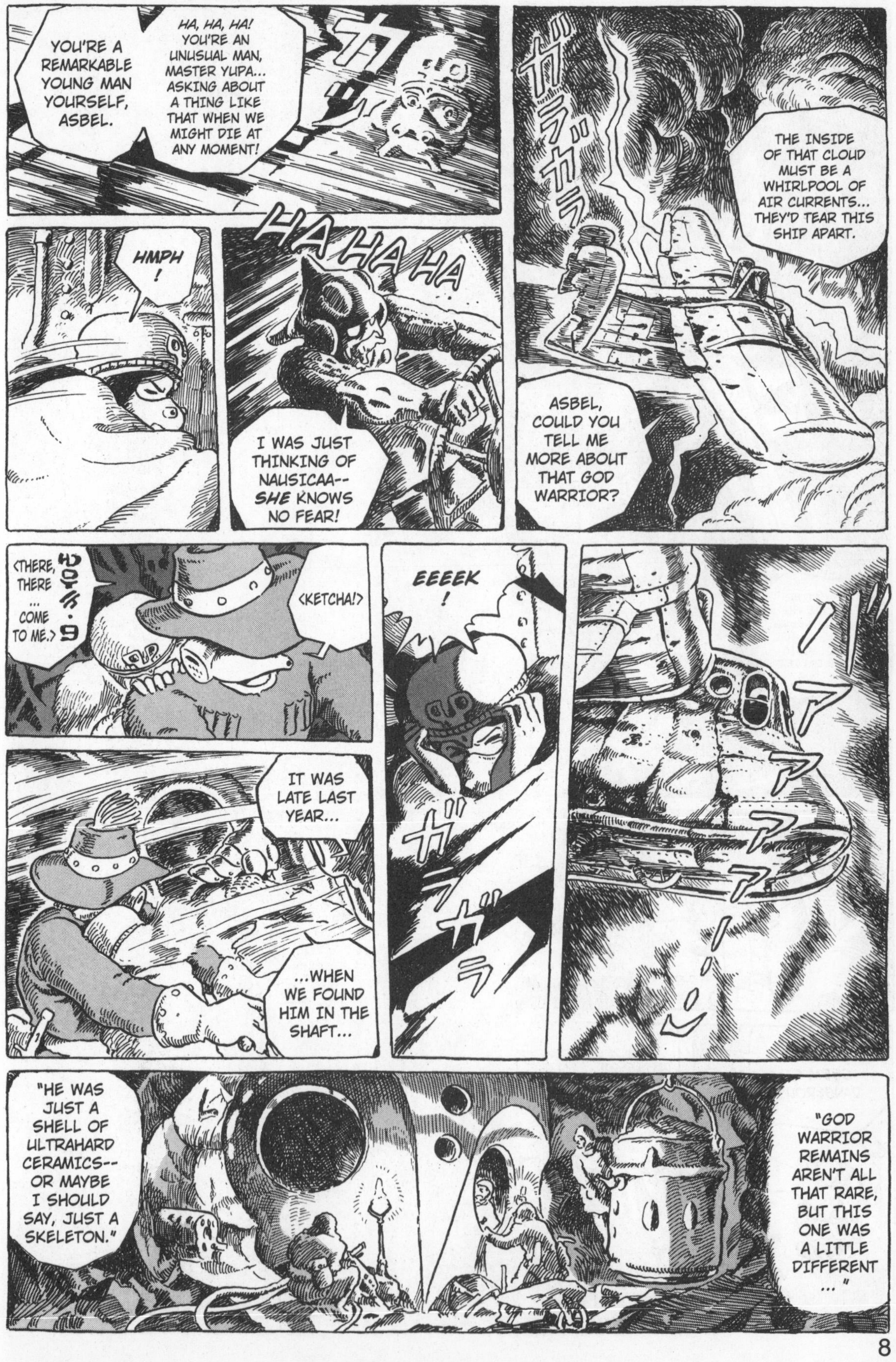
THE INSIDE OF THAT CLOUD MUST BE A WHIRLPOOL OF AIR CURRENTS... THEY'D TEAR THIS SHIP APART.
ASBEL, COULD YOU TELL ME MORE ABOUT THAT GOD WARRIOR?
HA, HA, HA! YOU'RE AN UNUSUAL MAN, MASTER YUPA... ASKING ABOUT A THING LIKE THAT WHEN WE MIGHT DIE AT ANY MOMENT!
YOU'RE A REMARKABLE YOUNG MAN YOURSELF, ASBEL.
HA HA HA HA
I WAS JUST THINKING OF NAUSICAA-- SHE KNOWS NO FEAR!
HMPH!
EEEEK!
<KETCHA!>
<THERE, THERE ... COME TO ME.>
IT WAS LATE LAST YEAR...
...WHEN WE FOUND HIM IN THE SHAFT...
"GOD WARRIOR REMAINS AREN'T ALL THAT RARE, BUT THIS ONE WAS A LITTLE DIFFERENT..."
"HE WAS JUST A SHELL OF ULTRAHARD CERAMICS--OR MAYBE I SHOULD SAY, JUST A SKELETON."

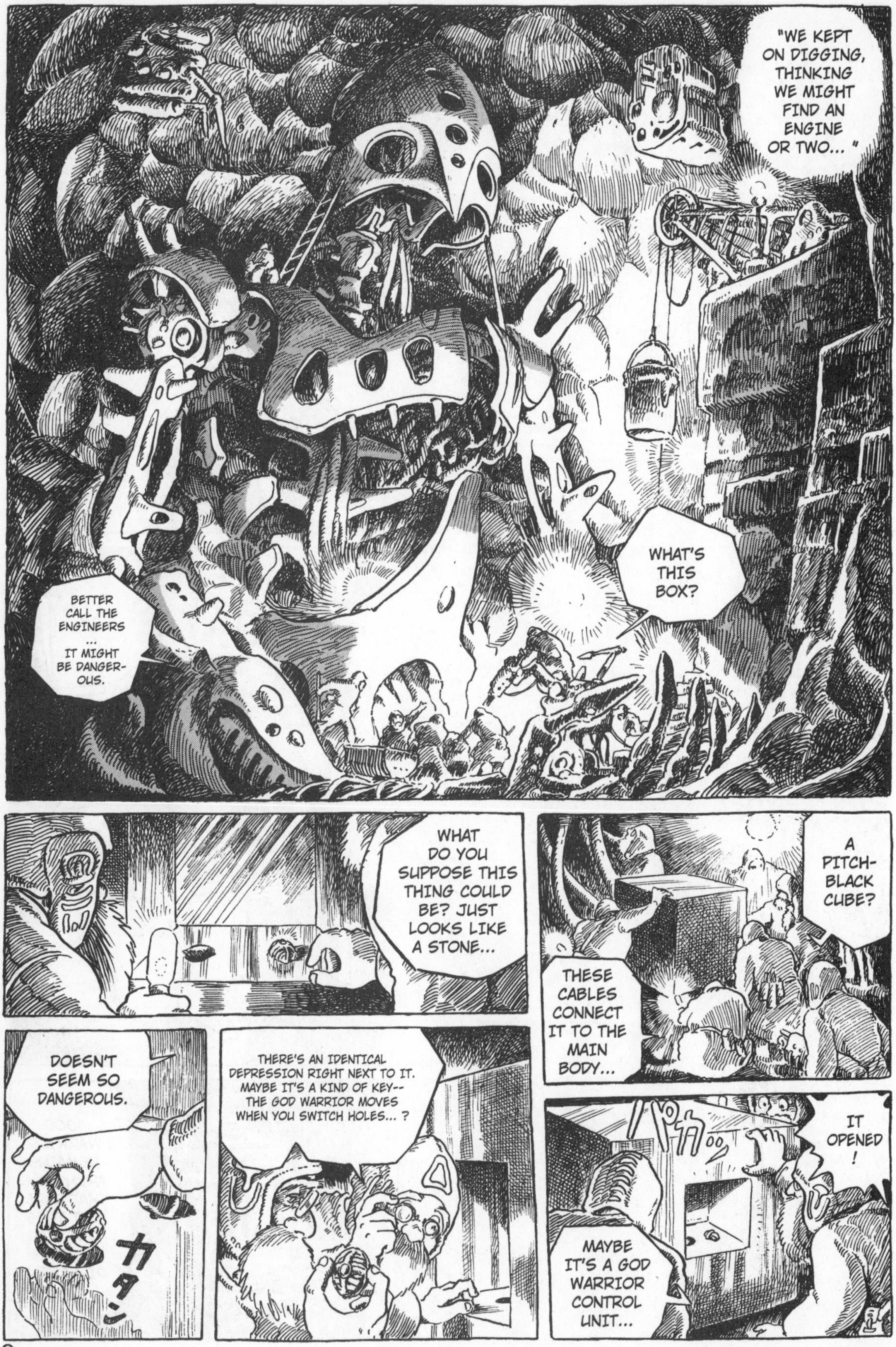

"WE KEPT ON DIGGING, THINKING WE MIGHT FIND AN ENGINE OR TWO..."
WHAT'S THIS BOX?
BETTER CALL THE ENGINEERS ... IT MIGHT BE DANGEROUS.
A PITCH-BLACK CUBE?
THESE CABLES CONNECT IT TO THE MAIN BODY...
WHAT DO YOU SUPPOSE THIS THING COULD BE? JUST LOOKS LIKE A STONE...
IT OPENED!
パカッ
MAYBE IT'S A GOD WARRIOR CONTROL UNIT...
THERE'S AN IDENTICAL DEPRESSION RIGHT NEXT TO IT. MAYBE IT'S A KIND OF KEY-- THE GOD WARRIOR MOVES WHEN YOU SWITCH HOLES... ?
DOESN'T SEEM SO DANGEROUS.
カタン

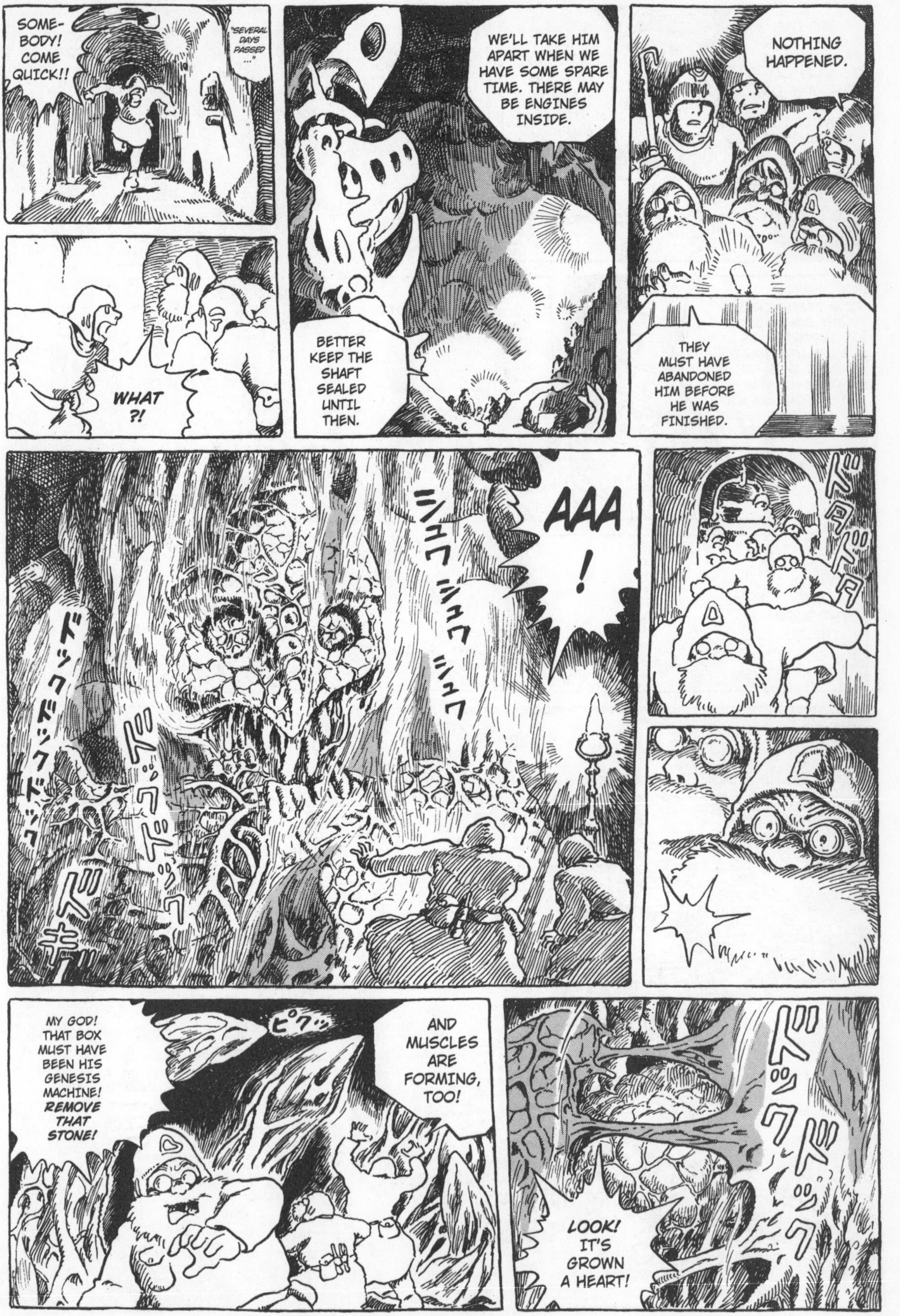

NOTHING HAPPENED.
THEY MUST HAVE ABANDONED HIM BEFORE HE WAS FINISHED.
WE'LL TAKE HIM APART WHEN WE HAVE SOME SPARE TIME. THERE MAY BE ENGINES INSIDE.
BETTER KEEP THE SHAFT SEALED UNTIL THEN.
"SEVERAL DAYS PASSED..."
SOME-BODY! COME QUICK!!
WHAT ?!
ドタドタ
AAA !
シュワ シュワ シュワ シュワ
ドックドックドック
ドックドック
ドキ
ドックドック
LOOK! IT'S GROWN A HEART!
AND MUSCLES ARE FORMING, TOO!
ピク
MY GOD! THAT BOX MUST HAVE BEEN HIS GENESIS MACHINE! *REMOVE THAT STONE!*

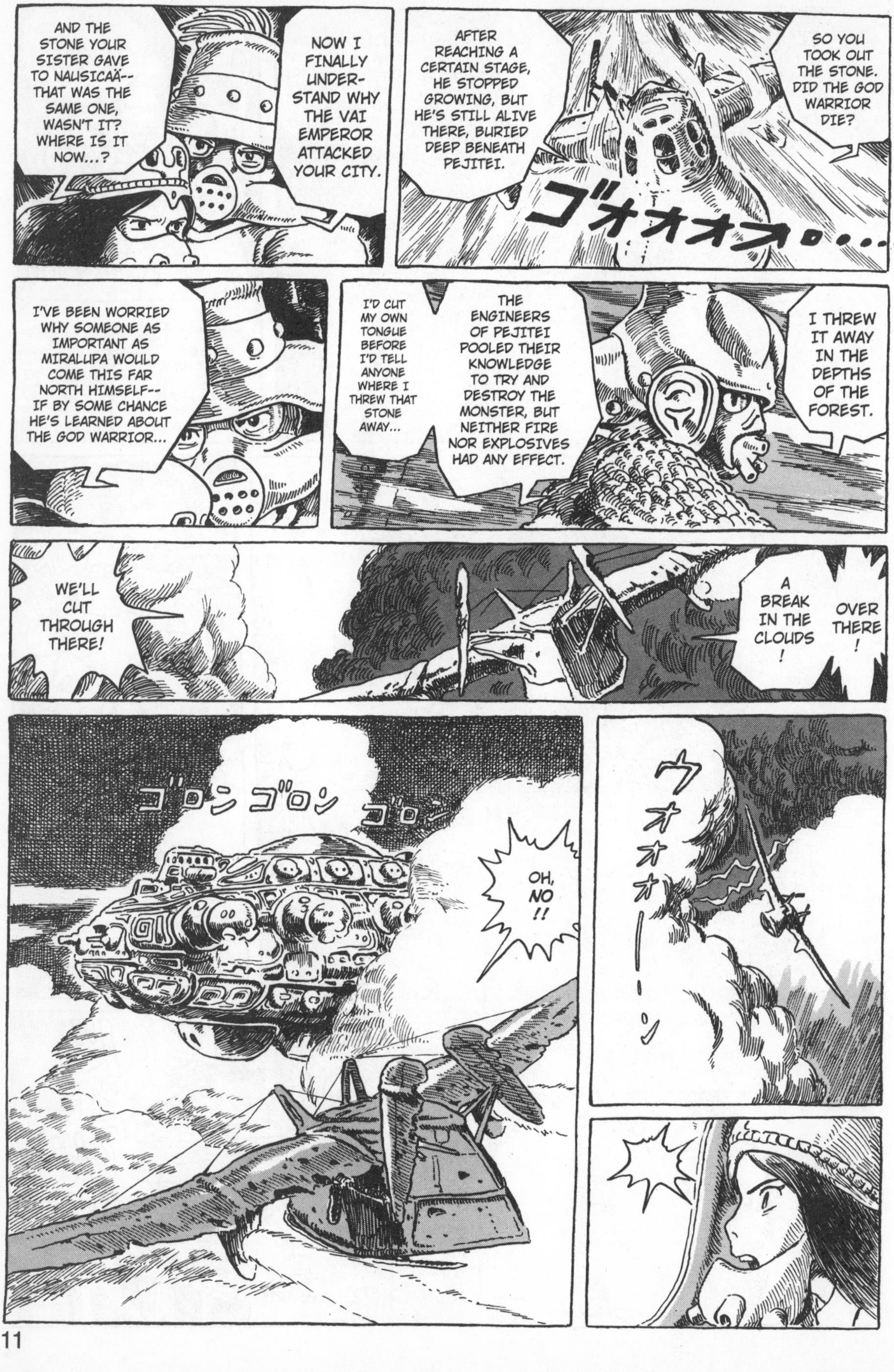
SO YOU TOOK OUT THE STONE. DID THE GOD WARRIOR DIE?
AFTER REACHING A CERTAIN STAGE, HE STOPPED GROWING, BUT HE'S STILL ALIVE THERE, BURIED DEEP BENEATH PEJITEI.
ゴオオオフ・・・
NOW I FINALLY UNDER-STAND WHY THE VAI EMPEROR ATTACKED YOUR CITY.
AND THE STONE YOUR SISTER GAVE TO NAUSICAÄ--THAT WAS THE SAME ONE, WASN'T IT? WHERE IS IT NOW...?
I THREW IT AWAY IN THE DEPTHS OF THE FOREST.
THE ENGINEERS OF PEJITEI POOLED THEIR KNOWLEDGE TO TRY AND DESTROY THE MONSTER, BUT NEITHER FIRE NOR EXPLOSIVES HAD ANY EFFECT.
I'D CUT MY OWN TONGUE BEFORE I'D TELL ANYONE WHERE I THREW THAT STONE AWAY...
I'VE BEEN WORRIED WHY SOMEONE AS IMPORTANT AS MIRALUPA WOULD COME THIS FAR NORTH HIMSELF--IF BY SOME CHANCE HE'S LEARNED ABOUT THE GOD WARRIOR...
OVER THERE!
A BREAK IN THE CLOUDS!
WE'LL CUT THROUGH THERE!
ウオオオーーン
ゴロンゴロン ゴロン
OH, NO!!

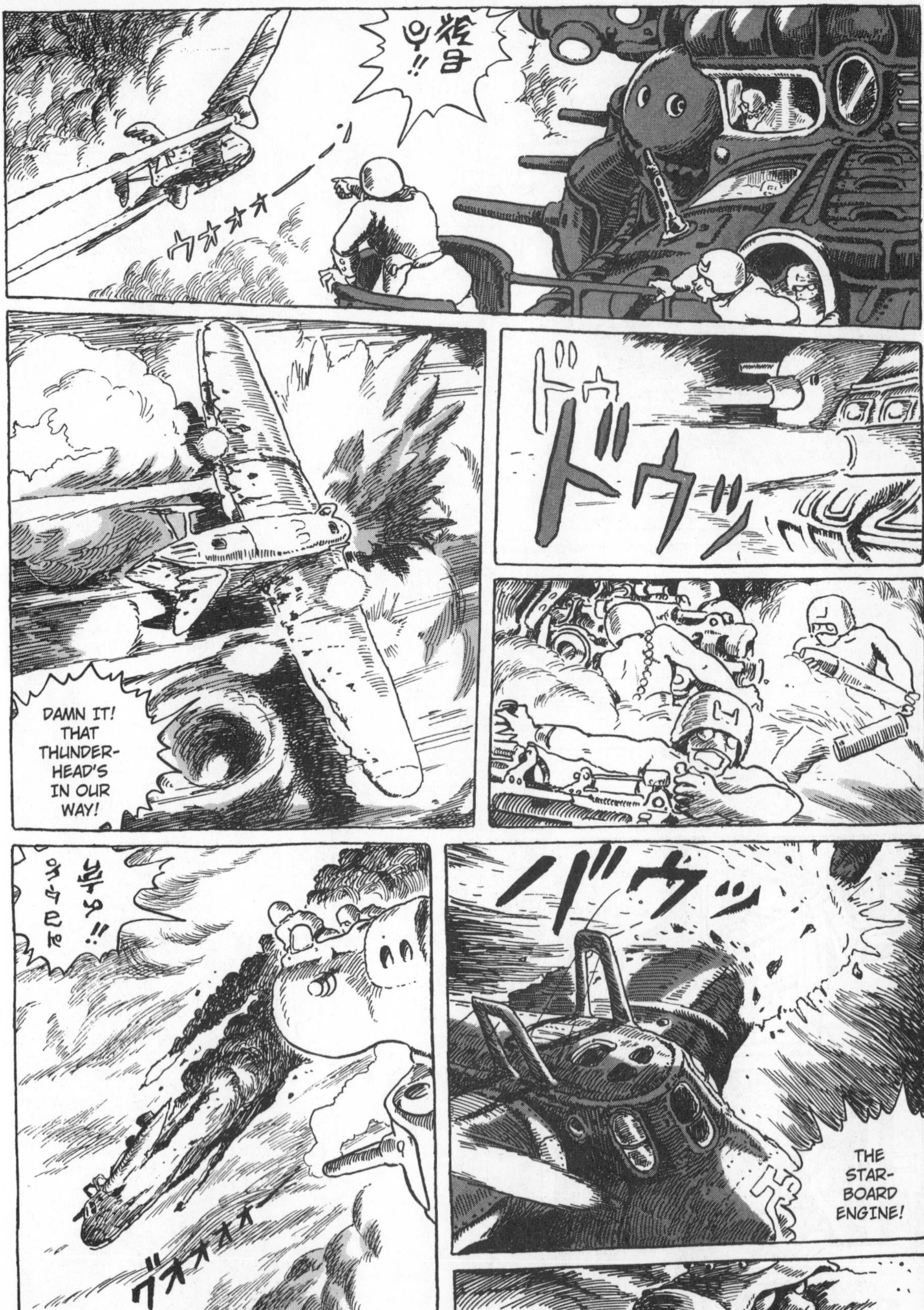
ウォォォー
ドゥ
ドゥッ
DAMN IT! THAT THUNDER-HEAD'S IN OUR WAY!
バウッ
THE STAR-BOARD ENGINE!
ヴォォォー

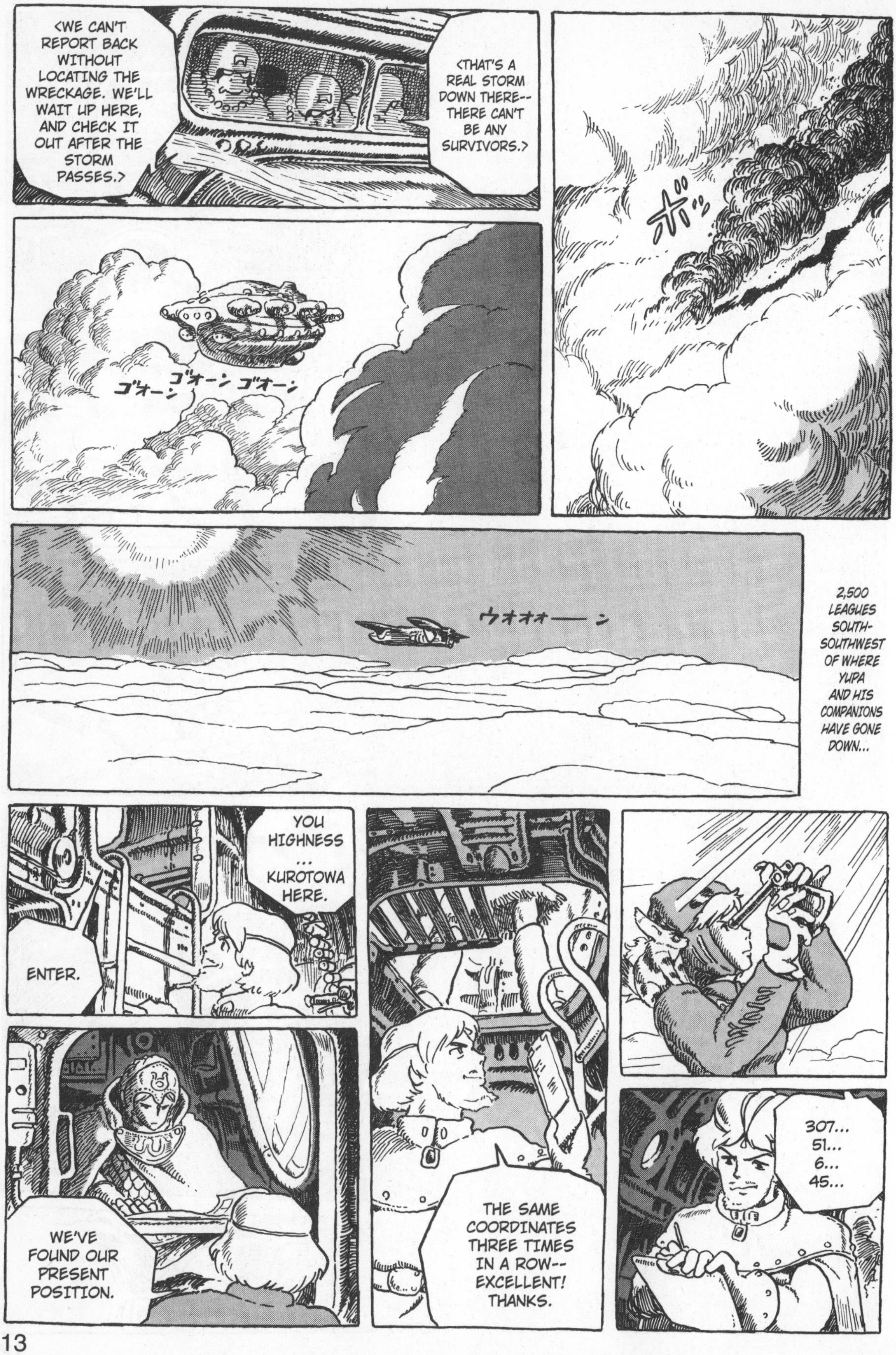
ボッ
<THAT'S A REAL STORM DOWN THERE-- THERE CAN'T BE ANY SURVIVORS.>
<WE CAN'T REPORT BACK WITHOUT LOCATING THE WRECKAGE. WE'LL WAIT UP HERE, AND CHECK IT OUT AFTER THE STORM PASSES.>
ゴォーン ゴォーン ゴォーン
2,500 LEAGUES SOUTH-SOUTHWEST OF WHERE YUPA AND HIS COMPANIONS HAVE GONE DOWN...
ウオオオーン
307... 51... 6... 45...
THE SAME COORDINATES THREE TIMES IN A ROW-- EXCELLENT! THANKS.
YOU HIGHNESS ... KUROTOWA HERE.
ENTER.
WE'VE FOUND OUR PRESENT POSITION.

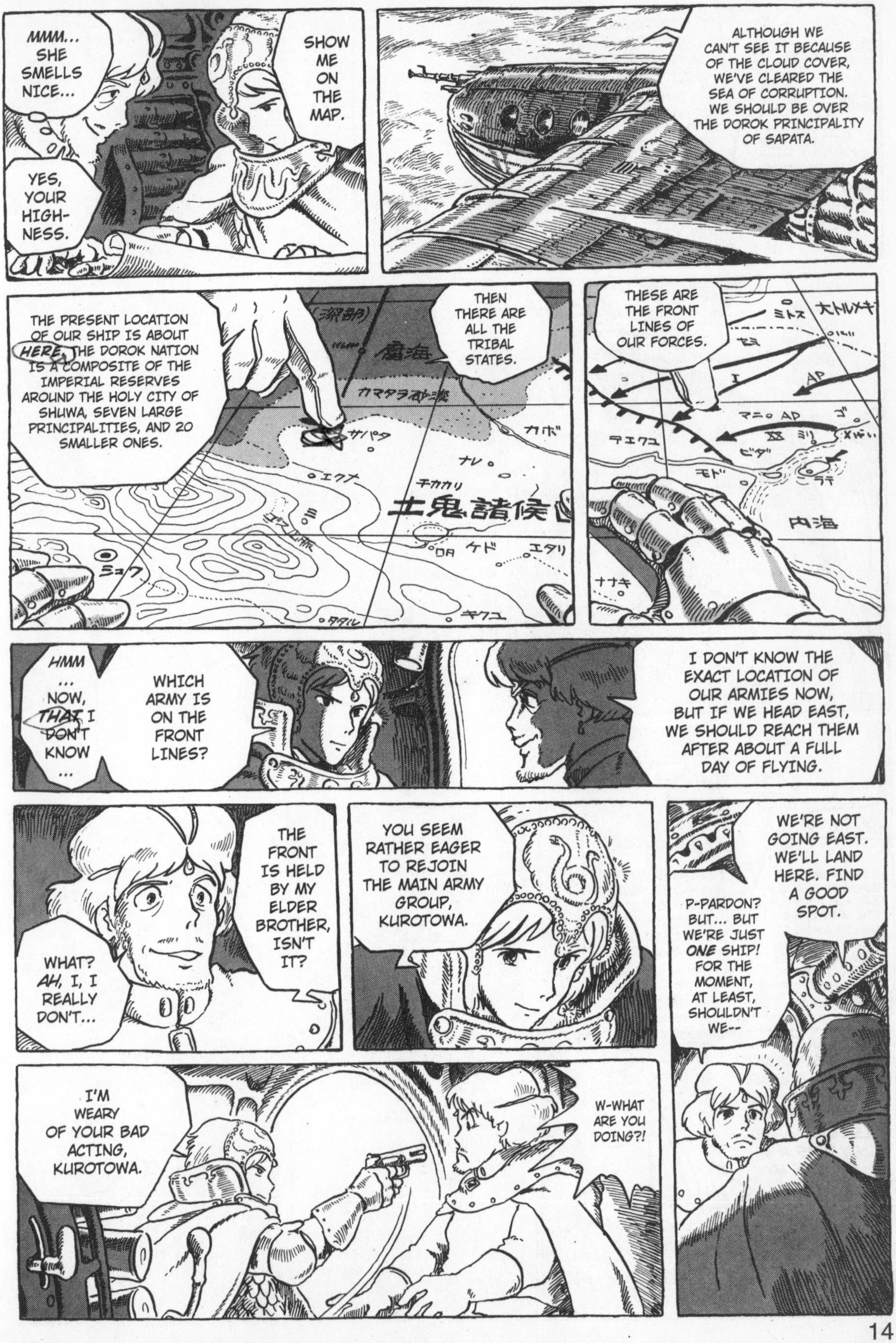
ALTHOUGH WE CAN'T SEE IT BECAUSE OF THE CLOUD COVER, WE'VE CLEARED THE SEA OF CORRUPTION. WE SHOULD BE OVER THE DOROK PRINCIPALITY OF SAPATA.
SHOW ME ON THE MAP.
MMM... SHE SMELLS NICE...
YES, YOUR HIGHNESS.
THESE ARE THE FRONT LINES OF OUR FORCES.
THEN THERE ARE ALL THE TRIBAL STATES.
THE PRESENT LOCATION OF OUR SHIP IS ABOUT HERE. THE DOROK NATION IS A COMPOSITE OF THE IMPERIAL RESERVES AROUND THE HOLY CITY OF SHUWA, SEVEN LARGE PRINCIPALITIES, AND 20 SMALLER ONES.
I DON'T KNOW THE EXACT LOCATION OF OUR ARMIES NOW, BUT IF WE HEAD EAST, WE SHOULD REACH THEM AFTER ABOUT A FULL DAY OF FLYING.
WHICH ARMY IS ON THE FRONT LINES?
HMM... NOW, THAT I DON'T KNOW...
WE'RE NOT GOING EAST. WE'LL LAND HERE. FIND A GOOD SPOT.
P-PARDON? BUT... BUT WE'RE JUST ONE SHIP! FOR THE MOMENT, AT LEAST, SHOULDN'T WE--
YOU SEEM RATHER EAGER TO REJOIN THE MAIN ARMY GROUP, KUROTOWA.
THE FRONT IS HELD BY MY ELDER BROTHER, ISN'T IT?
WHAT? AH, I, I REALLY DON'T...
W-WHAT ARE YOU DOING?!
I'M WEARY OF YOUR BAD ACTING, KUROTOWA.

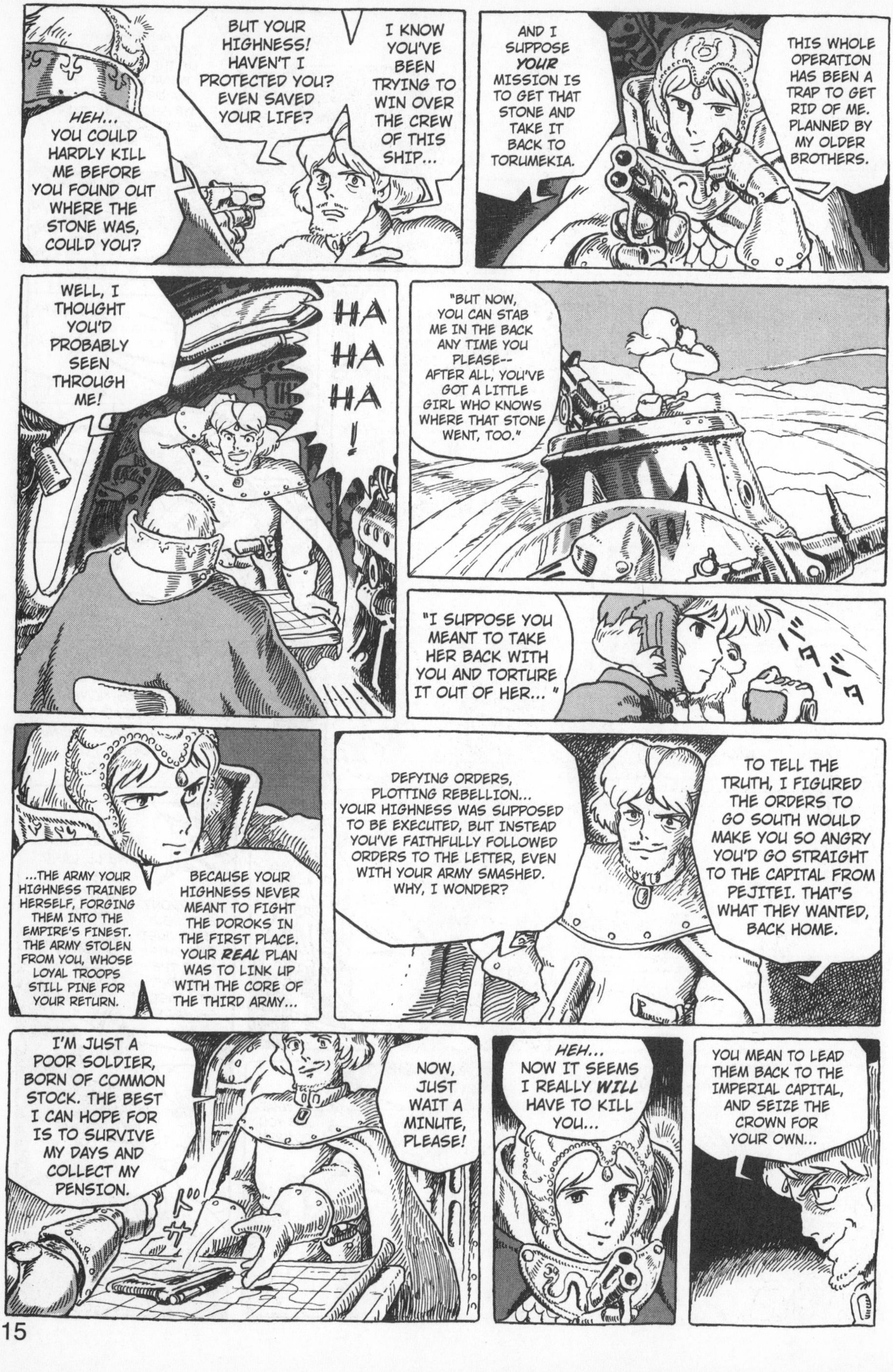
THIS WHOLE OPERATION HAS BEEN A TRAP TO GET RID OF ME. PLANNED BY MY OLDER BROTHERS.
AND I SUPPOSE *YOUR* MISSION IS TO GET THAT STONE AND TAKE IT BACK TO TORUMEKIA.
I KNOW YOU'VE BEEN TRYING TO WIN OVER THE CREW OF THIS SHIP...
BUT YOUR HIGHNESS! HAVEN'T I PROTECTED YOU? EVEN SAVED YOUR LIFE?
HEH... YOU COULD HARDLY KILL ME BEFORE YOU FOUND OUT WHERE THE STONE WAS, COULD YOU?
"BUT NOW, YOU CAN STAB ME IN THE BACK ANY TIME YOU PLEASE-- AFTER ALL, YOU'VE GOT A LITTLE GIRL WHO KNOWS WHERE THAT STONE WENT, TOO."
バタバタ
"I SUPPOSE YOU MEANT TO TAKE HER BACK WITH YOU AND TORTURE IT OUT OF HER..."
HA HA HA!
WELL, I THOUGHT YOU'D PROBABLY SEEN THROUGH ME!
TO TELL THE TRUTH, I FIGURED THE ORDERS TO GO SOUTH WOULD MAKE YOU SO ANGRY YOU'D GO STRAIGHT TO THE CAPITAL FROM PEJITEI. THAT'S WHAT THEY WANTED, BACK HOME.
DEFYING ORDERS, PLOTTING REBELLION... YOUR HIGHNESS WAS SUPPOSED TO BE EXECUTED, BUT INSTEAD YOU'VE FAITHFULLY FOLLOWED ORDERS TO THE LETTER, EVEN WITH YOUR ARMY SMASHED. WHY, I WONDER?
BECAUSE YOUR HIGHNESS NEVER MEANT TO FIGHT THE DOROKS IN THE FIRST PLACE. YOUR *REAL* PLAN WAS TO LINK UP WITH THE CORE OF THE THIRD ARMY...
...THE ARMY YOUR HIGHNESS TRAINED HERSELF, FORGING THEM INTO THE EMPIRE'S FINEST. THE ARMY STOLEN FROM YOU, WHOSE LOYAL TROOPS STILL PINE FOR YOUR RETURN.
YOU MEAN TO LEAD THEM BACK TO THE IMPERIAL CAPITAL, AND SEIZE THE CROWN FOR YOUR OWN...
HEH... NOW IT SEEMS I REALLY *WILL* HAVE TO KILL YOU...
NOW, JUST WAIT A MINUTE, PLEASE!
I'M JUST A POOR SOLDIER, BORN OF COMMON STOCK. THE BEST I CAN HOPE FOR IS TO SURVIVE MY DAYS AND COLLECT MY PENSION.

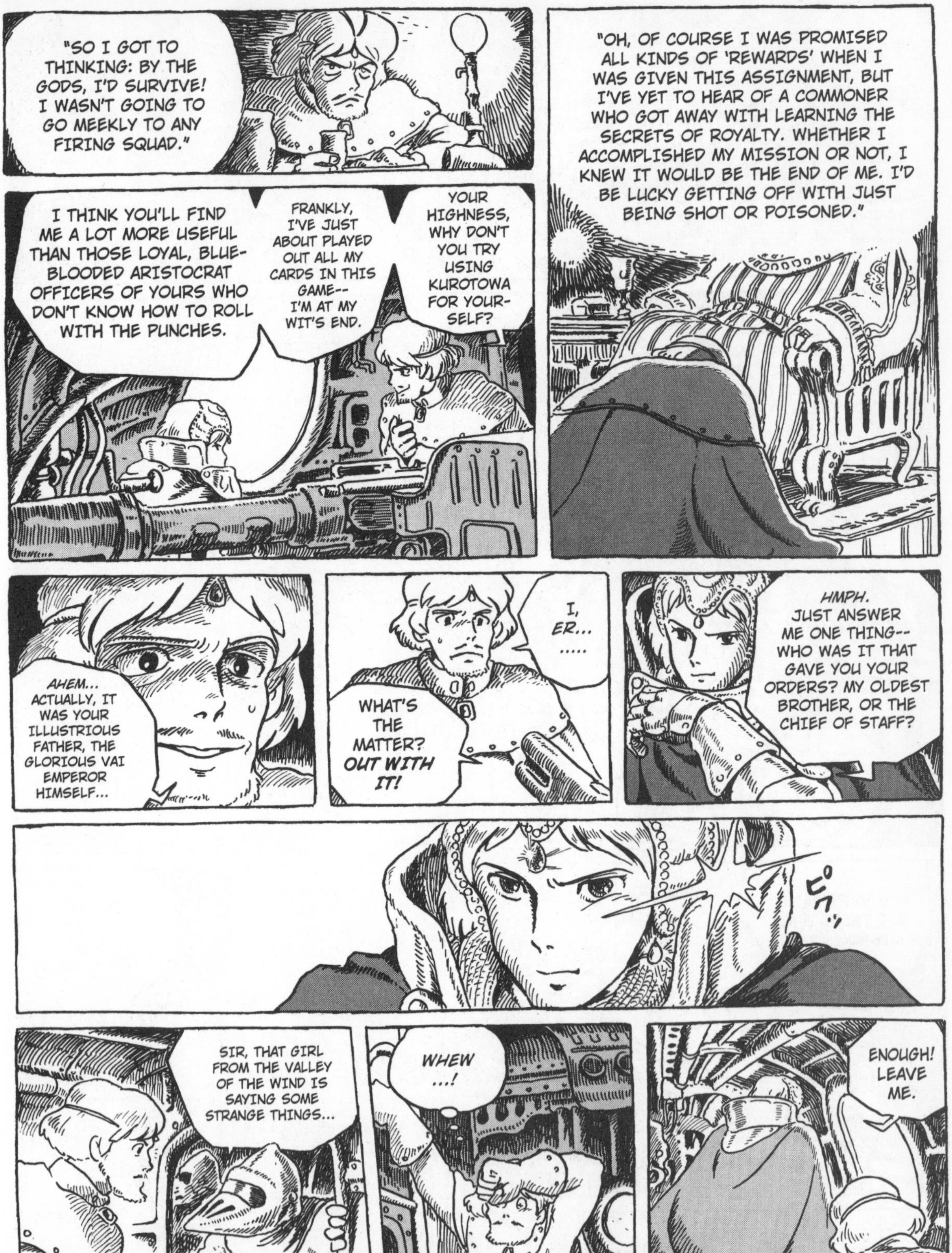
"OH, OF COURSE I WAS PROMISED ALL KINDS OF 'REWARDS' WHEN I WAS GIVEN THIS ASSIGNMENT, BUT I'VE YET TO HEAR OF A COMMONER WHO GOT AWAY WITH LEARNING THE SECRETS OF ROYALTY. WHETHER I ACCOMPLISHED MY MISSION OR NOT, I KNEW IT WOULD BE THE END OF ME. I'D BE LUCKY GETTING OFF WITH JUST BEING SHOT OR POISONED."
"SO I GOT TO THINKING: BY THE GODS, I'D SURVIVE! I WASN'T GOING TO GO MEEKLY TO ANY FIRING SQUAD."
YOUR HIGHNESS, WHY DON'T YOU TRY USING KUROTOWA FOR YOURSELF?
FRANKLY, I'VE JUST ABOUT PLAYED OUT ALL MY CARDS IN THIS GAME-- I'M AT MY WIT'S END.
I THINK YOU'LL FIND ME A LOT MORE USEFUL THAN THOSE LOYAL, BLUE-BLOODED ARISTOCRAT OFFICERS OF YOURS WHO DON'T KNOW HOW TO ROLL WITH THE PUNCHES.
HMPH. JUST ANSWER ME ONE THING-- WHO WAS IT THAT GAVE YOU YOUR ORDERS? MY OLDEST BROTHER, OR THE CHIEF OF STAFF?
I, ER... .....
WHAT'S THE MATTER? OUT WITH IT!
AHEM... ACTUALLY, IT WAS YOUR ILLUSTRIOUS FATHER, THE GLORIOUS VAI EMPEROR HIMSELF...
ピクッ
ENOUGH! LEAVE ME.
YOUR HIGHNESS?
WHEW ...!
SIR, THAT GIRL FROM THE VALLEY OF THE WIND IS SAYING SOME STRANGE THINGS...
HMM ...?

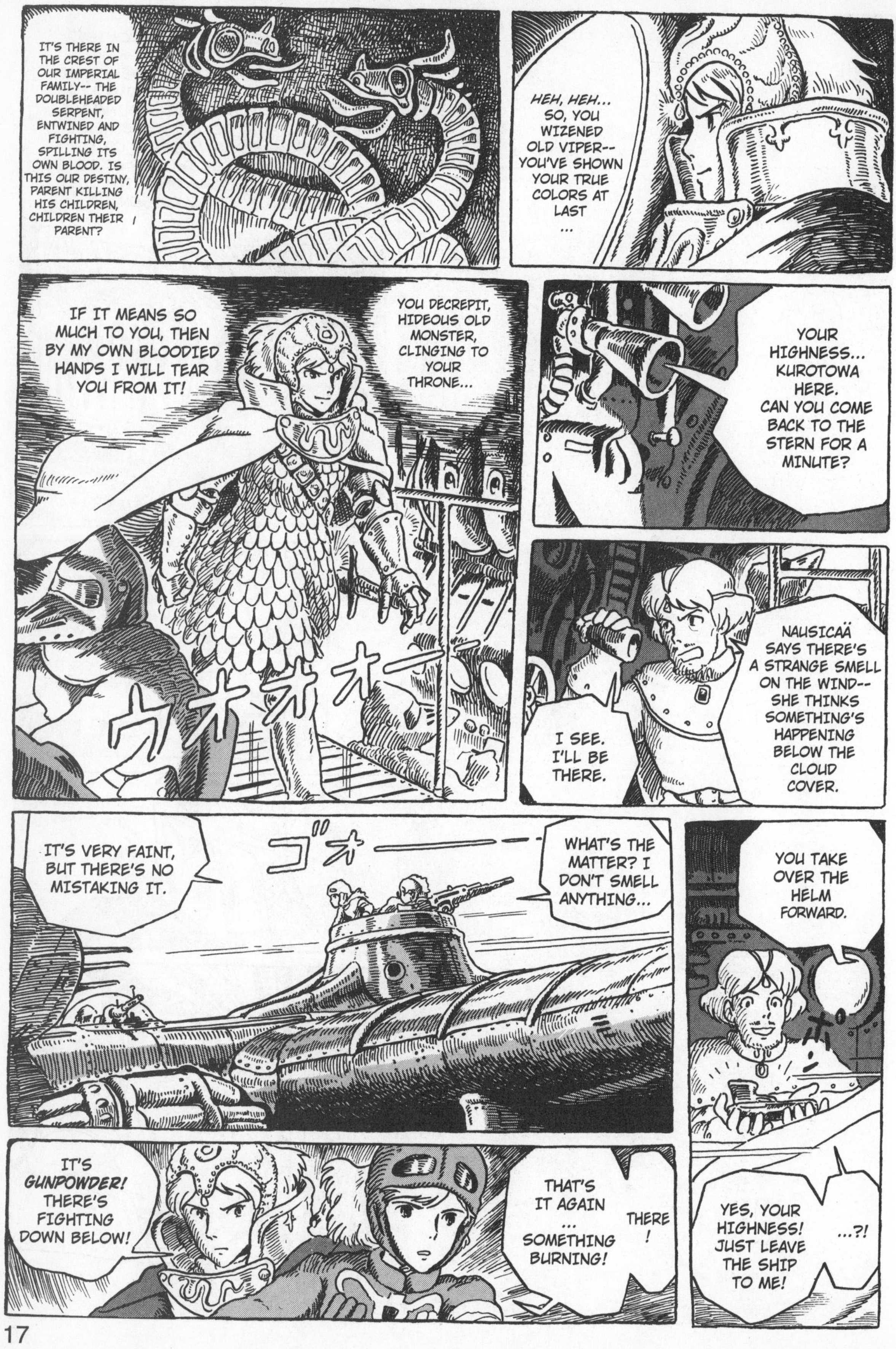
HEH, HEH... SO, YOU WIZENED OLD VIPER-- YOU'VE SHOWN YOUR TRUE COLORS AT LAST ...
IT'S THERE IN THE CREST OF OUR IMPERIAL FAMILY-- THE DOUBLEHEADED SERPENT, ENTWINED AND FIGHTING, SPILLING ITS OWN BLOOD. IS THIS OUR DESTINY, PARENT KILLING HIS CHILDREN, CHILDREN THEIR PARENT?
YOUR HIGHNESS... KUROTOWA HERE. CAN YOU COME BACK TO THE STERN FOR A MINUTE?
NAUSICAÄ SAYS THERE'S A STRANGE SMELL ON THE WIND-- SHE THINKS SOMETHING'S HAPPENING BELOW THE CLOUD COVER.
I SEE. I'LL BE THERE.
YOU DECREPIT, HIDEOUS OLD MONSTER, CLINGING TO YOUR THRONE...
IF IT MEANS SO MUCH TO YOU, THEN BY MY OWN BLOODIED HANDS I WILL TEAR YOU FROM IT!
ウオオオオー
YOU TAKE OVER THE HELM FORWARD.
YES, YOUR HIGHNESS! JUST LEAVE THE SHIP TO ME!
...?!
WHAT'S THE MATTER? I DON'T SMELL ANYTHING...
ゴオーーー
IT'S VERY FAINT, BUT THERE'S NO MISTAKING IT.
THERE!
THAT'S IT AGAIN ... SOMETHING BURNING!
IT'S GUNPOWDER! THERE'S FIGHTING DOWN BELOW!

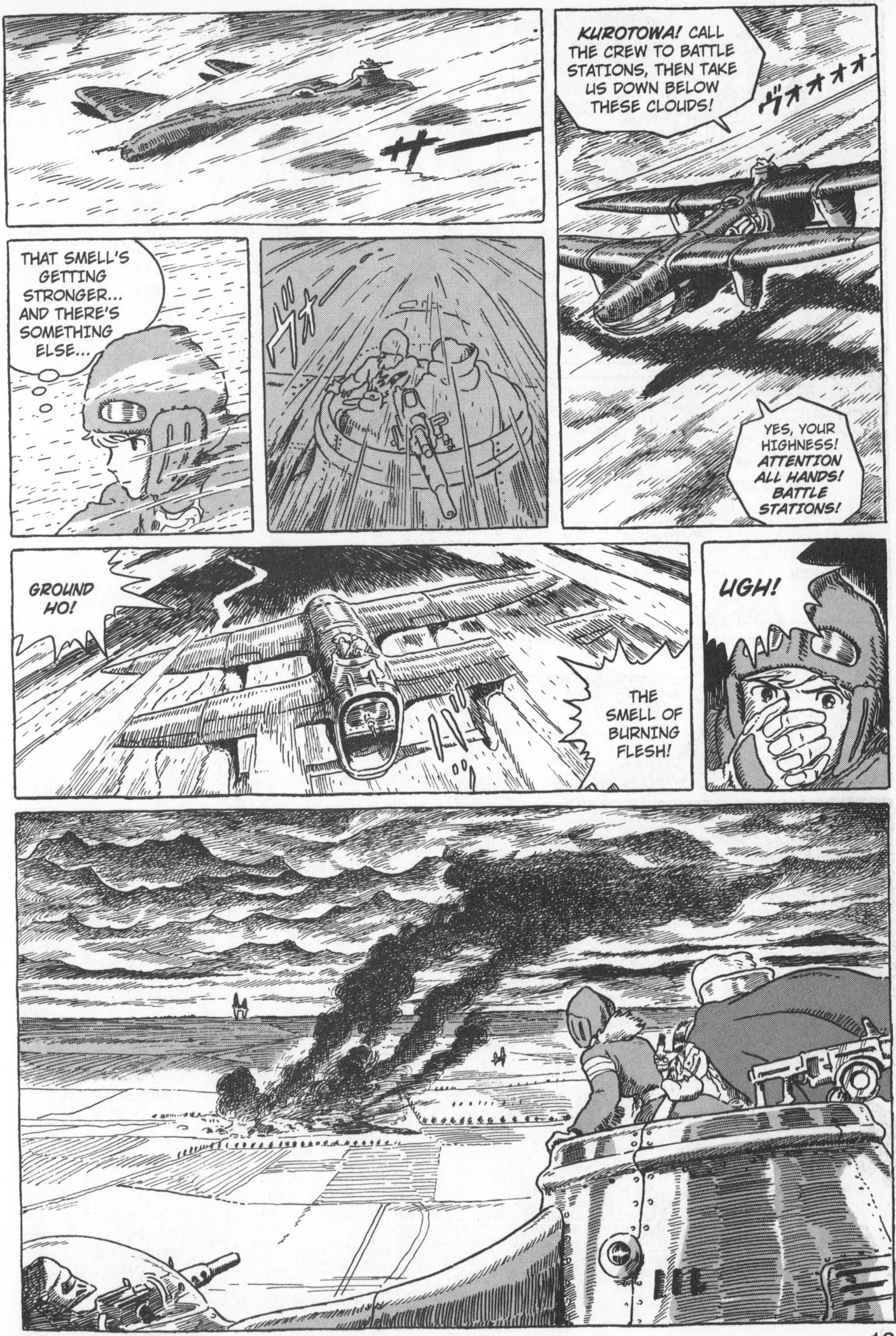
KUROTOWA! CALL THE CREW TO BATTLE STATIONS, THEN TAKE US DOWN BELOW THESE CLOUDS!
ヴォオオオ
YES, YOUR HIGHNESS! ATTENTION ALL HANDS! BATTLE STATIONS!
ザ
ヴォ
THAT SMELL'S GETTING STRONGER... AND THERE'S SOMETHING ELSE...
UGH!
GROUND HO!
THE SMELL OF BURNING FLESH!

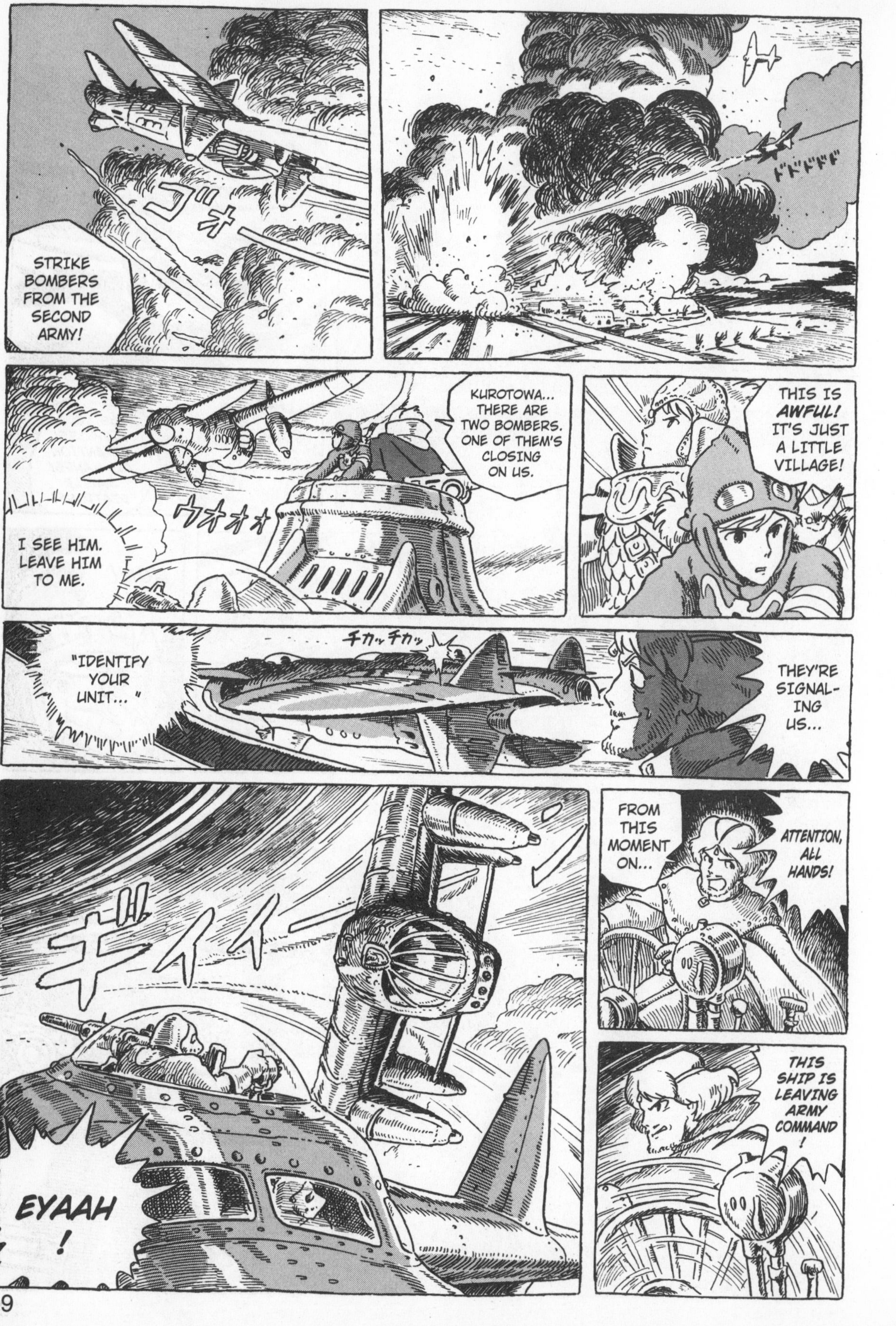
ドドドドド
STRIKE BOMBERS FROM THE SECOND ARMY!
ゴォー
THIS IS **AWFUL!** IT'S JUST A LITTLE VILLAGE!
KUROTOWA... THERE ARE TWO BOMBERS. ONE OF THEM'S CLOSING ON US.
ウオオオ
I SEE HIM. LEAVE HIM TO ME.
チカッチカッ
THEY'RE SIGNAL-ING US...
"IDENTIFY YOUR UNIT..."
ATTENTION, ALL HANDS!
FROM THIS MOMENT ON...
THIS SHIP IS LEAVING ARMY COMMAND!
ギイイー
EYAAH!

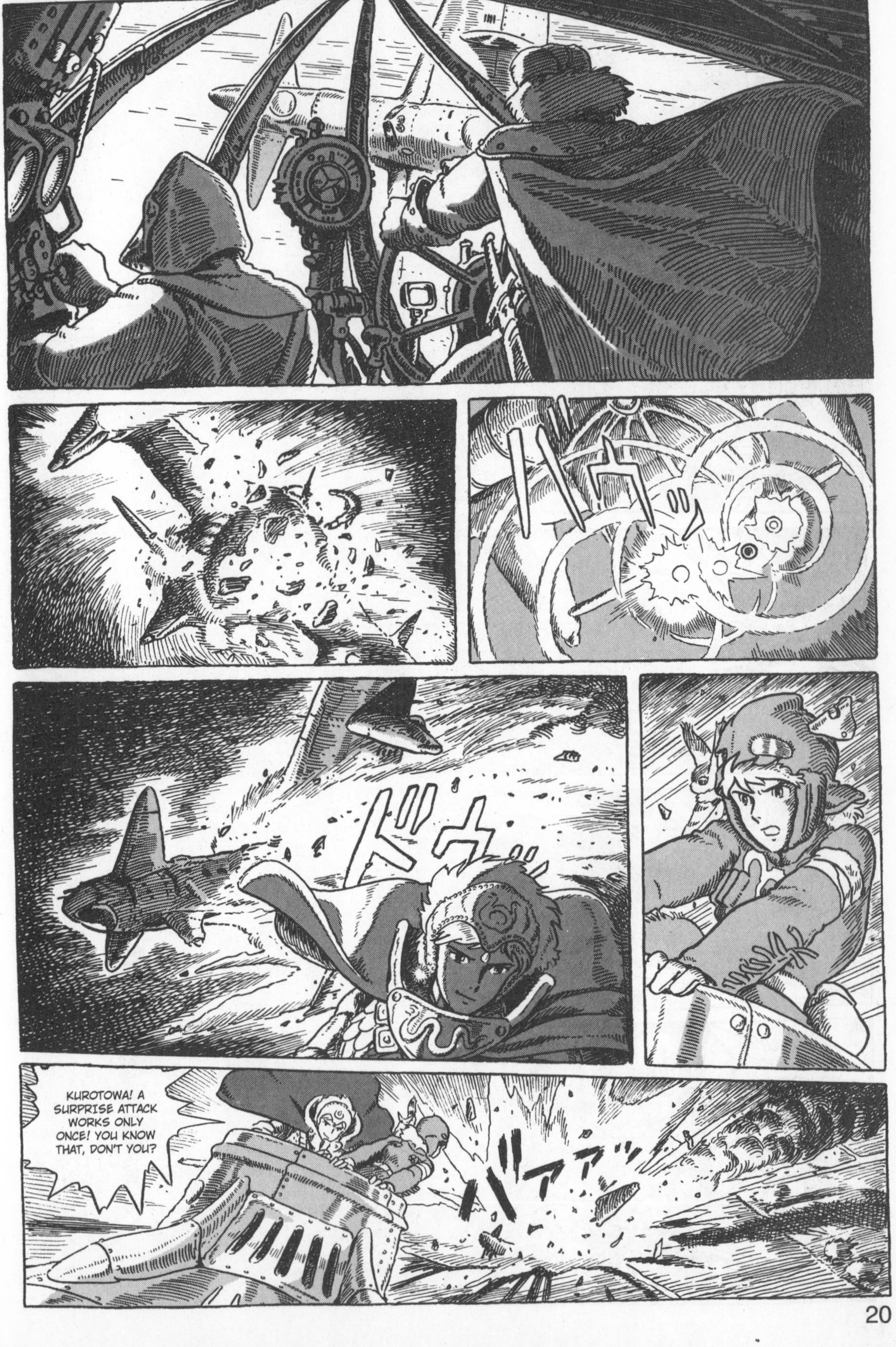
KUROTOWA! A SURPRISE ATTACK WORKS ONLY ONCE! YOU KNOW THAT, DON'T YOU?

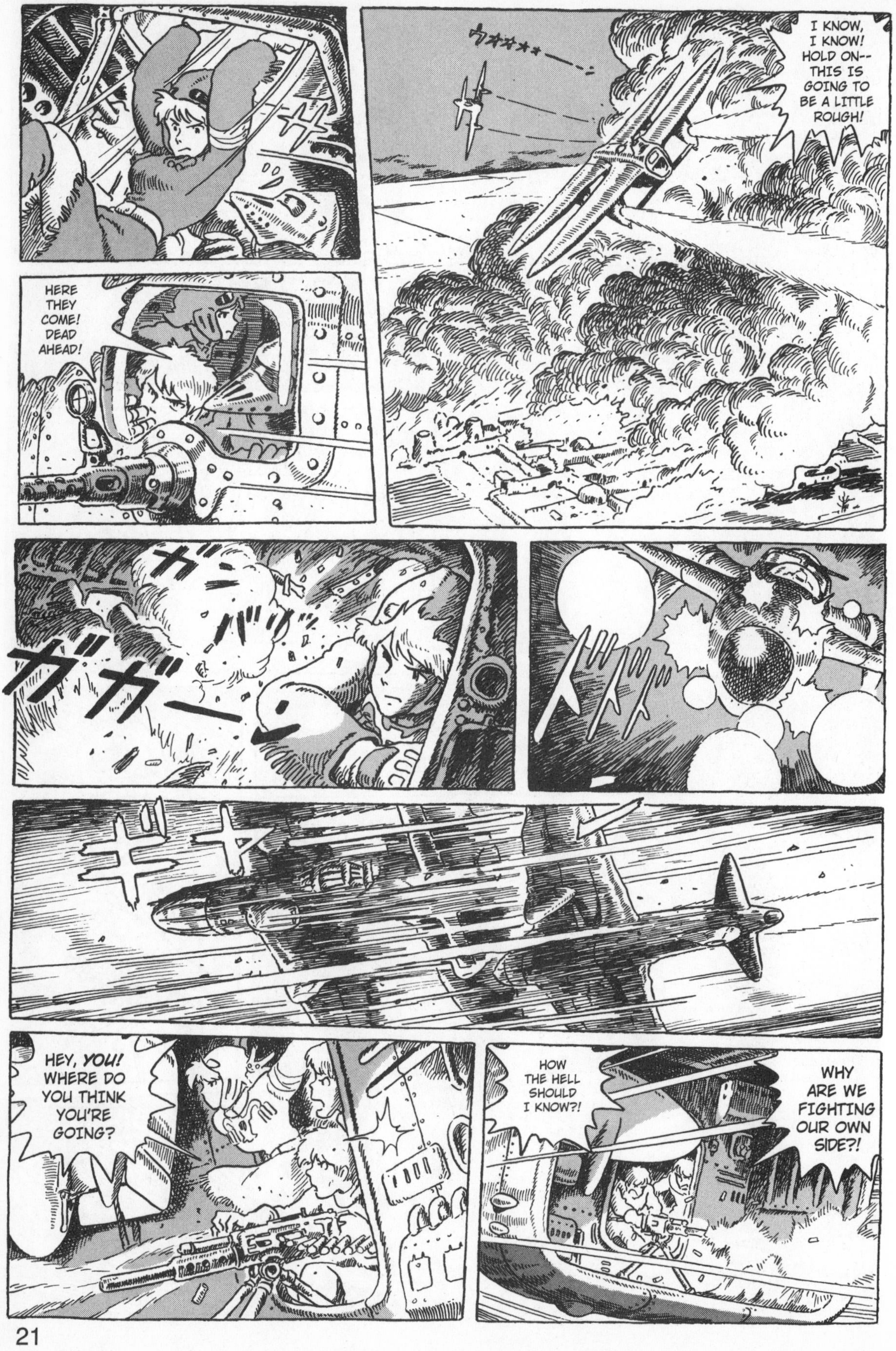

I KNOW, I KNOW! HOLD ON-- THIS IS GOING TO BE A LITTLE ROUGH!
HERE THEY COME! DEAD AHEAD!
WHY ARE WE FIGHTING OUR OWN SIDE?!
HOW THE HELL SHOULD I KNOW?!
HEY, *YOU!* WHERE DO YOU THINK YOU'RE GOING?

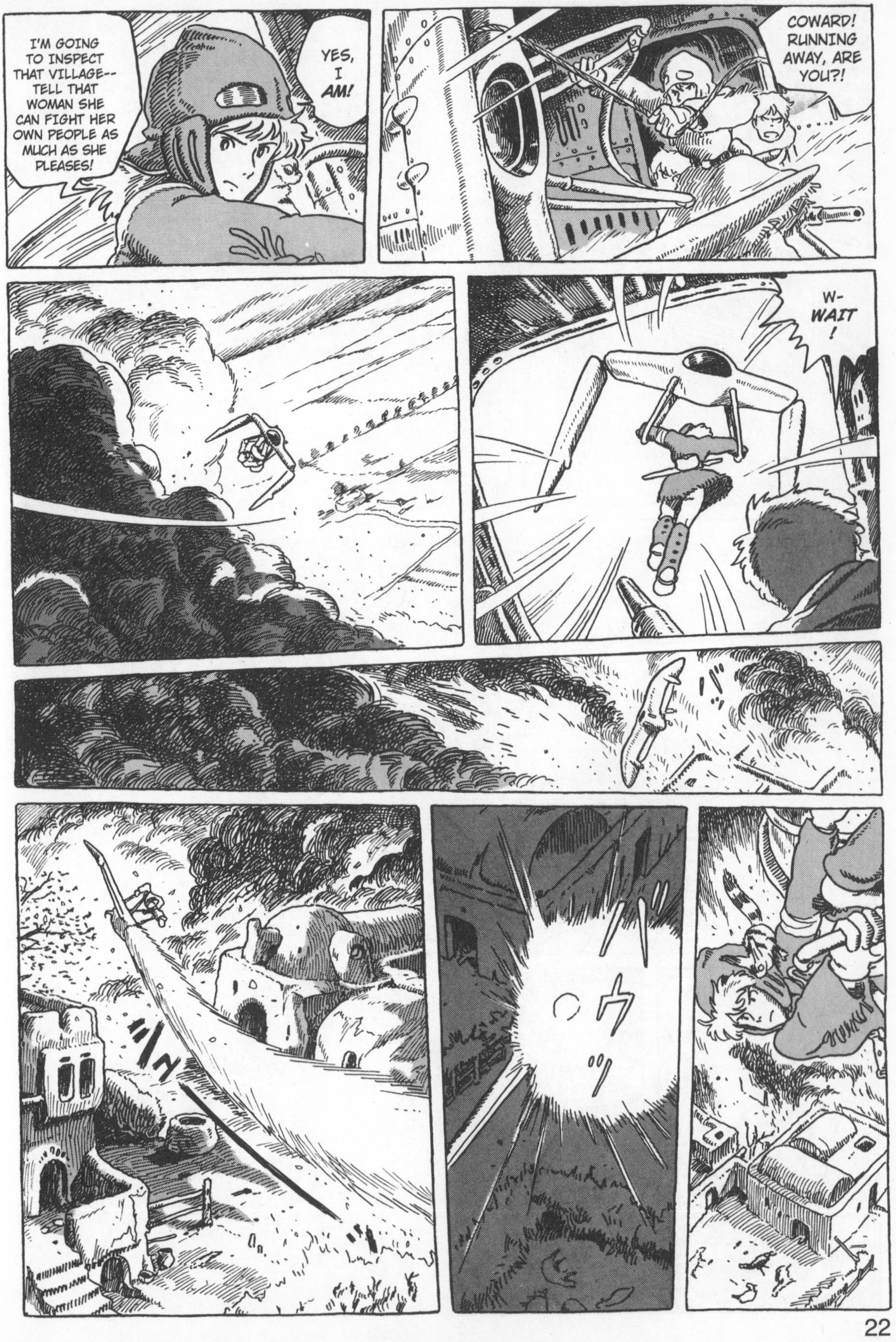
COWARD! RUNNING AWAY, ARE YOU?!
YES, I AM!
I'M GOING TO INSPECT THAT VILLAGE-- TELL THAT WOMAN SHE CAN FIGHT HER OWN PEOPLE AS MUCH AS SHE PLEASES!
W- WAIT!

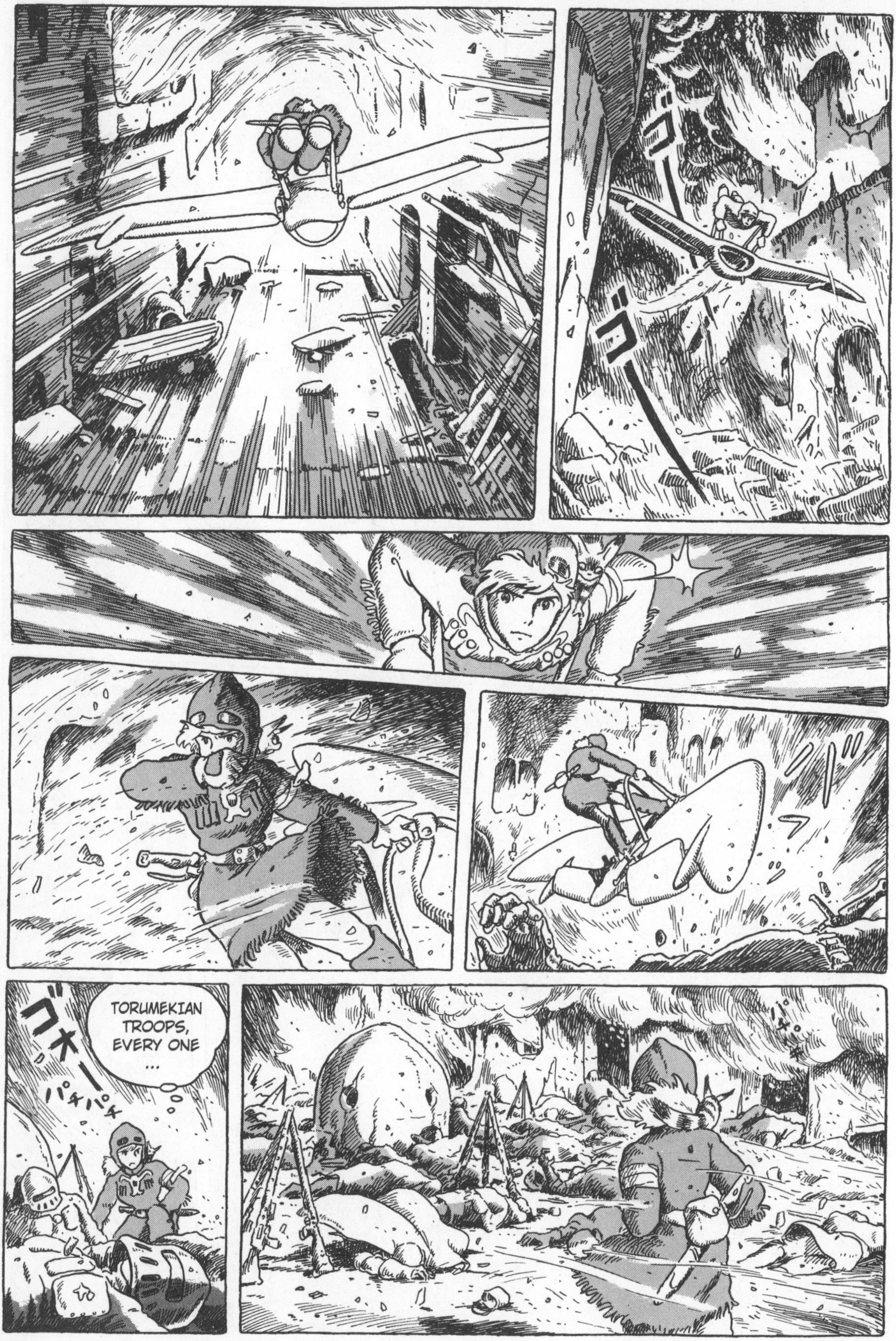
TORUMEKIAN
TROOPS,
EVERY ONE
...

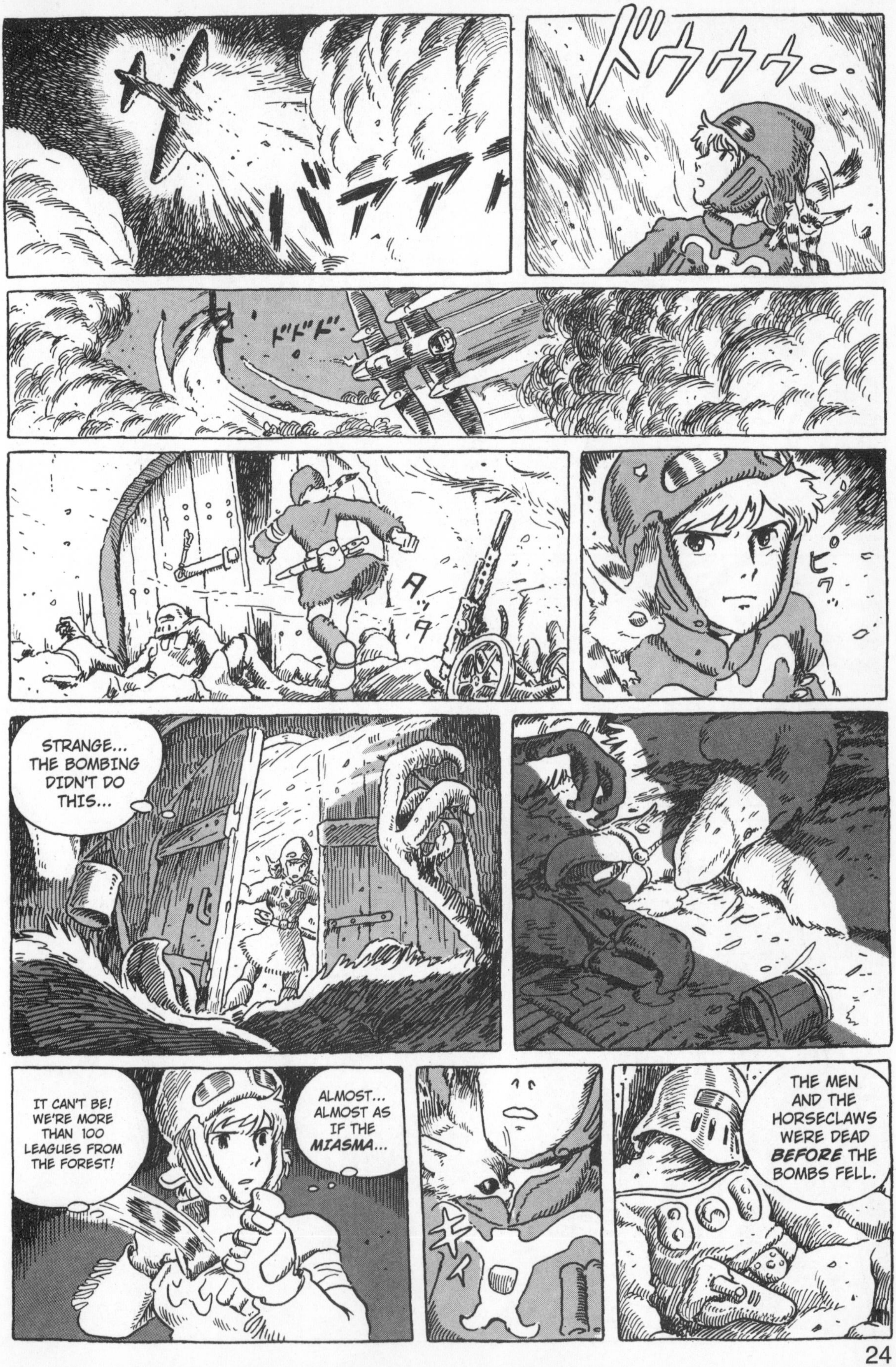
ドウウウ
バアア
ドドド
ピク
タッタ
STRANGE... THE BOMBING DIDN'T DO THIS...
THE MEN AND THE HORSECLAWS WERE DEAD *BEFORE* THE BOMBS FELL.
キィ
ALMOST... ALMOST AS IF THE *MIASMA*...
IT CAN'T BE! WE'RE MORE THAN 100 LEAGUES FROM THE FOREST!

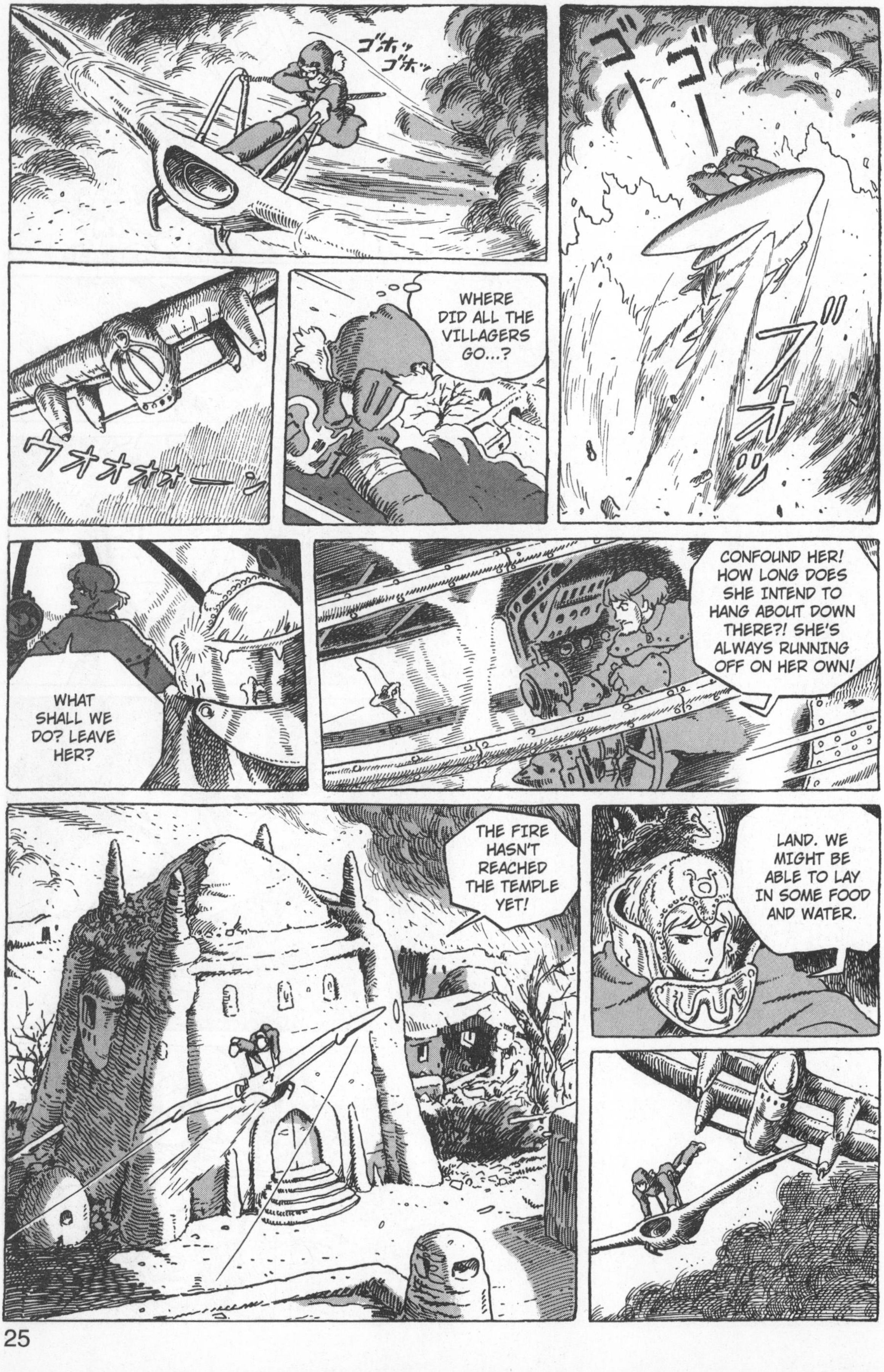
ゴーゴー
ブフオッ
ゴホッ ゴホッ
WHERE DID ALL THE VILLAGERS GO...?
ウオオオオオーン
CONFOUND HER! HOW LONG DOES SHE INTEND TO HANG ABOUT DOWN THERE?! SHE'S ALWAYS RUNNING OFF ON HER OWN!
WHAT SHALL WE DO? LEAVE HER?
LAND. WE MIGHT BE ABLE TO LAY IN SOME FOOD AND WATER.
THE FIRE HASN'T REACHED THE TEMPLE YET!

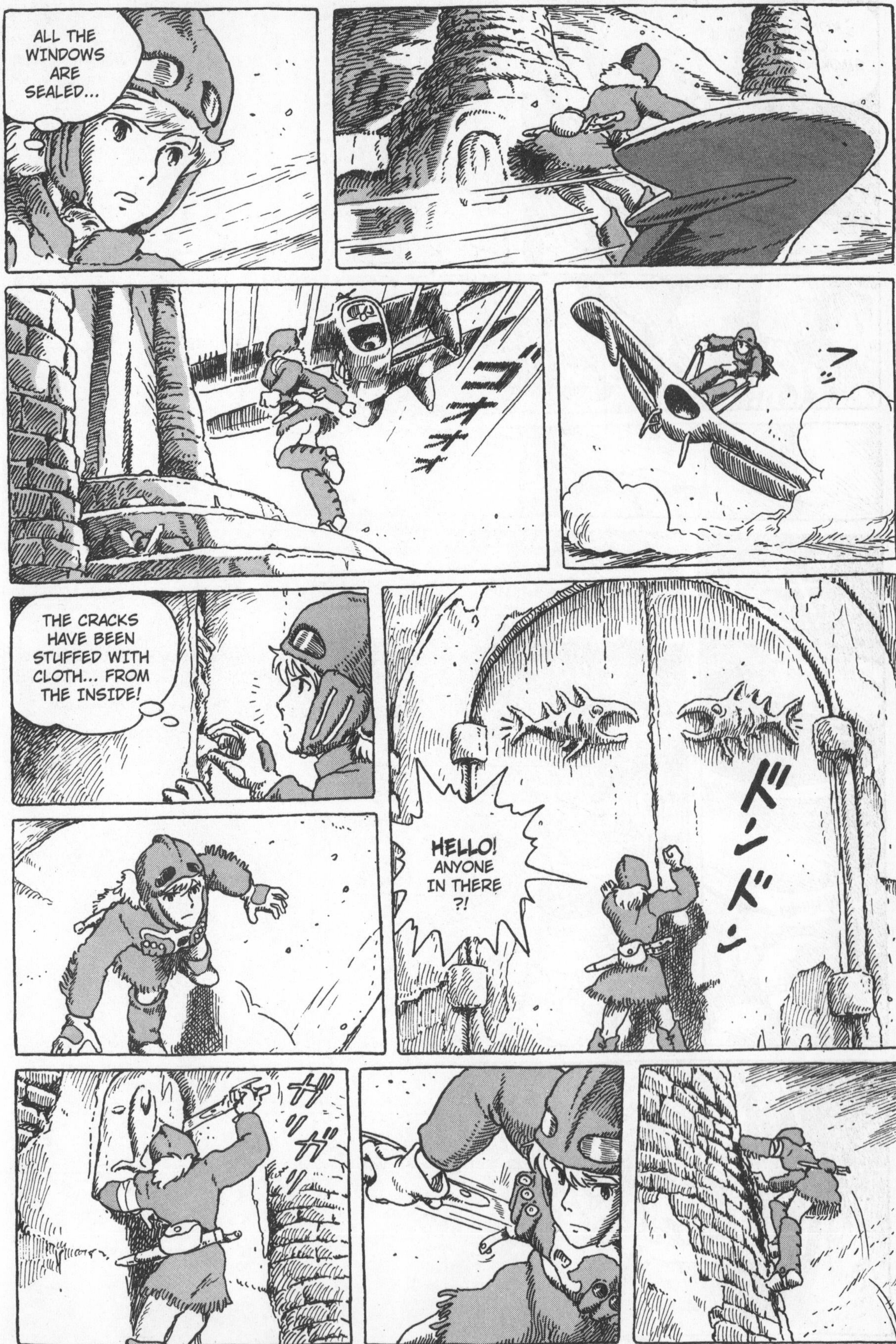
ALL THE WINDOWS ARE SEALED...
HELLO! ANYONE IN THERE ?!
THE CRACKS HAVE BEEN STUFFED WITH CLOTH... FROM THE INSIDE!

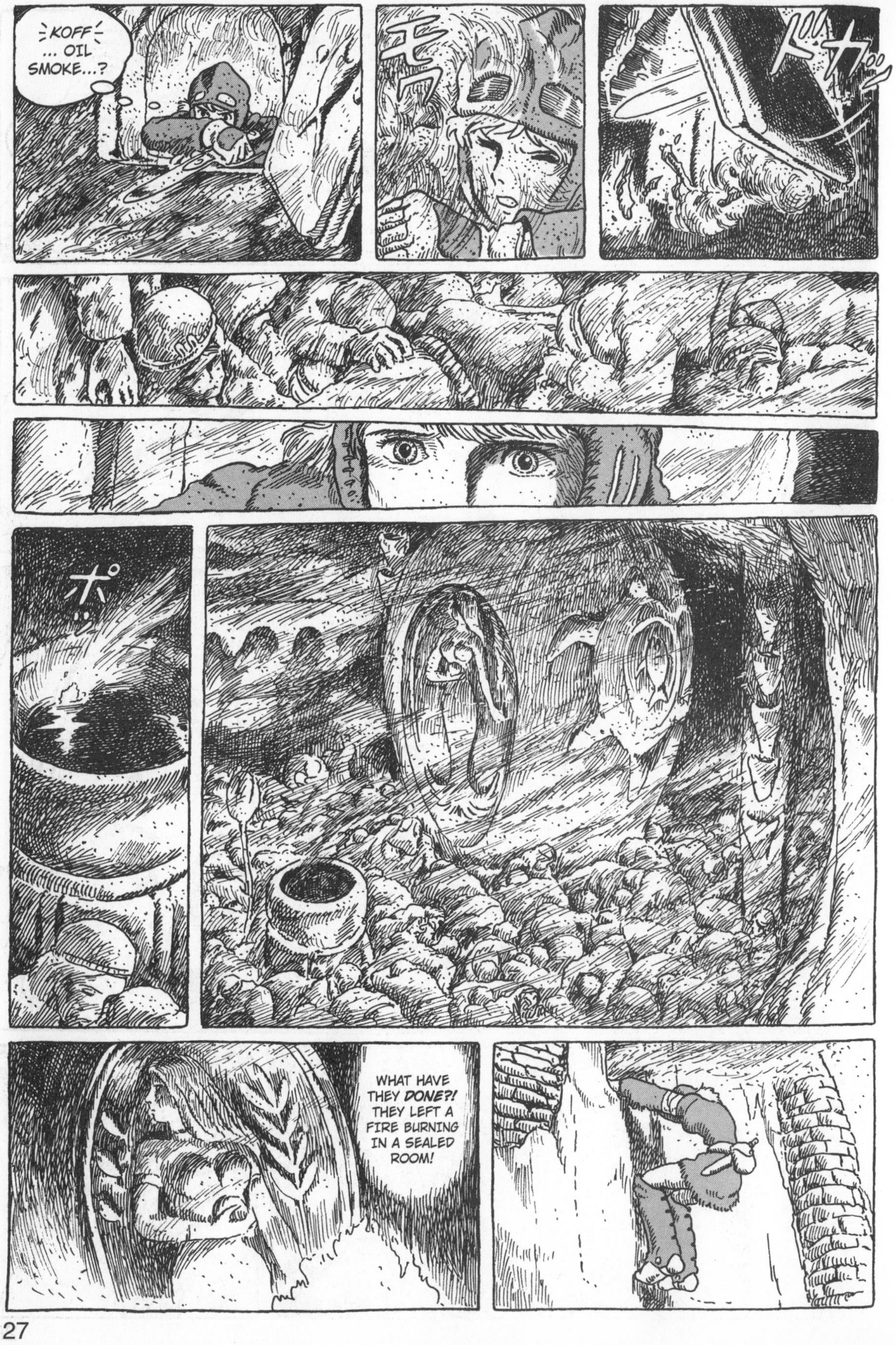
KOFF ... OIL SMOKE...?
WHAT HAVE THEY DONE?! THEY LEFT A FIRE BURNING IN A SEALED ROOM!

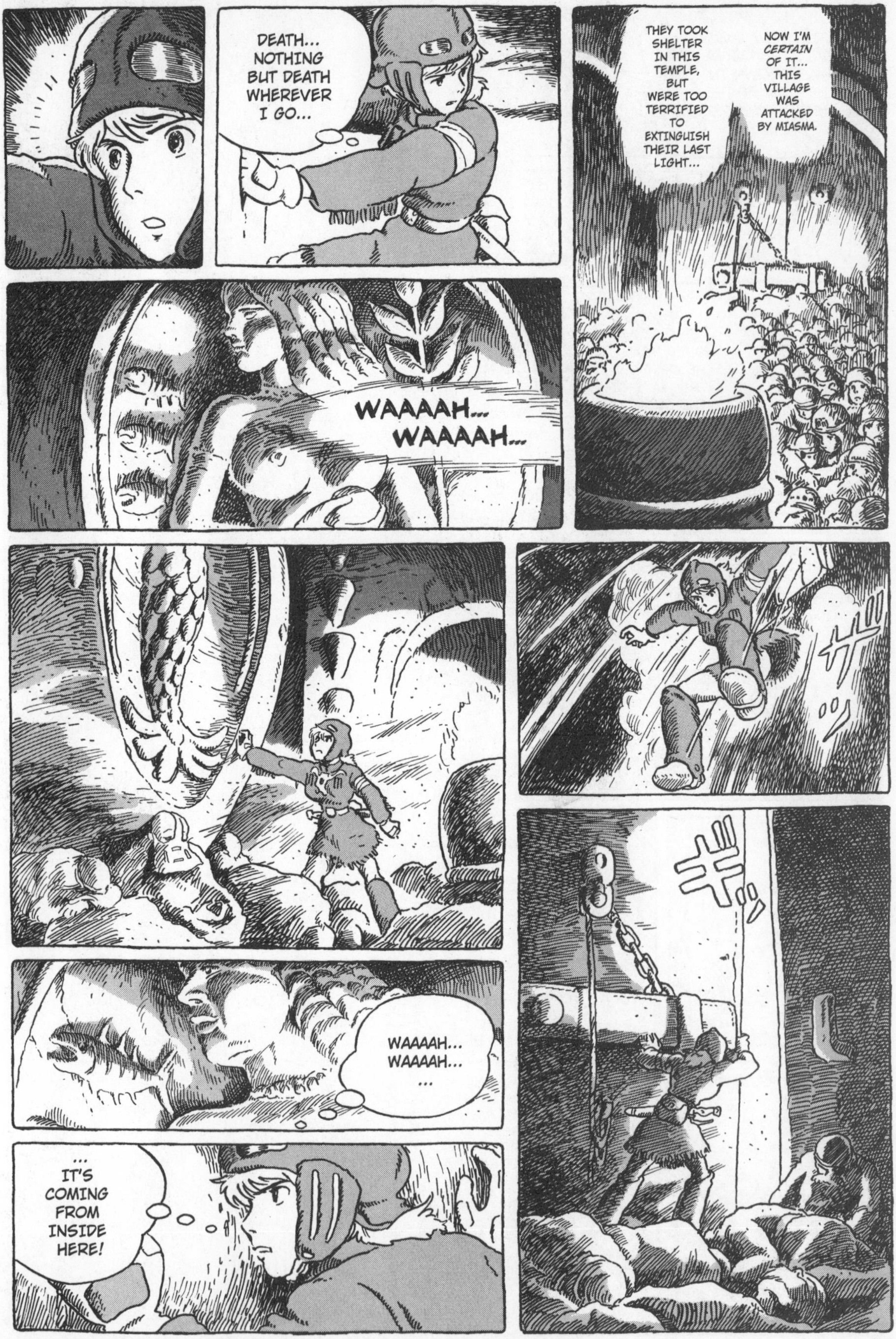
NOW I'M *CERTAIN* OF IT... THIS VILLAGE WAS ATTACKED BY MIASMA.
THEY TOOK SHELTER IN THIS TEMPLE, BUT WERE TOO TERRIFIED TO EXTINGUISH THEIR LAST LIGHT...
DEATH... NOTHING BUT DEATH WHEREVER I GO...
WAAAAH... WAAAAH...
ザッ
ギッ
WAAAAH... WAAAAH... ...
... IT'S COMING FROM INSIDE HERE!

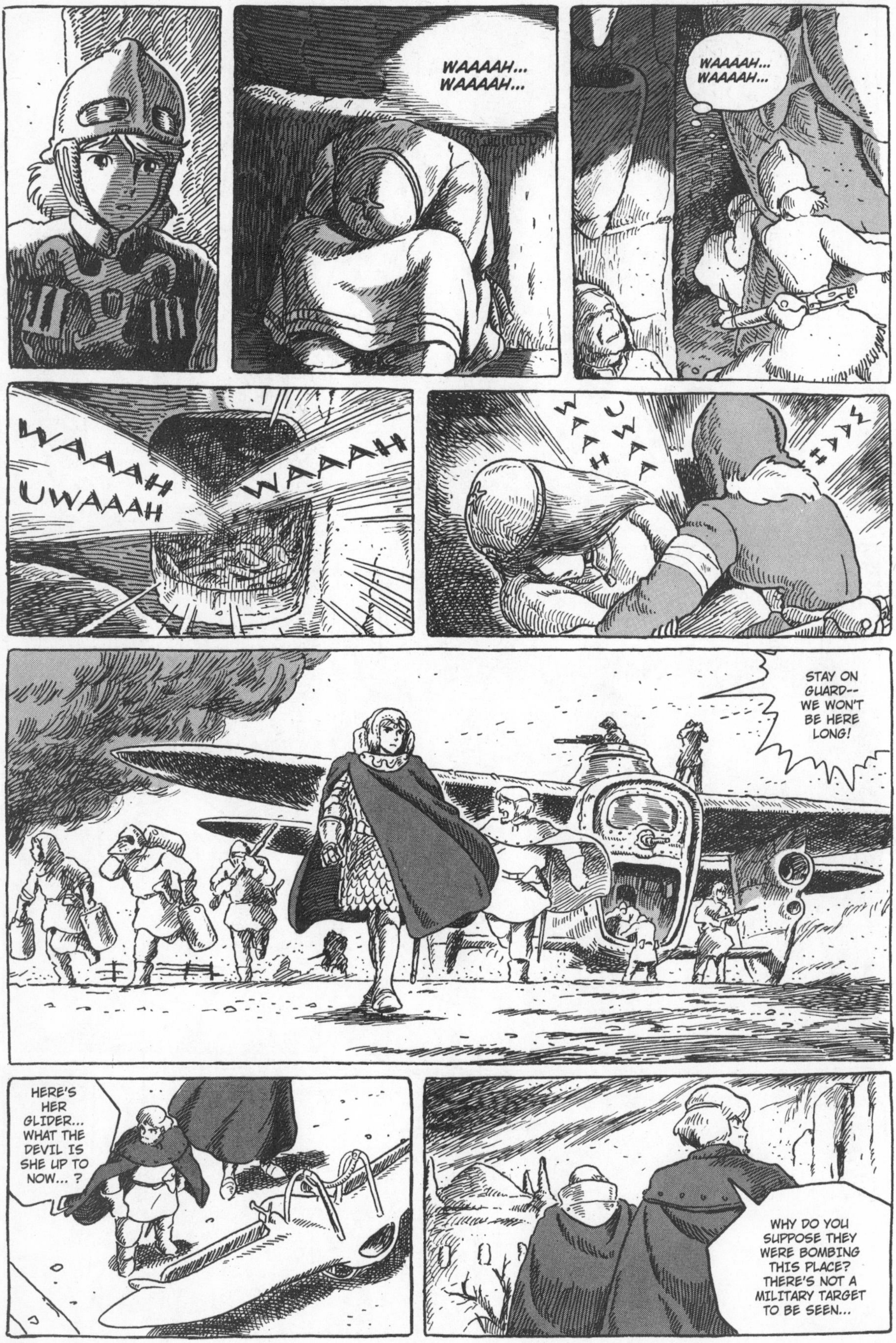
WAAAAH... WAAAAH...
WAAAAH... WAAAAH...
WAAH
UWAAA
WAAH
WAAAAH
WAAAAH
UWAAAH
STAY ON GUARD-- WE WON'T BE HERE LONG!
WHY DO YOU SUPPOSE THEY WERE BOMBING THIS PLACE? THERE'S NOT A MILITARY TARGET TO BE SEEN...
HERE'S HER GLIDER... WHAT THE DEVIL IS SHE UP TO NOW... ?

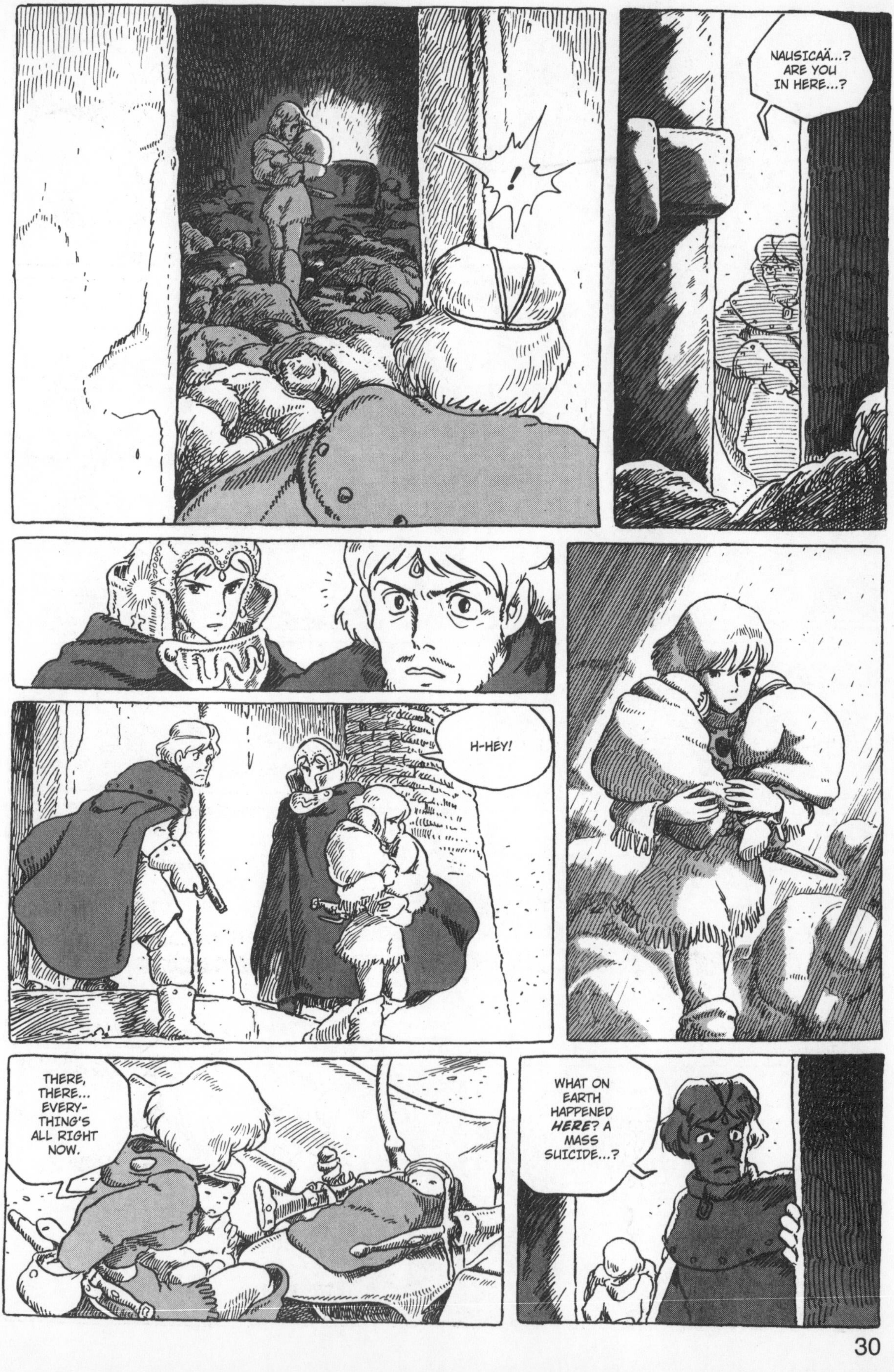
NAUSICAÄ...? ARE YOU IN HERE...?
!
H-HEY!
WHAT ON EARTH HAPPENED *HERE*? A MASS SUICIDE...?
THERE, THERE... EVERY-THING'S ALL RIGHT NOW.

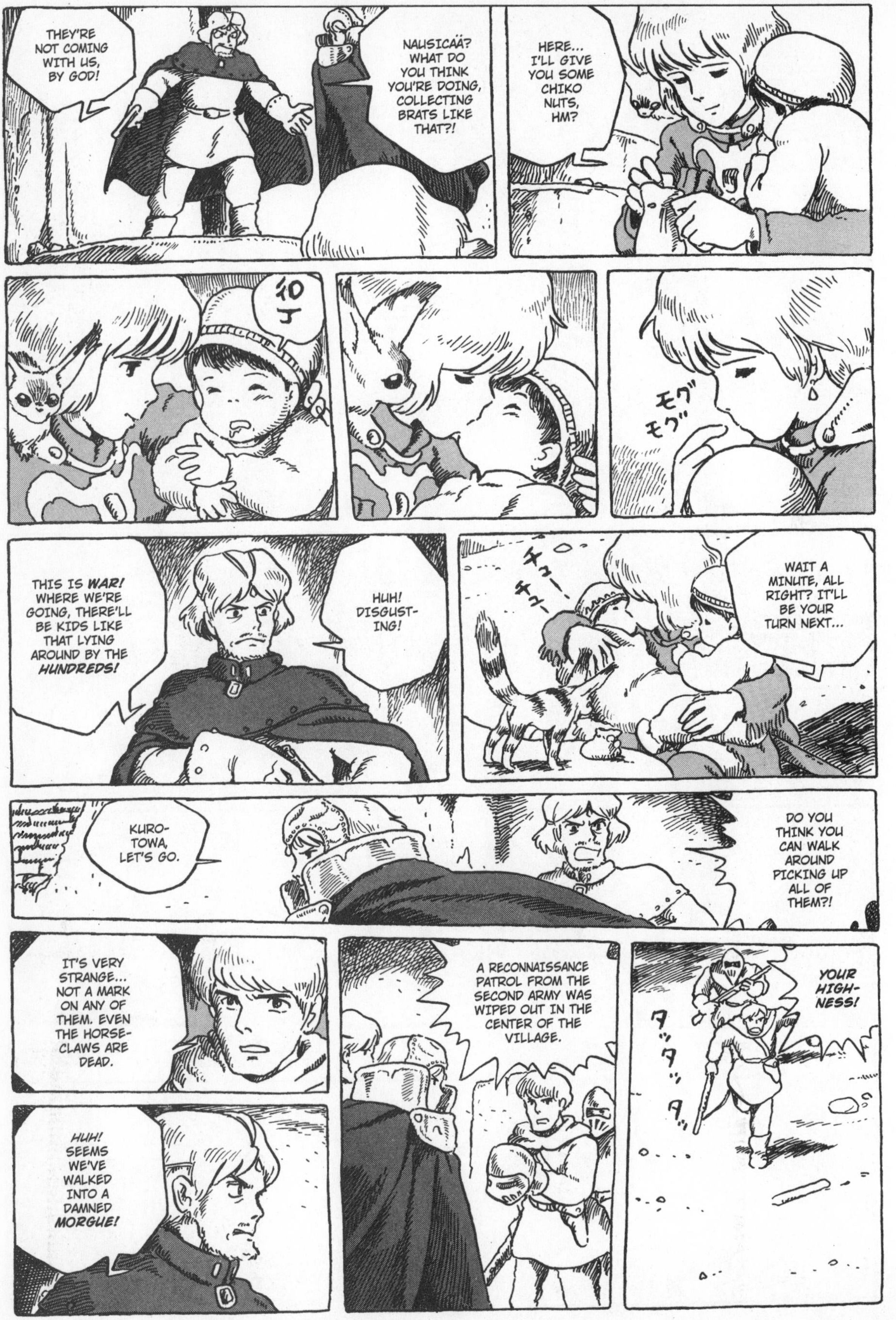
HERE... I'LL GIVE YOU SOME CHIKO NUTS, HM?
NAUSICAÄ? WHAT DO YOU THINK YOU'RE DOING, COLLECTING BRATS LIKE THAT?!
THEY'RE NOT COMING WITH US, BY GOD!
モグ モグ
チュー チュー
WAIT A MINUTE, ALL RIGHT? IT'LL BE YOUR TURN NEXT...
HUH! DISGUSTING!
THIS IS *WAR!* WHERE WE'RE GOING, THERE'LL BE KIDS LIKE THAT LYING AROUND BY THE ***HUNDREDS!***
DO YOU THINK YOU CAN WALK AROUND PICKING UP ALL OF THEM?!
KUROTOWA, LET'S GO.
YOUR HIGHNESS!
タッ タッ タッ
A RECONNAISSANCE PATROL FROM THE SECOND ARMY WAS WIPED OUT IN THE CENTER OF THE VILLAGE.
IT'S VERY STRANGE... NOT A MARK ON ANY OF THEM. EVEN THE HORSE-CLAWS ARE DEAD.
HUH! SEEMS WE'VE WALKED INTO A DAMNED ***MORGUE!***

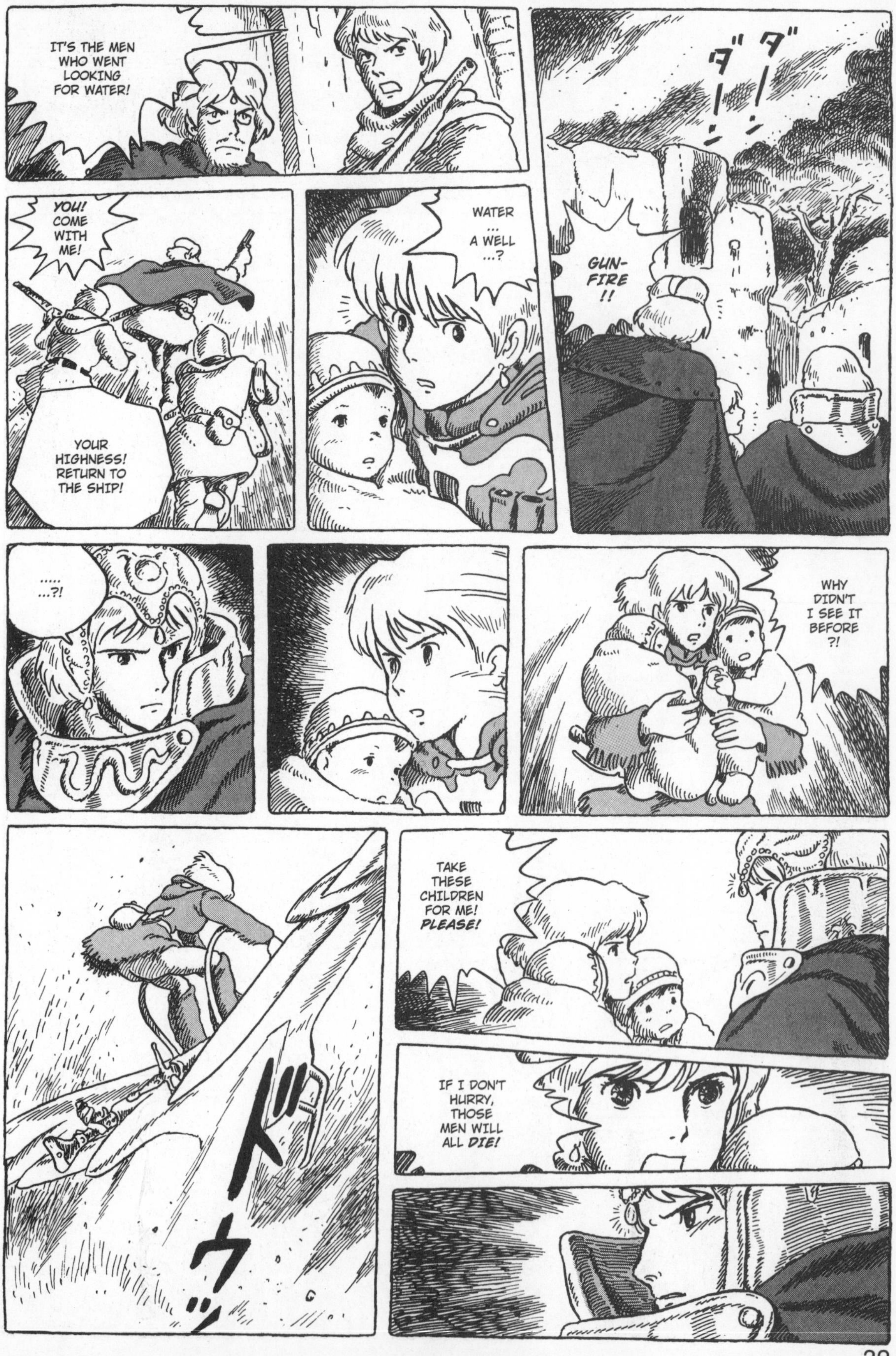
ダーン
ダーン
GUN-FIRE !!
IT'S THE MEN WHO WENT LOOKING FOR WATER!
WATER ... A WELL ...?
YOU! COME WITH ME!
YOUR HIGHNESS! RETURN TO THE SHIP!
WHY DIDN'T I SEE IT BEFORE ?!
....?!
TAKE THESE CHILDREN FOR ME! PLEASE!
IF I DON'T HURRY, THOSE MEN WILL ALL DIE!
ドゥッ

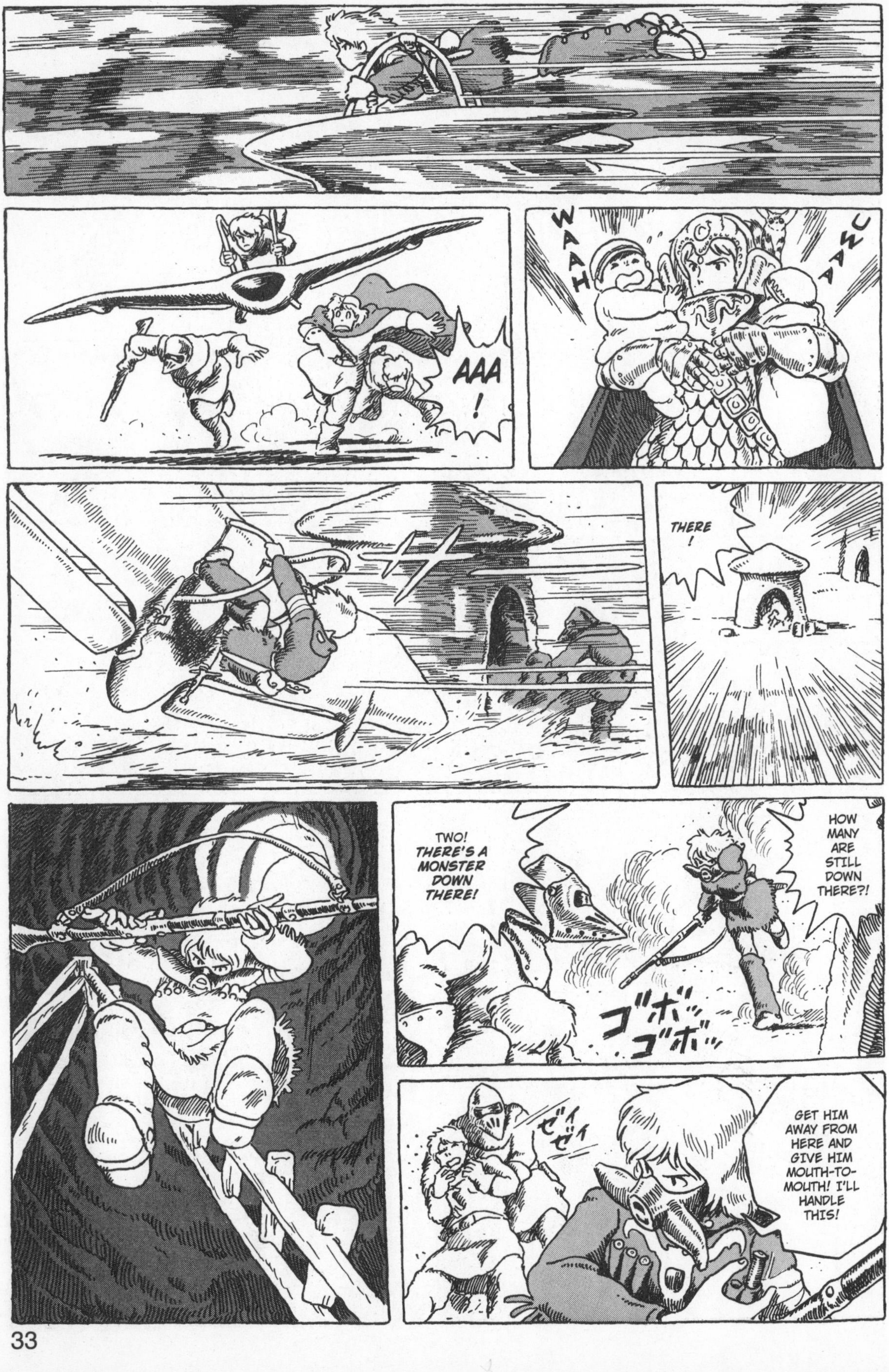
UWAAA
WAAH
AAA!
THERE!
HOW MANY ARE STILL DOWN THERE?!
TWO! THERE'S A MONSTER DOWN THERE!
ゴボッ
ゴボッ
ゼイ
ゼイ
GET HIM AWAY FROM HERE AND GIVE HIM MOUTH-TO-MOUTH! I'LL HANDLE THIS!

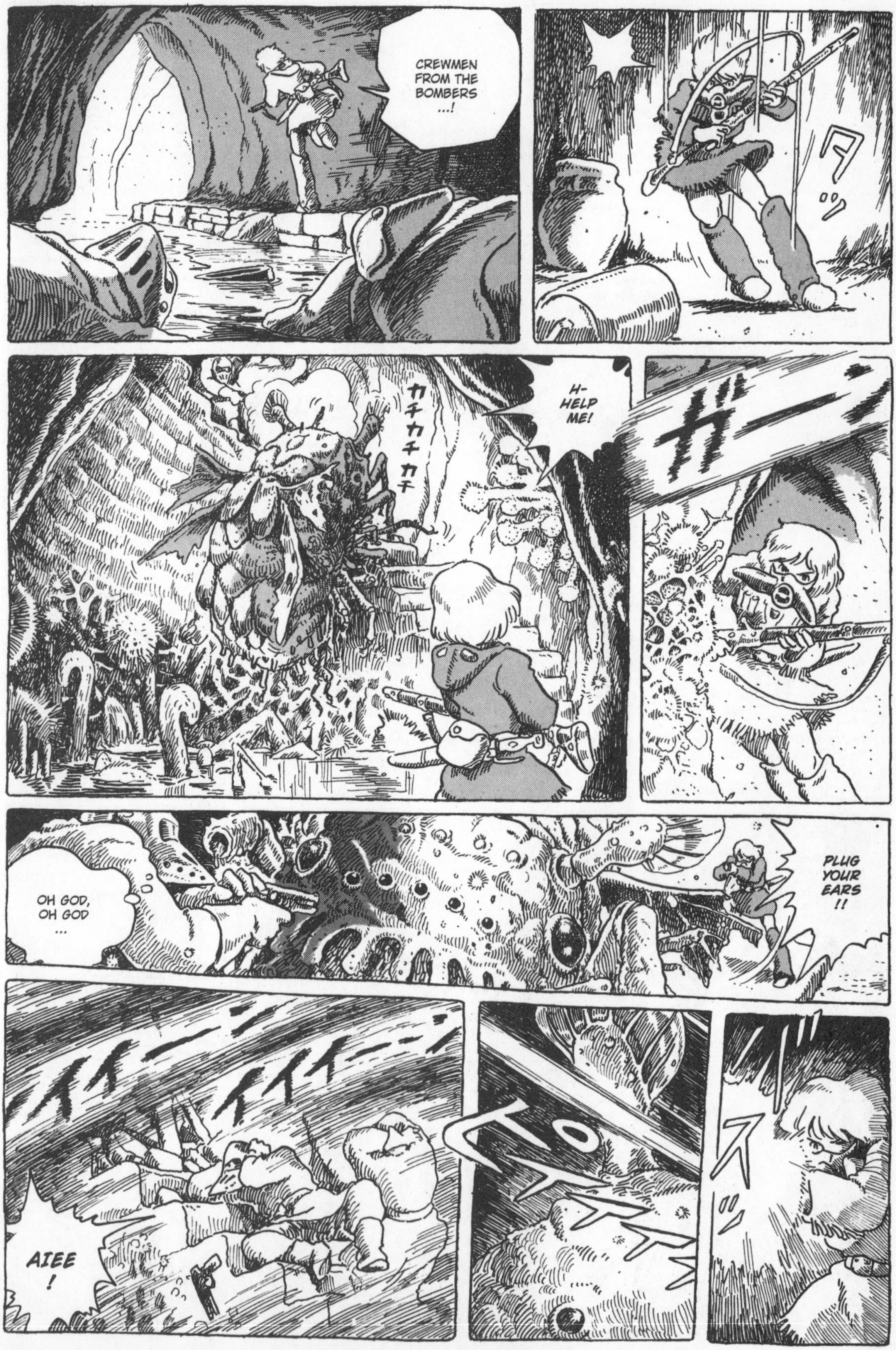

タッ
CREWMEN FROM THE BOMBERS ...!
H-HELP ME!
カチカチカチ
PLUG YOUR EARS !!
OH GOD, OH GOD ...
AIEE !

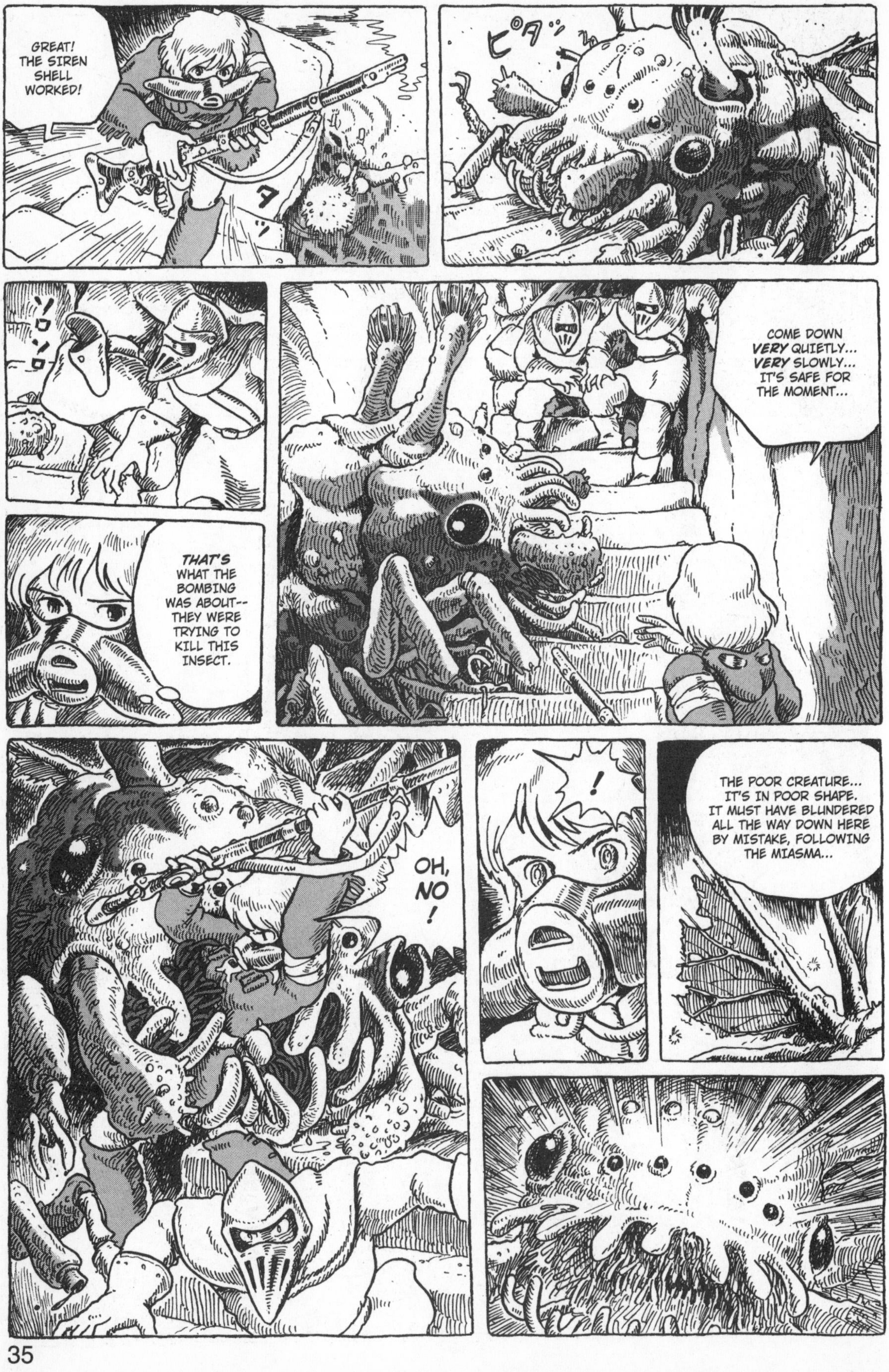
GREAT! THE SIREN SHELL WORKED!
COME DOWN VERY QUIETLY... VERY SLOWLY... IT'S SAFE FOR THE MOMENT...
THAT'S WHAT THE BOMBING WAS ABOUT-- THEY WERE TRYING TO KILL THIS INSECT.
THE POOR CREATURE... IT'S IN POOR SHAPE. IT MUST HAVE BLUNDERED ALL THE WAY DOWN HERE BY MISTAKE, FOLLOWING THE MIASMA...
!
OH, NO!

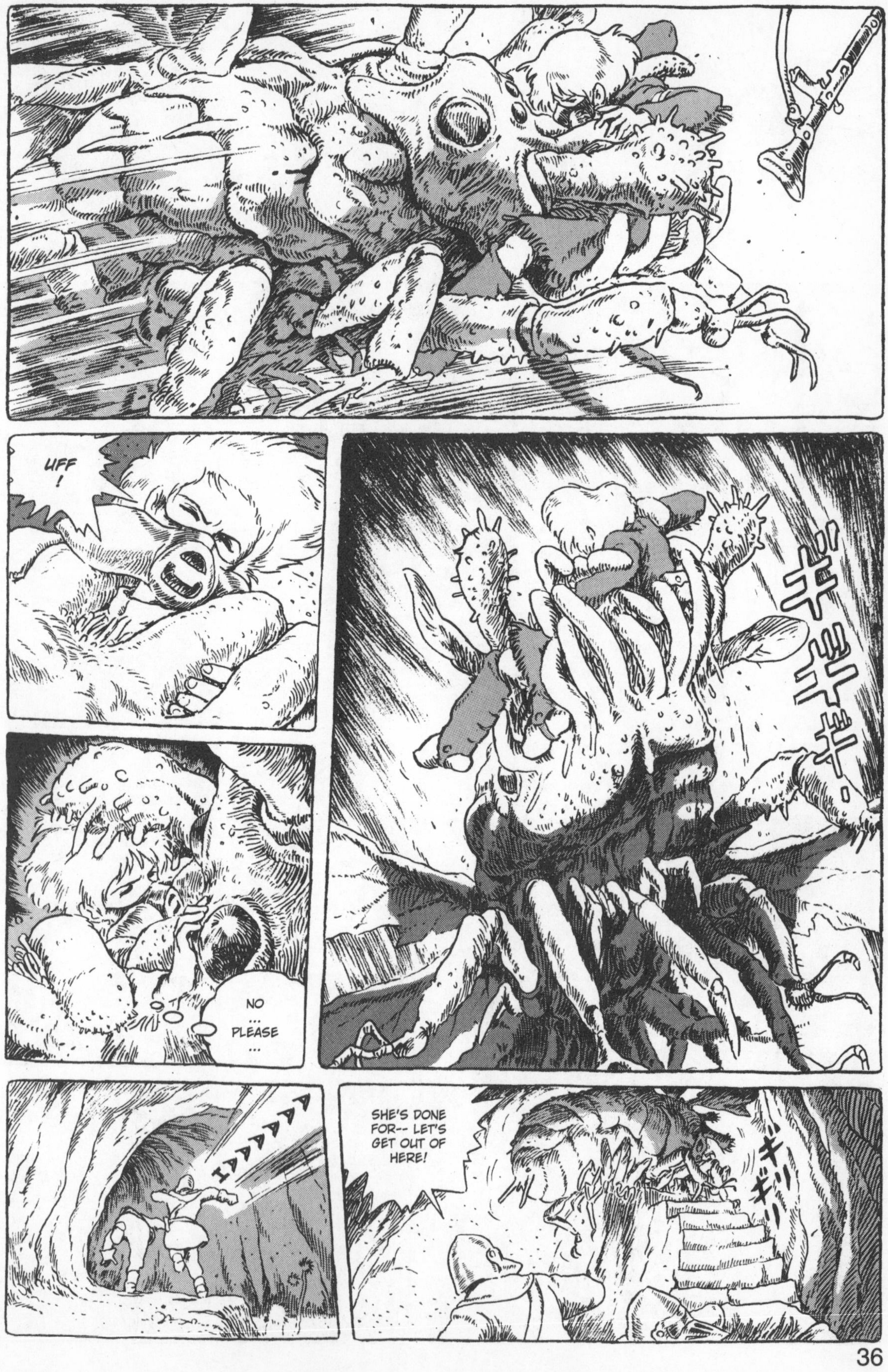
ギチギチ
UFF!
NO ... PLEASE ...
SHE'S DONE FOR-- LET'S GET OUT OF HERE!
ギリギリ

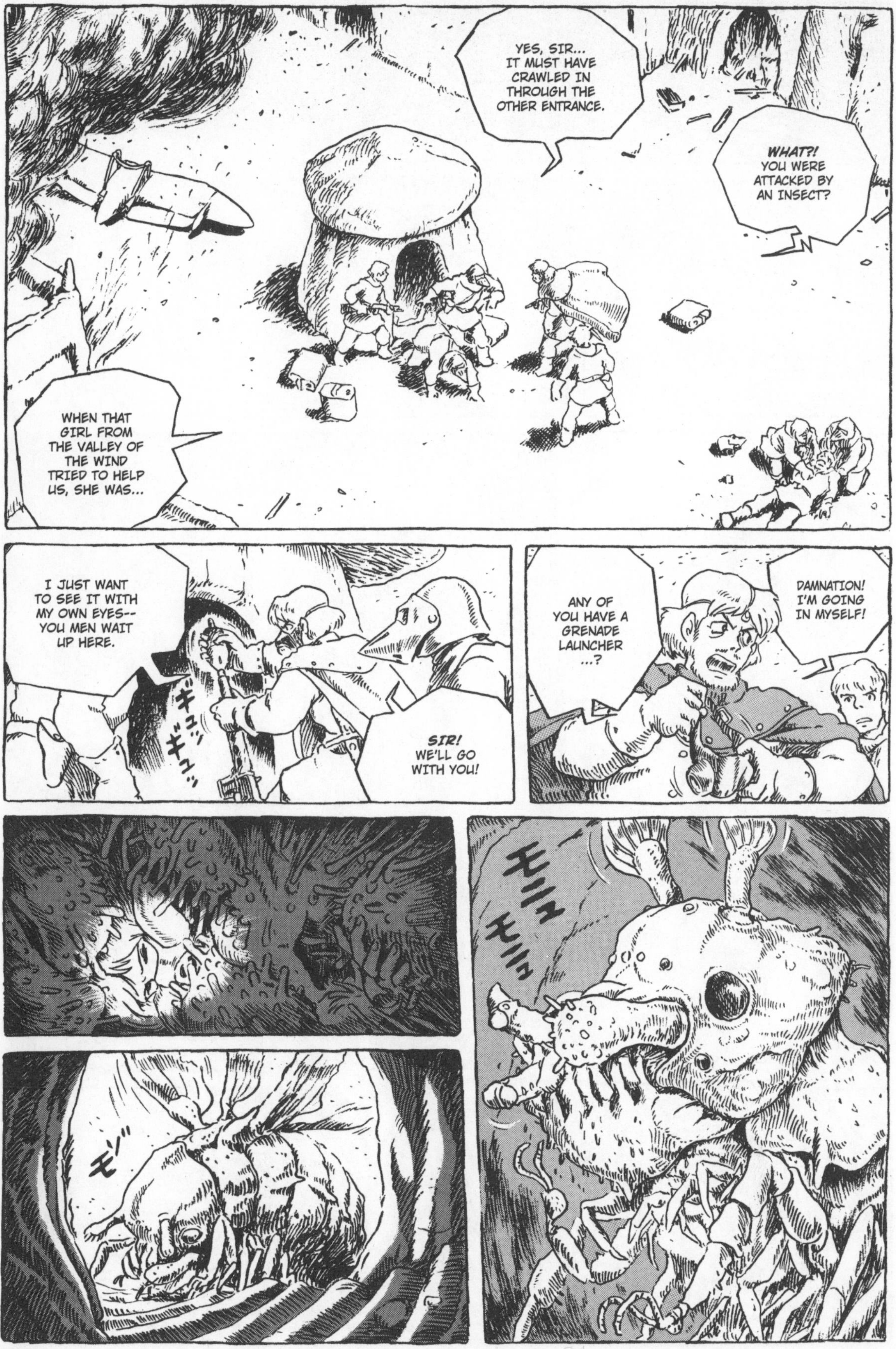
WHAT?! YOU WERE ATTACKED BY AN INSECT?
YES, SIR... IT MUST HAVE CRAWLED IN THROUGH THE OTHER ENTRANCE.
WHEN THAT GIRL FROM THE VALLEY OF THE WIND TRIED TO HELP US, SHE WAS...
DAMNATION! I'M GOING IN MYSELF!
ANY OF YOU HAVE A GRENADE LAUNCHER ...?
SIR! WE'LL GO WITH YOU!
I JUST WANT TO SEE IT WITH MY OWN EYES-- YOU MEN WAIT UP HERE.
ギュッ ギュッ
モニュ モニュ
モゾ

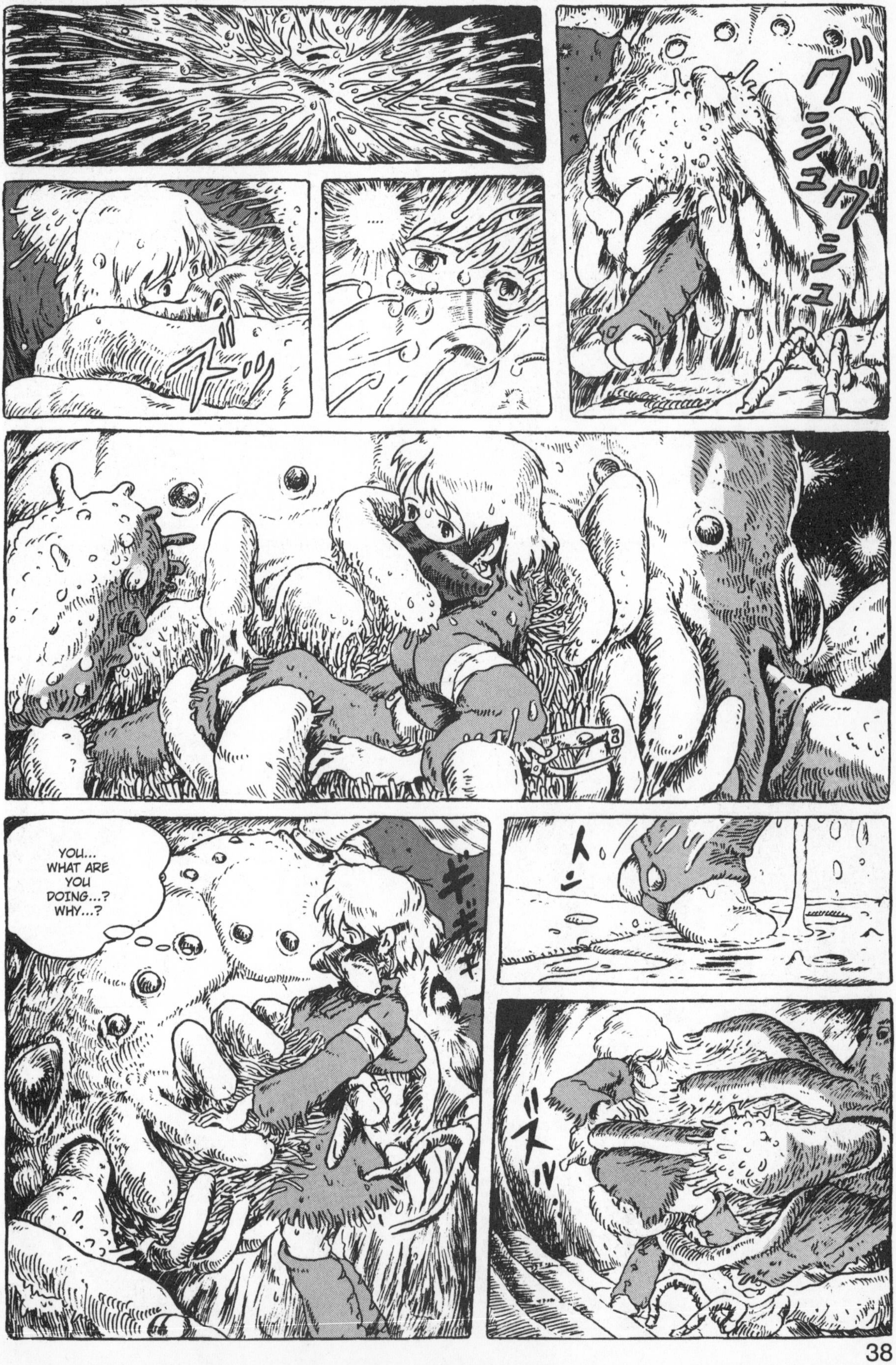
グシュグシュ
YOU... WHAT ARE YOU DOING...? WHY...?

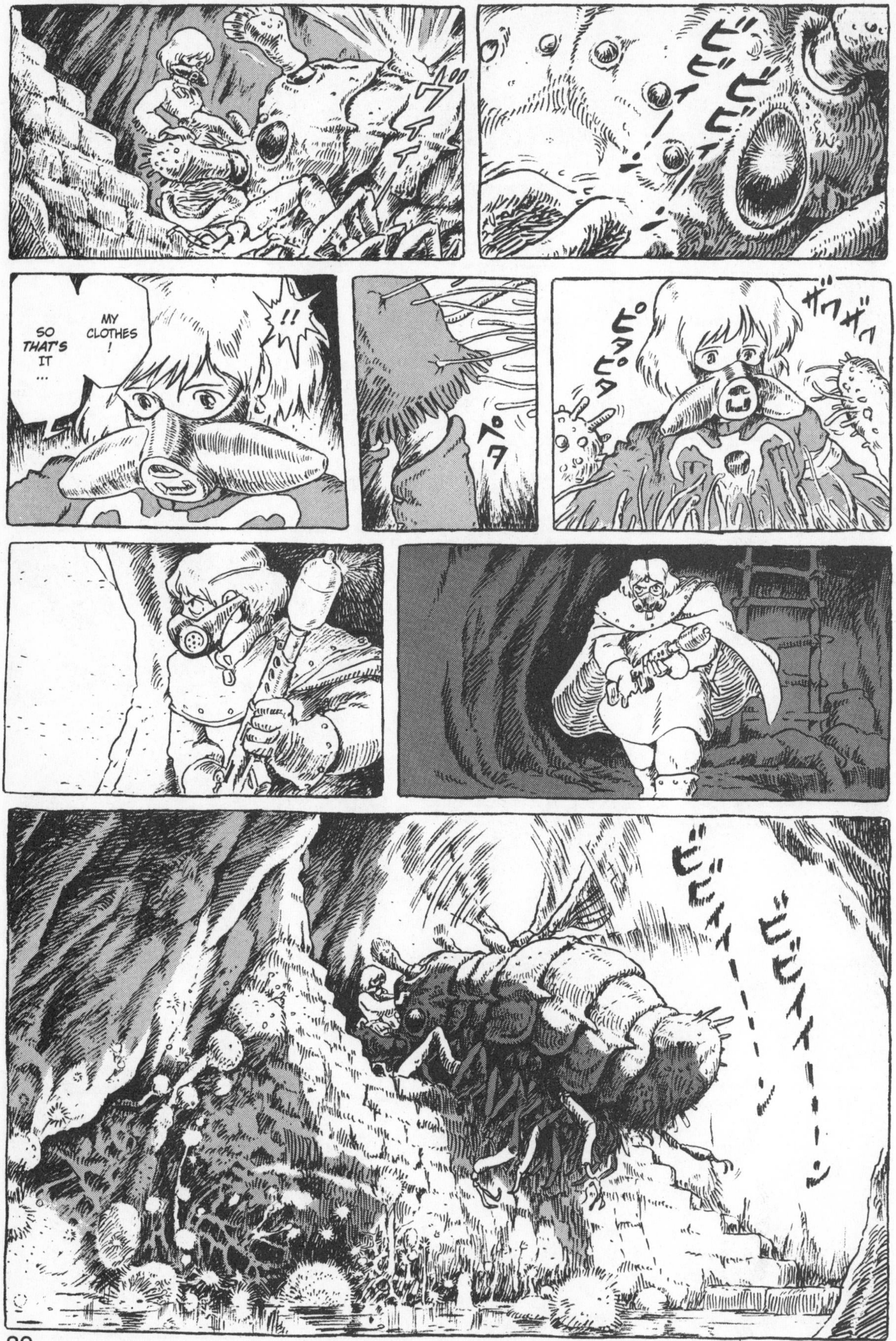
!!
MY CLOTHES !
SO THAT'S IT ...

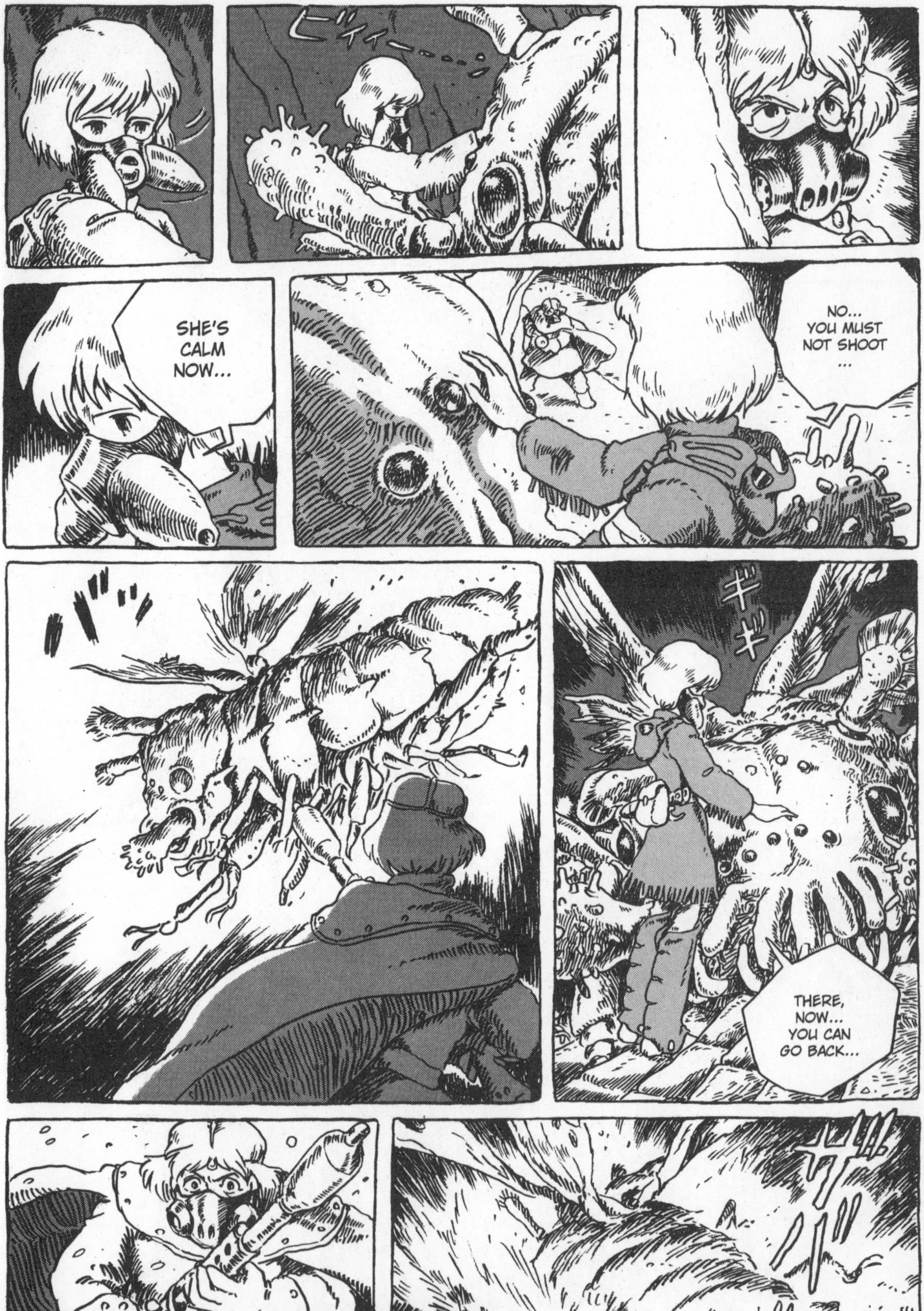
NO... YOU MUST NOT SHOOT ...
SHE'S CALM NOW...
THERE, NOW... YOU CAN GO BACK...

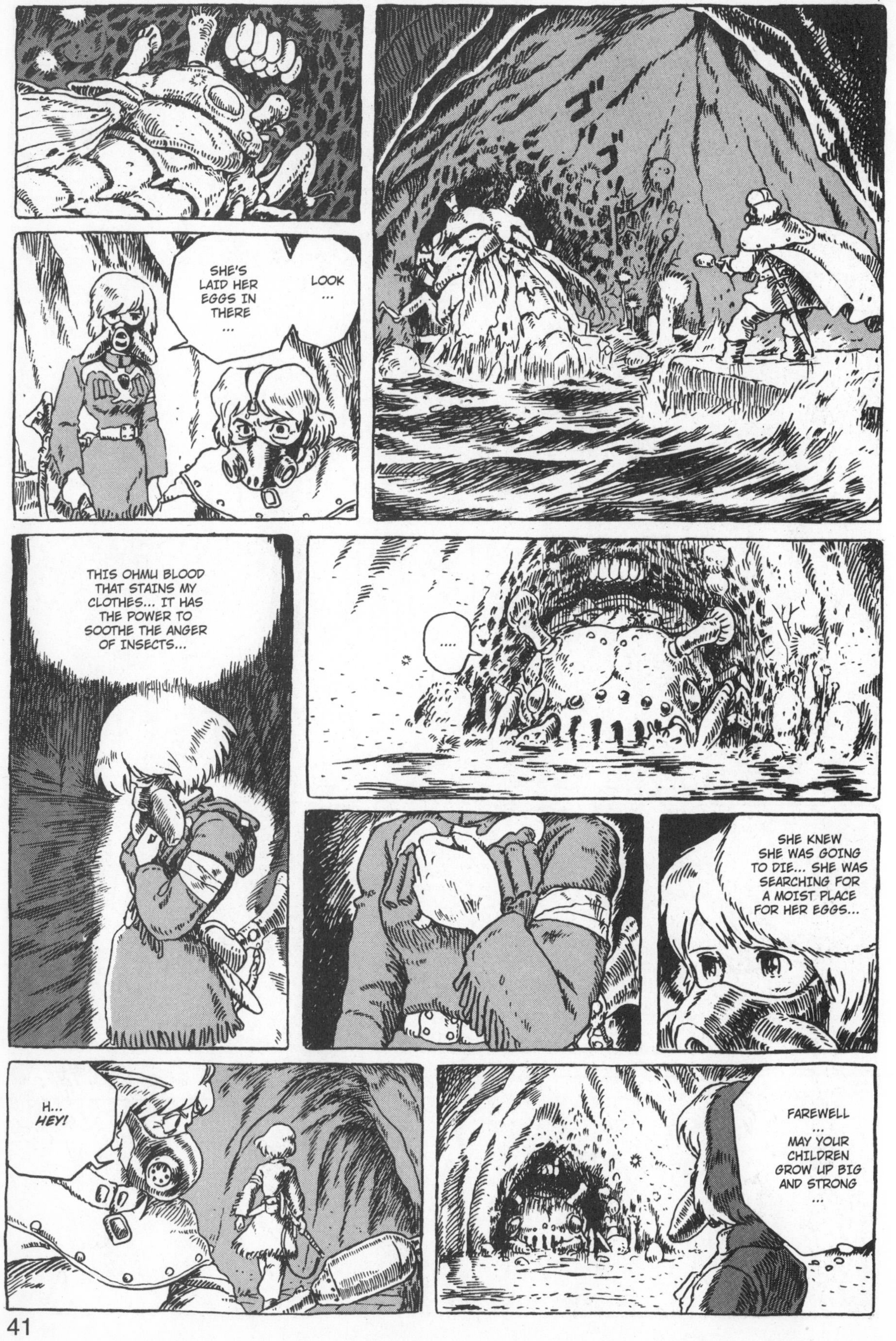
LOOK ...
SHE'S LAID HER EGGS IN THERE ...
....
SHE KNEW SHE WAS GOING TO DIE... SHE WAS SEARCHING FOR A MOIST PLACE FOR HER EGGS...
THIS OHMU BLOOD THAT STAINS MY CLOTHES... IT HAS THE POWER TO SOOTHE THE ANGER OF INSECTS...
FAREWELL ... MAY YOUR CHILDREN GROW UP BIG AND STRONG ...
H... *HEY!*

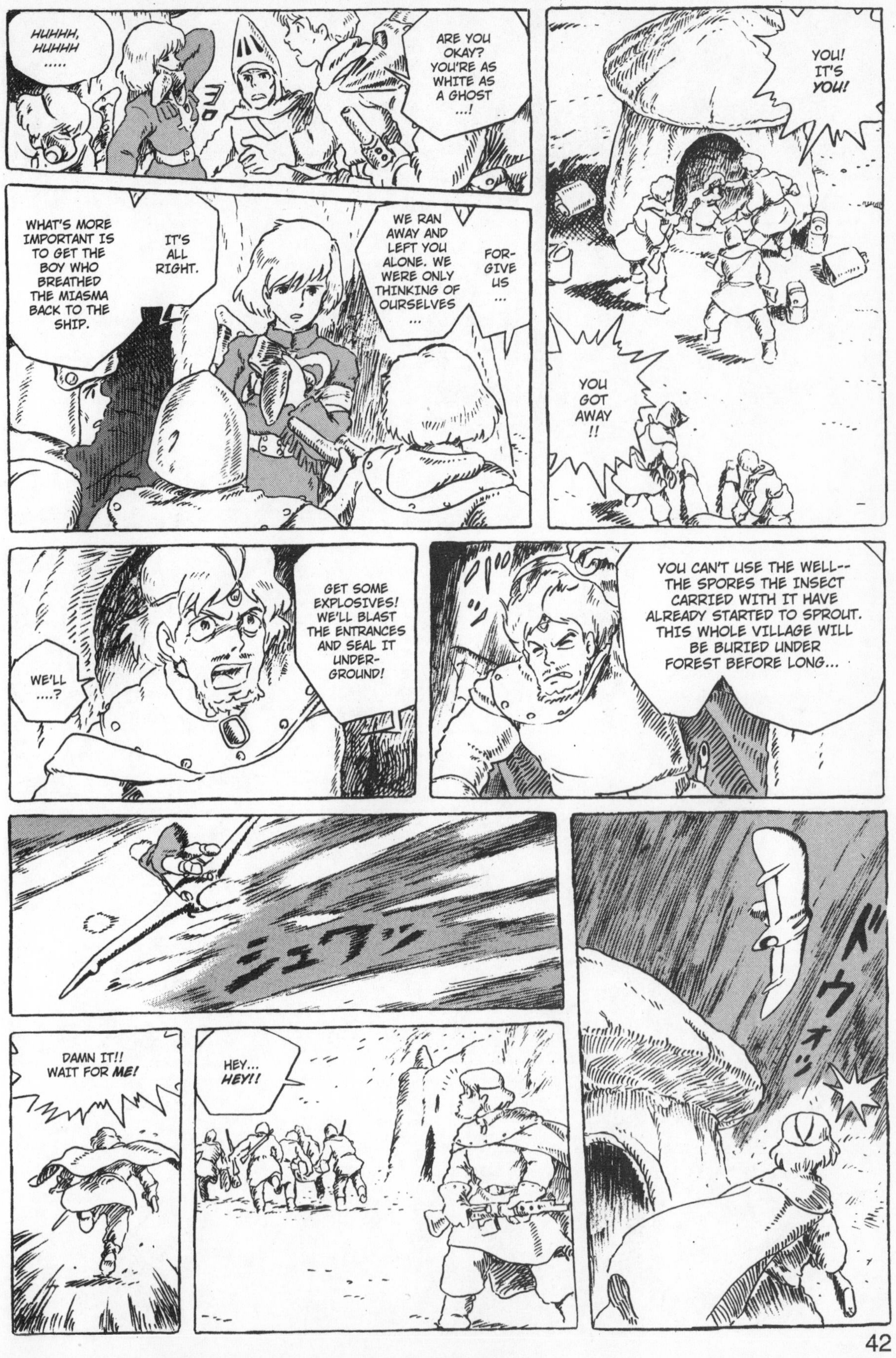
YOU! IT'S YOU!
YOU GOT AWAY !!
ARE YOU OKAY? YOU'RE AS WHITE AS A GHOST ...!
HUHHH, HUHHH .....
FOR-GIVE US ...
WE RAN AWAY AND LEFT YOU ALONE. WE WERE ONLY THINKING OF OURSELVES ...
IT'S ALL RIGHT.
WHAT'S MORE IMPORTANT IS TO GET THE BOY WHO BREATHED THE MIASMA BACK TO THE SHIP.
YOU CAN'T USE THE WELL-- THE SPORES THE INSECT CARRIED WITH IT HAVE ALREADY STARTED TO SPROUT. THIS WHOLE VILLAGE WILL BE BURIED UNDER FOREST BEFORE LONG...
GET SOME EXPLOSIVES! WE'LL BLAST THE ENTRANCES AND SEAL IT UNDER-GROUND!
WE'LL ....?
シュワッ
HEY... HEY!!
DAMN IT!! WAIT FOR ME!

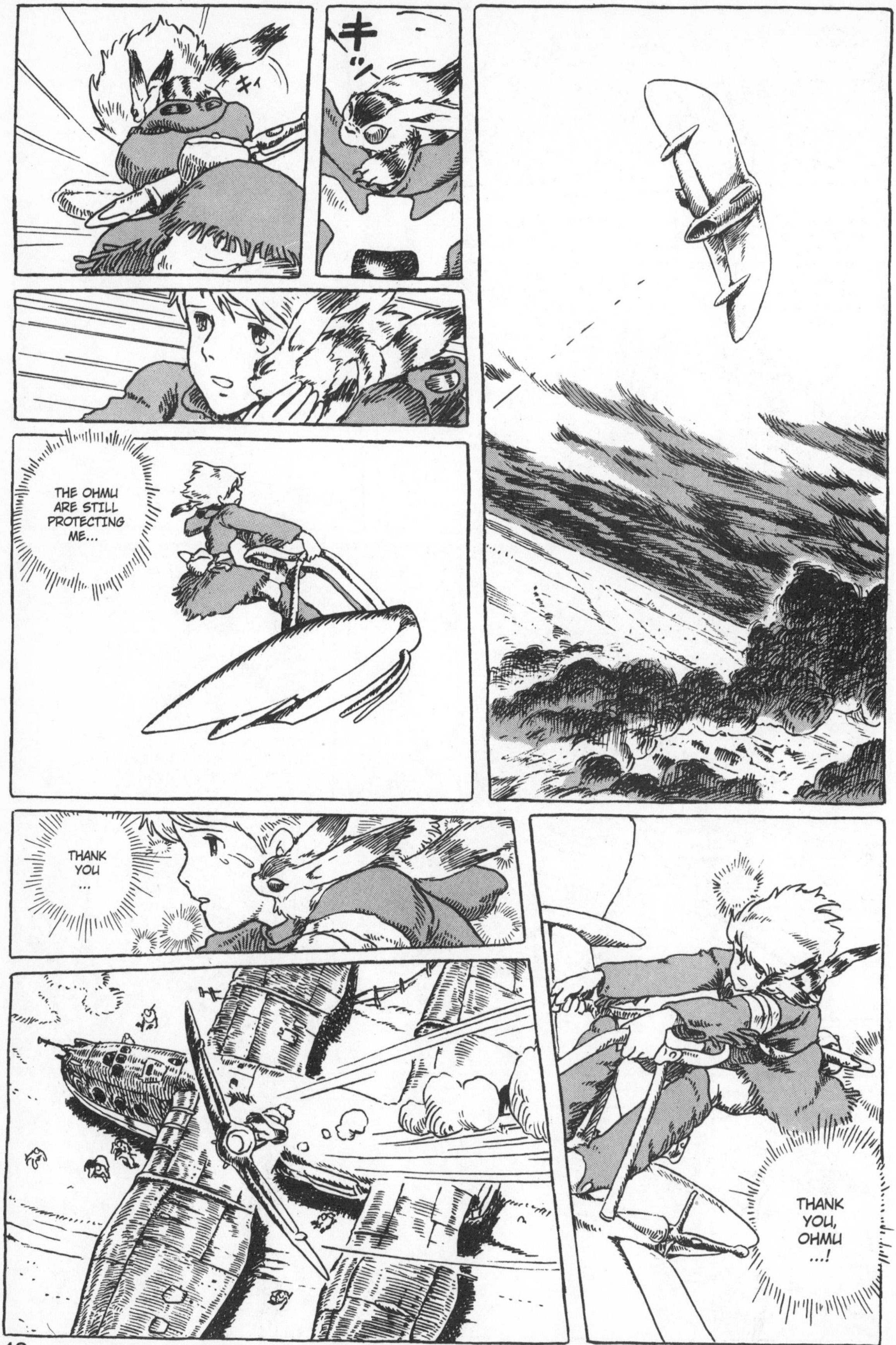

キッ
キィ
THE OHMU ARE STILL PROTECTING ME...
THANK YOU, OHMU ...!
THANK YOU ...

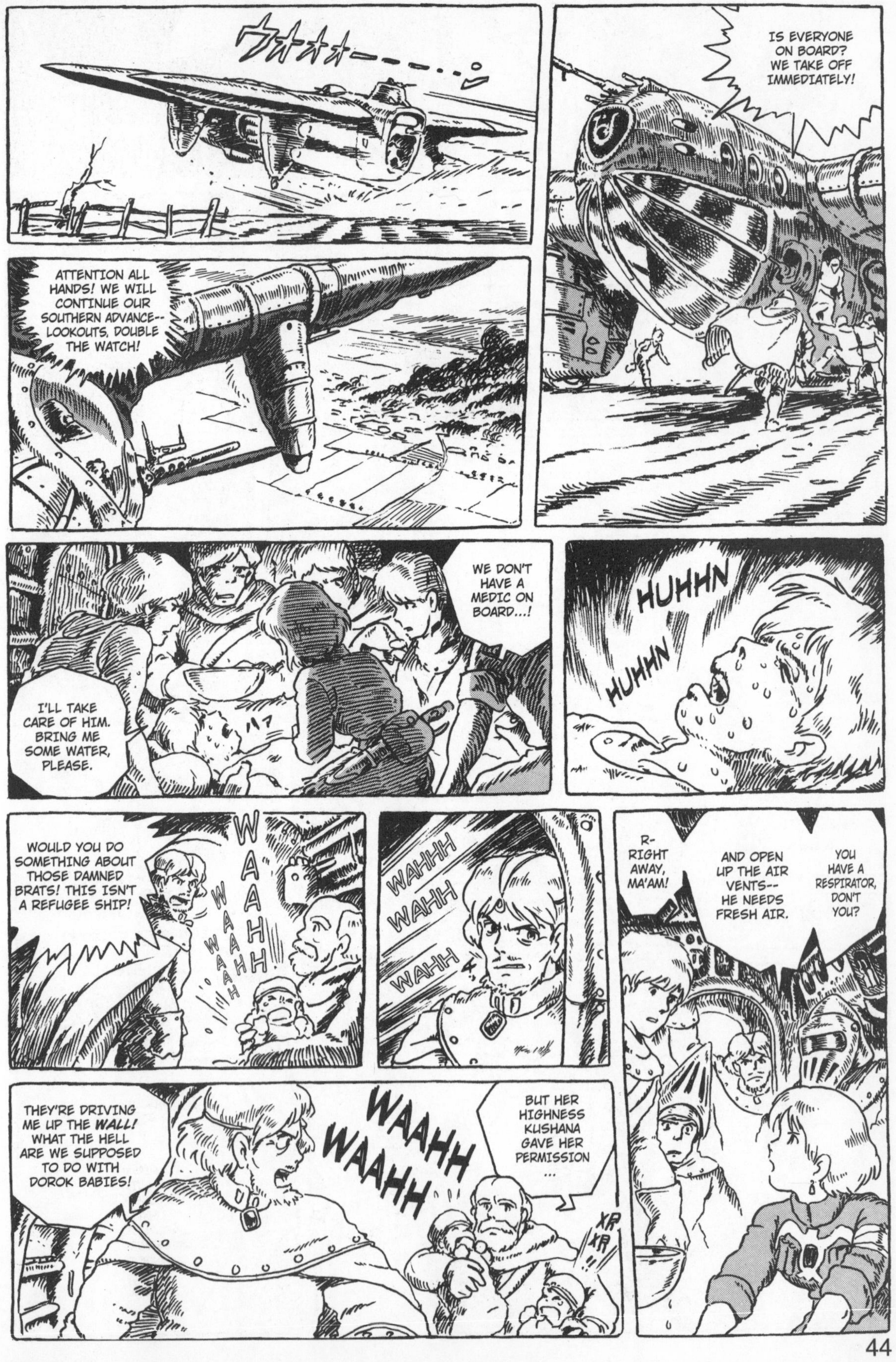
IS EVERYONE ON BOARD? WE TAKE OFF IMMEDIATELY!
ウォォォーーー‥ン
ATTENTION ALL HANDS! WE WILL CONTINUE OUR SOUTHERN ADVANCE-- LOOKOUTS, DOUBLE THE WATCH!
HUHHN
HUHHN
WE DON'T HAVE A MEDIC ON BOARD...!
ハッ
I'LL TAKE CARE OF HIM. BRING ME SOME WATER, PLEASE.
YOU HAVE A RESPIRATOR, DON'T YOU?
AND OPEN UP THE AIR VENTS-- HE NEEDS FRESH AIR.
R- RIGHT AWAY, MA'AM!
WAHHH
WAHH
WAHH
WAAHH
WAAHH
WAAHH
WOULD YOU DO SOMETHING ABOUT THOSE DAMNED BRATS! THIS ISN'T A REFUGEE SHIP!
BUT HER HIGHNESS KUSHANA GAVE HER PERMISSION ...
WAAHH
WAAHH
XR XR
THEY'RE DRIVING ME UP THE WALL! WHAT THE HELL ARE WE SUPPOSED TO DO WITH DOROK BABIES!

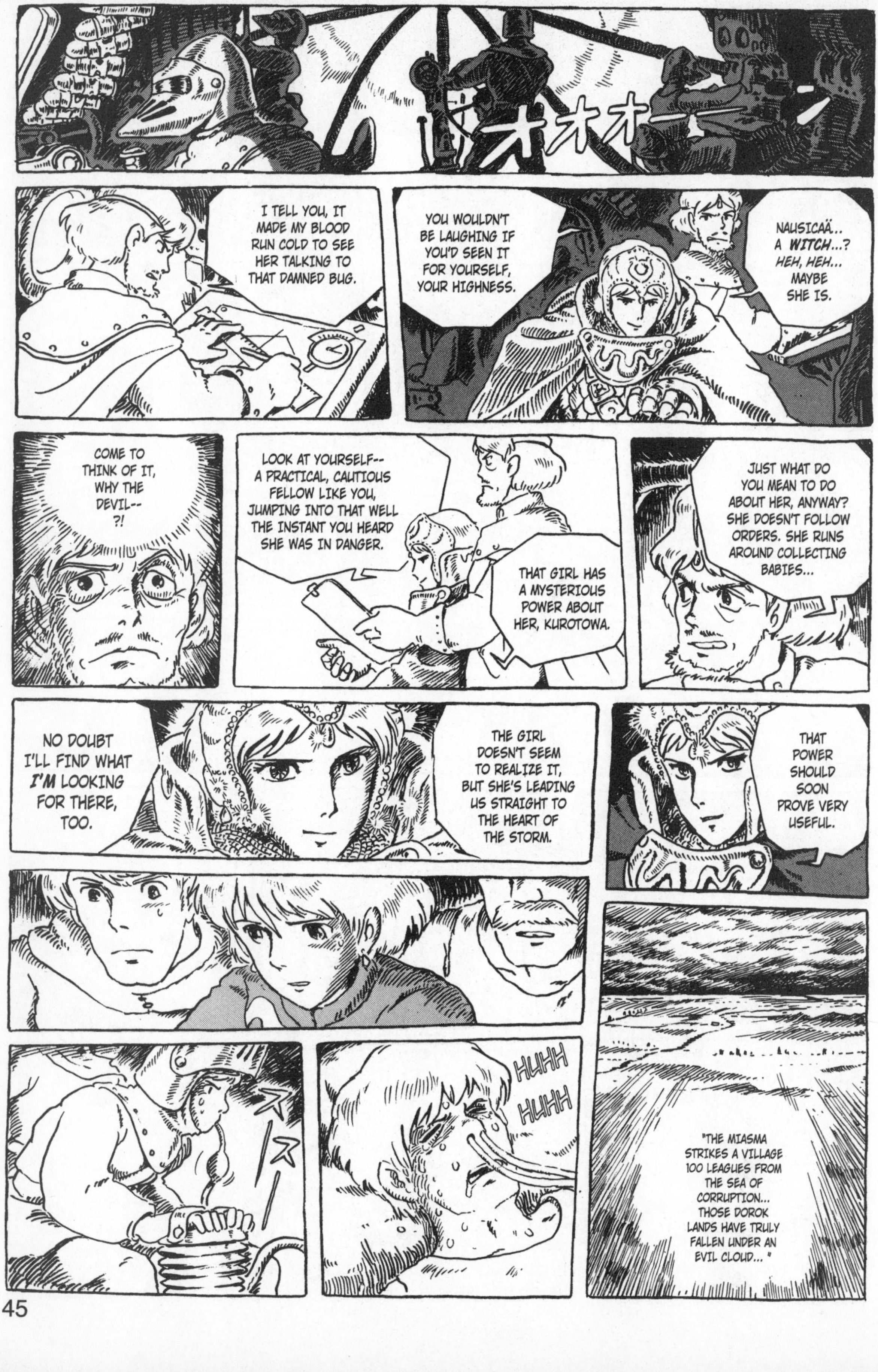
オオオーーン
NAUSICAÄ... A ***WITCH***...? *HEH, HEH...* MAYBE SHE IS.
YOU WOULDN'T BE LAUGHING IF YOU'D SEEN IT FOR YOURSELF, YOUR HIGHNESS.
I TELL YOU, IT MADE MY BLOOD RUN COLD TO SEE HER TALKING TO THAT DAMNED BUG.
JUST WHAT DO YOU MEAN TO DO ABOUT HER, ANYWAY? SHE DOESN'T FOLLOW ORDERS. SHE RUNS AROUND COLLECTING BABIES...
LOOK AT YOURSELF-- A PRACTICAL, CAUTIOUS FELLOW LIKE YOU, JUMPING INTO THAT WELL THE INSTANT YOU HEARD SHE WAS IN DANGER.
THAT GIRL HAS A MYSTERIOUS POWER ABOUT HER, KUROTOWA.
COME TO THINK OF IT, WHY THE DEVIL-- ?!
THAT POWER SHOULD SOON PROVE VERY USEFUL.
THE GIRL DOESN'T SEEM TO REALIZE IT, BUT SHE'S LEADING US STRAIGHT TO THE HEART OF THE STORM.
NO DOUBT I'LL FIND WHAT ***I'M*** LOOKING FOR THERE, TOO.
"THE MIASMA STRIKES A VILLAGE 100 LEAGUES FROM THE SEA OF CORRUPTION... THOSE DOROK LANDS HAVE TRULY FALLEN UNDER AN EVIL CLOUD..."
HUHH
HUHH
ス
ス

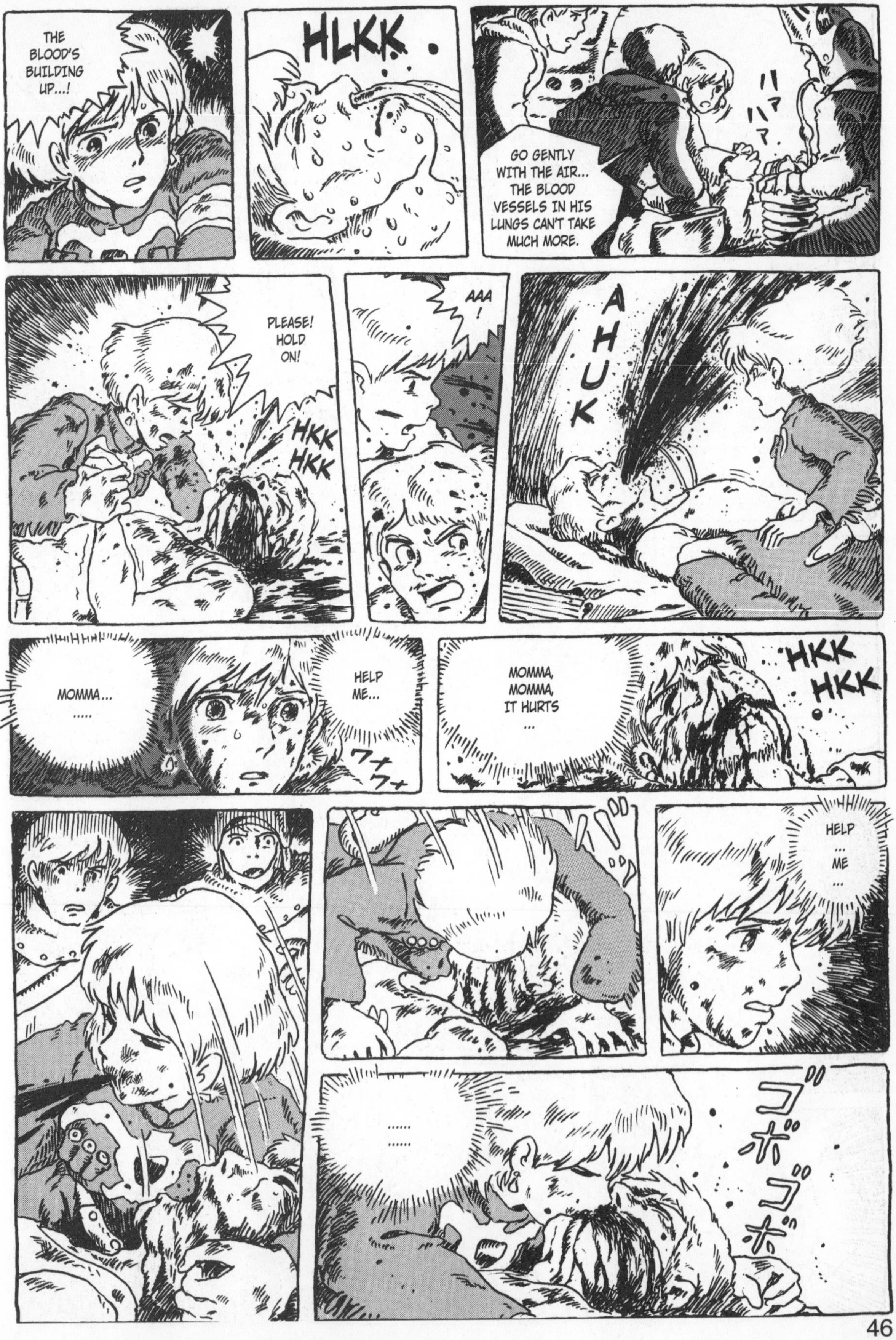
ハァハァ
GO GENTLY WITH THE AIR... THE BLOOD VESSELS IN HIS LUNGS CAN'T TAKE MUCH MORE.
HLKK
THE BLOOD'S BUILDING UP...!
AHUK
AAA!
PLEASE! HOLD ON!
HKK HKK
HKK HKK
MOMMA, MOMMA, IT HURTS ...
HELP ME...
MOMMA... .....
ワナワナ
HELP ... ME ...
ゴボゴボ
....

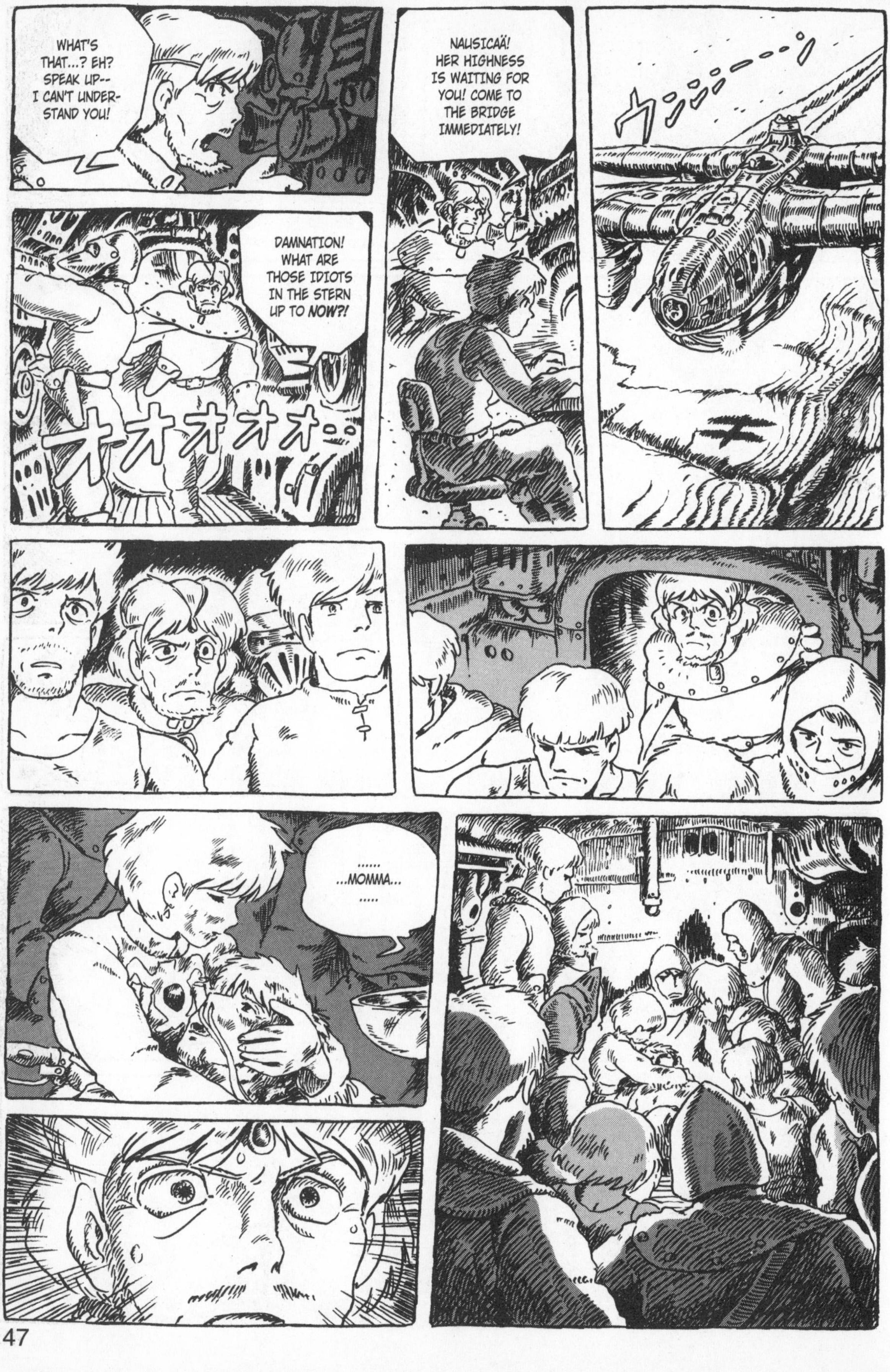
NAUSICAÄ! HER HIGHNESS IS WAITING FOR YOU! COME TO THE BRIDGE IMMEDIATELY!
WHAT'S THAT...? EH? SPEAK UP-- I CAN'T UNDER-STAND YOU!
DAMNATION! WHAT ARE THOSE IDIOTS IN THE STERN UP TO ***NOW?!***
....MOMMA... .....

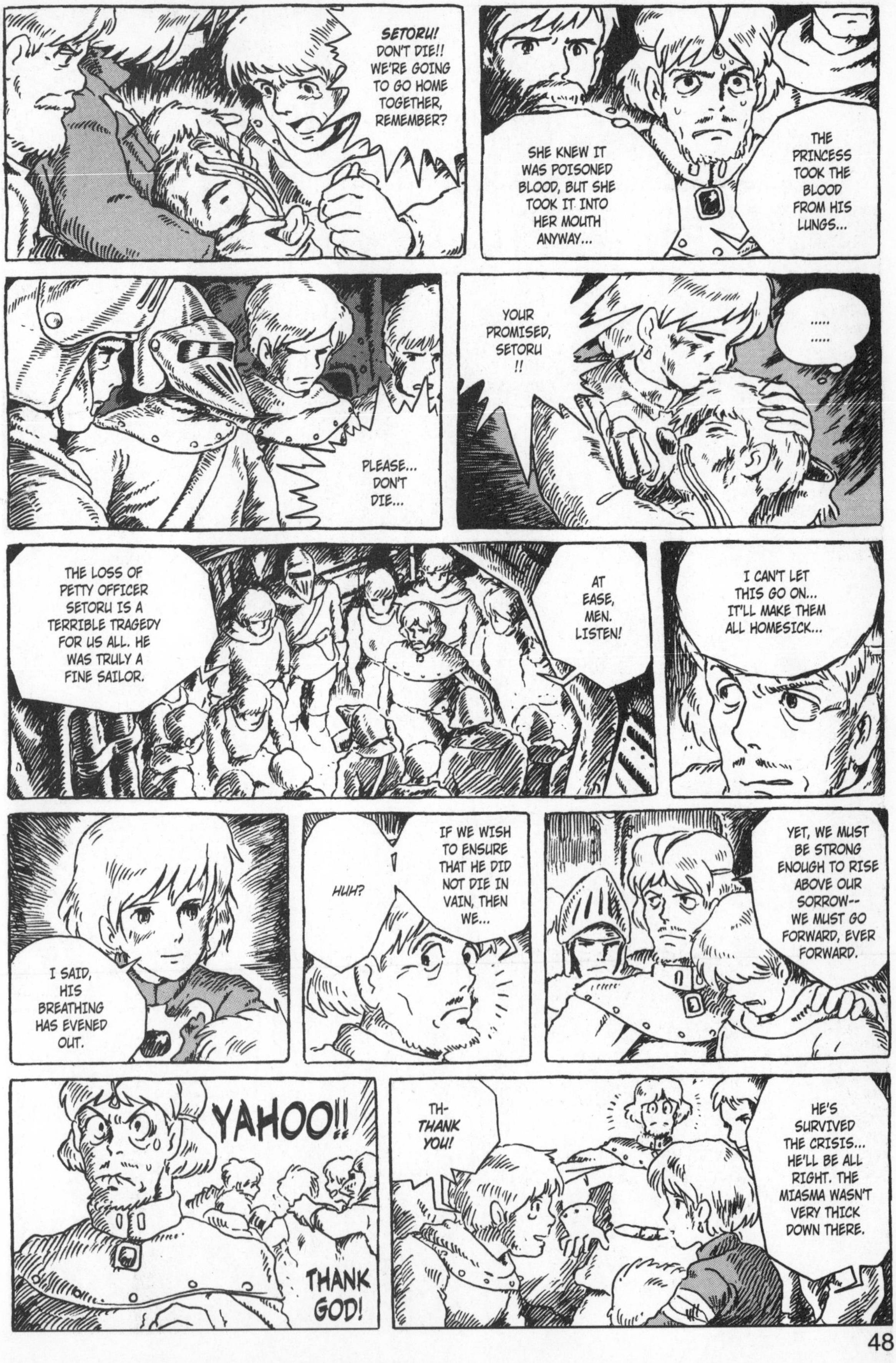
SETORU! DON'T DIE!! WE'RE GOING TO GO HOME TOGETHER, REMEMBER?
THE PRINCESS TOOK THE BLOOD FROM HIS LUNGS...
SHE KNEW IT WAS POISONED BLOOD, BUT SHE TOOK IT INTO HER MOUTH ANYWAY...
YOUR PROMISED, SETORU !!
.....
.....
PLEASE... DON'T DIE...
THE LOSS OF PETTY OFFICER SETORU IS A TERRIBLE TRAGEDY FOR US ALL. HE WAS TRULY A FINE SAILOR.
AT EASE, MEN. LISTEN!
I CAN'T LET THIS GO ON... IT'LL MAKE THEM ALL HOMESICK...
YET, WE MUST BE STRONG ENOUGH TO RISE ABOVE OUR SORROW-- WE MUST GO FORWARD, EVER FORWARD.
IF WE WISH TO ENSURE THAT HE DID NOT DIE IN VAIN, THEN WE...
HUH?
I SAID, HIS BREATHING HAS EVENED OUT.
HE'S SURVIVED THE CRISIS... HE'LL BE ALL RIGHT. THE MIASMA WASN'T VERY THICK DOWN THERE.
TH- THANK YOU!
YAHOO!!
THANK GOD!

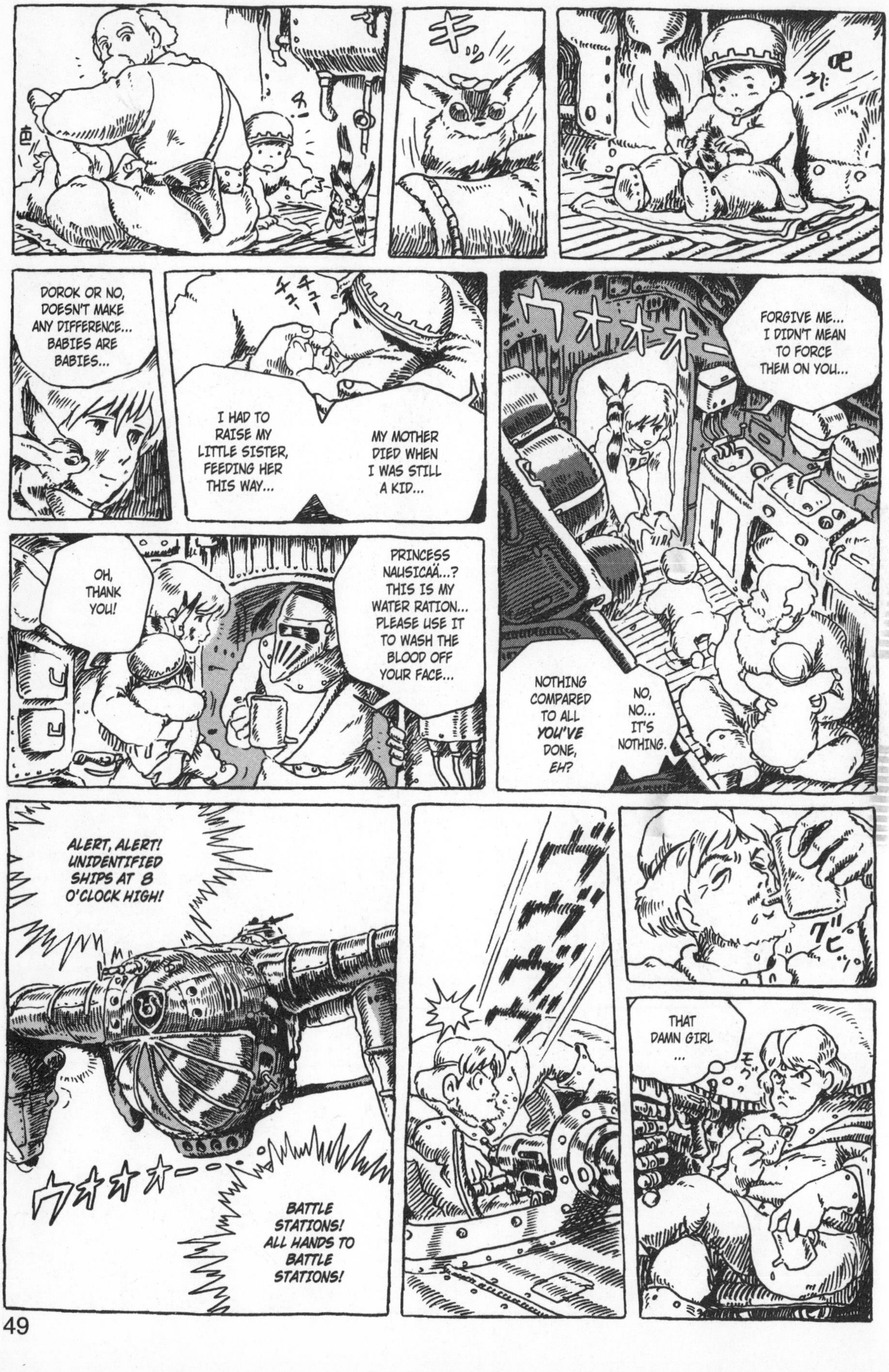
FORGIVE ME... I DIDN'T MEAN TO FORCE THEM ON YOU...
NO, NO... IT'S NOTHING.
NOTHING COMPARED TO ALL YOU'VE DONE, EH?
MY MOTHER DIED WHEN I WAS STILL A KID...
I HAD TO RAISE MY LITTLE SISTER, FEEDING HER THIS WAY...
DOROK OR NO, DOESN'T MAKE ANY DIFFERENCE... BABIES ARE BABIES...
PRINCESS NAUSICAÄ...? THIS IS MY WATER RATION... PLEASE USE IT TO WASH THE BLOOD OFF YOUR FACE...
OH, THANK YOU!
THAT DAMN GIRL ...
ALERT, ALERT! UNIDENTIFIED SHIPS AT 8 O'CLOCK HIGH!
BATTLE STATIONS! ALL HANDS TO BATTLE STATIONS!

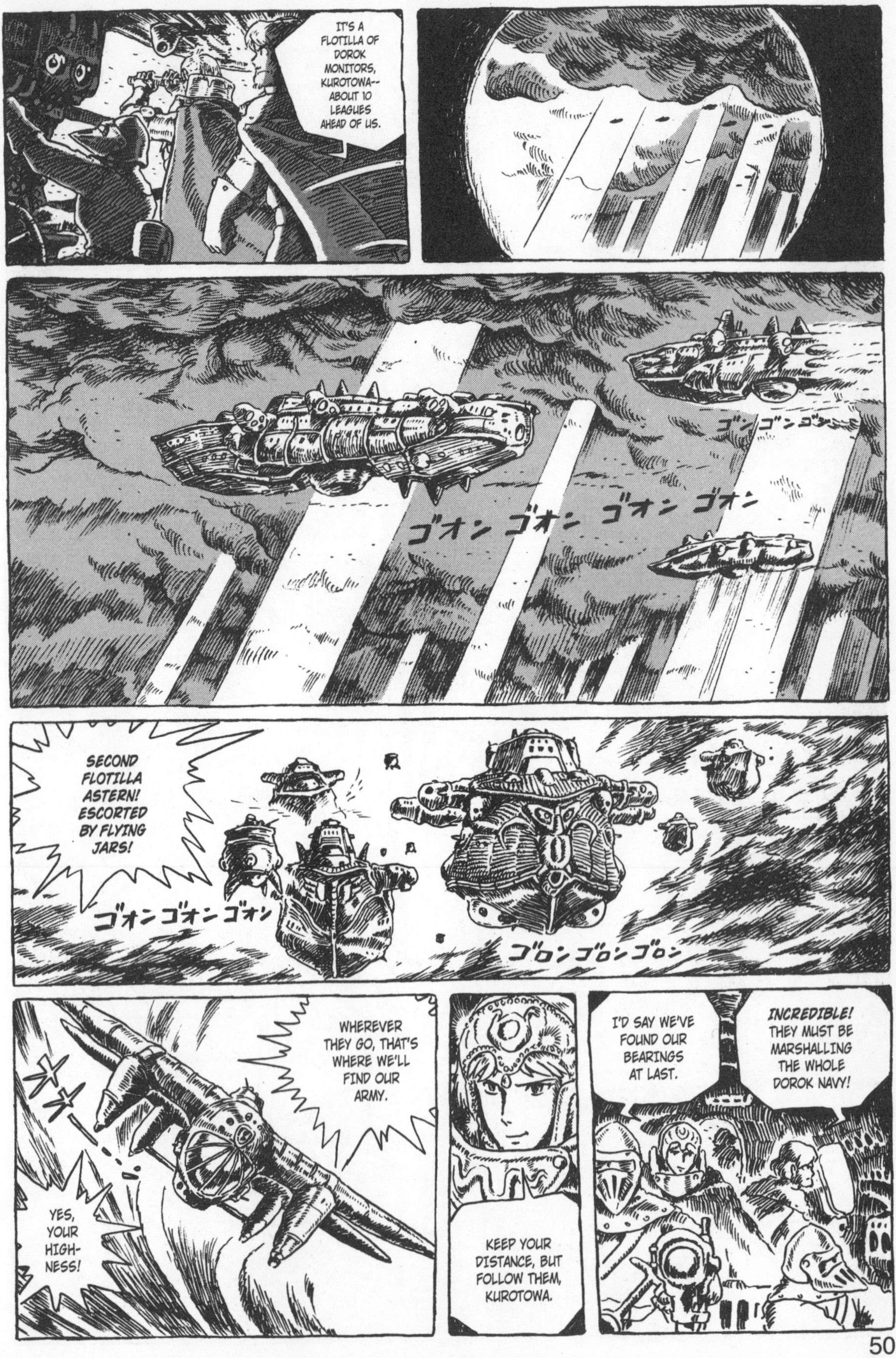
IT'S A FLOTILLA OF DOROK MONITORS, KUROTOWA-- ABOUT 10 LEAGUES AHEAD OF US.
ゴンゴンゴン
ゴオンゴオン ゴオン ゴオン
SECOND FLOTILLA ASTERN! ESCORTED BY FLYING JARS!
ゴオンゴオンゴオン
ゴロンゴロンゴロン
INCREDIBLE! THEY MUST BE MARSHALLING THE WHOLE DOROK NAVY!
I'D SAY WE'VE FOUND OUR BEARINGS AT LAST.
KEEP YOUR DISTANCE, BUT FOLLOW THEM, KUROTOWA.
WHEREVER THEY GO, THAT'S WHERE WE'LL FIND OUR ARMY.
YES, YOUR HIGH-NESS!

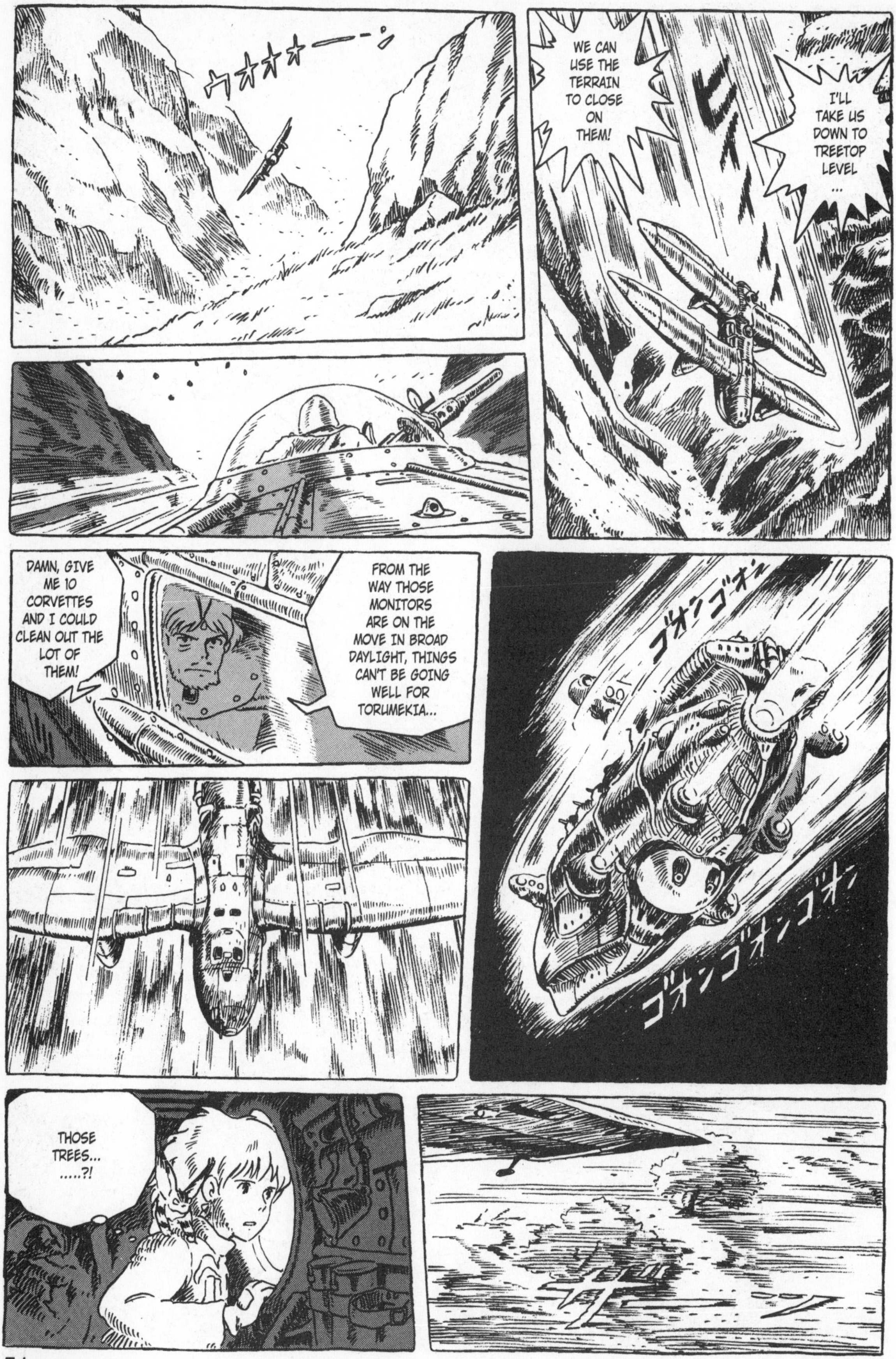
WE CAN USE THE TERRAIN TO CLOSE ON THEM!
I'LL TAKE US DOWN TO TREETOP LEVEL ...
ヒィィィ
ウオオオオーーン
ゴオンゴオン
ゴオンゴオンゴオン
FROM THE WAY THOSE MONITORS ARE ON THE MOVE IN BROAD DAYLIGHT, THINGS CAN'T BE GOING WELL FOR TORUMEKIA...
DAMN, GIVE ME 10 CORVETTES AND I COULD CLEAN OUT THE LOT OF THEM!
THOSE TREES... .....?!

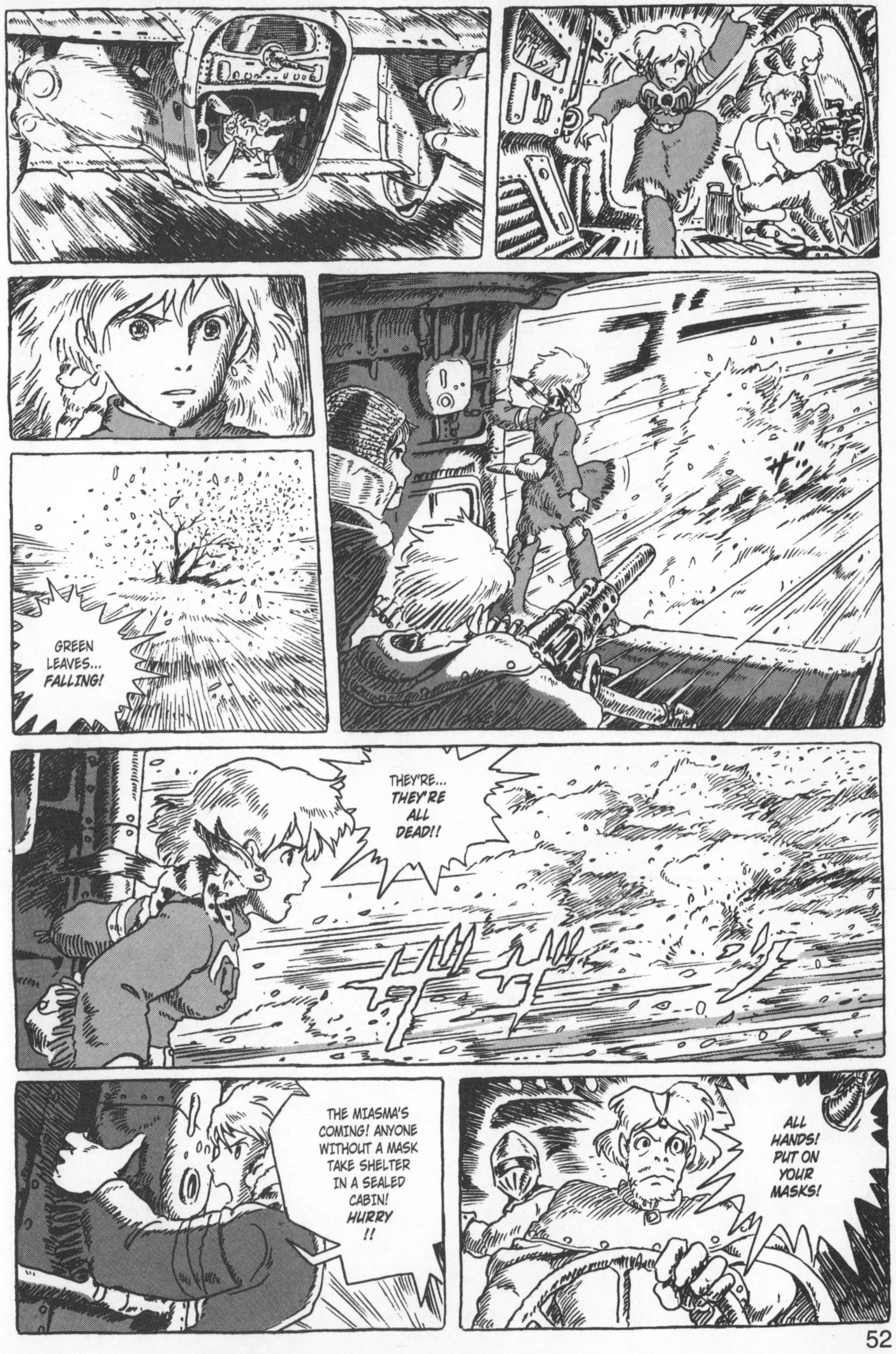
ゴー
ザッ
GREEN LEAVES... FALLING!
THEY'RE... THEY'RE ALL DEAD!!
ザザザッ
ALL HANDS! PUT ON YOUR MASKS!
THE MIASMA'S COMING! ANYONE WITHOUT A MASK TAKE SHELTER IN A SEALED CABIN! HURRY !!

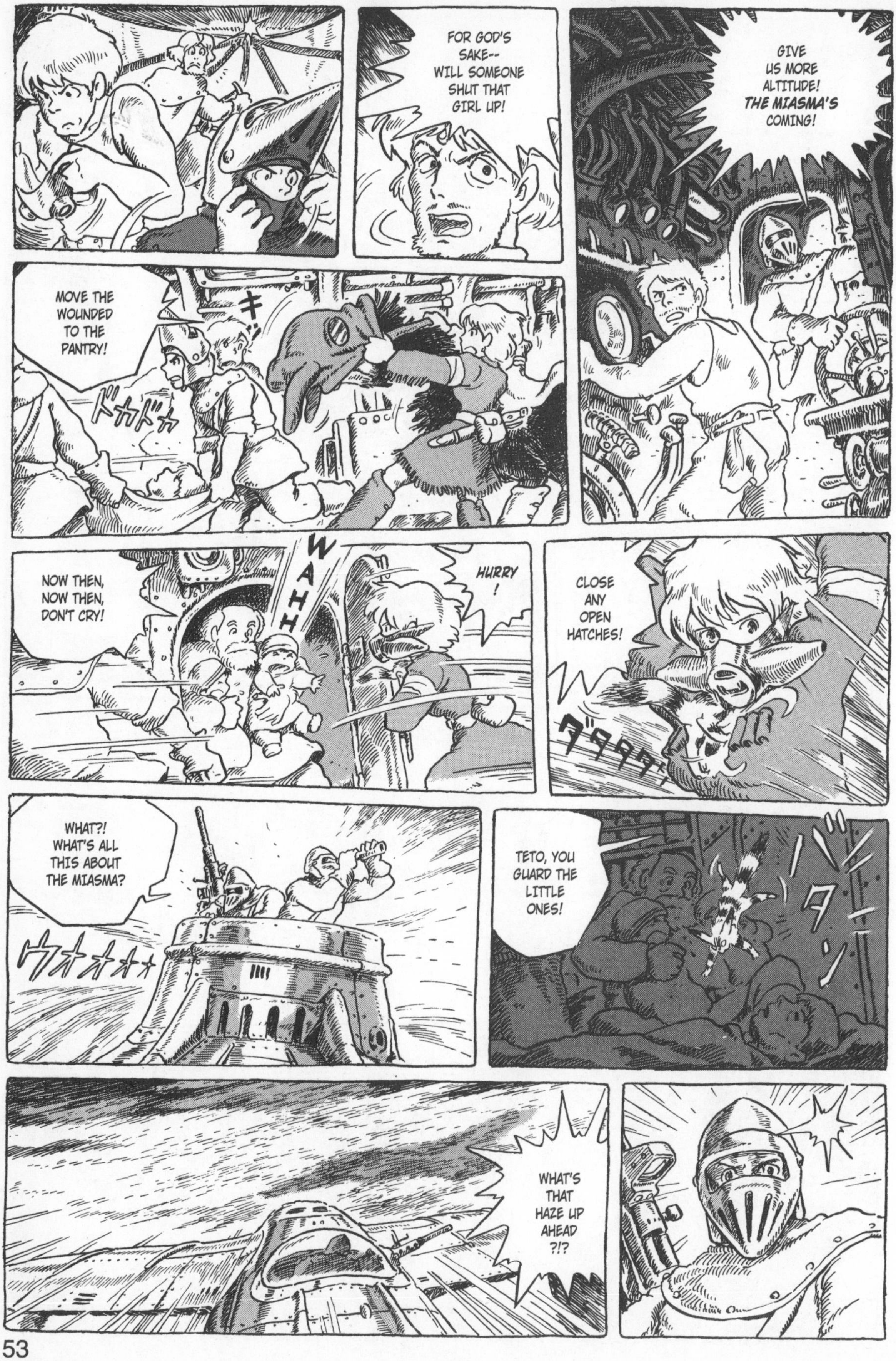
GIVE US MORE ALTITUDE! THE MIASMA'S COMING!
FOR GOD'S SAKE-- WILL SOMEONE SHUT THAT GIRL UP!
キ
MOVE THE WOUNDED TO THE PANTRY!
ドカドカ
CLOSE ANY OPEN HATCHES!
ダダダダ
HURRY!
WAHHH
NOW THEN, NOW THEN, DON'T CRY!
バタン
TETO, YOU GUARD THE LITTLE ONES!
WHAT?! WHAT'S ALL THIS ABOUT THE MIASMA?
ウォォォォォ
WHAT'S THAT HAZE UP AHEAD ?!?

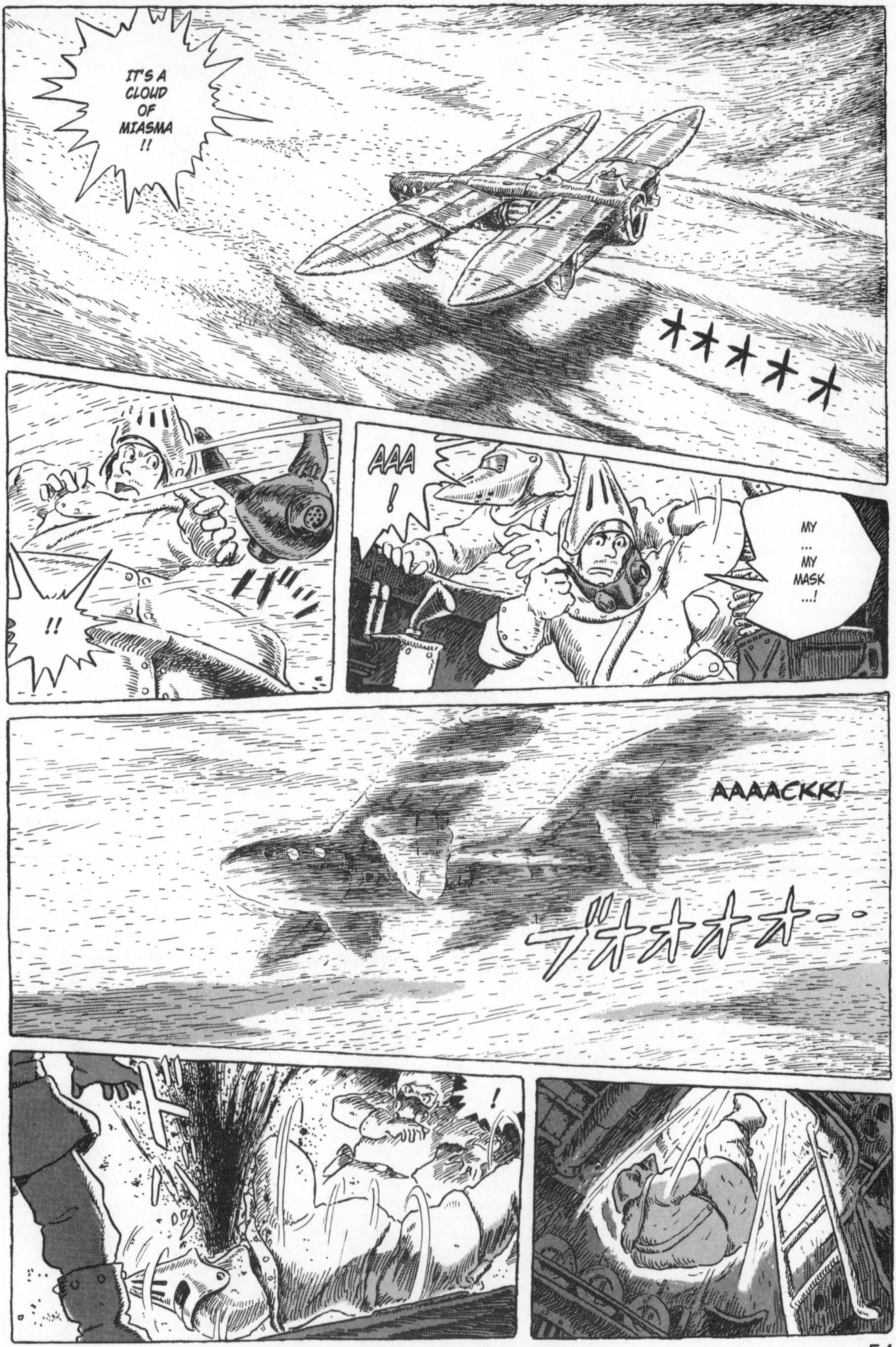
IT'S A CLOUD OF MIASMA !!
AAA !
MY ... MY MASK ...!
!!
AAAACKK!
ブオオオオー
!

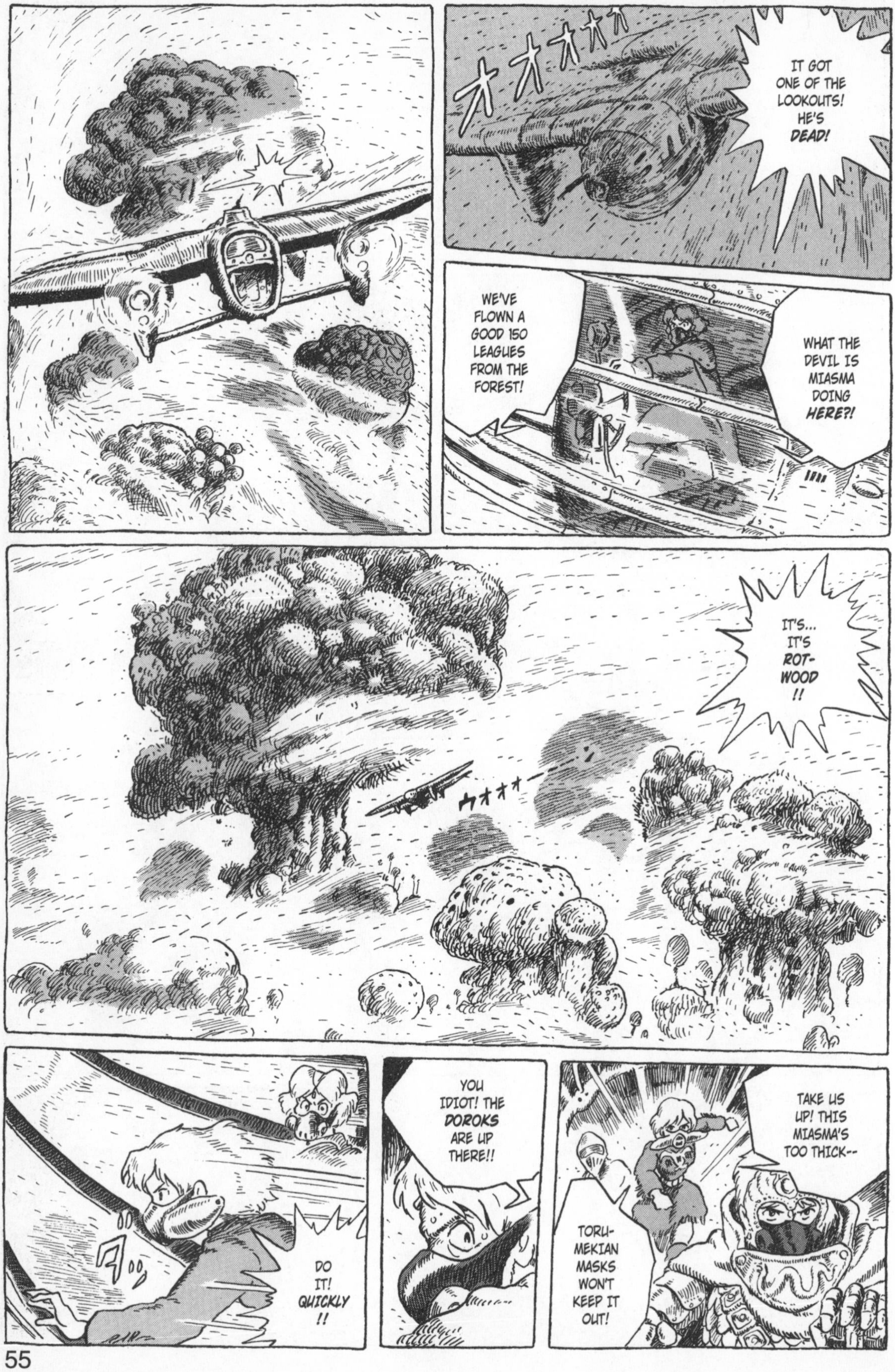
オオオオオオ
IT GOT ONE OF THE LOOKOUTS! HE'S **DEAD!**
WE'VE FLOWN A GOOD 150 LEAGUES FROM THE FOREST!
WHAT THE DEVIL IS MIASMA DOING **HERE?!**
IT'S... IT'S **ROT-WOOD** !!
ウオオオー
TAKE US UP! THIS MIASMA'S TOO THICK--
TORU-MEKIAN MASKS WON'T KEEP IT OUT!
YOU IDIOT! THE **DOROKS** ARE UP THERE!!
DO IT! **QUICKLY** !!

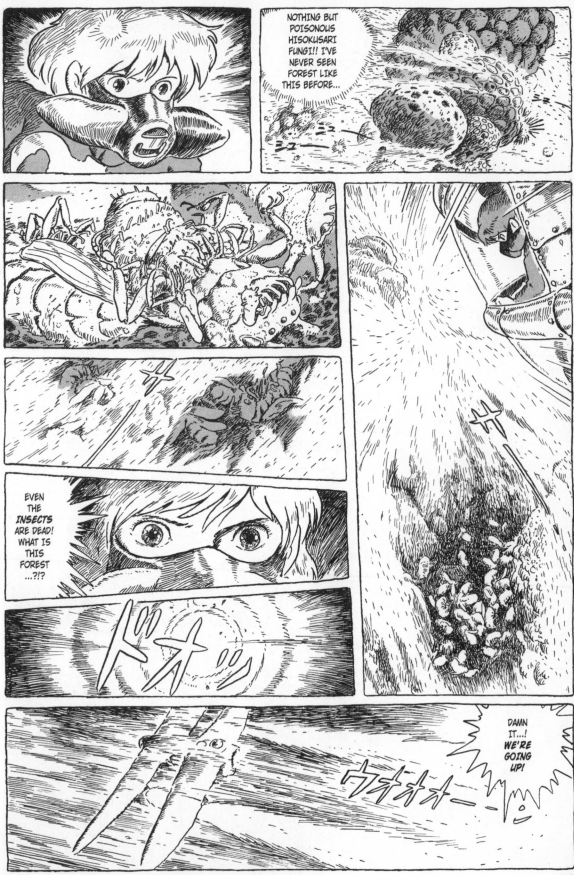

NOTHING BUT POISONOUS HISOKUSARI FUNGI!! I'VE NEVER SEEN FOREST LIKE THIS BEFORE...

EVEN THE *INSECTS* ARE DEAD! WHAT IS THIS FOREST ...?!?

DAMN IT...! *WE'RE GOING UP!*

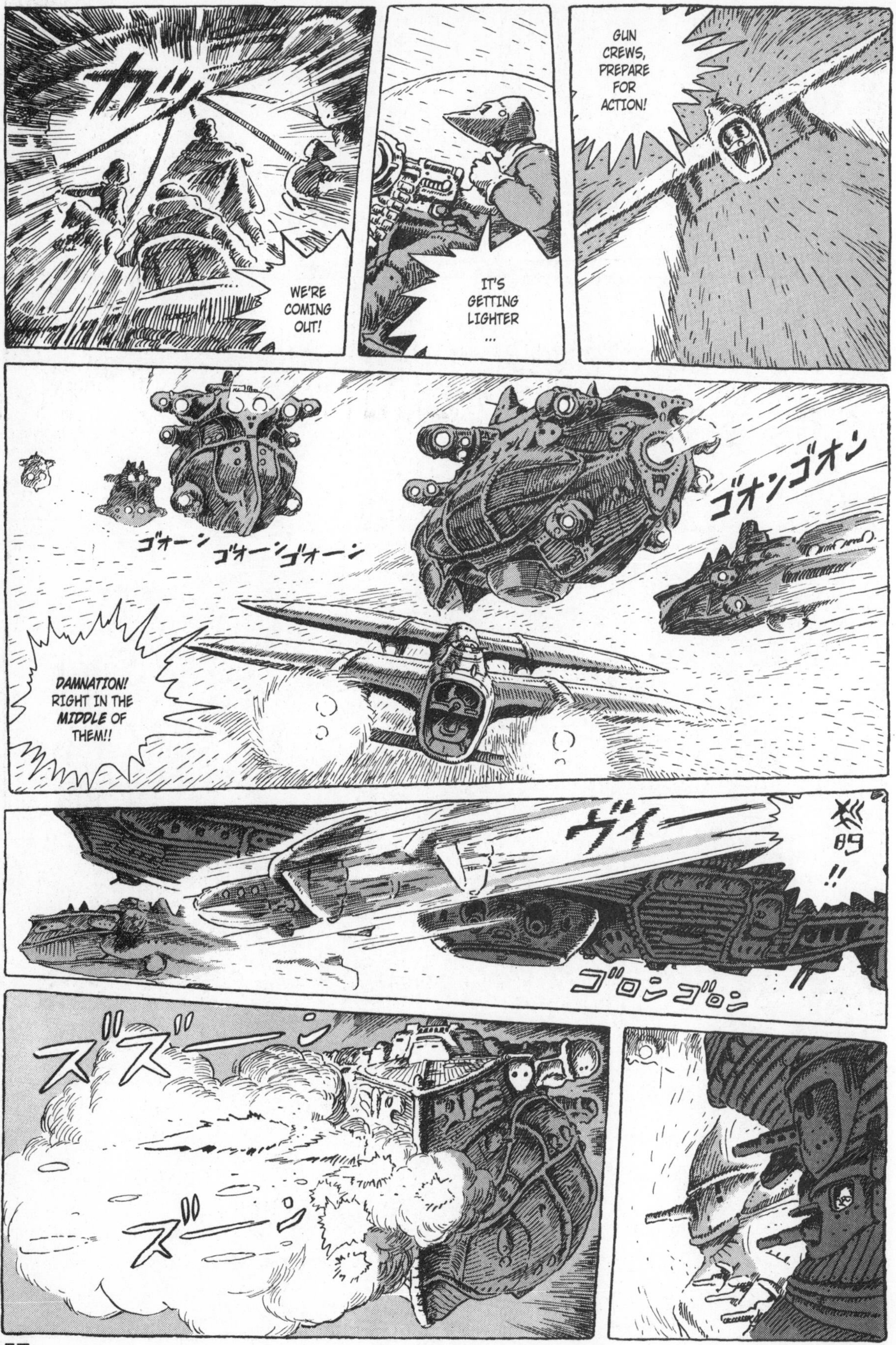
GUN CREWS, PREPARE FOR ACTION!
IT'S GETTING LIGHTER ...
WE'RE COMING OUT!
カッ
ゴオンゴオン
ゴォーン ゴォーン ゴォーン
DAMNATION! RIGHT IN THE **MIDDLE** OF THEM!!
ヴィー
ゴロンゴロン
ズズーン
ズーン

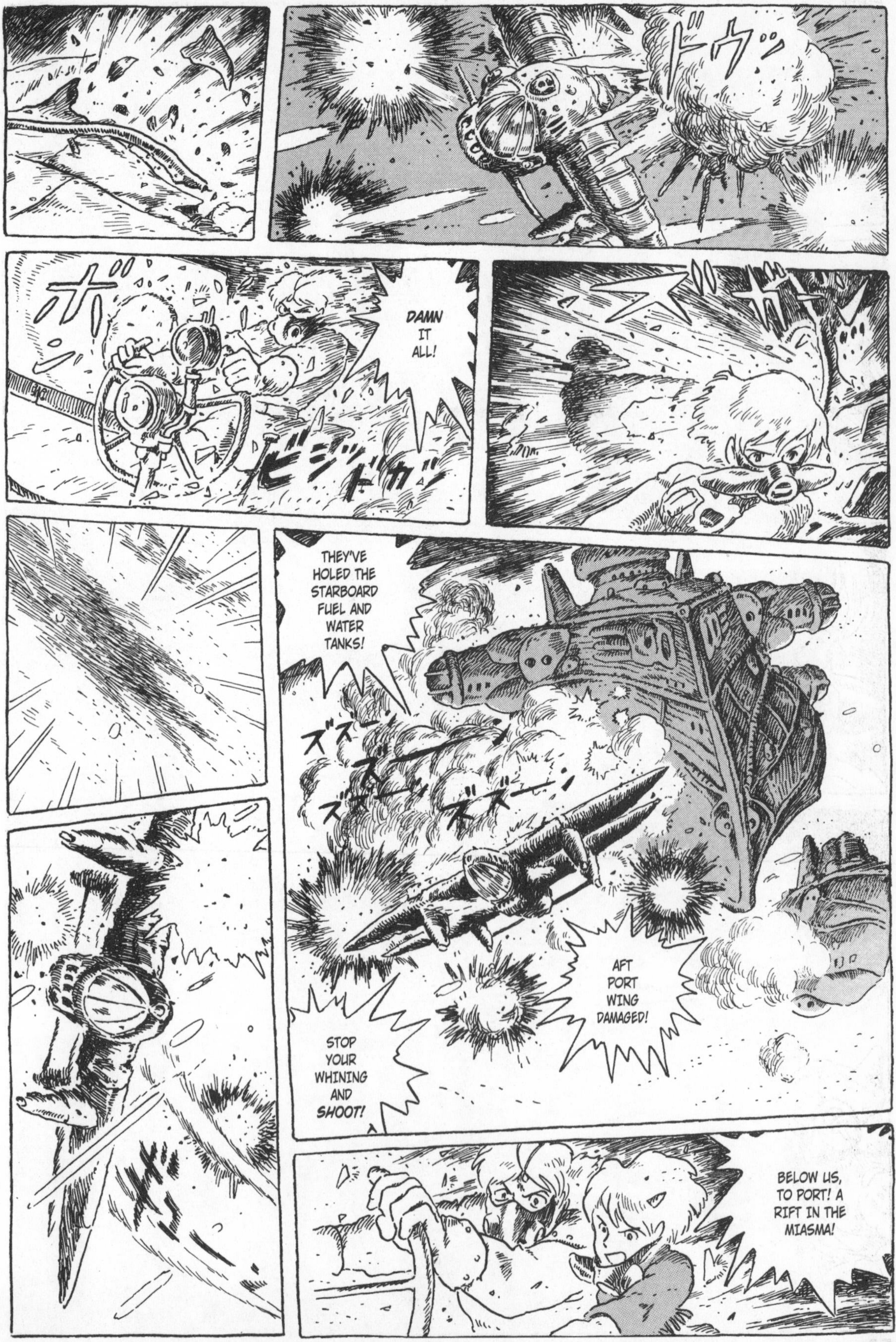

DAMN IT ALL!
THEY'VE HOLED THE STARBOARD FUEL AND WATER TANKS!
AFT PORT WING DAMAGED!
STOP YOUR WHINING AND SHOOT!
BELOW US, TO PORT! A RIFT IN THE MIASMA!

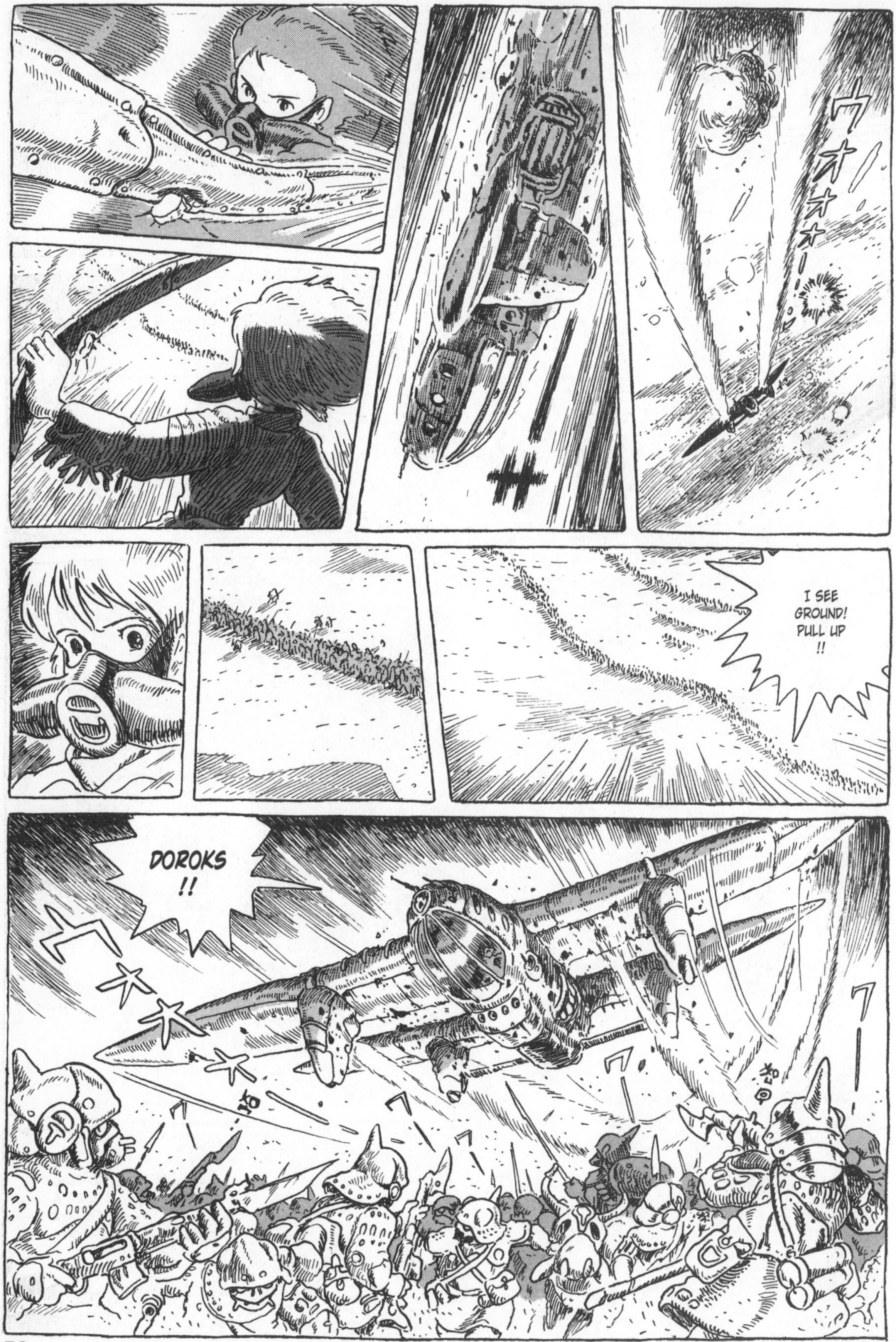
I SEE GROUND! PULL UP !!
DOROKS !!

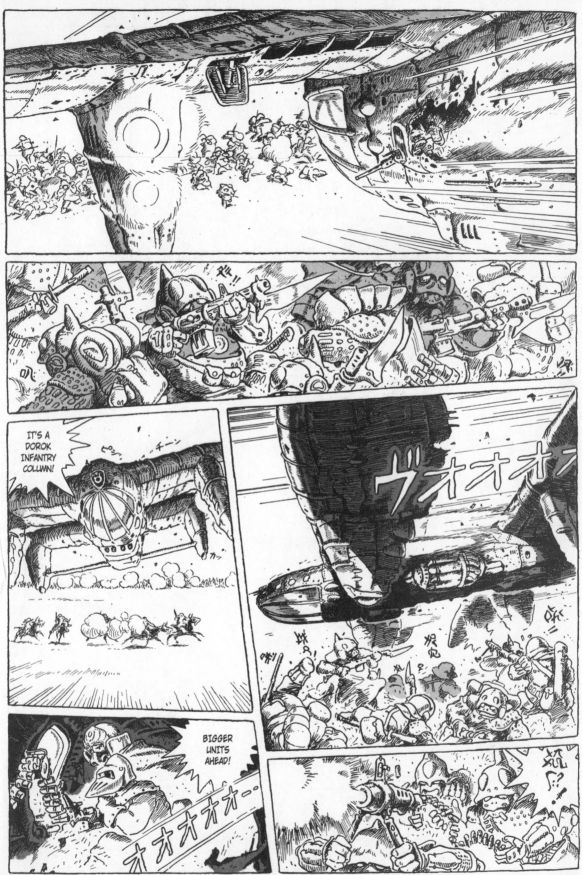

IT'S A DOROK INFANTRY COLUMN!

BIGGER UNITS AHEAD!

60

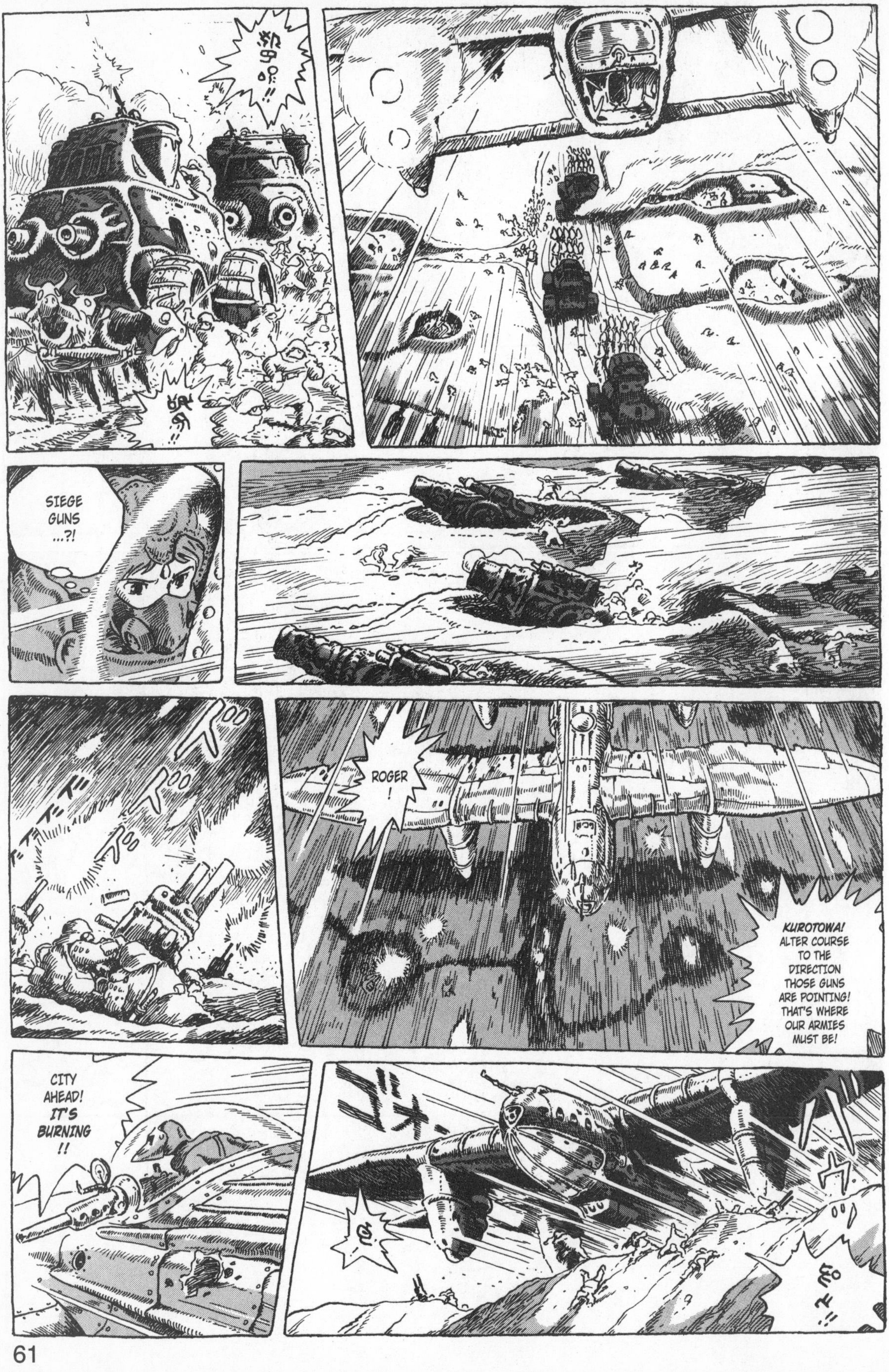
SIEGE GUNS ...?!
KUROTOWA! ALTER COURSE TO THE DIRECTION THOSE GUNS ARE POINTING! THAT'S WHERE OUR ARMIES MUST BE!
ROGER !
CITY AHEAD! IT'S BURNING !!

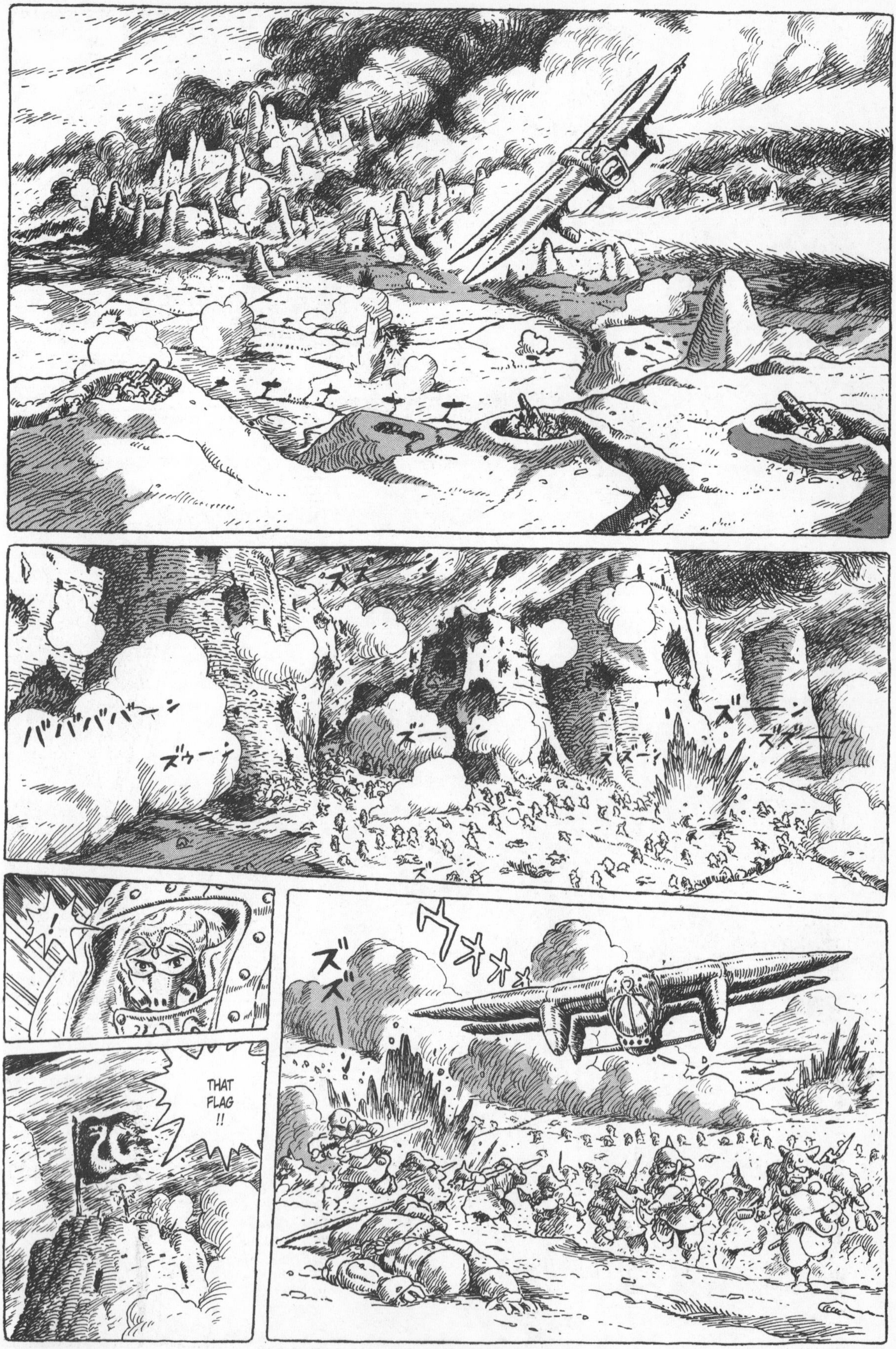
ズズ
ズーーン
ズズーーン
ズズーン
ズー
ババババーン
ズウーン
ズーン
ウオオオォ
ズズー
!
THAT FLAG !!

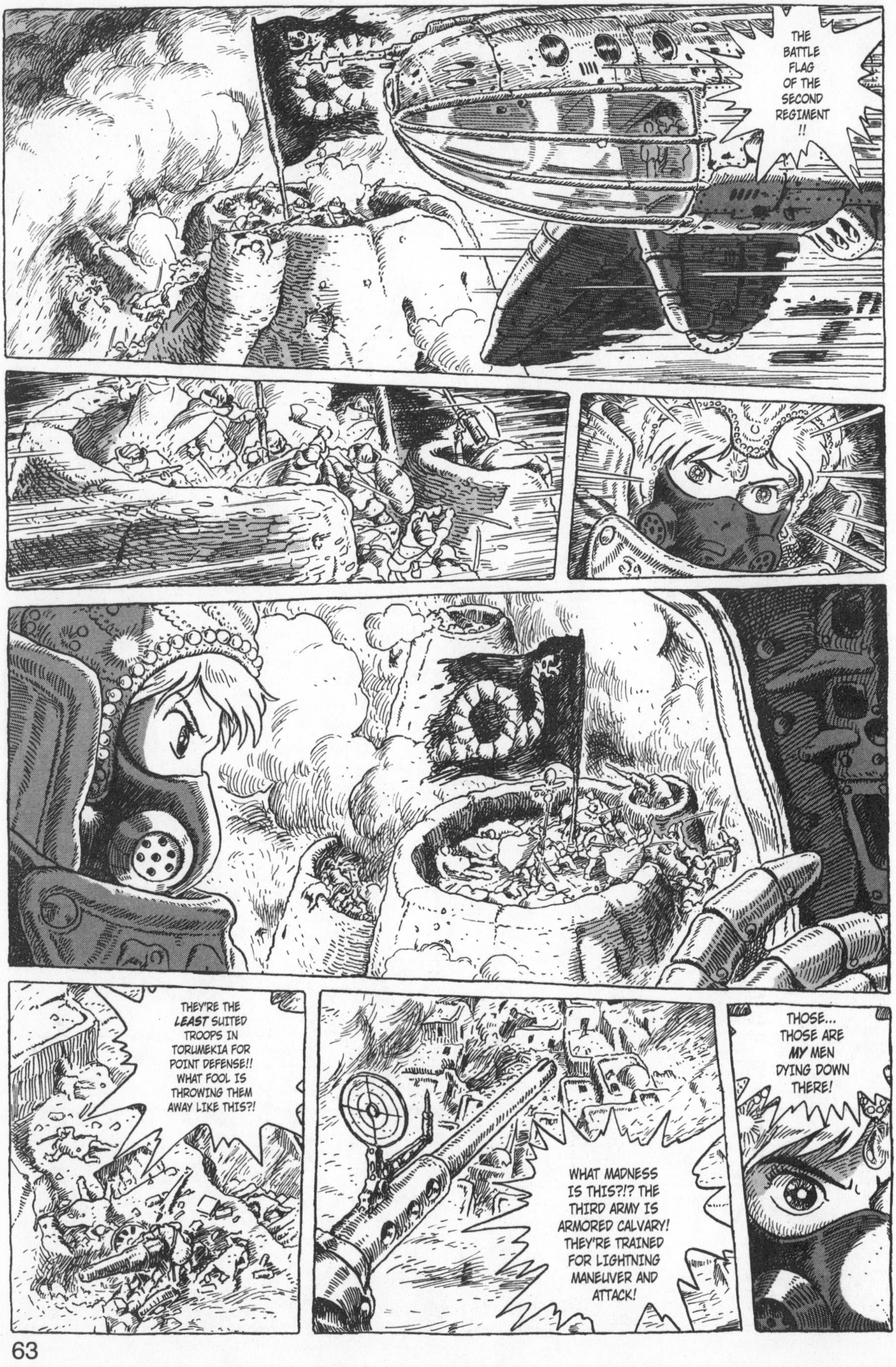
THE BATTLE FLAG OF THE SECOND REGIMENT !!
THOSE... THOSE ARE MY MEN DYING DOWN THERE!
WHAT MADNESS IS THIS?!? THE THIRD ARMY IS ARMORED CALVARY! THEY'RE TRAINED FOR LIGHTNING MANEUVER AND ATTACK!
THEY'RE THE LEAST SUITED TROOPS IN TORUMEKIA FOR POINT DEFENSE!! WHAT FOOL IS THROWING THEM AWAY LIKE THIS?!

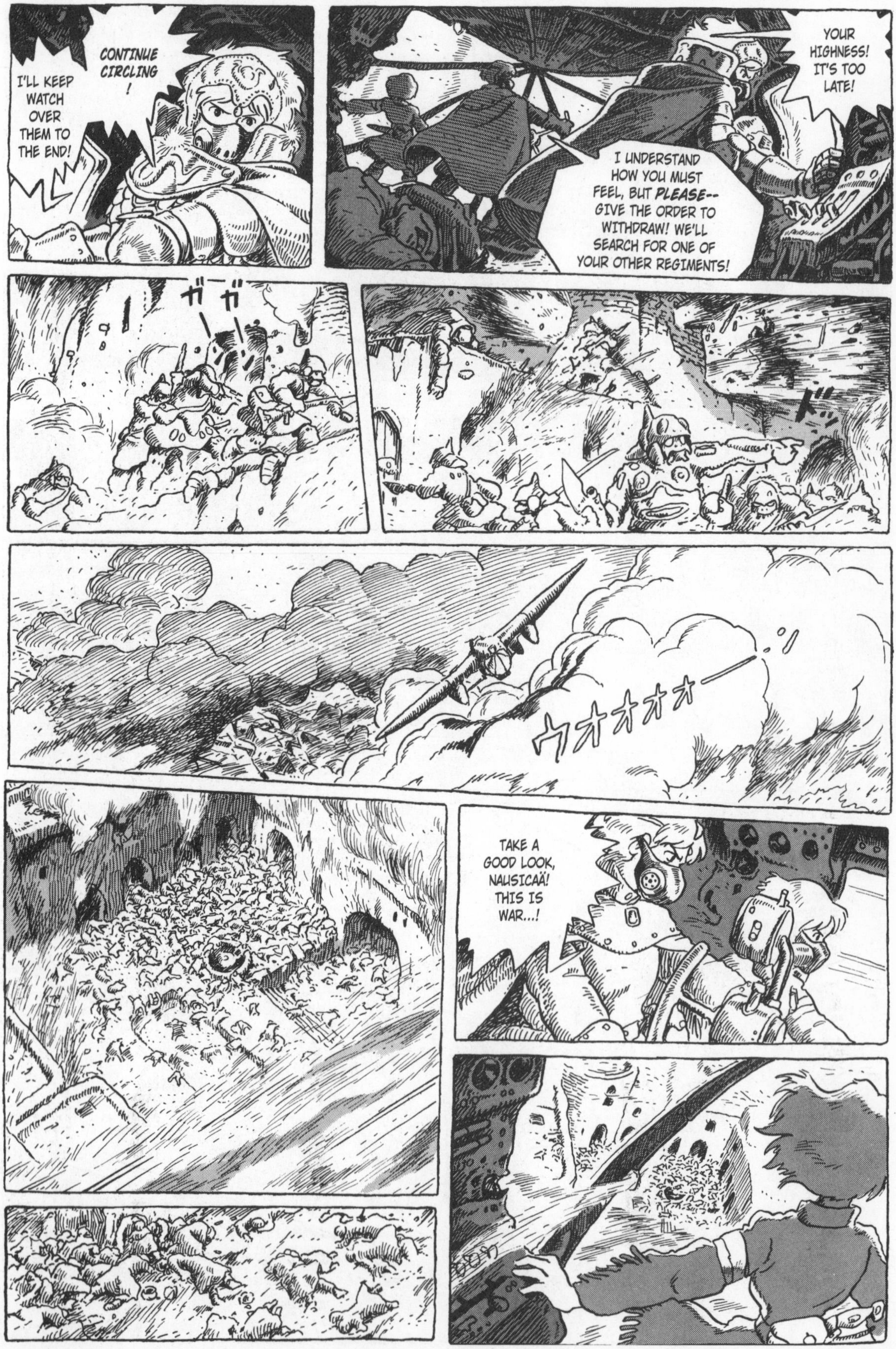
YOUR HIGHNESS! IT'S TOO LATE!
I UNDERSTAND HOW YOU MUST FEEL, BUT **PLEASE--** GIVE THE ORDER TO WITHDRAW! WE'LL SEARCH FOR ONE OF YOUR OTHER REGIMENTS!
CONTINUE CIRCLING !
I'LL KEEP WATCH OVER THEM TO THE END!
ド
ガガーン
ウオオオオー
TAKE A GOOD LOOK, NAUSICAÄ! THIS IS WAR...!

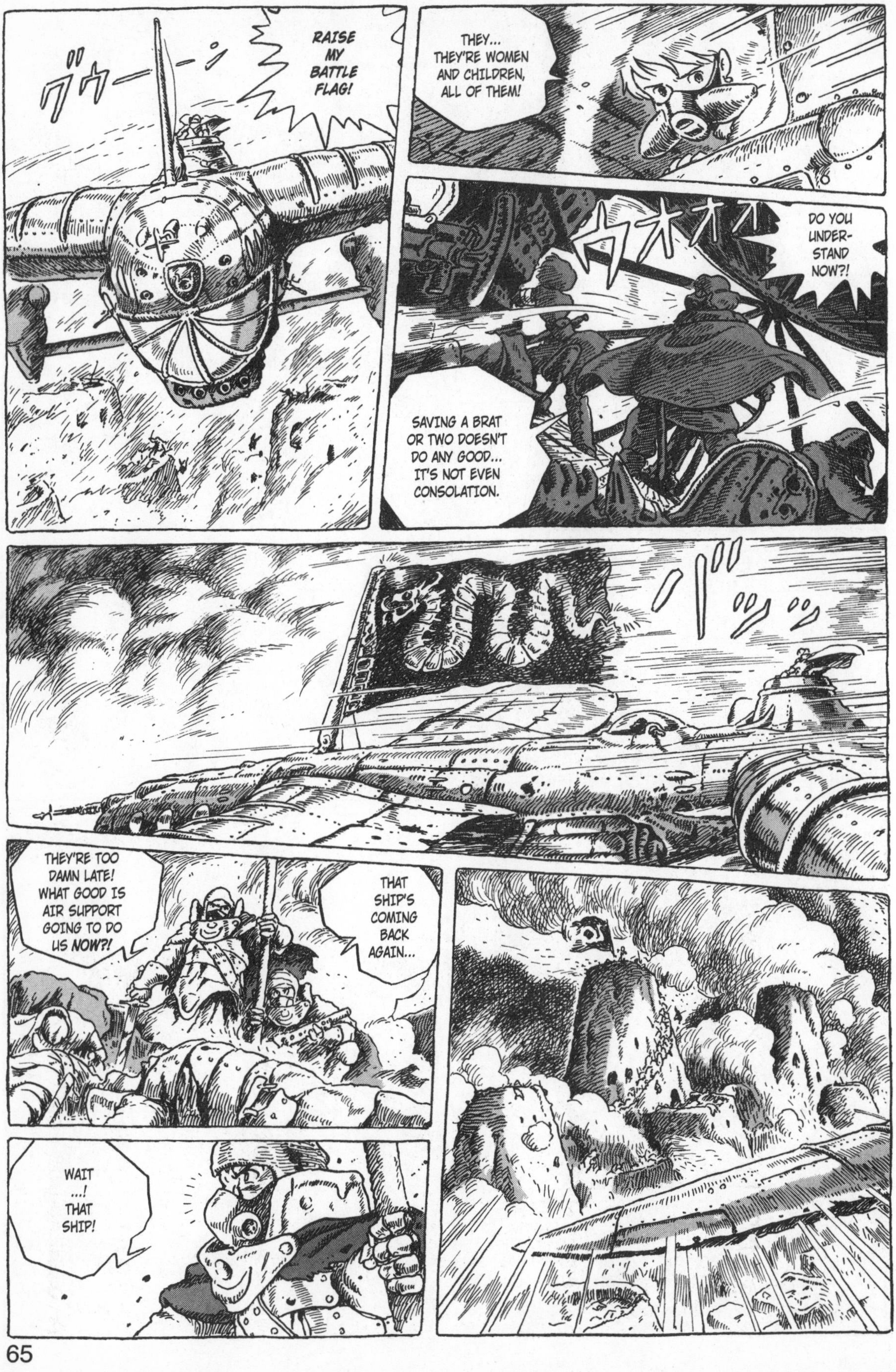
THEY... THEY'RE WOMEN AND CHILDREN, ALL OF THEM!
ウオオオ
DO YOU UNDERSTAND NOW?!
SAVING A BRAT OR TWO DOESN'T DO ANY GOOD... IT'S NOT EVEN CONSOLATION.
RAISE MY BATTLE FLAG!
THAT SHIP'S COMING BACK AGAIN...
THEY'RE TOO DAMN LATE! WHAT GOOD IS AIR SUPPORT GOING TO DO US NOW?!
WAIT ...! THAT SHIP!

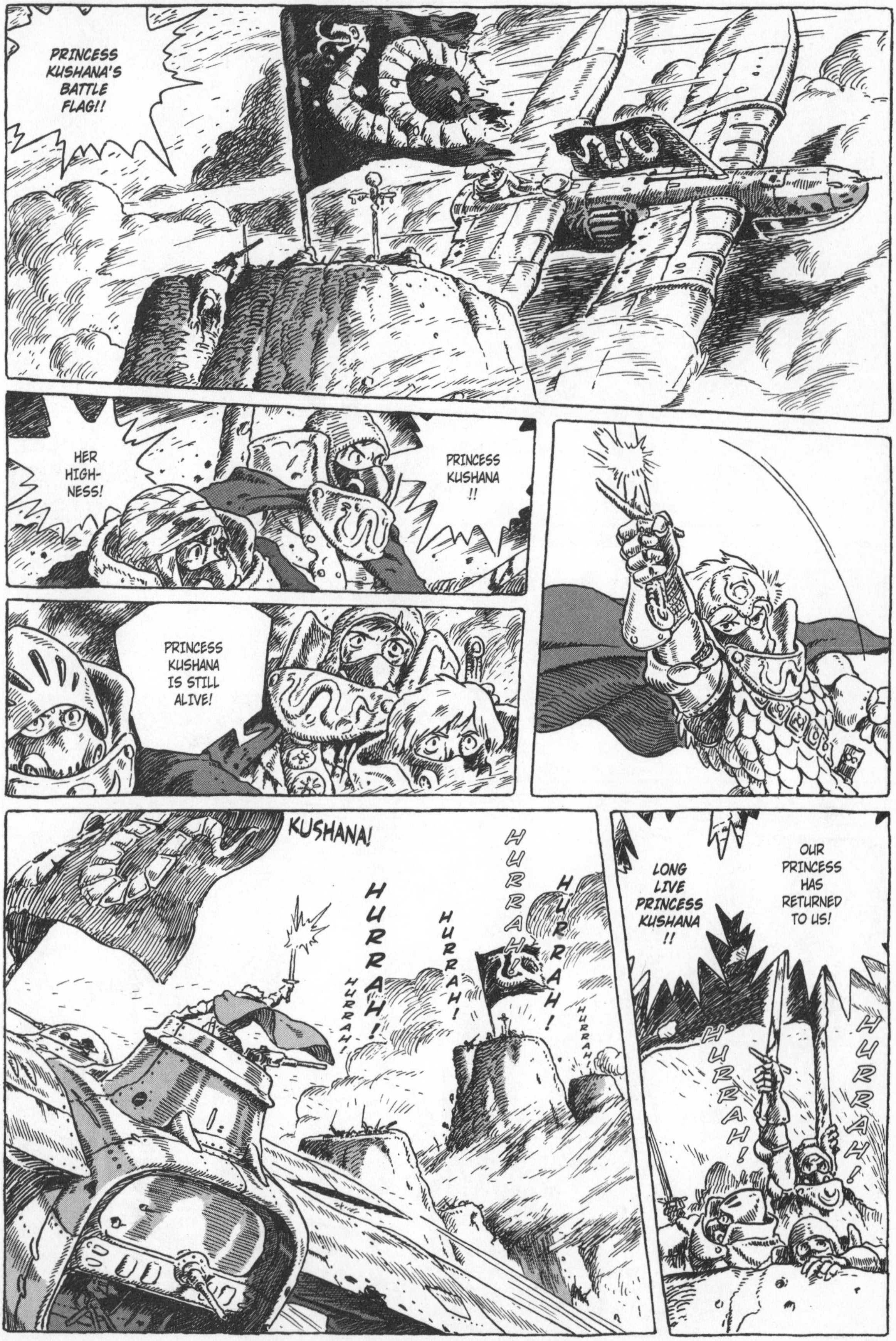
PRINCESS KUSHANA'S BATTLE FLAG!!
PRINCESS KUSHANA !!
HER HIGH-NESS!
PRINCESS KUSHANA IS STILL ALIVE!
OUR PRINCESS HAS RETURNED TO US!
LONG LIVE PRINCESS KUSHANA !!
HURRAH!
HURRAH!
KUSHANA!
HURRAH!
HURRAH!
HURRAH!
HURRAH!
HURRAH!
HURRAH

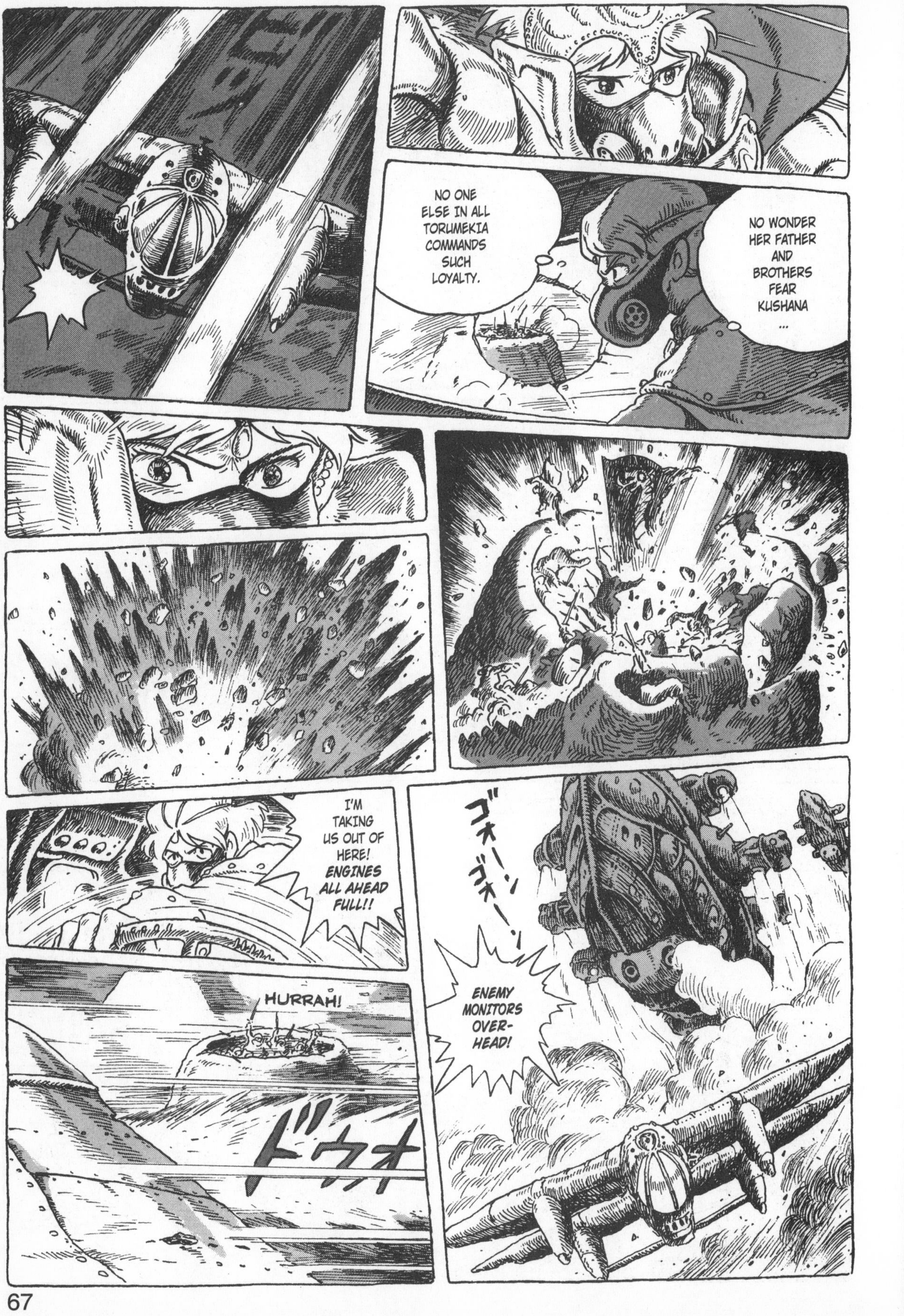
NO WONDER HER FATHER AND BROTHERS FEAR KUSHANA ...
NO ONE ELSE IN ALL TORUMEKIA COMMANDS SUCH LOYALTY.
ゴオーン
ゴオーン
ENEMY MONITORS OVER-HEAD!
I'M TAKING US OUT OF HERE! ENGINES ALL AHEAD FULL!!
HURRAH!
ドウオ

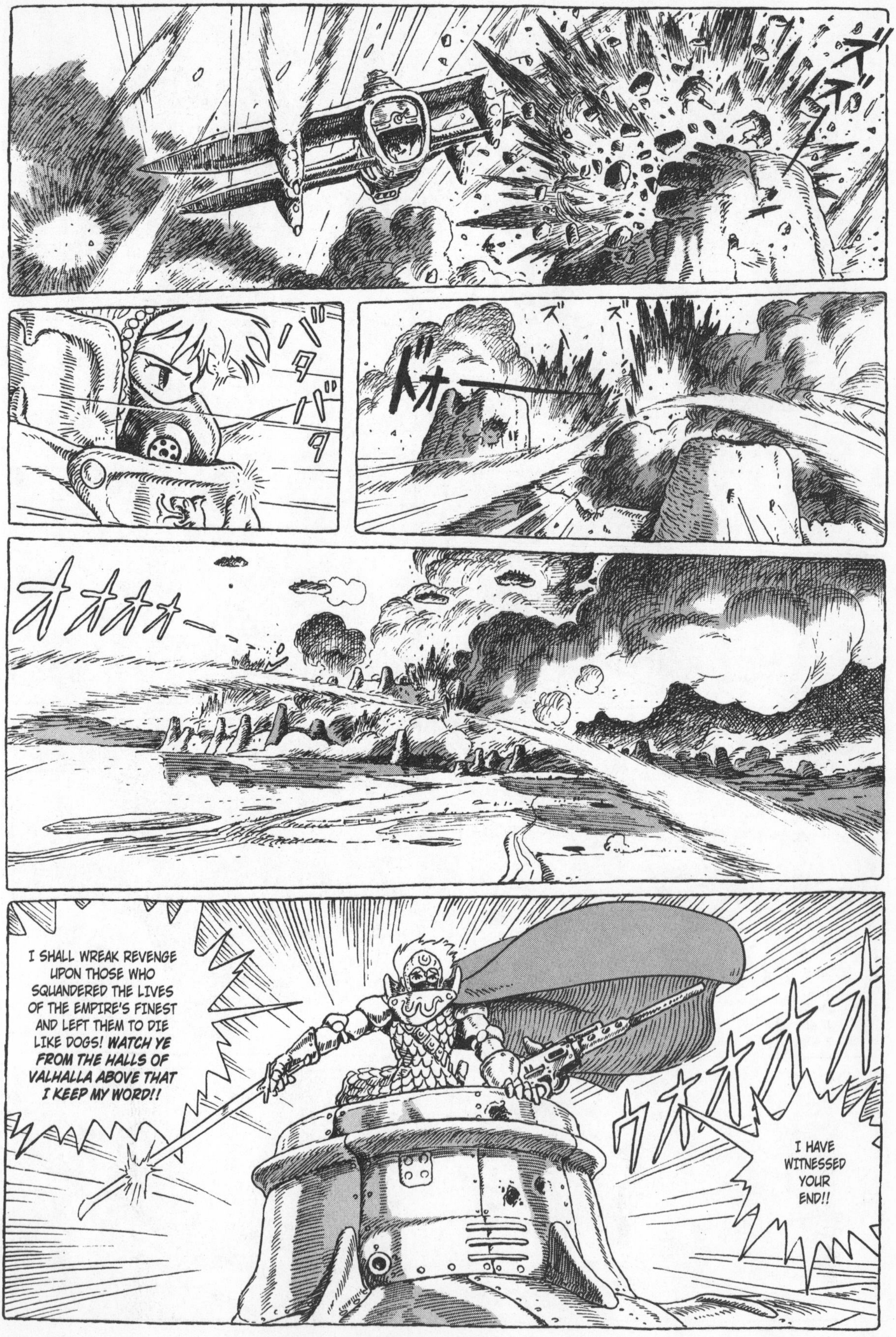
ズズ
ズズ
ドオー
バタバタ
オオオオー
ウオオオオ
I SHALL WREAK REVENGE UPON THOSE WHO SQUANDERED THE LIVES OF THE EMPIRE'S FINEST AND LEFT THEM TO DIE LIKE DOGS! ***WATCH YE FROM THE HALLS OF VALHALLA ABOVE THAT I KEEP MY WORD!!***
I HAVE WITNESSED YOUR END!!

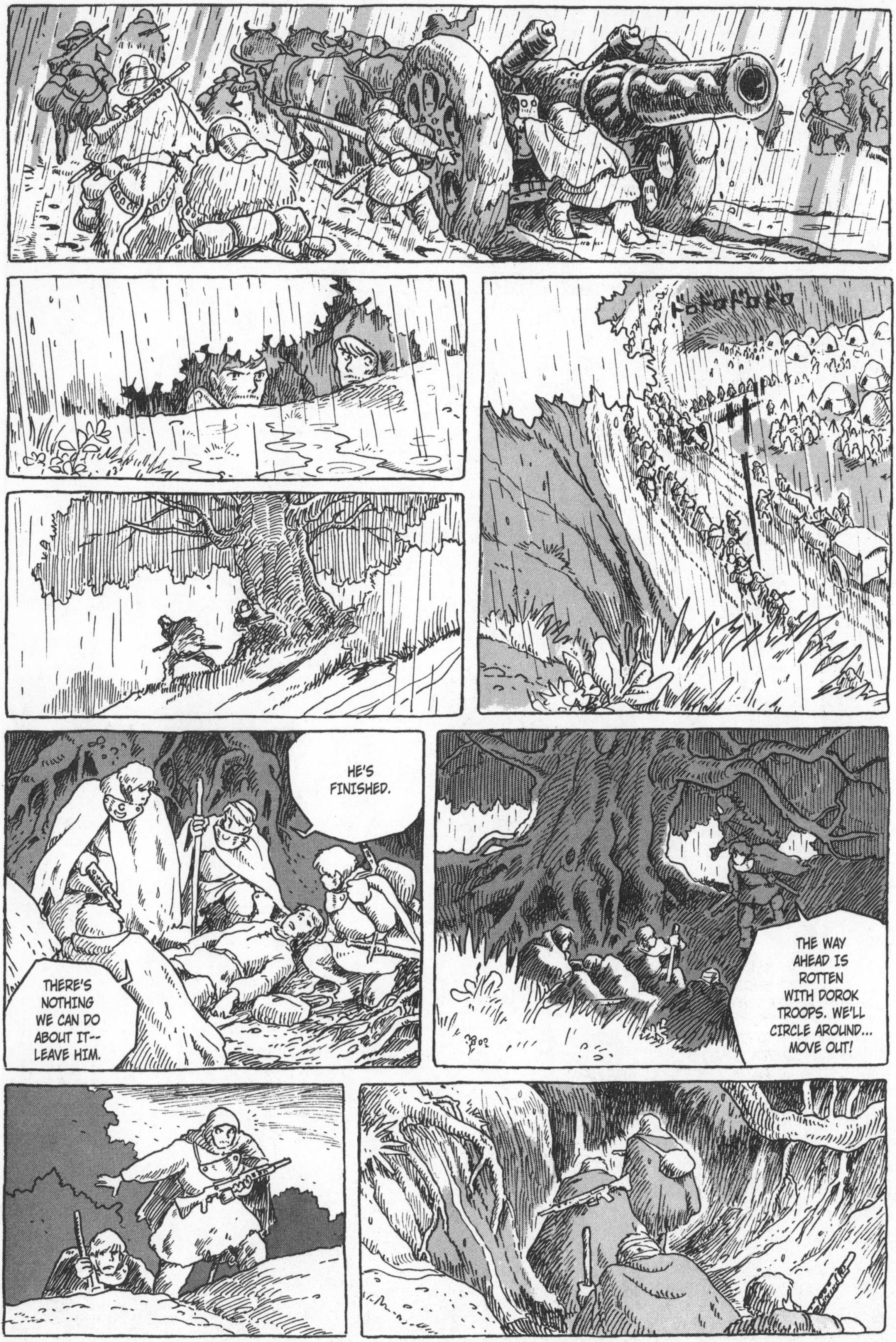
THE WAY AHEAD IS ROTTEN WITH DOROK TROOPS. WE'LL CIRCLE AROUND... MOVE OUT!
HE'S FINISHED.
THERE'S NOTHING WE CAN DO ABOUT IT-- LEAVE HIM.

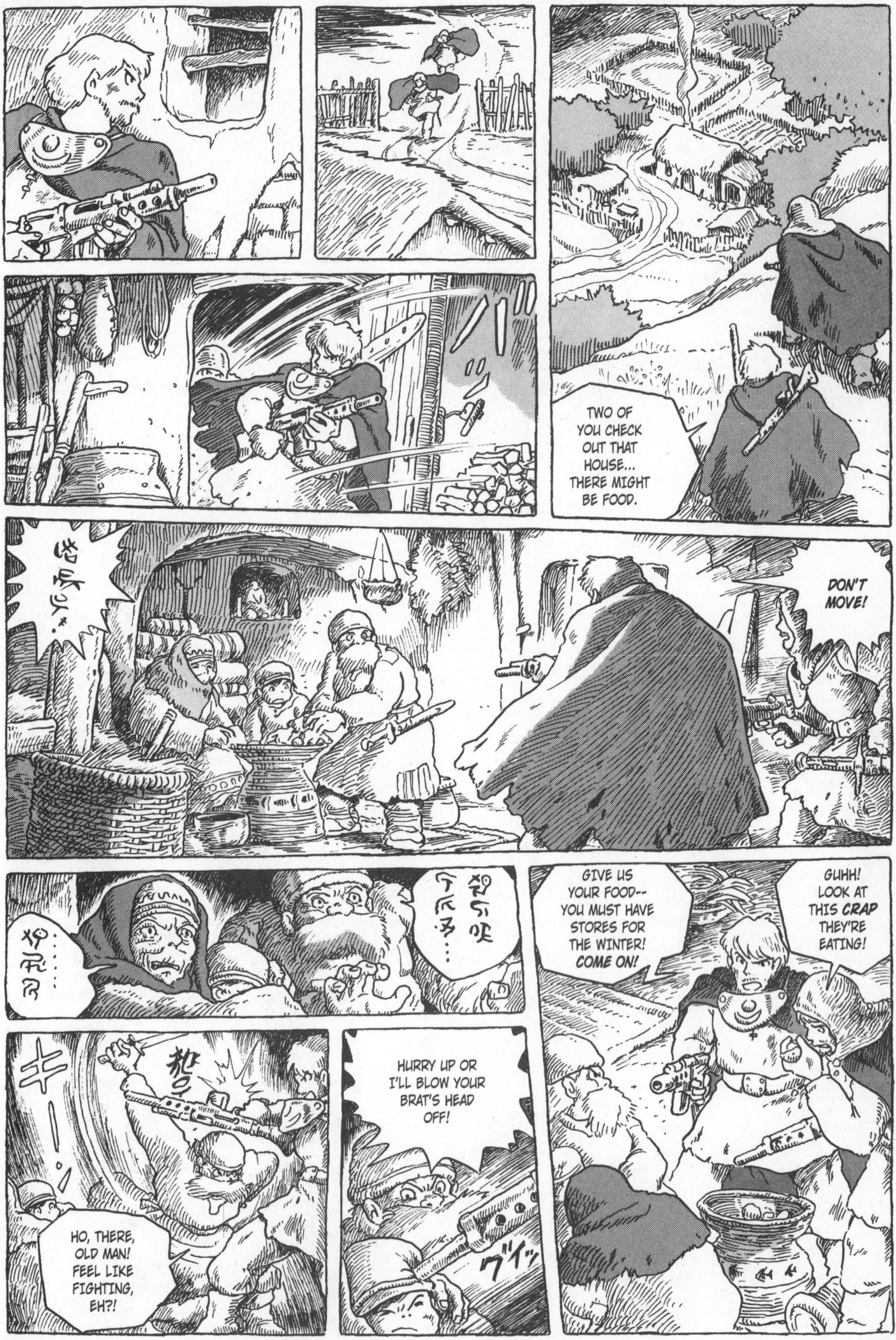
TWO OF YOU CHECK OUT THAT HOUSE... THERE MIGHT BE FOOD.
DON'T MOVE!
GUHH! LOOK AT THIS CRAP THEY'RE EATING!
GIVE US YOUR FOOD-- YOU MUST HAVE STORES FOR THE WINTER! COME ON!
HURRY UP OR I'LL BLOW YOUR BRAT'S HEAD OFF!
グイッ
HO, THERE, OLD MAN! FEEL LIKE FIGHTING, EH?!

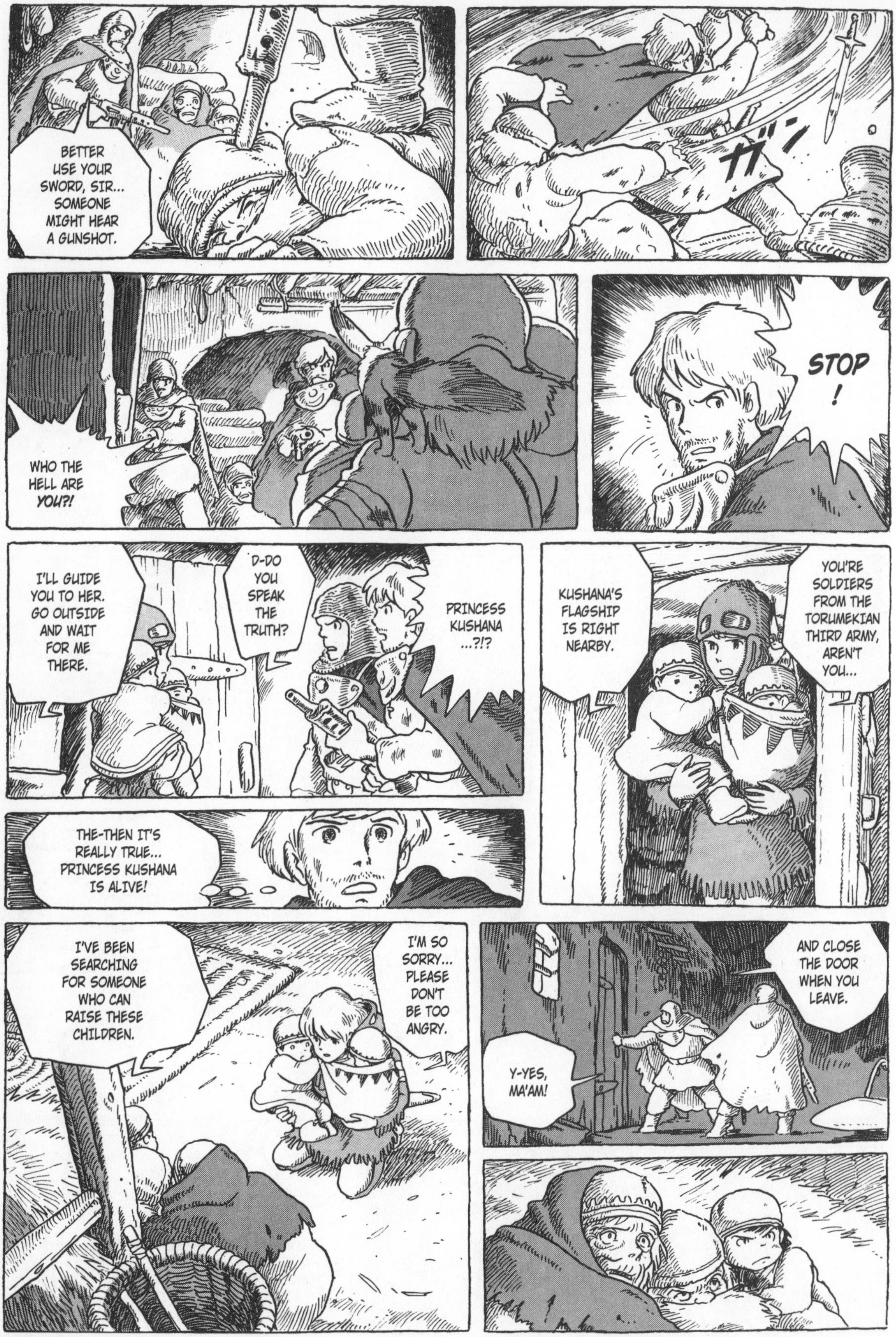
ガン
BETTER USE YOUR SWORD, SIR... SOMEONE MIGHT HEAR A GUNSHOT.
STOP!
WHO THE HELL ARE *YOU?!*
YOU'RE SOLDIERS FROM THE TORUMEKIAN THIRD ARMY, AREN'T YOU...
KUSHANA'S FLAGSHIP IS RIGHT NEARBY.
PRINCESS KUSHANA ...?!?
D-DO YOU SPEAK THE TRUTH?
I'LL GUIDE YOU TO HER. GO OUTSIDE AND WAIT FOR ME THERE.
THE-THEN IT'S REALLY TRUE... PRINCESS KUSHANA IS ALIVE!
AND CLOSE THE DOOR WHEN YOU LEAVE.
Y-YES, MA'AM!
I'M SO SORRY... PLEASE DON'T BE TOO ANGRY.
I'VE BEEN SEARCHING FOR SOMEONE WHO CAN RAISE THESE CHILDREN.

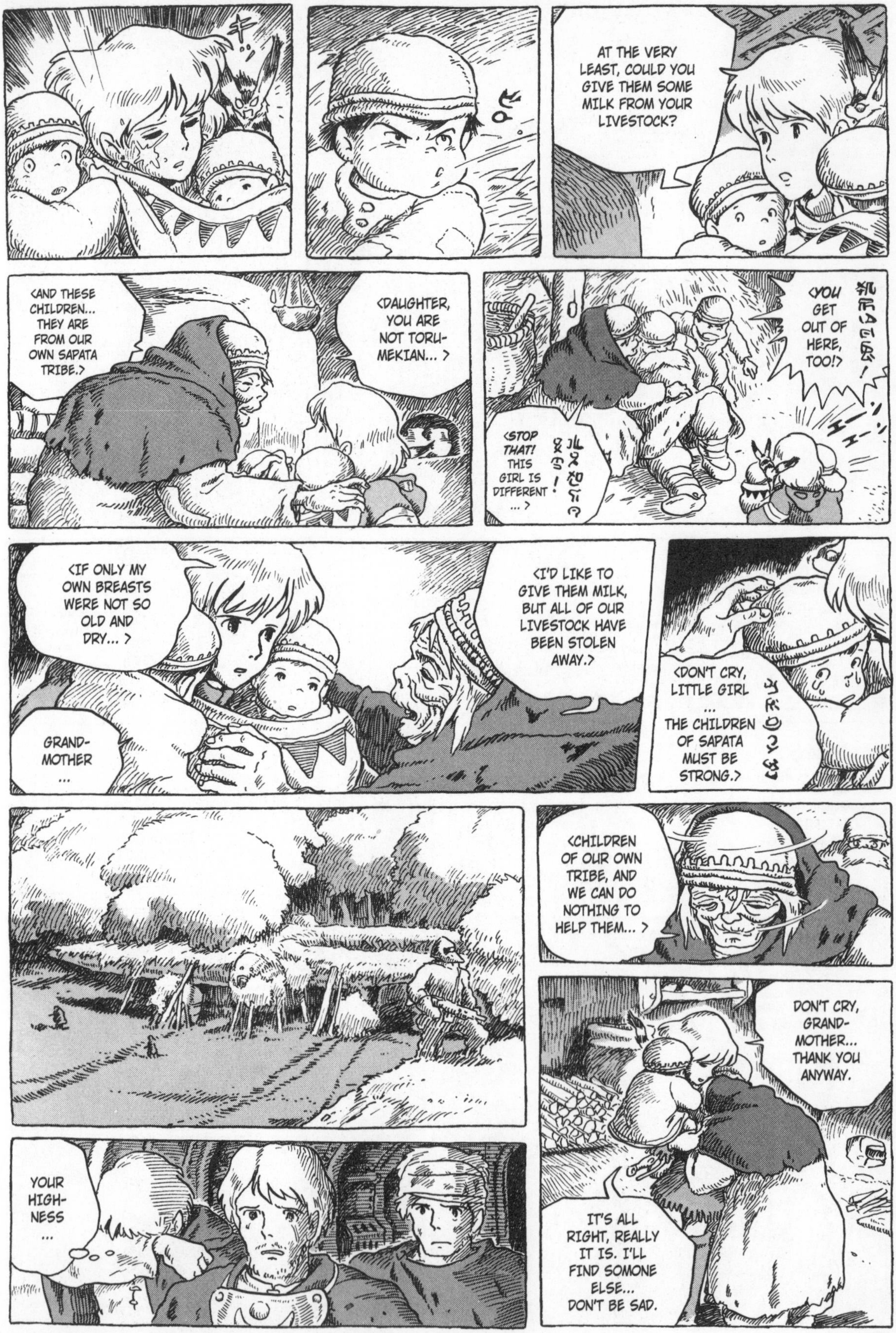
AT THE VERY LEAST, COULD YOU GIVE THEM SOME MILK FROM YOUR LIVESTOCK?
<YOU GET OUT OF HERE, TOO!>
<STOP THAT! THIS GIRL IS DIFFERENT ... >
<DAUGHTER, YOU ARE NOT TORU-MEKIAN... >
<AND THESE CHILDREN... THEY ARE FROM OUR OWN SAPATA TRIBE.>
<DON'T CRY, LITTLE GIRL ... THE CHILDREN OF SAPATA MUST BE STRONG.>
<I'D LIKE TO GIVE THEM MILK, BUT ALL OF OUR LIVESTOCK HAVE BEEN STOLEN AWAY.>
<IF ONLY MY OWN BREASTS WERE NOT SO OLD AND DRY... >
GRAND-MOTHER ...
<CHILDREN OF OUR OWN TRIBE, AND WE CAN DO NOTHING TO HELP THEM... >
DON'T CRY, GRAND-MOTHER... THANK YOU ANYWAY.
IT'S ALL RIGHT, REALLY IT IS. I'LL FIND SOMONE ELSE... DON'T BE SAD.
YOUR HIGH-NESS ...

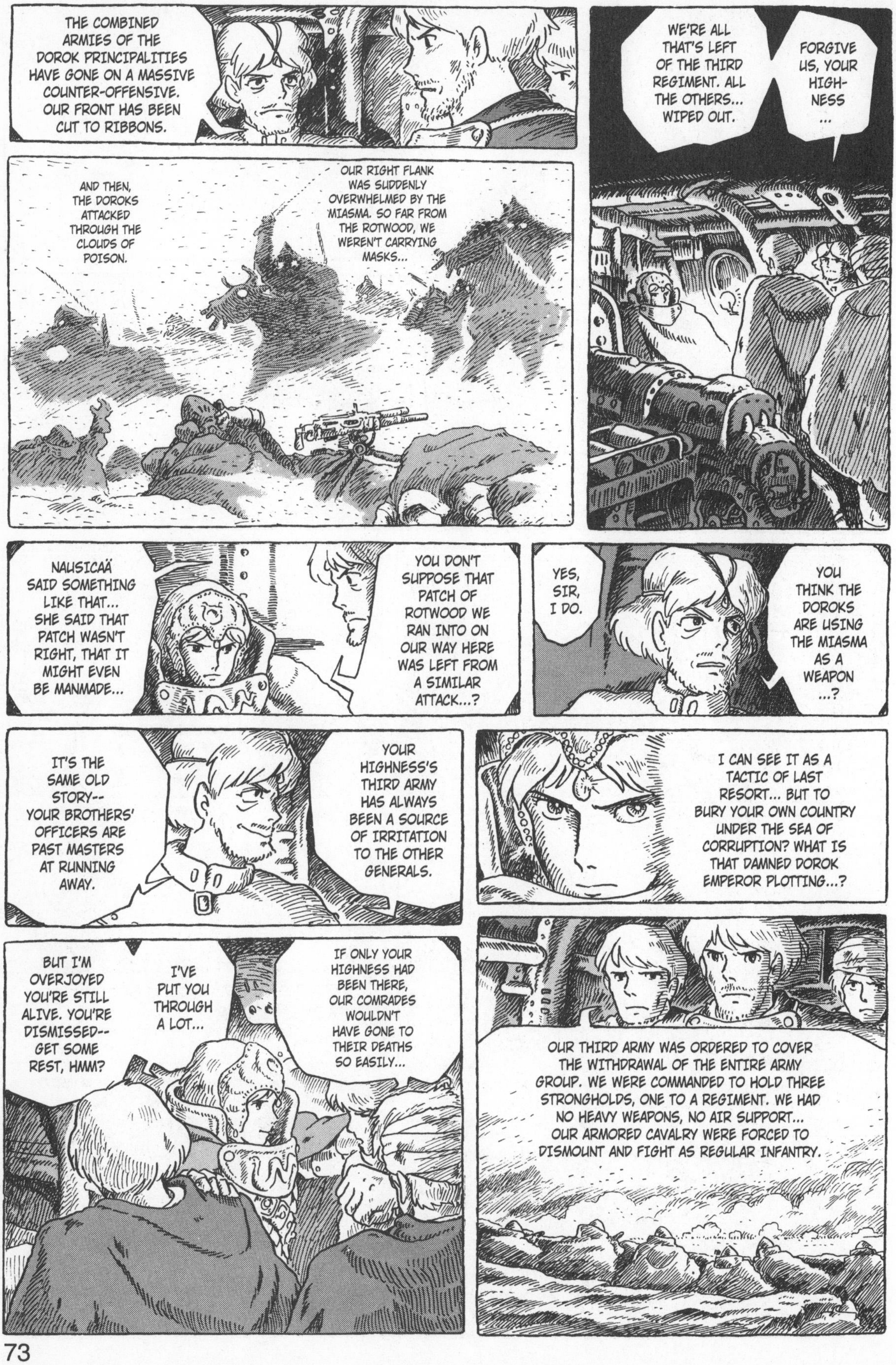
FORGIVE US, YOUR HIGHNESS ...
WE'RE ALL THAT'S LEFT OF THE THIRD REGIMENT. ALL THE OTHERS... WIPED OUT.
THE COMBINED ARMIES OF THE DOROK PRINCIPALITIES HAVE GONE ON A MASSIVE COUNTER-OFFENSIVE. OUR FRONT HAS BEEN CUT TO RIBBONS.
OUR RIGHT FLANK WAS SUDDENLY OVERWHELMED BY THE MIASMA. SO FAR FROM THE ROTWOOD, WE WEREN'T CARRYING MASKS...
AND THEN, THE DOROKS ATTACKED THROUGH THE CLOUDS OF POISON.
YOU THINK THE DOROKS ARE USING THE MIASMA AS A WEAPON ...?
YES, SIR, I DO.
YOU DON'T SUPPOSE THAT PATCH OF ROTWOOD WE RAN INTO ON OUR WAY HERE WAS LEFT FROM A SIMILAR ATTACK...?
NAUSICAÄ SAID SOMETHING LIKE THAT... SHE SAID THAT PATCH WASN'T RIGHT, THAT IT MIGHT EVEN BE MANMADE...
I CAN SEE IT AS A TACTIC OF LAST RESORT... BUT TO BURY YOUR OWN COUNTRY UNDER THE SEA OF CORRUPTION? WHAT IS THAT DAMNED DOROK EMPEROR PLOTTING...?
YOUR HIGHNESS'S THIRD ARMY HAS ALWAYS BEEN A SOURCE OF IRRITATION TO THE OTHER GENERALS.
IT'S THE SAME OLD STORY-- YOUR BROTHERS' OFFICERS ARE PAST MASTERS AT RUNNING AWAY.
OUR THIRD ARMY WAS ORDERED TO COVER THE WITHDRAWAL OF THE ENTIRE ARMY GROUP. WE WERE COMMANDED TO HOLD THREE STRONGHOLDS, ONE TO A REGIMENT. WE HAD NO HEAVY WEAPONS, NO AIR SUPPORT... OUR ARMORED CAVALRY WERE FORCED TO DISMOUNT AND FIGHT AS REGULAR INFANTRY.
IF ONLY YOUR HIGHNESS HAD BEEN THERE, OUR COMRADES WOULDN'T HAVE GONE TO THEIR DEATHS SO EASILY...
I'VE PUT YOU THROUGH A LOT...
BUT I'M OVERJOYED YOU'RE STILL ALIVE. YOU'RE DISMISSED-- GET SOME REST, HMM?

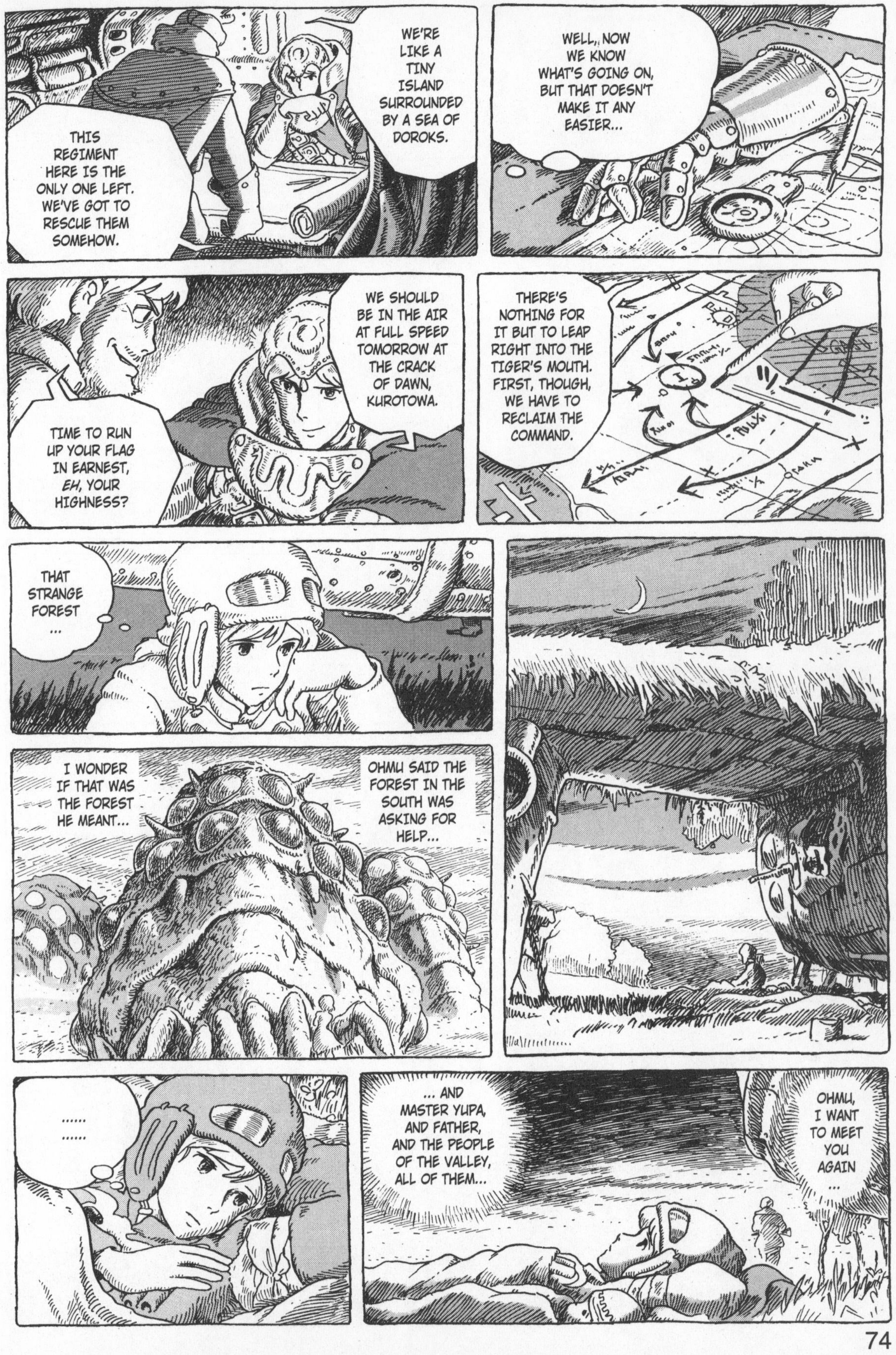
WELL, NOW WE KNOW WHAT'S GOING ON, BUT THAT DOESN'T MAKE IT ANY EASIER...
WE'RE LIKE A TINY ISLAND SURROUNDED BY A SEA OF DOROKS.
THIS REGIMENT HERE IS THE ONLY ONE LEFT. WE'VE GOT TO RESCUE THEM SOMEHOW.
THERE'S NOTHING FOR IT BUT TO LEAP RIGHT INTO THE TIGER'S MOUTH. FIRST, THOUGH, WE HAVE TO RECLAIM THE COMMAND.
WE SHOULD BE IN THE AIR AT FULL SPEED TOMORROW AT THE CRACK OF DAWN, KUROTOWA.
TIME TO RUN UP YOUR FLAG IN EARNEST, *EH*, YOUR HIGHNESS?
THAT STRANGE FOREST ...
OHMU SAID THE FOREST IN THE SOUTH WAS ASKING FOR HELP...
I WONDER IF THAT WAS THE FOREST HE MEANT...
OHMU, I WANT TO MEET YOU AGAIN ...
... AND MASTER YUPA, AND FATHER, AND THE PEOPLE OF THE VALLEY, ALL OF THEM...
....

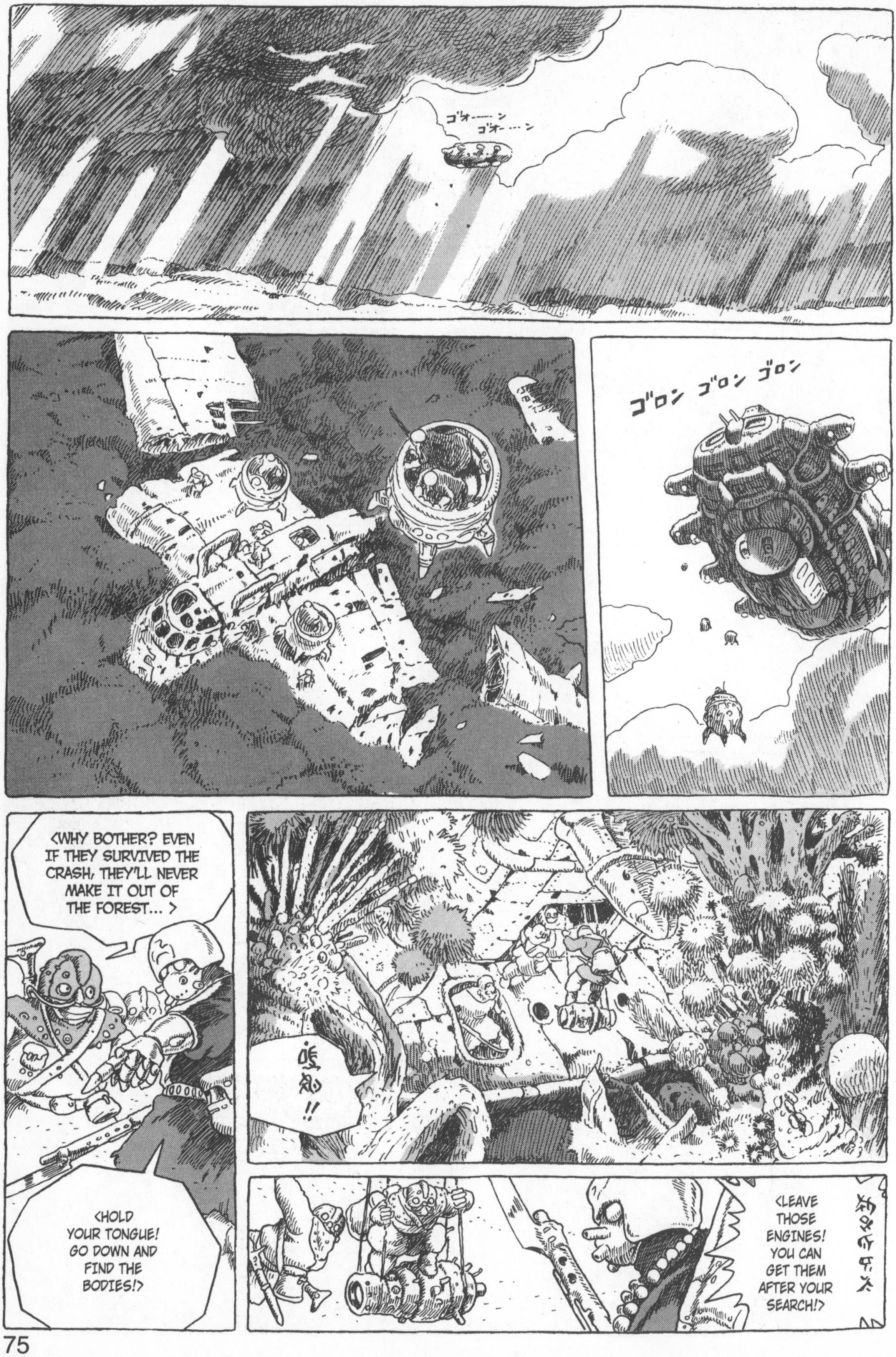
ゴオーーン
ゴオーーン
ゴロン ゴロン ゴロン
<LEAVE THOSE ENGINES! YOU CAN GET THEM AFTER YOUR SEARCH!>
<WHY BOTHER? EVEN IF THEY SURVIVED THE CRASH, THEY'LL NEVER MAKE IT OUT OF THE FOREST... >
<HOLD YOUR TONGUE! GO DOWN AND FIND THE BODIES!>

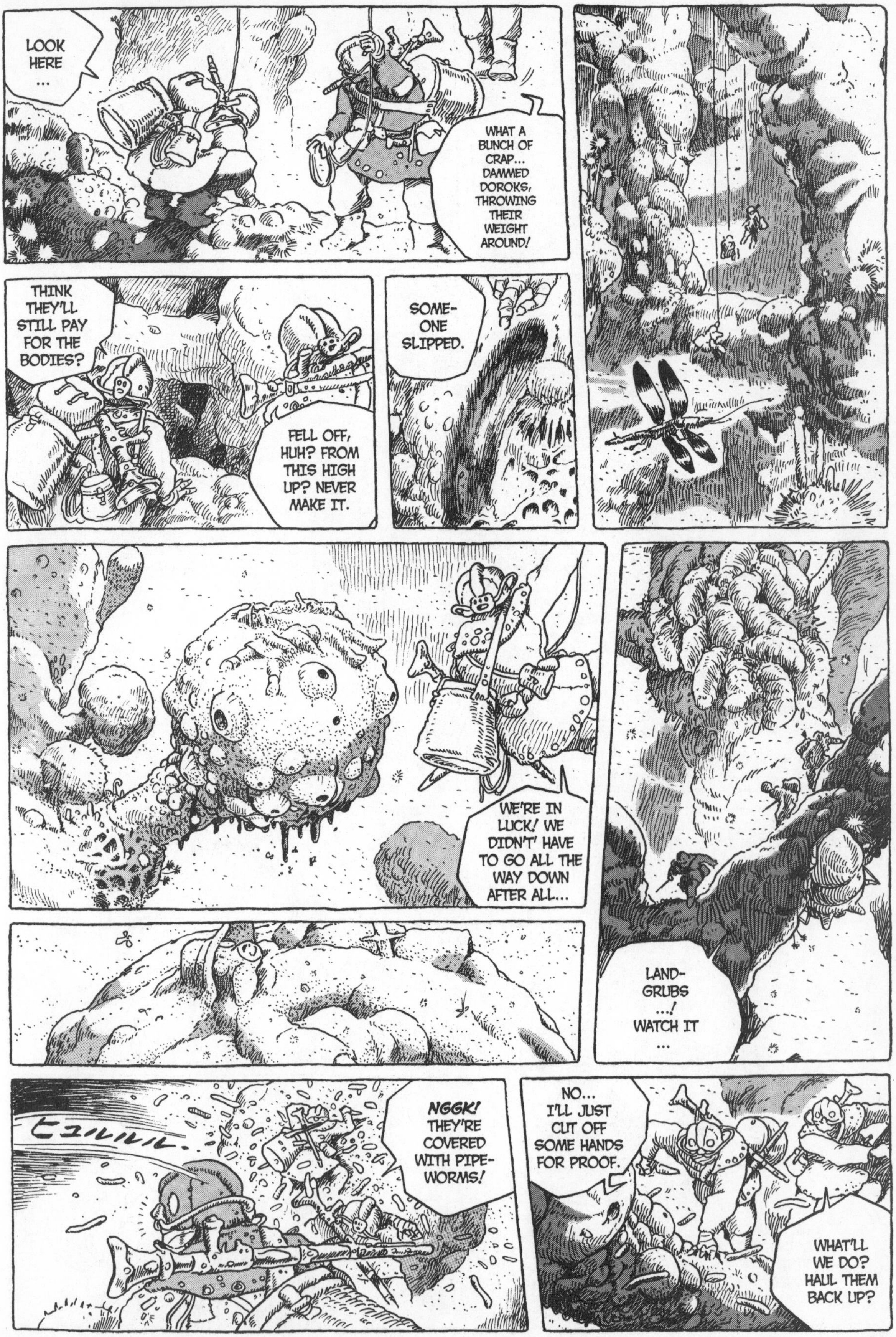
WHAT A BUNCH OF CRAP... DAMMED DOROKS, THROWING THEIR WEIGHT AROUND!
LOOK HERE ...
SOME-ONE SLIPPED.
FELL OFF, HUH? FROM THIS HIGH UP? NEVER MAKE IT.
THINK THEY'LL STILL PAY FOR THE BODIES?
LAND-GRUBS ...! WATCH IT ...
WE'RE IN LUCK! WE DIDN'T HAVE TO GO ALL THE WAY DOWN AFTER ALL...
WHAT'LL WE DO? HAUL THEM BACK UP?
NO... I'LL JUST CUT OFF SOME HANDS FOR PROOF.
NGGK! THEY'RE COVERED WITH PIPE-WORMS!
ヒュルルルル...

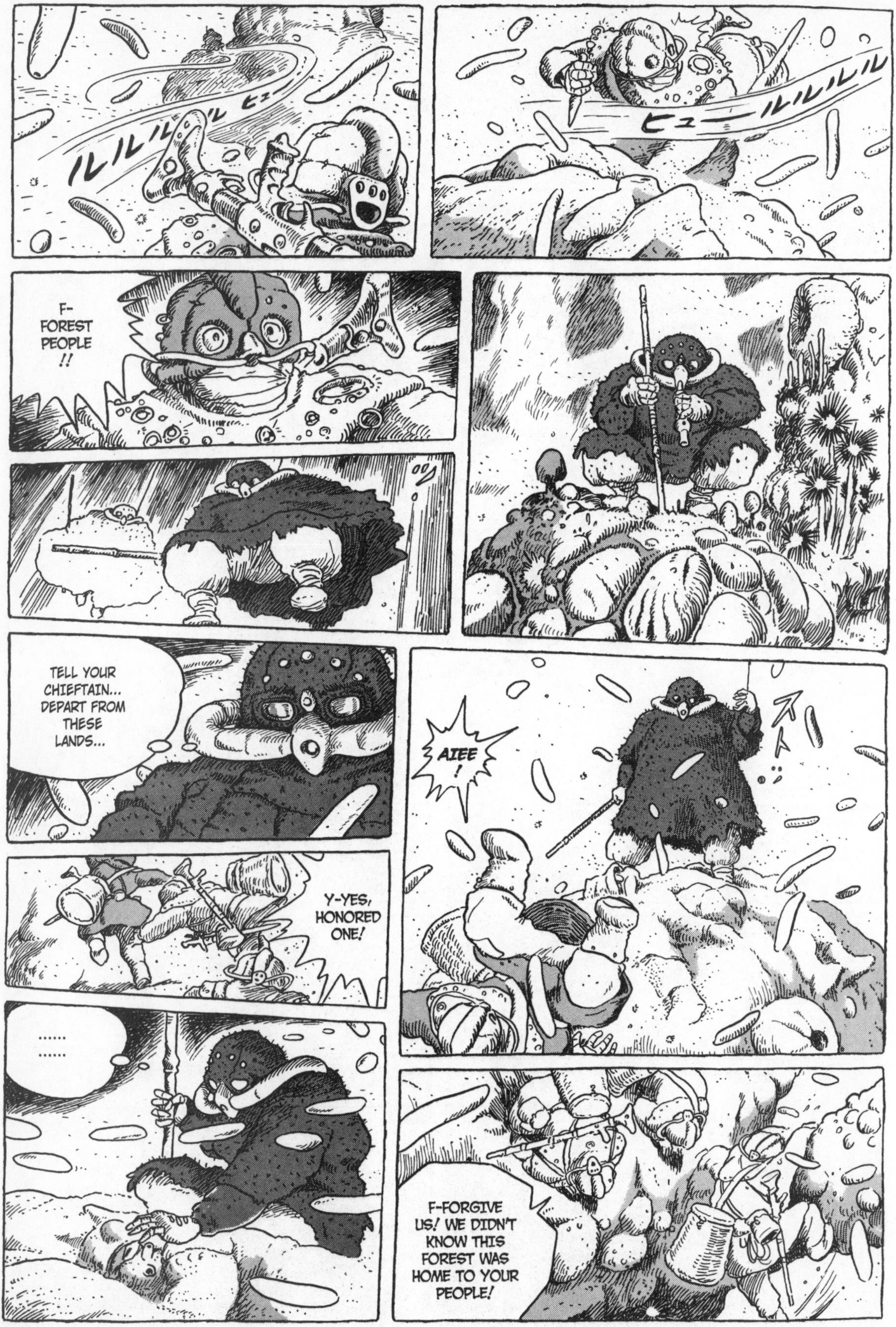
F-FOREST PEOPLE!!
AIEE!
TELL YOUR CHIEFTAIN... DEPART FROM THESE LANDS...
Y-YES, HONORED ONE!
F-FORGIVE US! WE DIDN'T KNOW THIS FOREST WAS HOME TO YOUR PEOPLE!
......
......

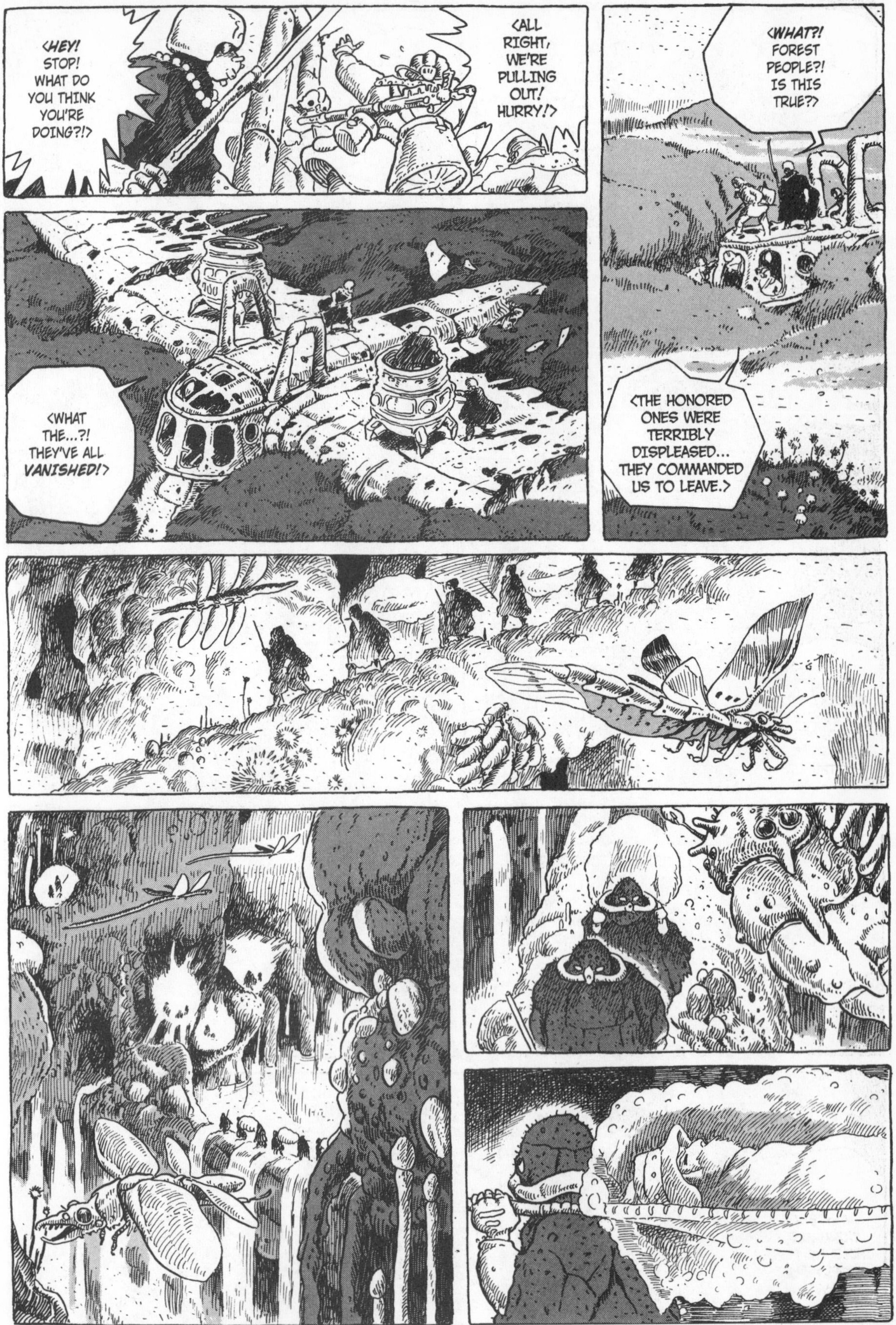
<WHAT?! FOREST PEOPLE?! IS THIS TRUE?>
<THE HONORED ONES WERE TERRIBLY DISPLEASED... THEY COMMANDED US TO LEAVE.>
<ALL RIGHT, WE'RE PULLING OUT! HURRY!>
<HEY! STOP! WHAT DO YOU THINK YOU'RE DOING?!>
<WHAT THE...?! THEY'VE ALL VANISHED!>

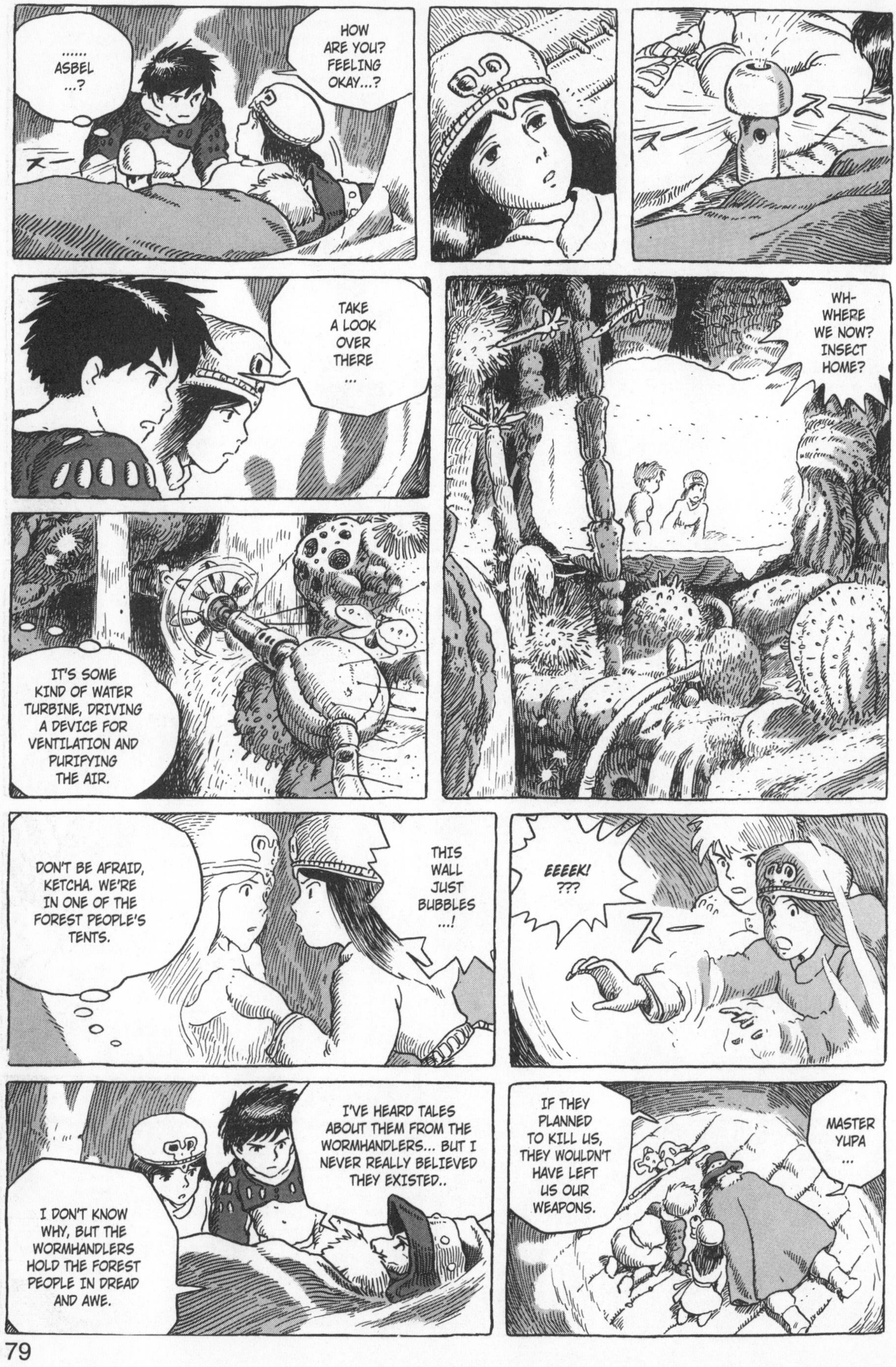
スー
スー
HOW ARE YOU? FEELING OKAY...?
...... ASBEL ...?
スー
WH- WHERE WE NOW? INSECT HOME?
TAKE A LOOK OVER THERE ...
IT'S SOME KIND OF WATER TURBINE, DRIVING A DEVICE FOR VENTILATION AND PURIFYING THE AIR.
EEEEK! ???
スー
THIS WALL JUST BUBBLES ...!
DON'T BE AFRAID, KETCHA. WE'RE IN ONE OF THE FOREST PEOPLE'S TENTS.
MASTER YUPA ...
IF THEY PLANNED TO KILL US, THEY WOULDN'T HAVE LEFT US OUR WEAPONS.
I'VE HEARD TALES ABOUT THEM FROM THE WORMHANDLERS... BUT I NEVER REALLY BELIEVED THEY EXISTED..
I DON'T KNOW WHY, BUT THE WORMHANDLERS HOLD THE FOREST PEOPLE IN DREAD AND AWE.

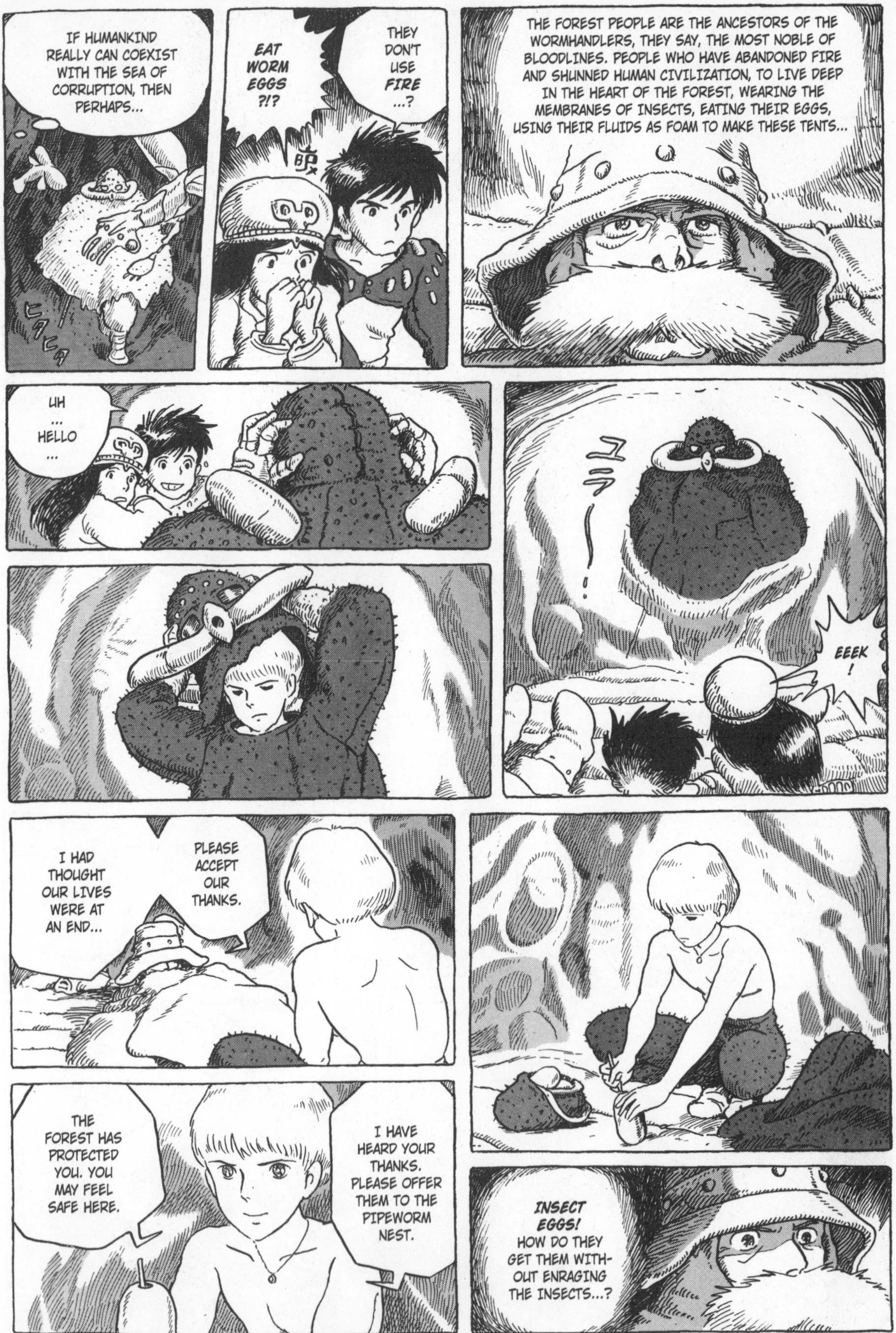
THE FOREST PEOPLE ARE THE ANCESTORS OF THE WORMHANDLERS, THEY SAY, THE MOST NOBLE OF BLOODLINES. PEOPLE WHO HAVE ABANDONED FIRE AND SHUNNED HUMAN CIVILIZATION, TO LIVE DEEP IN THE HEART OF THE FOREST, WEARING THE MEMBRANES OF INSECTS, EATING THEIR EGGS, USING THEIR FLUIDS AS FOAM TO MAKE THESE TENTS...
THEY DON'T USE ***FIRE*** ...?
EAT WORM EGGS ?!?
IF HUMANKIND REALLY CAN COEXIST WITH THE SEA OF CORRUPTION, THEN PERHAPS...
ユラ〜!
EEEK !
UH ... HELLO ...
INSECT EGGS! HOW DO THEY GET THEM WITH-OUT ENRAGING THE INSECTS...?
PLEASE ACCEPT OUR THANKS.
I HAD THOUGHT OUR LIVES WERE AT AN END...
I HAVE HEARD YOUR THANKS. PLEASE OFFER THEM TO THE PIPEWORM NEST.
THE FOREST HAS PROTECTED YOU. YOU MAY FEEL SAFE HERE.

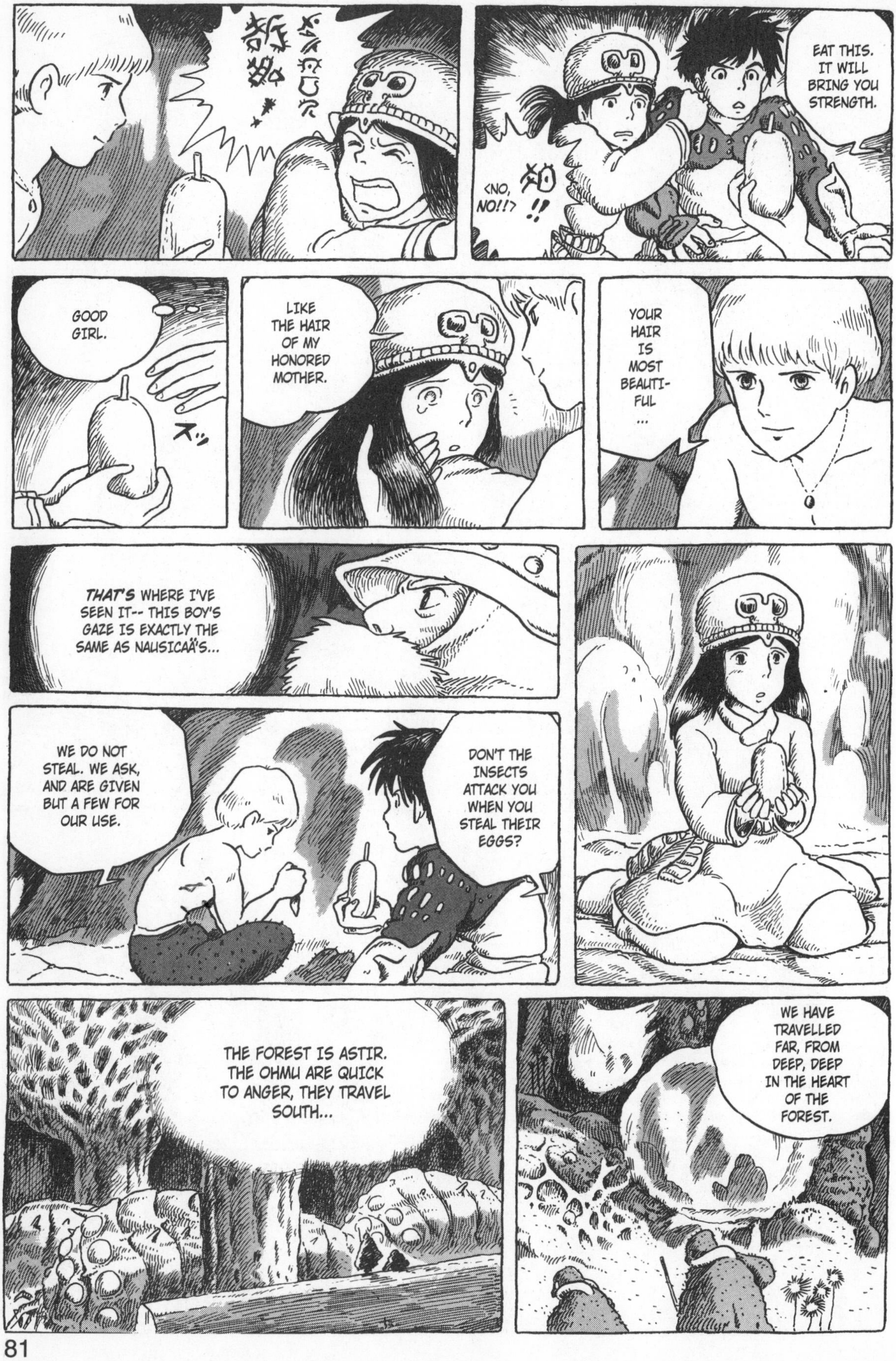
EAT THIS. IT WILL BRING YOU STRENGTH.
<NO, NO!!>
YOUR HAIR IS MOST BEAUTIFUL ...
LIKE THE HAIR OF MY HONORED MOTHER.
GOOD GIRL.
THAT'S WHERE I'VE SEEN IT-- THIS BOY'S GAZE IS EXACTLY THE SAME AS NAUSICAÄ'S...
DON'T THE INSECTS ATTACK YOU WHEN YOU STEAL THEIR EGGS?
WE DO NOT STEAL. WE ASK, AND ARE GIVEN BUT A FEW FOR OUR USE.
WE HAVE TRAVELLED FAR, FROM DEEP, DEEP IN THE HEART OF THE FOREST.
THE FOREST IS ASTIR. THE OHMU ARE QUICK TO ANGER, THEY TRAVEL SOUTH...

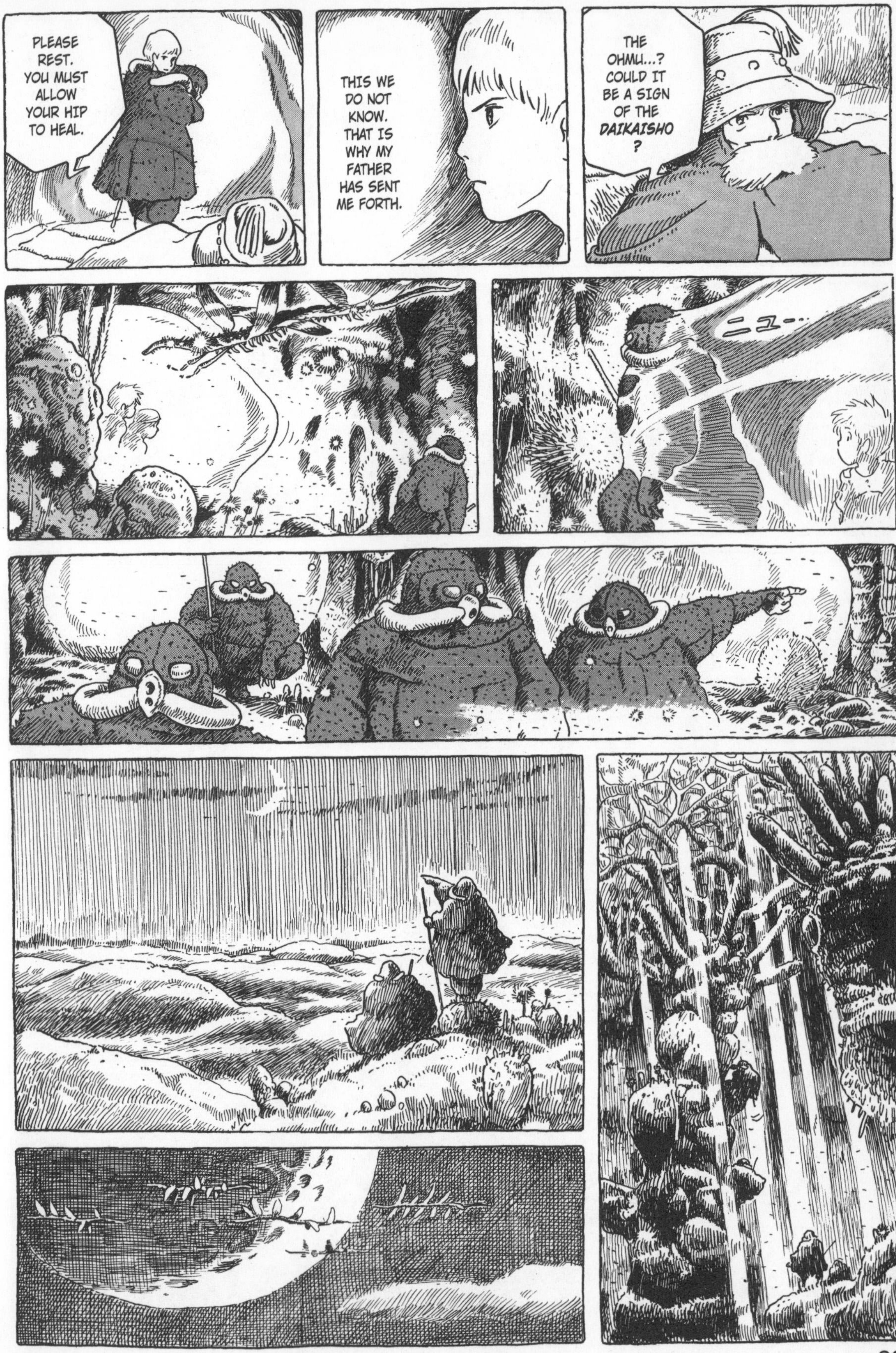
THE OHMU...? COULD IT BE A SIGN OF THE *DAIKAISHO* ?
THIS WE DO NOT KNOW. THAT IS WHY MY FATHER HAS SENT ME FORTH.
PLEASE REST. YOU MUST ALLOW YOUR HIP TO HEAL.
ニュ‥

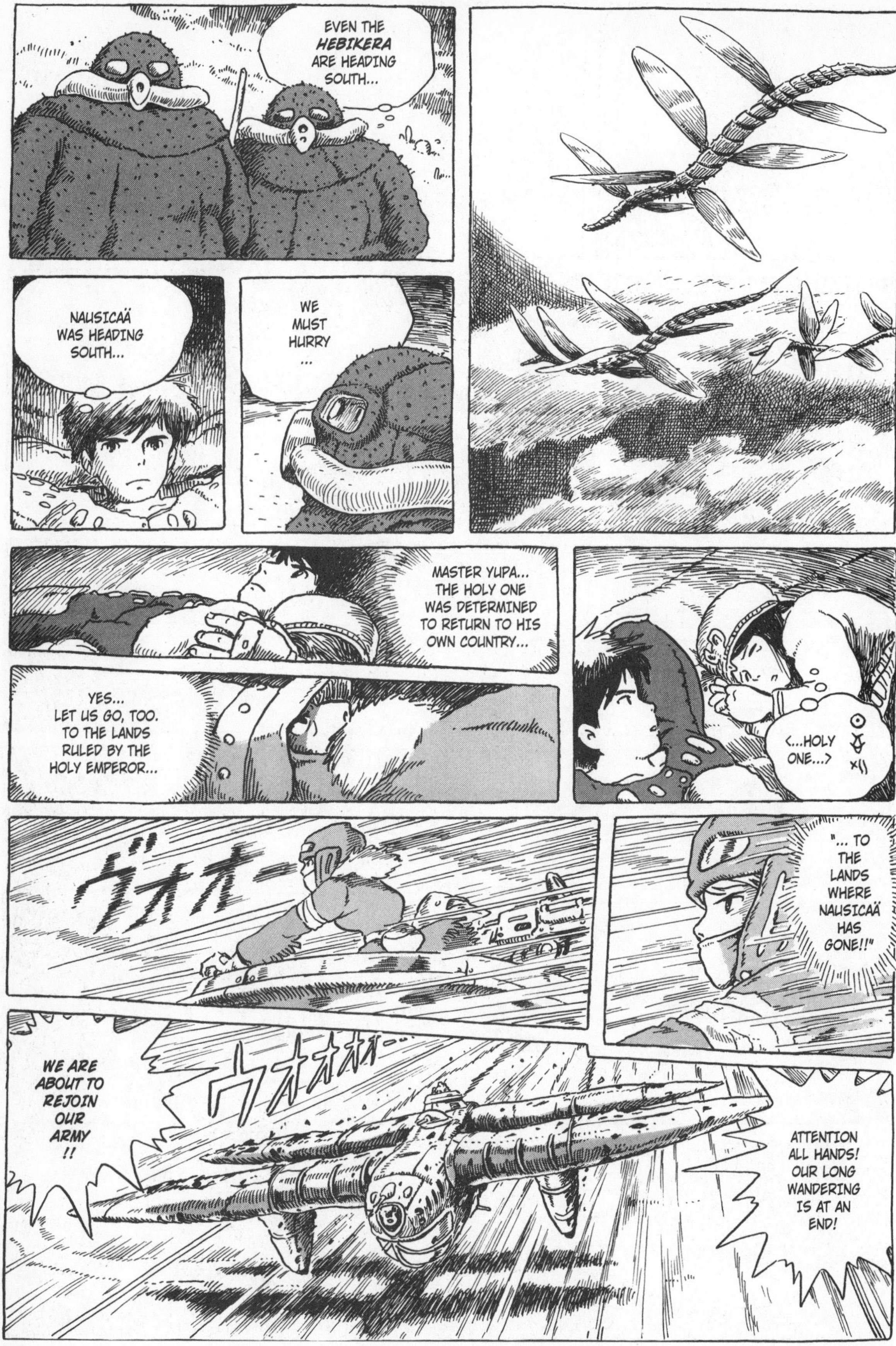
EVEN THE **HEBIKERA** ARE HEADING SOUTH...
WE MUST HURRY ...
NAUSICAÄ WAS HEADING SOUTH...
<...HOLY ONE...>
MASTER YUPA... THE HOLY ONE WAS DETERMINED TO RETURN TO HIS OWN COUNTRY...
YES... LET US GO, TOO. TO THE LANDS RULED BY THE HOLY EMPEROR...
"... TO THE LANDS WHERE NAUSICAÄ HAS GONE!!"
ヴオオー
ウオオオオー…
ATTENTION ALL HANDS! OUR LONG WANDERING IS AT AN END!
WE ARE ABOUT TO REJOIN OUR ARMY !!

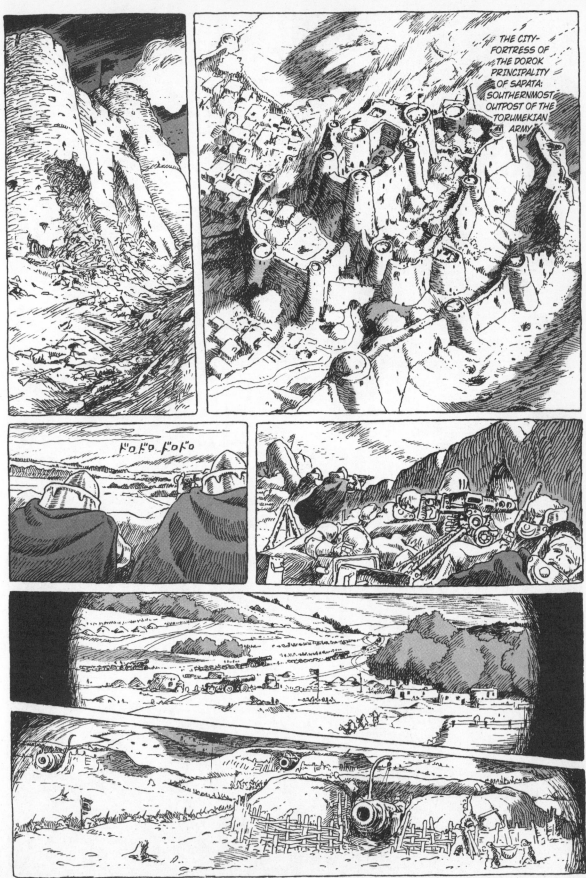

THE CITY-FORTRESS OF THE DOROK PRINCIPALITY OF SAPATA: SOUTHERNMOST OUTPOST OF THE TORUMEKIAN ARMY!!

ドォドォ ドォドォ

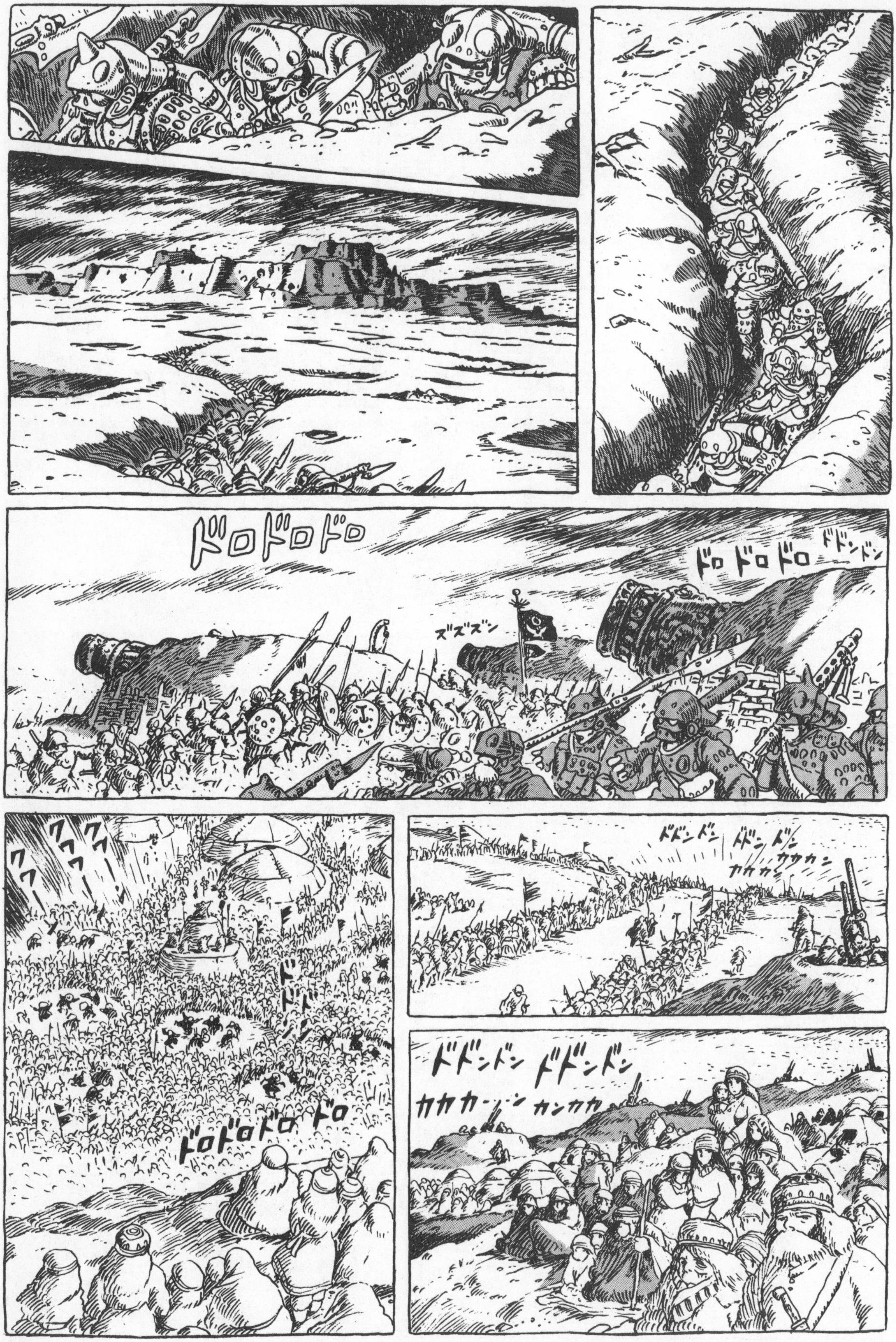
ドドンドン
ドロドロドロ
ズズズン
ドロドロドロ
ドドンドン ドドンドン
カカカン カカカン
ドドンドン ドドンドン
カカカーン カンカカ
ワワー
ワワワー
ワァー
ドドドーン
ドロドロドロ ドロ

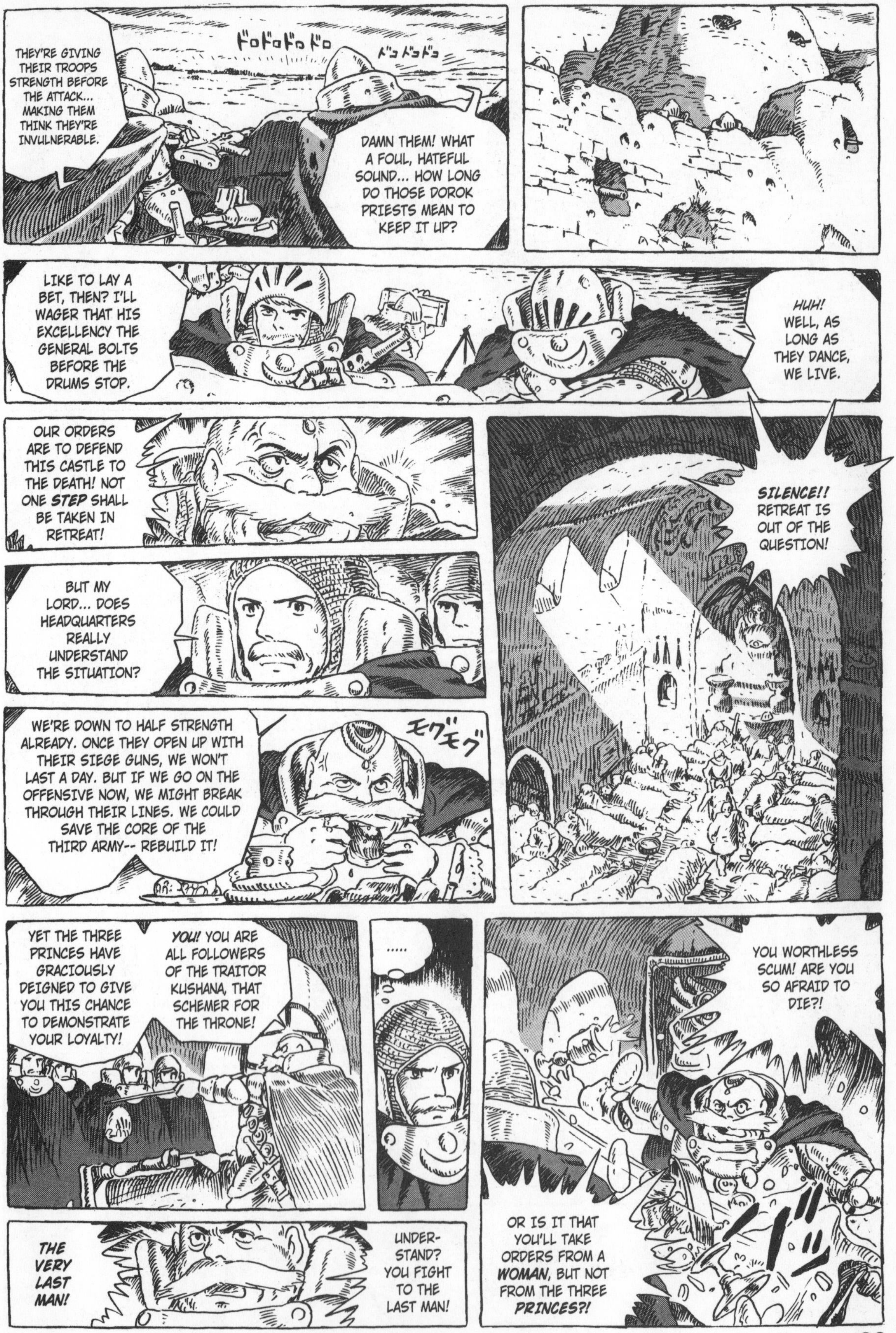

THEY'RE GIVING THEIR TROOPS STRENGTH BEFORE THE ATTACK... MAKING THEM THINK THEY'RE INVULNERABLE.
DAMN THEM! WHAT A FOUL, HATEFUL SOUND... HOW LONG DO THOSE DOROK PRIESTS MEAN TO KEEP IT UP?
LIKE TO LAY A BET, THEN? I'LL WAGER THAT HIS EXCELLENCY THE GENERAL BOLTS BEFORE THE DRUMS STOP.
HUH! WELL, AS LONG AS THEY DANCE, WE LIVE.
OUR ORDERS ARE TO DEFEND THIS CASTLE TO THE DEATH! NOT ONE STEP SHALL BE TAKEN IN RETREAT!
BUT MY LORD... DOES HEADQUARTERS REALLY UNDERSTAND THE SITUATION?
WE'RE DOWN TO HALF STRENGTH ALREADY. ONCE THEY OPEN UP WITH THEIR SIEGE GUNS, WE WON'T LAST A DAY. BUT IF WE GO ON THE OFFENSIVE NOW, WE MIGHT BREAK THROUGH THEIR LINES. WE COULD SAVE THE CORE OF THE THIRD ARMY-- REBUILD IT!
モグモグ
SILENCE!! RETREAT IS OUT OF THE QUESTION!
YOU! YOU ARE ALL FOLLOWERS OF THE TRAITOR KUSHANA, THAT SCHEMER FOR THE THRONE!
YET THE THREE PRINCES HAVE GRACIOUSLY DEIGNED TO GIVE YOU THIS CHANCE TO DEMONSTRATE YOUR LOYALTY!
.....
YOU WORTHLESS SCUM! ARE YOU SO AFRAID TO DIE?!
OR IS IT THAT YOU'LL TAKE ORDERS FROM A WOMAN, BUT NOT FROM THE THREE PRINCES?!
UNDERSTAND? YOU FIGHT TO THE LAST MAN!
THE VERY LAST MAN!

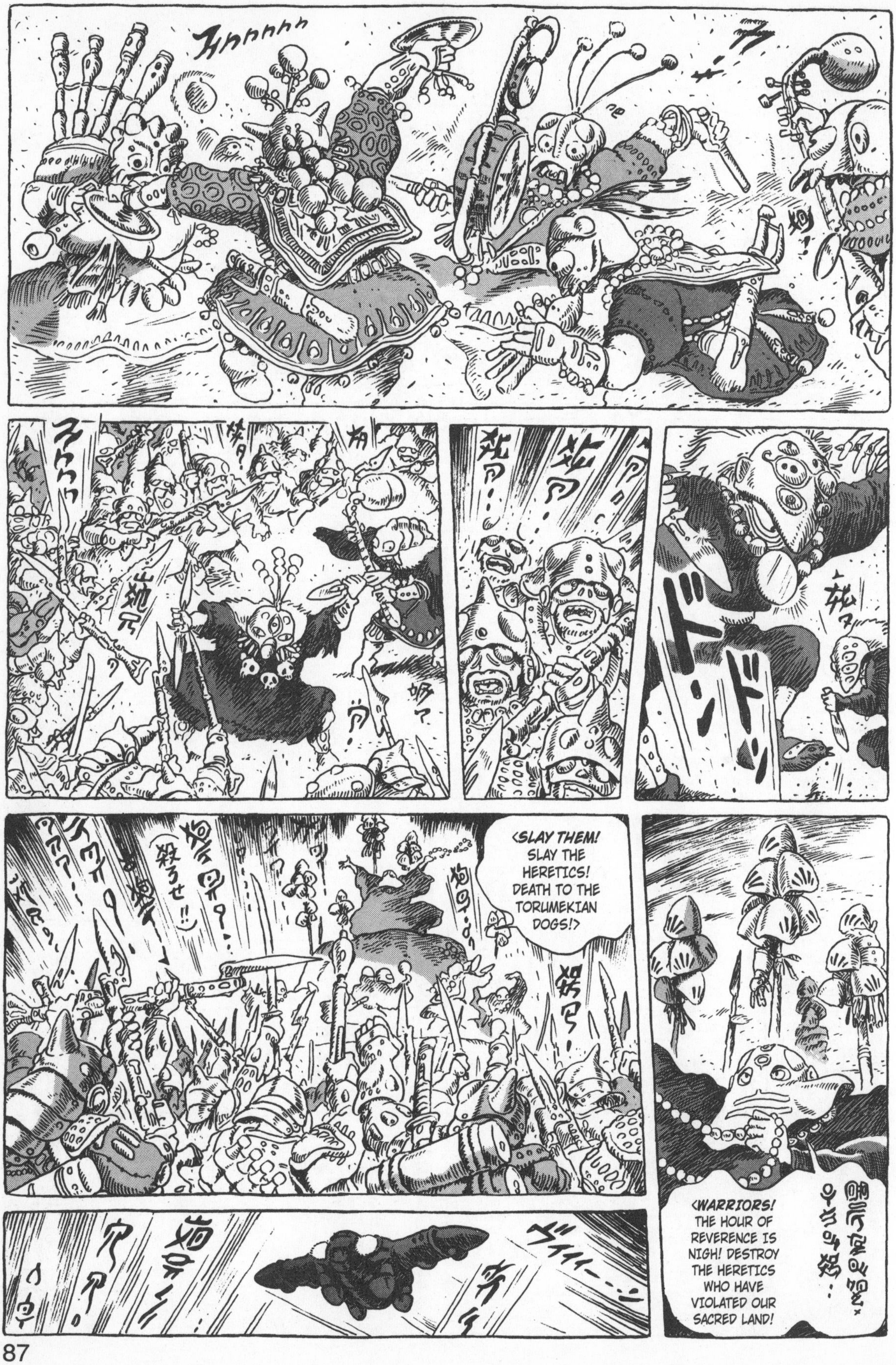
<WARRIORS! THE HOUR OF REVERENCE IS NIGH! DESTROY THE HERETICS WHO HAVE VIOLATED OUR SACRED LAND!>
<SLAY THEM! SLAY THE HERETICS! DEATH TO THE TORUMEKIAN DOGS!>

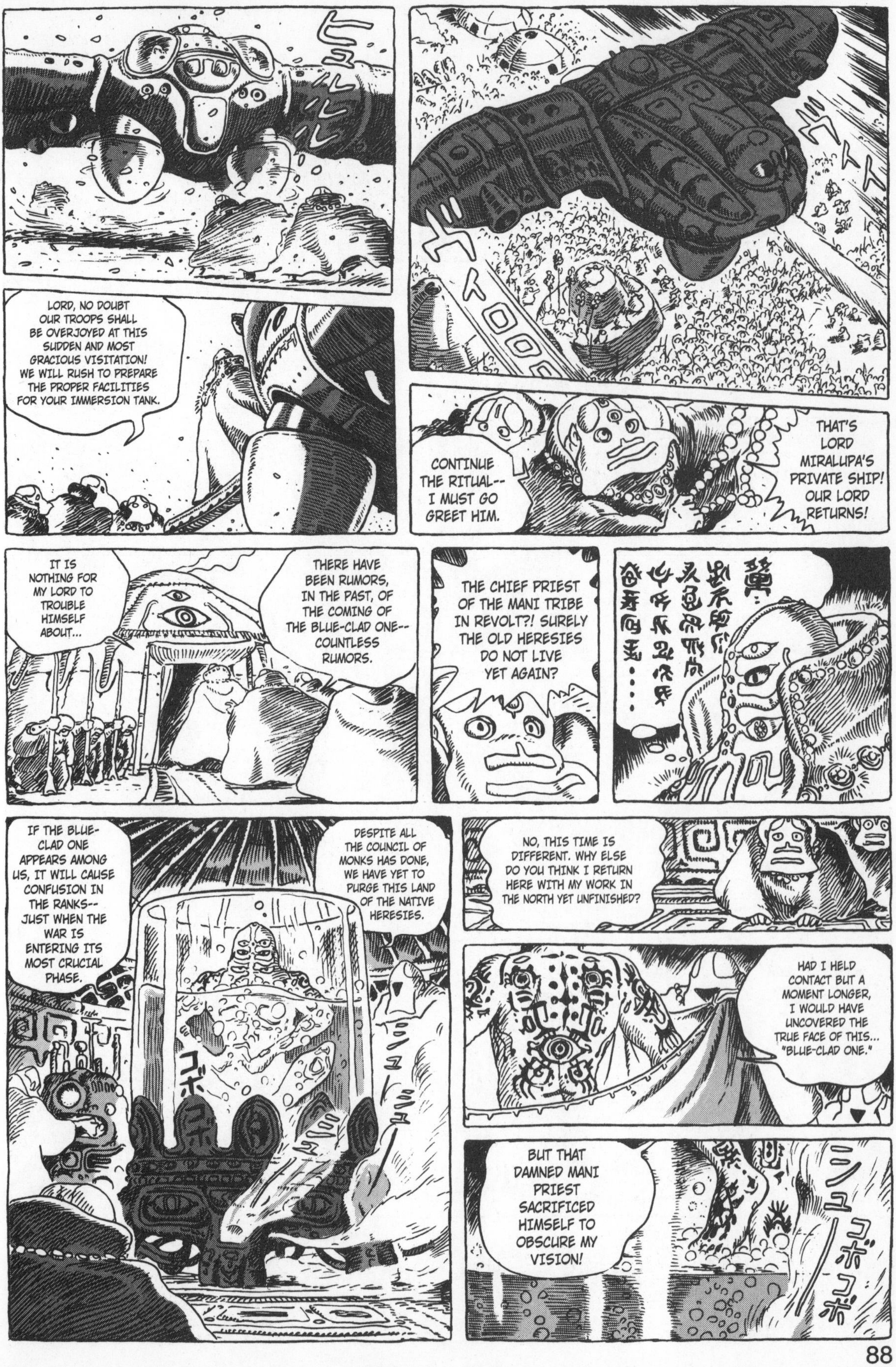
THAT'S LORD MIRALUPA'S PRIVATE SHIP! OUR LORD RETURNS!
CONTINUE THE RITUAL-- I MUST GO GREET HIM.
LORD, NO DOUBT OUR TROOPS SHALL BE OVERJOYED AT THIS SUDDEN AND MOST GRACIOUS VISITATION! WE WILL RUSH TO PREPARE THE PROPER FACILITIES FOR YOUR IMMERSION TANK.
THE CHIEF PRIEST OF THE MANI TRIBE IN REVOLT?! SURELY THE OLD HERESIES DO NOT LIVE YET AGAIN?
THERE HAVE BEEN RUMORS, IN THE PAST, OF THE COMING OF THE BLUE-CLAD ONE-- COUNTLESS RUMORS.
IT IS NOTHING FOR MY LORD TO TROUBLE HIMSELF ABOUT...
NO, THIS TIME IS DIFFERENT. WHY ELSE DO YOU THINK I RETURN HERE WITH MY WORK IN THE NORTH YET UNFINISHED?
HAD I HELD CONTACT BUT A MOMENT LONGER, I WOULD HAVE UNCOVERED THE TRUE FACE OF THIS... "BLUE-CLAD ONE."
BUT THAT DAMNED MANI PRIEST SACRIFICED HIMSELF TO OBSCURE MY VISION!
DESPITE ALL THE COUNCIL OF MONKS HAS DONE, WE HAVE YET TO PURGE THIS LAND OF THE NATIVE HERESIES.
IF THE BLUE-CLAD ONE APPEARS AMONG US, IT WILL CAUSE CONFUSION IN THE RANKS-- JUST WHEN THE WAR IS ENTERING ITS MOST CRUCIAL PHASE.

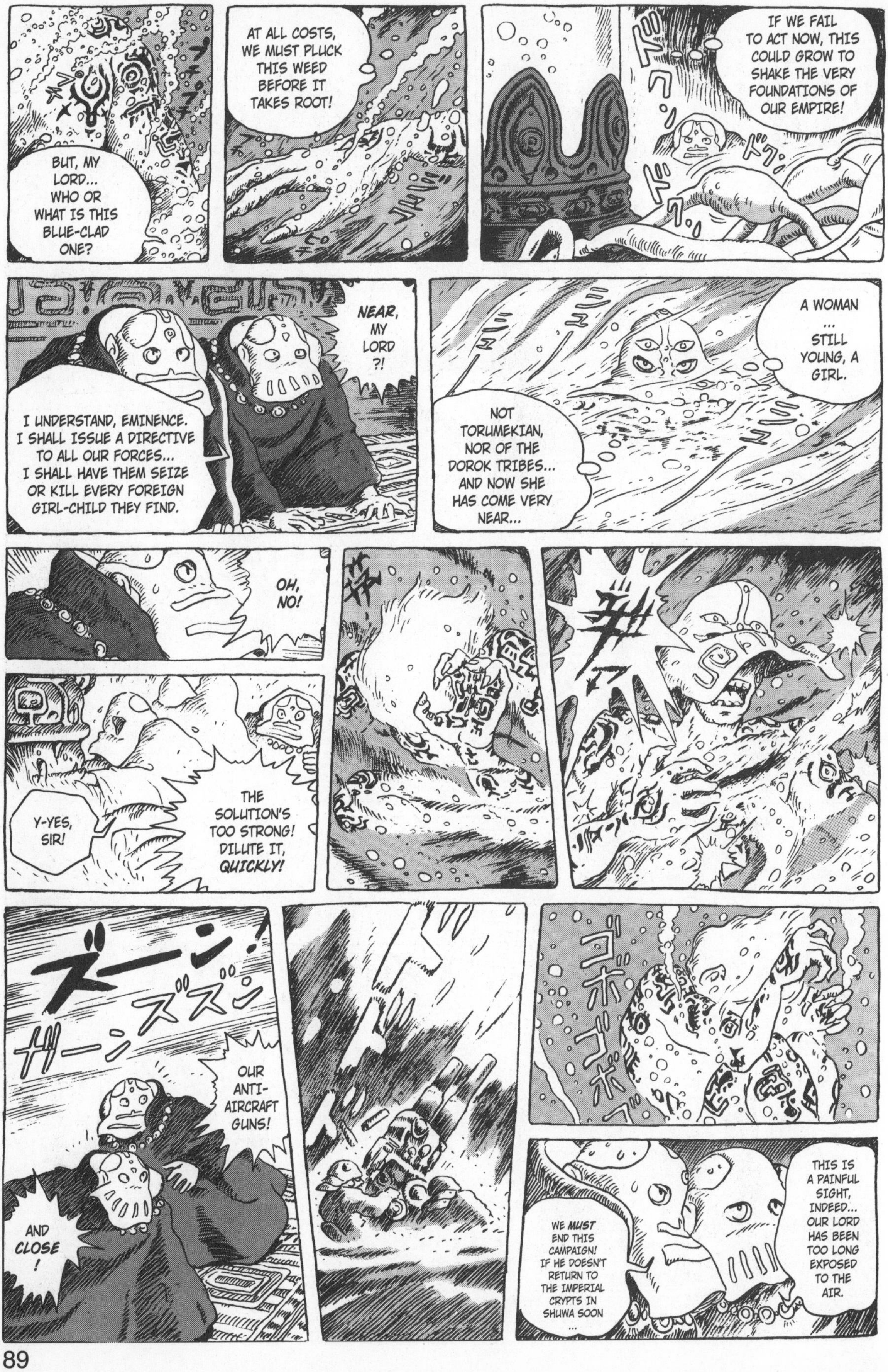
IF WE FAIL TO ACT NOW, THIS COULD GROW TO SHAKE THE VERY FOUNDATIONS OF OUR EMPIRE!
AT ALL COSTS, WE MUST PLUCK THIS WEED BEFORE IT TAKES ROOT!
BUT, MY LORD... WHO OR WHAT IS THIS BLUE-CLAD ONE?
A WOMAN ... STILL YOUNG, A GIRL.
NOT TORUMEKIAN, NOR OF THE DOROK TRIBES... AND NOW SHE HAS COME VERY NEAR...
NEAR, MY LORD ?!
I UNDERSTAND, EMINENCE. I SHALL ISSUE A DIRECTIVE TO ALL OUR FORCES... I SHALL HAVE THEM SEIZE OR KILL EVERY FOREIGN GIRL-CHILD THEY FIND.
OH, NO!
THE SOLUTION'S TOO STRONG! DILUTE IT, QUICKLY!
Y-YES, SIR!
THIS IS A PAINFUL SIGHT, INDEED... OUR LORD HAS BEEN TOO LONG EXPOSED TO THE AIR.
WE MUST END THIS CAMPAIGN! IF HE DOESN'T RETURN TO THE IMPERIAL CRYPTS IN SHUWA SOON ...
OUR ANTI-AIRCRAFT GUNS!
AND CLOSE !

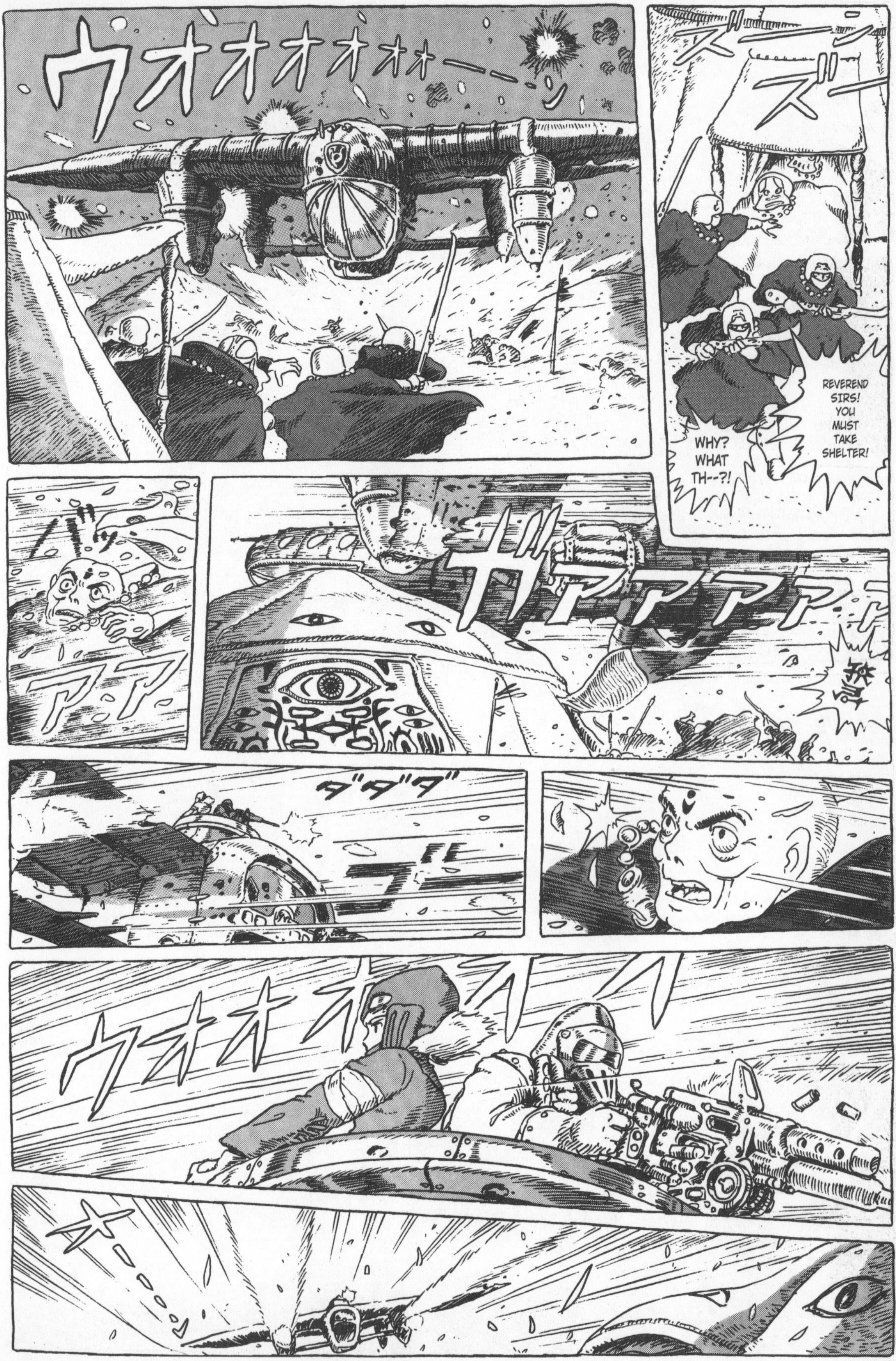
REVEREND SIRS! YOU MUST TAKE SHELTER!
WHY? WHAT TH--?!

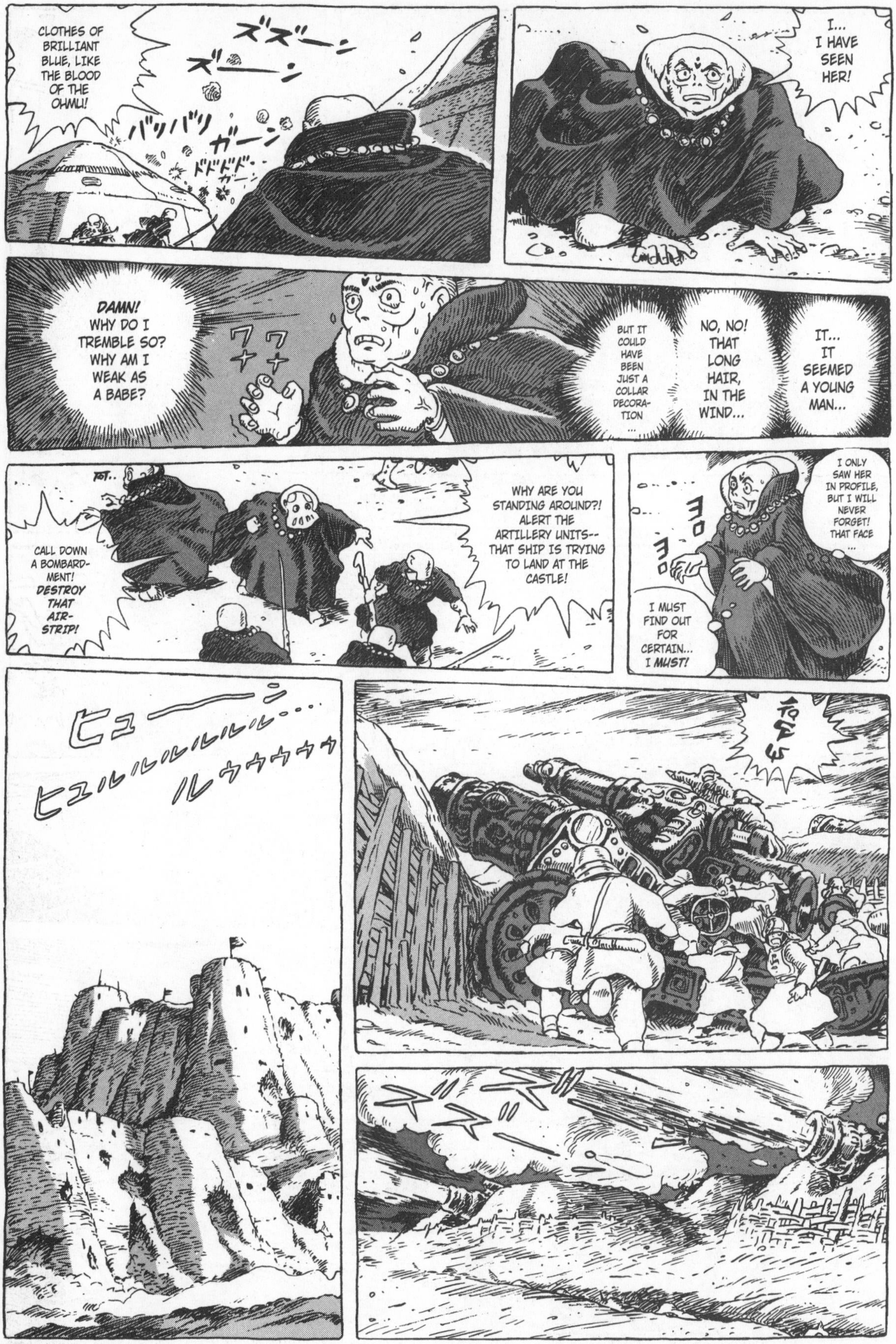
I... I HAVE SEEN HER!
CLOTHES OF BRILLIANT BLUE, LIKE THE BLOOD OF THE OHMU!
ズズーン
ズーン
バッバリ
ガーン
ドドドド
IT... IT SEEMED A YOUNG MAN...
NO, NO! THAT LONG HAIR, IN THE WIND...
BUT IT COULD HAVE BEEN JUST A COLLAR DECORATION ...
ワナ ワナ
DAMN! WHY DO I TREMBLE SO? WHY AM I WEAK AS A BABE?
I ONLY SAW HER IN PROFILE, BUT I WILL NEVER FORGET! THAT FACE ...
ヨロ ヨロ
I MUST FIND OUT FOR CERTAIN... I ***MUST!***
WHY ARE YOU STANDING AROUND?! ALERT THE ARTILLERY UNITS-- THAT SHIP IS TRYING TO LAND AT THE CASTLE!
CALL DOWN A BOMBARDMENT! ***DESTROY THAT AIRSTRIP!***
ズズーン
ヒューーン
ヒュルルルルルル....
ルウウウウ

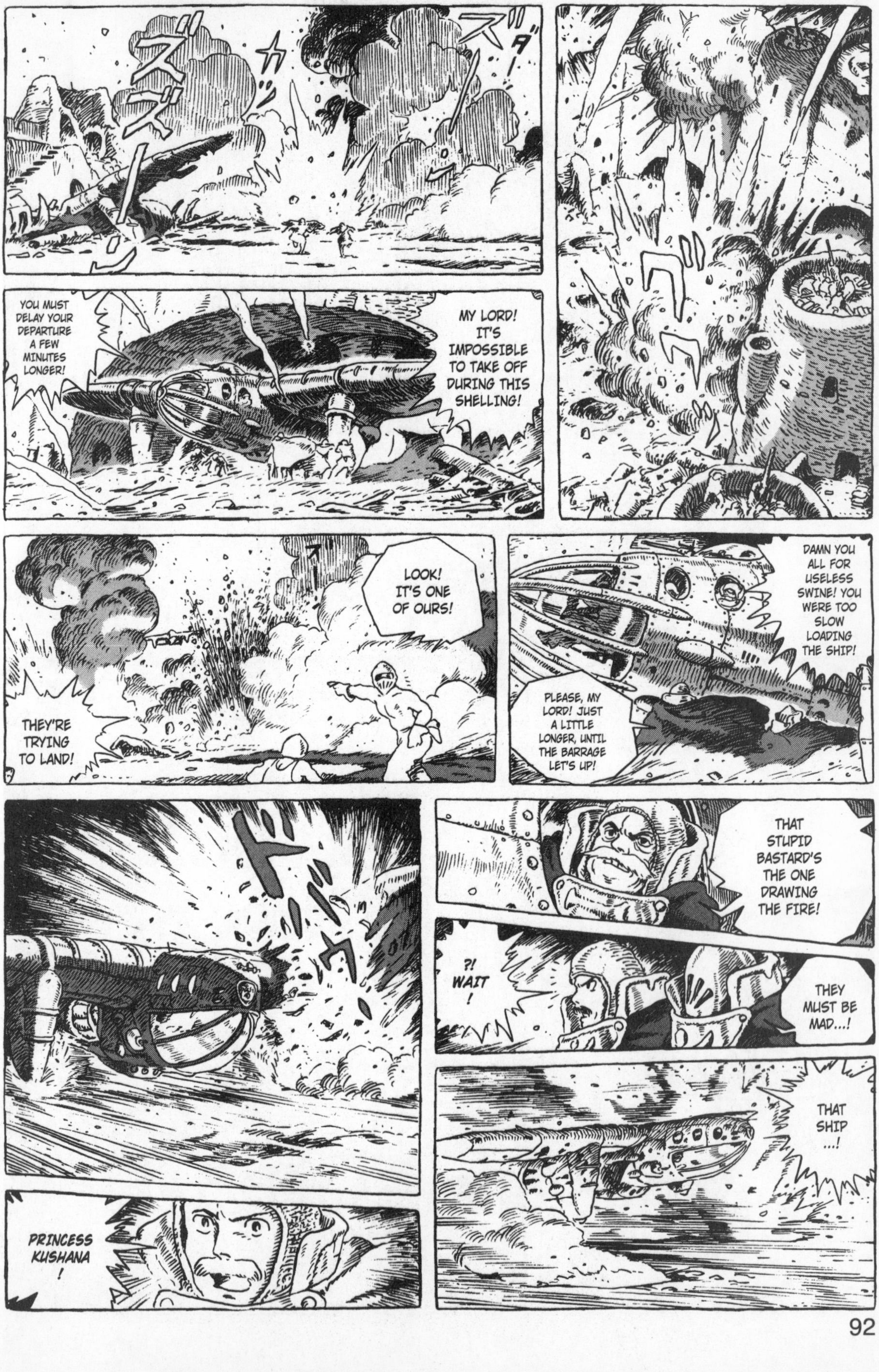
MY LORD! IT'S IMPOSSIBLE TO TAKE OFF DURING THIS SHELLING!
YOU MUST DELAY YOUR DEPARTURE A FEW MINUTES LONGER!
DAMN YOU ALL FOR USELESS SWINE! YOU WERE TOO SLOW LOADING THE SHIP!
PLEASE, MY LORD! JUST A LITTLE LONGER, UNTIL THE BARRAGE LET'S UP!
LOOK! IT'S ONE OF OURS!
THEY'RE TRYING TO LAND!
THAT STUPID BASTARD'S THE ONE DRAWING THE FIRE!
THEY MUST BE MAD...!
?! WAIT!
THAT SHIP ...!
PRINCESS KUSHANA!

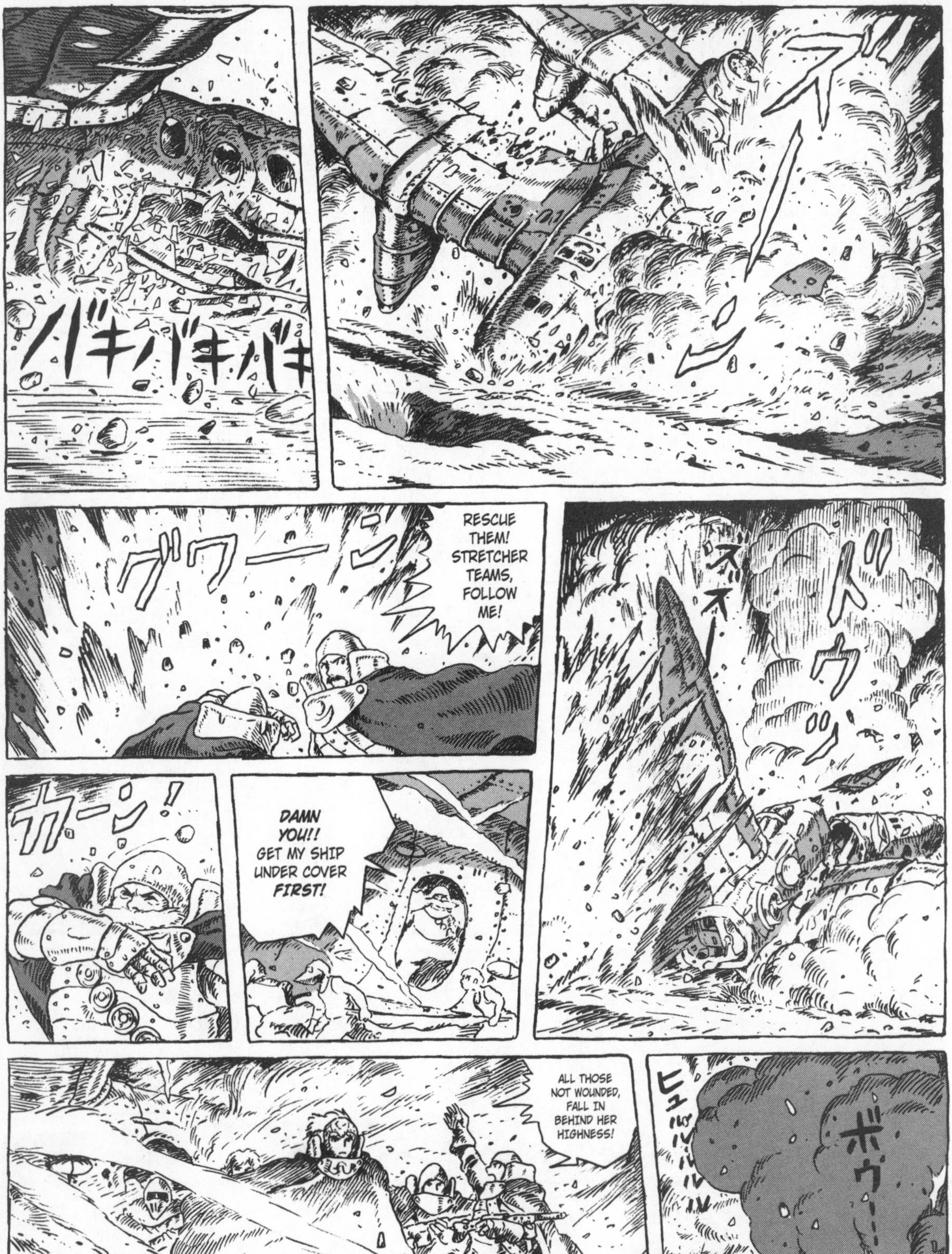
バキ!バキバキ
ドウウッ
RESCUE THEM! STRETCHER TEAMS, FOLLOW ME!
グワーン
DAMN YOU!! GET MY SHIP UNDER COVER FIRST!
カーン!
ボウ
ALL THOSE NOT WOUNDED, FALL IN BEHIND HER HIGHNESS!

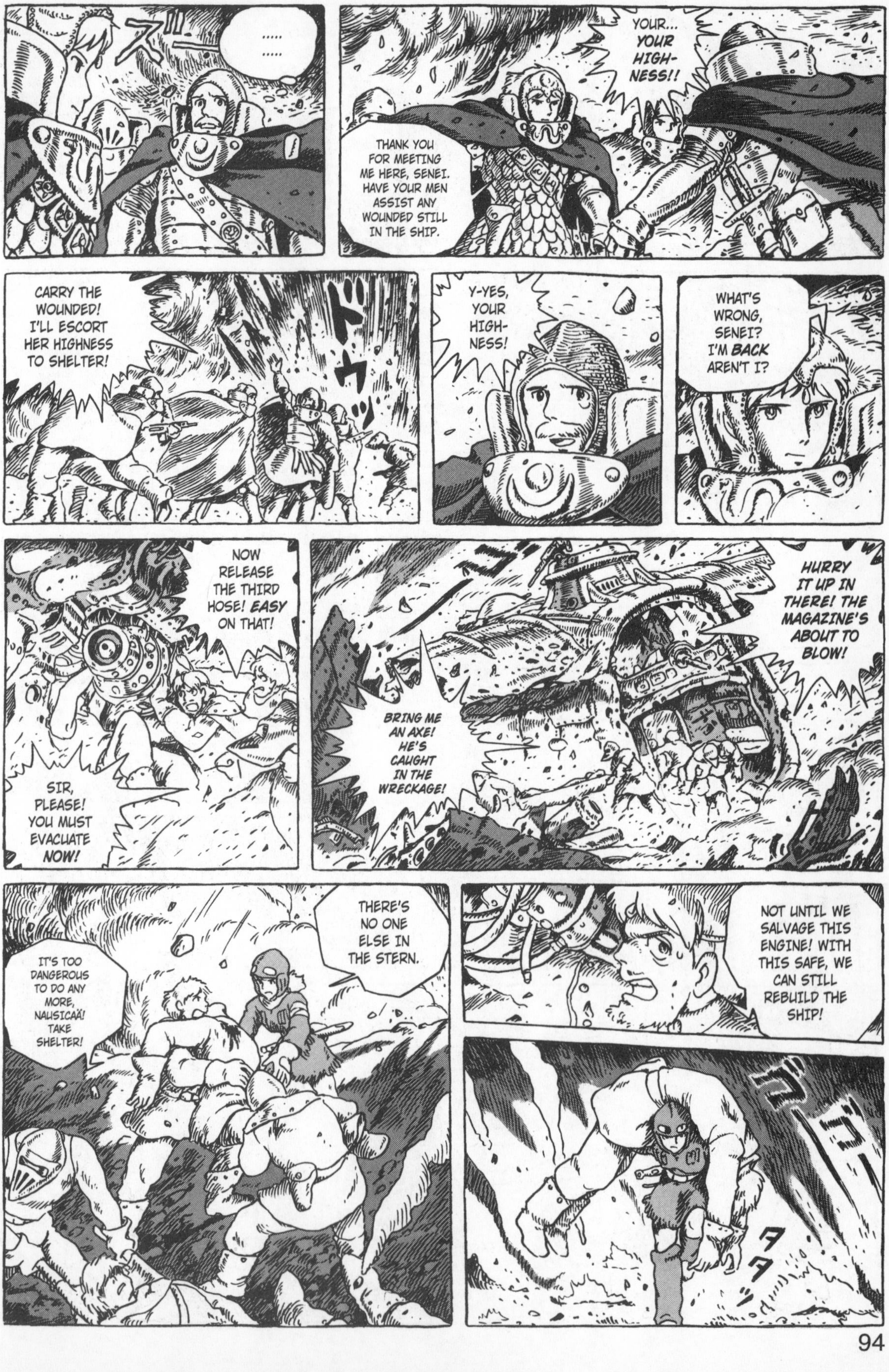
YOUR... YOUR HIGH-NESS!!
THANK YOU FOR MEETING ME HERE, SENEI. HAVE YOUR MEN ASSIST ANY WOUNDED STILL IN THE SHIP.
....
WHAT'S WRONG, SENEI? I'M BACK AREN'T I?
Y-YES, YOUR HIGH-NESS!
CARRY THE WOUNDED! I'LL ESCORT HER HIGHNESS TO SHELTER!
HURRY IT UP IN THERE! THE MAGAZINE'S ABOUT TO BLOW!
BRING ME AN AXE! HE'S CAUGHT IN THE WRECKAGE!
NOW RELEASE THE THIRD HOSE! EASY ON THAT!
SIR, PLEASE! YOU MUST EVACUATE NOW!
NOT UNTIL WE SALVAGE THIS ENGINE! WITH THIS SAFE, WE CAN STILL REBUILD THE SHIP!
THERE'S NO ONE ELSE IN THE STERN.
IT'S TOO DANGEROUS TO DO ANY MORE, NAUSICAÄ! TAKE SHELTER!

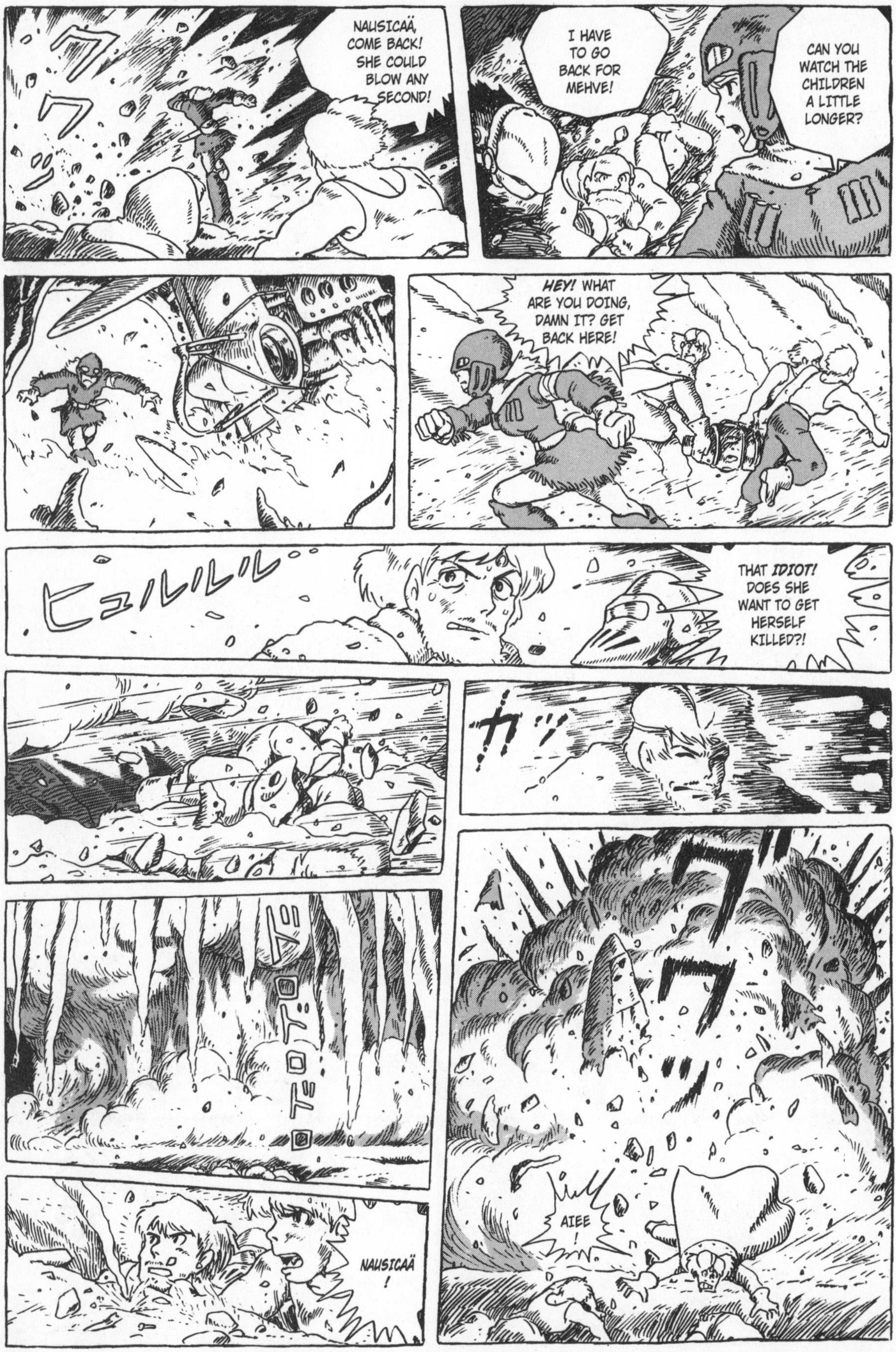
CAN YOU WATCH THE CHILDREN A LITTLE LONGER?
I HAVE TO GO BACK FOR MEHVE!
NAUSICAÄ, COME BACK! SHE COULD BLOW ANY SECOND!
HEY! WHAT ARE YOU DOING, DAMN IT? GET BACK HERE!
THAT **IDIOT!** DOES SHE WANT TO GET HERSELF KILLED?!
ヒュルルルル
カッ
AIEE!
NAUSICAÄ!

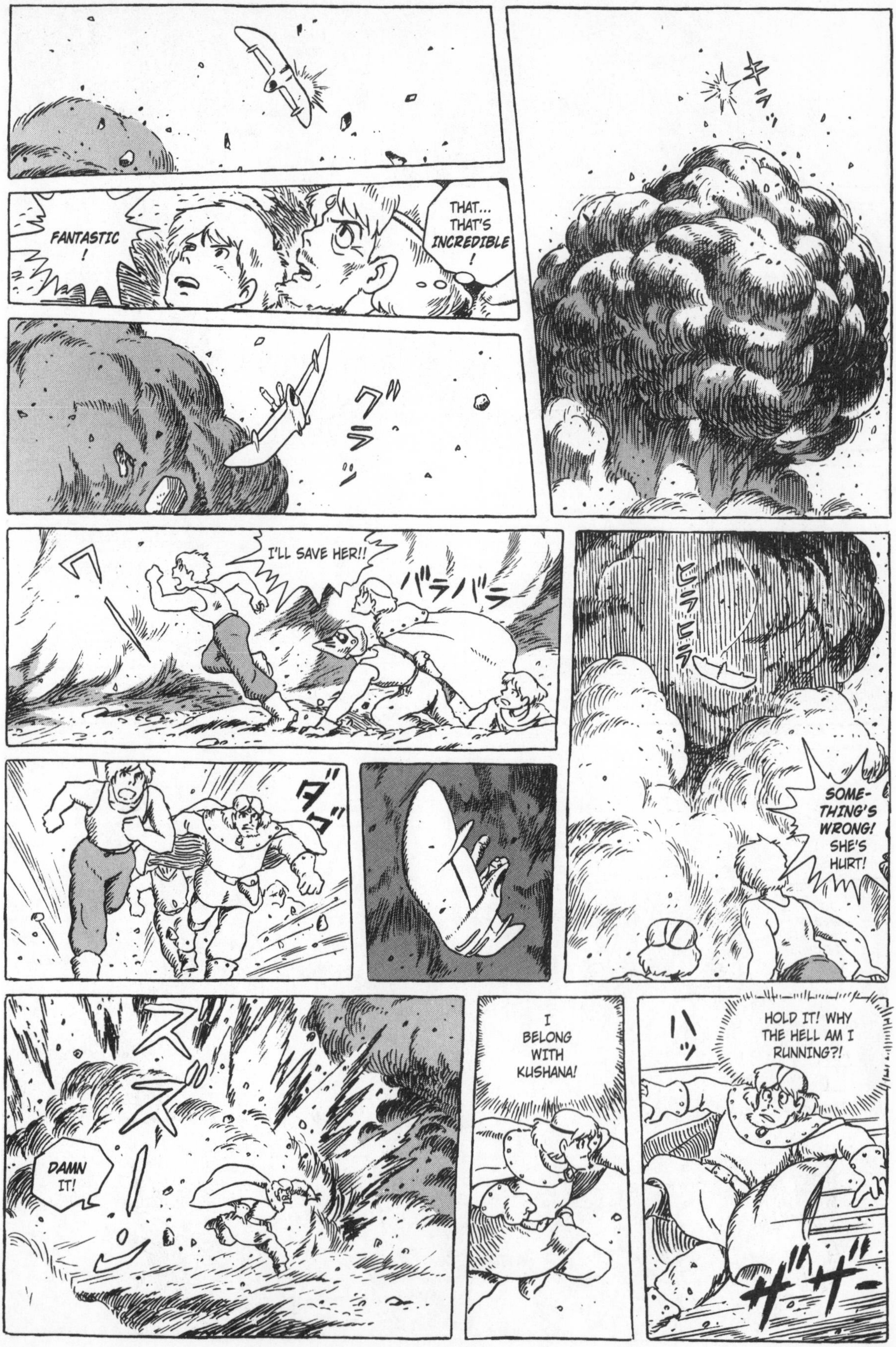
キラッ
THAT... THAT'S INCREDIBLE!
FANTASTIC!
グラッ
ヒラヒラ
SOME-THING'S WRONG! SHE'S HURT!
バラバラ
I'LL SAVE HER!!
ワーッ
HOLD IT! WHY THE HELL AM I RUNNING?!
ハッ
ザザー
I BELONG WITH KUSHANA!
DAMN IT!

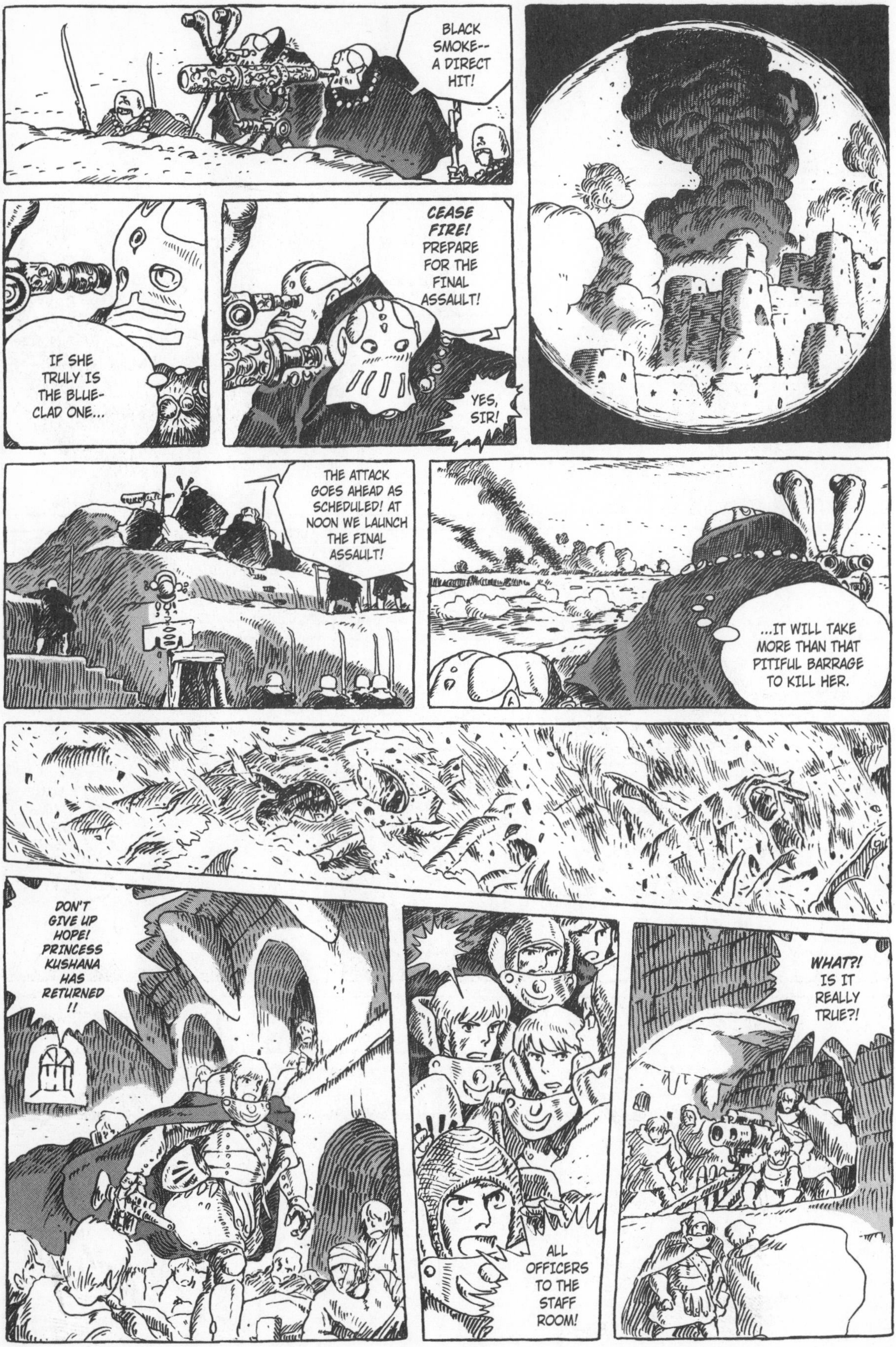
BLACK SMOKE--A DIRECT HIT!
CEASE FIRE! PREPARE FOR THE FINAL ASSAULT!
YES, SIR!
IF SHE TRULY IS THE BLUE-CLAD ONE...
...IT WILL TAKE MORE THAN THAT PITIFUL BARRAGE TO KILL HER.
THE ATTACK GOES AHEAD AS SCHEDULED! AT NOON WE LAUNCH THE FINAL ASSAULT!
WHAT?! IS IT REALLY TRUE?!
ALL OFFICERS TO THE STAFF ROOM!
DON'T GIVE UP HOPE! PRINCESS KUSHANA HAS RETURNED!!

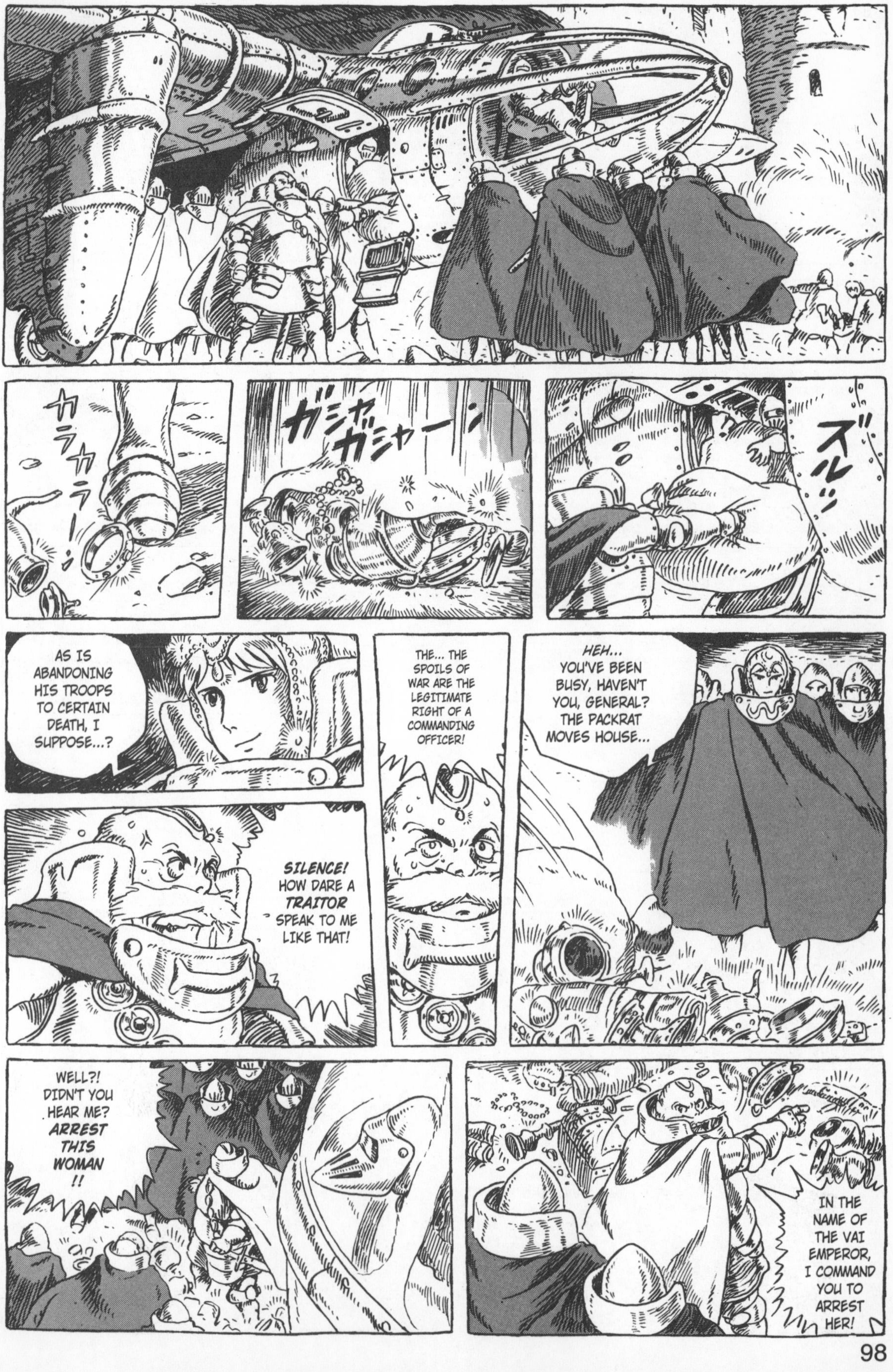
ズルッ
ガシャ
ガシャーン
カラカラー！
HEH... YOU'VE BEEN BUSY, HAVEN'T YOU, GENERAL? THE PACKRAT MOVES HOUSE...
THE... THE SPOILS OF WAR ARE THE LEGITIMATE RIGHT OF A COMMANDING OFFICER!
AS IS ABANDONING HIS TROOPS TO CERTAIN DEATH, I SUPPOSE...?
SILENCE! HOW DARE A TRAITOR SPEAK TO ME LIKE THAT!
IN THE NAME OF THE VAI EMPEROR, I COMMAND YOU TO ARREST HER!
WELL?! DIDN'T YOU HEAR ME? ARREST THIS WOMAN!!

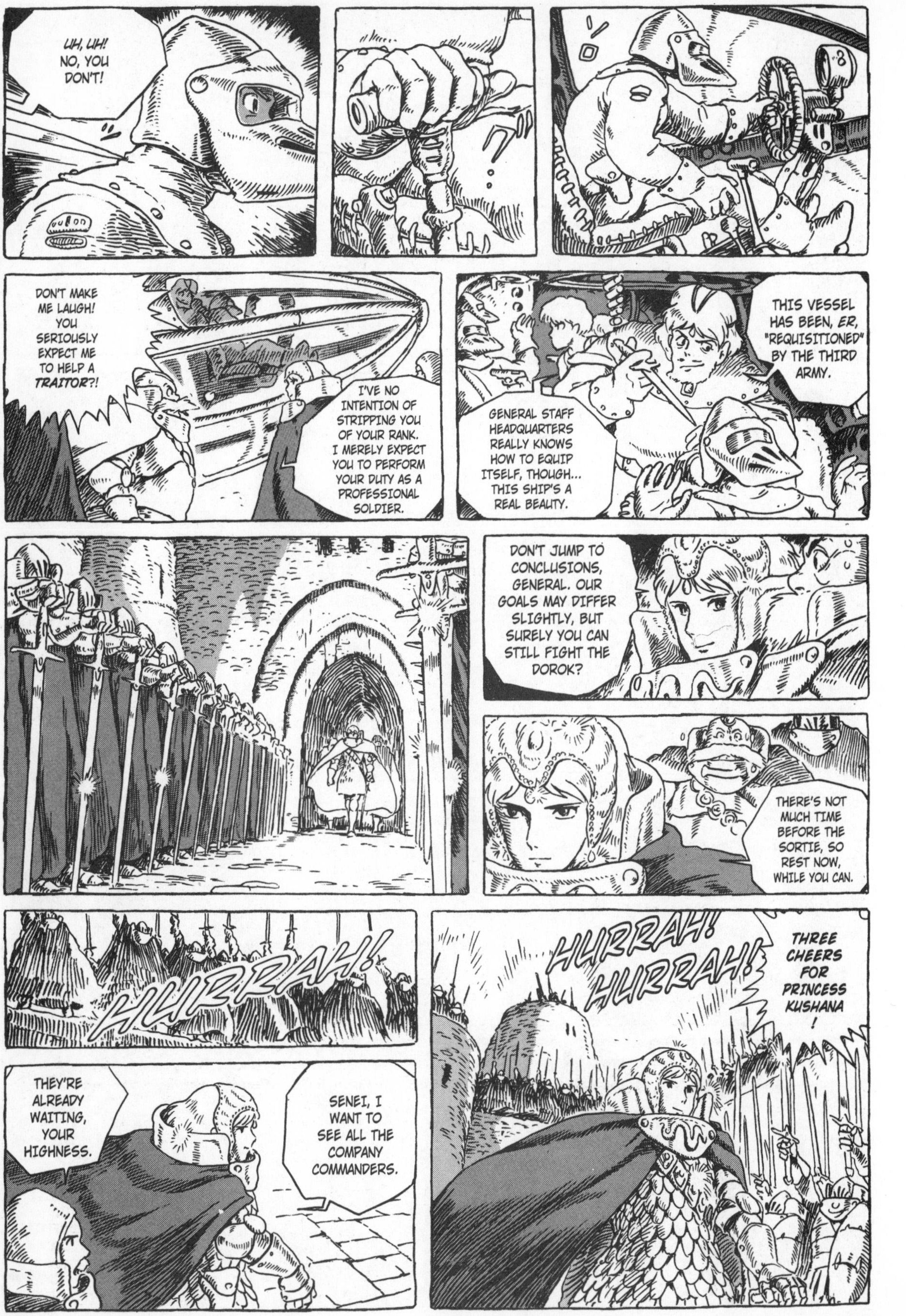
UH, UH! NO, YOU DON'T!
THIS VESSEL HAS BEEN, *ER*, "REQUISITIONED" BY THE THIRD ARMY.
GENERAL STAFF HEADQUARTERS REALLY KNOWS HOW TO EQUIP ITSELF, THOUGH... THIS SHIP'S A REAL BEAUTY.
DON'T MAKE ME LAUGH! YOU SERIOUSLY EXPECT ME TO HELP A *TRAITOR*?!
I'VE NO INTENTION OF STRIPPING YOU OF YOUR RANK. I MERELY EXPECT YOU TO PERFORM YOUR DUTY AS A PROFESSIONAL SOLDIER.
DON'T JUMP TO CONCLUSIONS, GENERAL. OUR GOALS MAY DIFFER SLIGHTLY, BUT SURELY YOU CAN STILL FIGHT THE DOROK?
THERE'S NOT MUCH TIME BEFORE THE SORTIE, SO REST NOW, WHILE YOU CAN.
THREE CHEERS FOR PRINCESS KUSHANA!
HURRAH! HURRAH!
HURRAH!
SENEI, I WANT TO SEE ALL THE COMPANY COMMANDERS.
THEY'RE ALREADY WAITING, YOUR HIGHNESS.

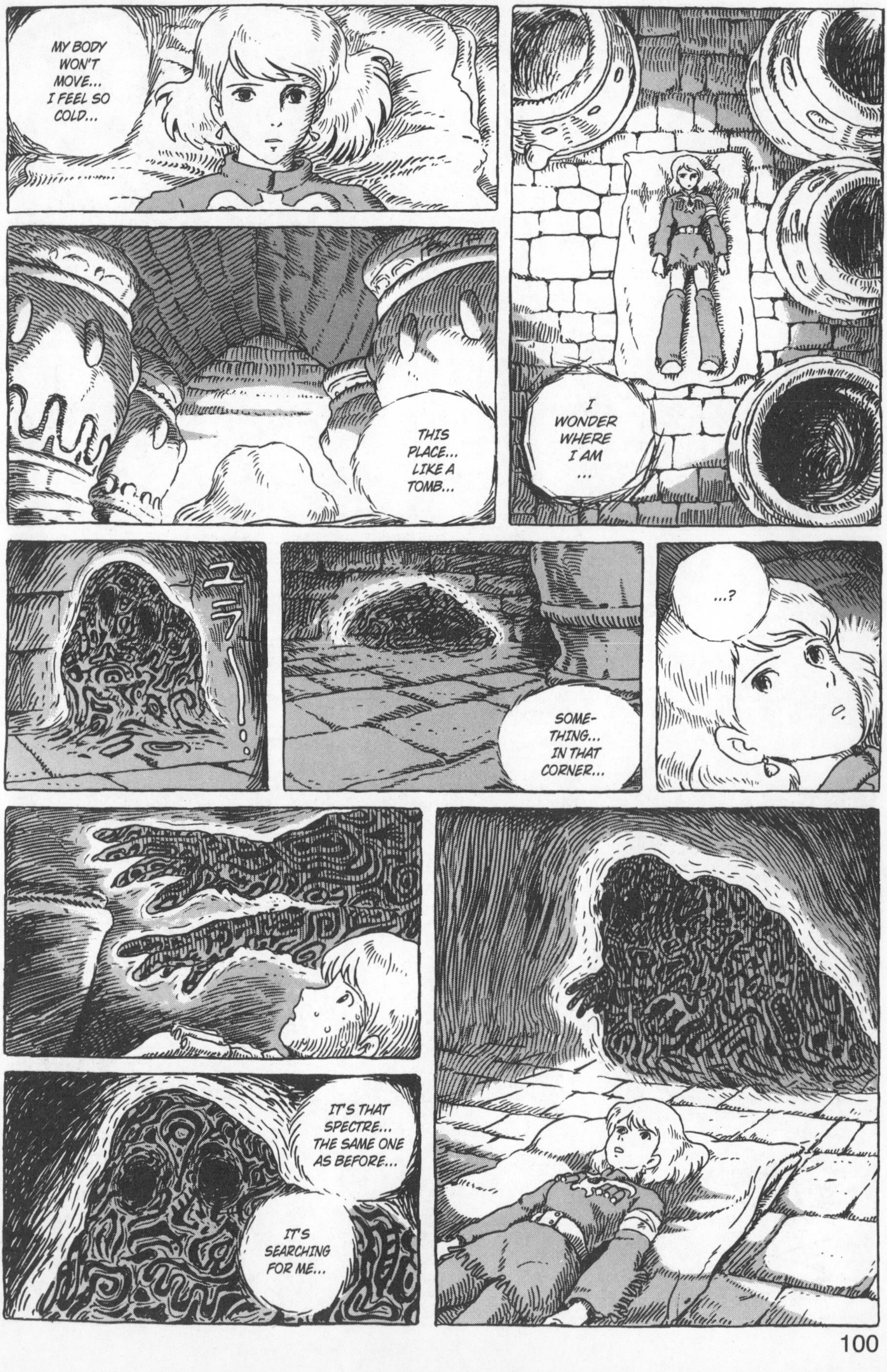
I WONDER WHERE I AM ...
MY BODY WON'T MOVE... I FEEL SO COLD...
THIS PLACE... LIKE A TOMB...
...?
SOME-THING... IN THAT CORNER...
ユラー!
IT'S THAT SPECTRE... THE SAME ONE AS BEFORE...
IT'S SEARCHING FOR ME...

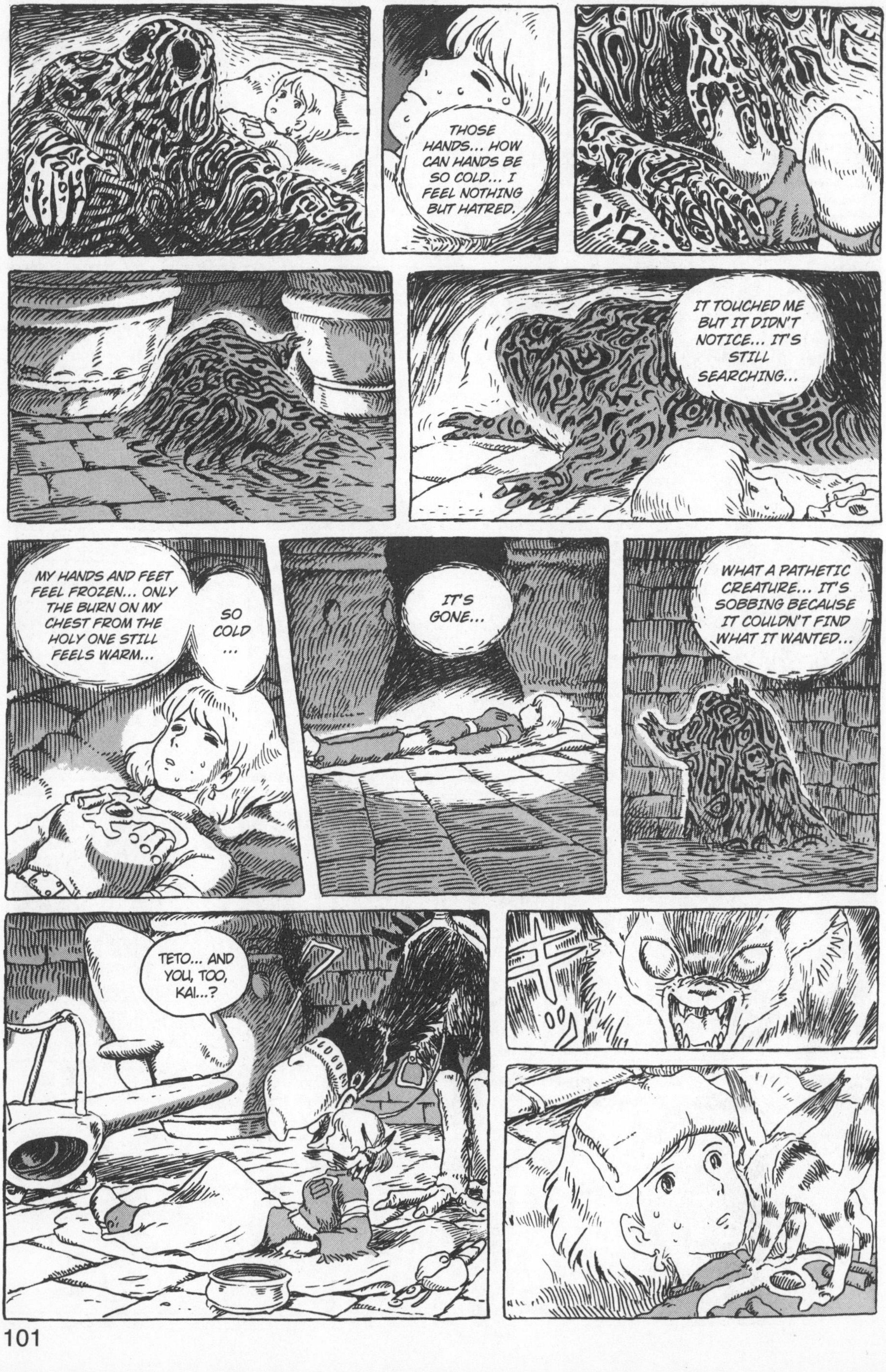
THOSE HANDS... HOW CAN HANDS BE SO COLD... I FEEL NOTHING BUT HATRED.
IT TOUCHED ME BUT IT DIDN'T NOTICE... IT'S STILL SEARCHING...
WHAT A PATHETIC CREATURE... IT'S SOBBING BECAUSE IT COULDN'T FIND WHAT IT WANTED...
IT'S GONE...
SO COLD ...
MY HANDS AND FEET FEEL FROZEN... ONLY THE BURN ON MY CHEST FROM THE HOLY ONE STILL FEELS WARM...
TETO... AND YOU, TOO, KAI...?

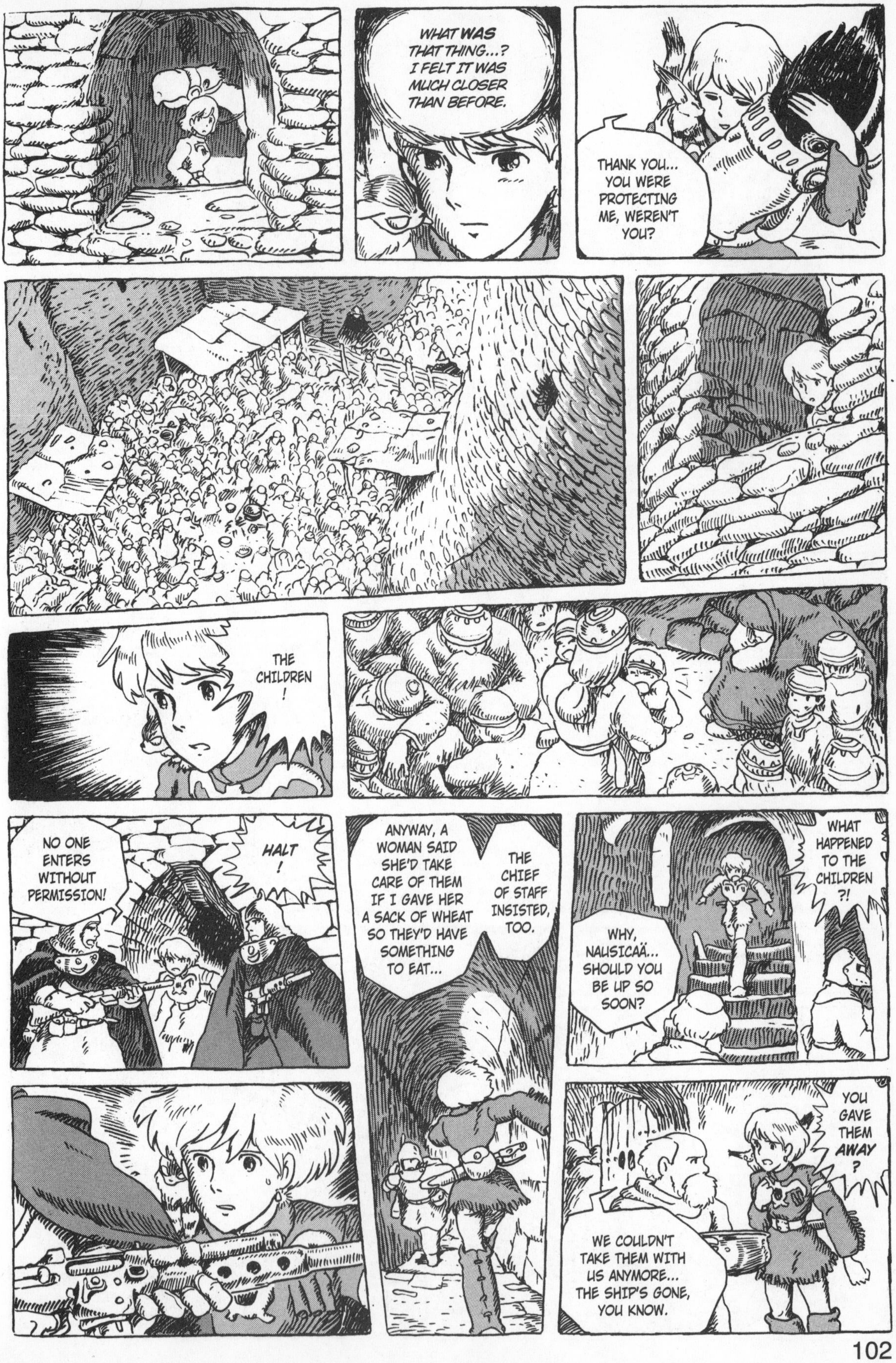
THANK YOU... YOU WERE PROTECTING ME, WEREN'T YOU?
WHAT **WAS** THAT THING...? I FELT IT WAS MUCH CLOSER THAN BEFORE.
THE CHILDREN!
WHAT HAPPENED TO THE CHILDREN?!
WHY, NAUSICAÄ... SHOULD YOU BE UP SO SOON?
YOU GAVE THEM **AWAY**?
WE COULDN'T TAKE THEM WITH US ANYMORE... THE SHIP'S GONE, YOU KNOW.
ANYWAY, A WOMAN SAID SHE'D TAKE CARE OF THEM IF I GAVE HER A SACK OF WHEAT SO THEY'D HAVE SOMETHING TO EAT...
THE CHIEF OF STAFF INSISTED, TOO.
HALT!
NO ONE ENTERS WITHOUT PERMISSION!

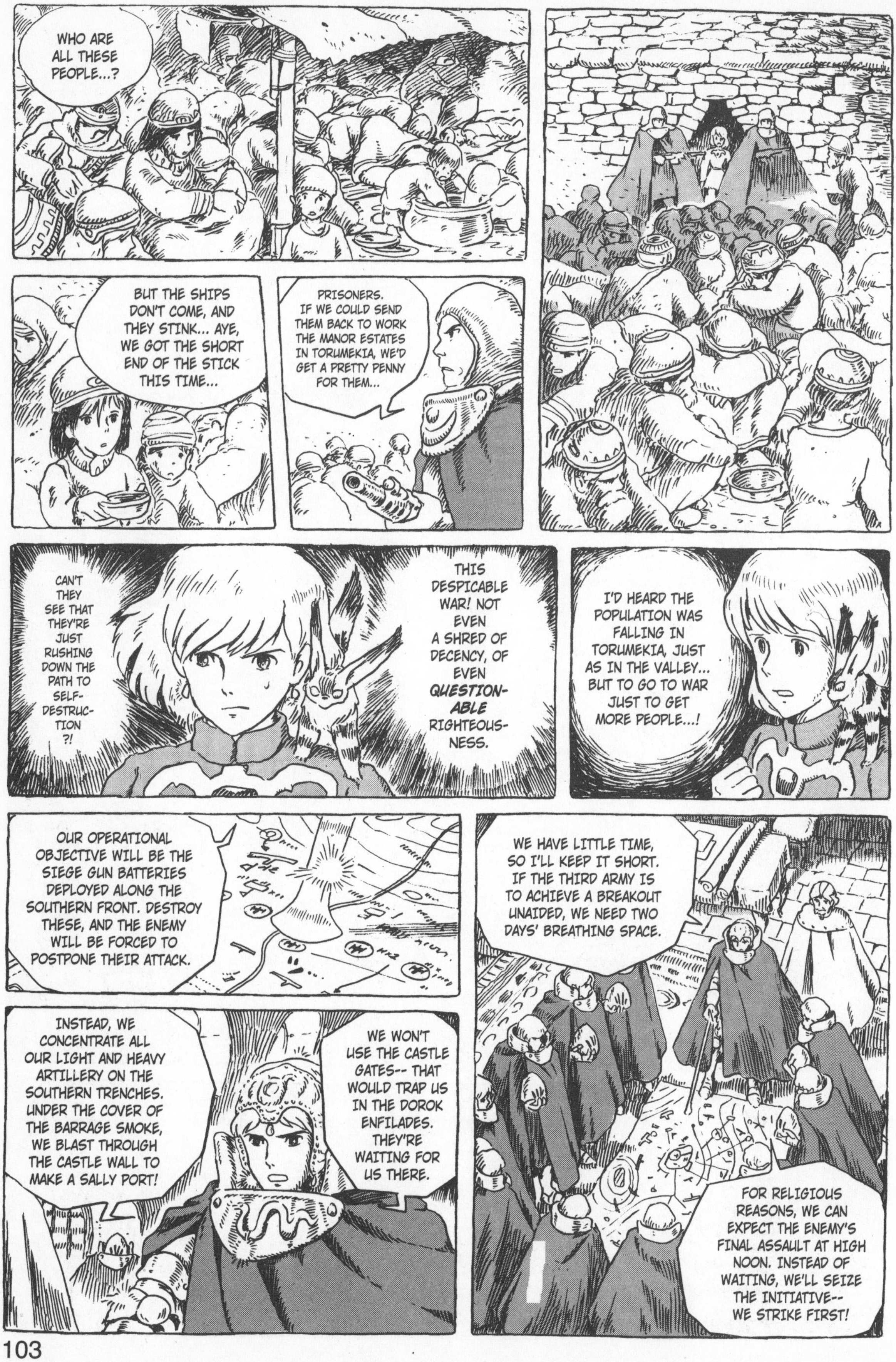
WHO ARE ALL THESE PEOPLE...?
PRISONERS. IF WE COULD SEND THEM BACK TO WORK THE MANOR ESTATES IN TORUMEKIA, WE'D GET A PRETTY PENNY FOR THEM...
BUT THE SHIPS DON'T COME, AND THEY STINK... AYE, WE GOT THE SHORT END OF THE STICK THIS TIME...
I'D HEARD THE POPULATION WAS FALLING IN TORUMEKIA, JUST AS IN THE VALLEY... BUT TO GO TO WAR JUST TO GET MORE PEOPLE...!
THIS DESPICABLE WAR! NOT EVEN A SHRED OF DECENCY, OF EVEN *QUESTIONABLE* RIGHTEOUSNESS.
CAN'T THEY SEE THAT THEY'RE JUST RUSHING DOWN THE PATH TO SELF-DESTRUCTION?!
WE HAVE LITTLE TIME, SO I'LL KEEP IT SHORT. IF THE THIRD ARMY IS TO ACHIEVE A BREAKOUT UNAIDED, WE NEED TWO DAYS' BREATHING SPACE.
FOR RELIGIOUS REASONS, WE CAN EXPECT THE ENEMY'S FINAL ASSAULT AT HIGH NOON. INSTEAD OF WAITING, WE'LL SEIZE THE INITIATIVE-- WE STRIKE FIRST!
OUR OPERATIONAL OBJECTIVE WILL BE THE SIEGE GUN BATTERIES DEPLOYED ALONG THE SOUTHERN FRONT. DESTROY THESE, AND THE ENEMY WILL BE FORCED TO POSTPONE THEIR ATTACK.
WE WON'T USE THE CASTLE GATES-- THAT WOULD TRAP US IN THE DOROK ENFILADES. THEY'RE WAITING FOR US THERE.
INSTEAD, WE CONCENTRATE ALL OUR LIGHT AND HEAVY ARTILLERY ON THE SOUTHERN TRENCHES. UNDER THE COVER OF THE BARRAGE SMOKE, WE BLAST THROUGH THE CASTLE WALL TO MAKE A SALLY PORT!

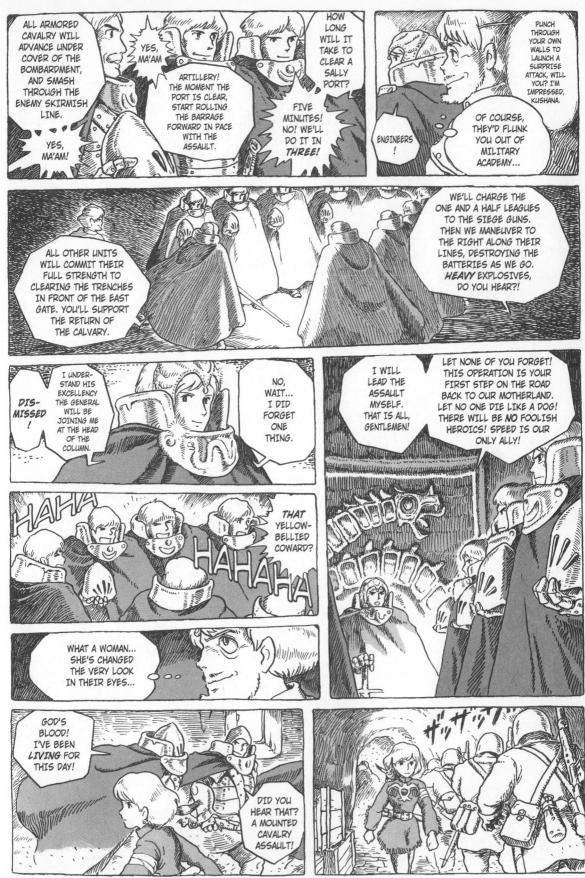

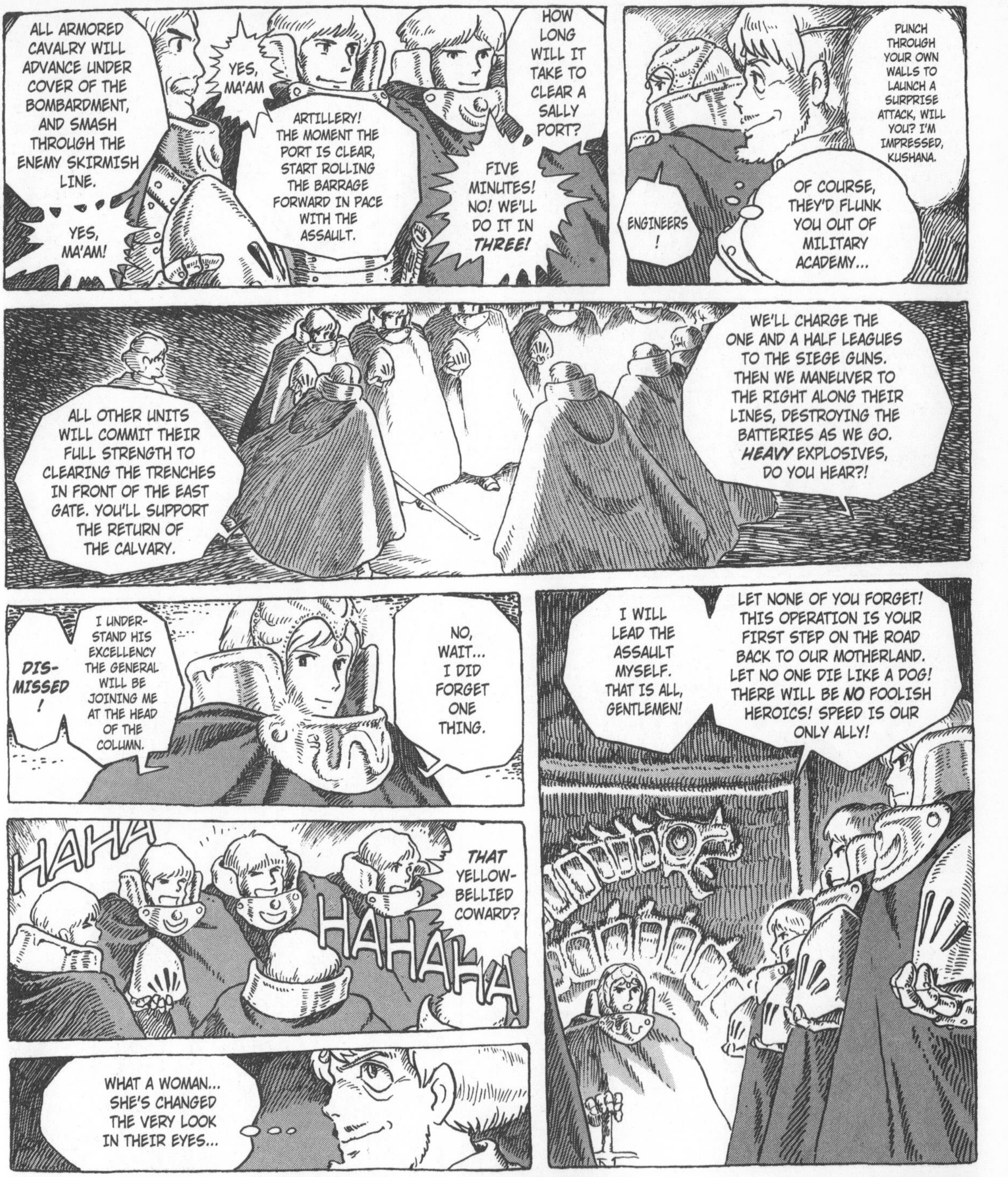
PUNCH THROUGH YOUR OWN WALLS TO LAUNCH A SURPRISE ATTACK, WILL YOU? I'M IMPRESSED, KUSHANA.
OF COURSE, THEY'D FLUNK YOU OUT OF MILITARY ACADEMY...
ENGINEERS!
HOW LONG WILL IT TAKE TO CLEAR A SALLY PORT?
FIVE MINUTES! NO! WE'LL DO IT IN *THREE!*
ALL ARMORED CAVALRY WILL ADVANCE UNDER COVER OF THE BOMBARDMENT, AND SMASH THROUGH THE ENEMY SKIRMISH LINE.
YES, MA'AM!
ARTILLERY! THE MOMENT THE PORT IS CLEAR, START ROLLING THE BARRAGE FORWARD IN PACE WITH THE ASSAULT.
YES, MA'AM
WE'LL CHARGE THE ONE AND A HALF LEAGUES TO THE SIEGE GUNS. THEN WE MANEUVER TO THE RIGHT ALONG THEIR LINES, DESTROYING THE BATTERIES AS WE GO. ***HEAVY*** EXPLOSIVES, DO YOU HEAR?!
ALL OTHER UNITS WILL COMMIT THEIR FULL STRENGTH TO CLEARING THE TRENCHES IN FRONT OF THE EAST GATE. YOU'LL SUPPORT THE RETURN OF THE CALVARY.
LET NONE OF YOU FORGET! THIS OPERATION IS YOUR FIRST STEP ON THE ROAD BACK TO OUR MOTHERLAND. LET NO ONE DIE LIKE A DOG! THERE WILL BE ***NO*** FOOLISH HEROICS! SPEED IS OUR ONLY ALLY!
I WILL LEAD THE ASSAULT MYSELF. THAT IS ALL, GENTLEMEN!
NO, WAIT... I DID FORGET ONE THING.
I UNDERSTAND HIS EXCELLENCY THE GENERAL WILL BE JOINING ME AT THE HEAD OF THE COLUMN.
DISMISSED!
HAHA
THAT YELLOW-BELLIED COWARD?
HAHAHAHA
WHAT A WOMAN... SHE'S CHANGED THE VERY LOOK IN THEIR EYES...
ザッザッ
GOD'S BLOOD! I'VE BEEN ***LIVING*** FOR THIS DAY!
DID YOU HEAR THAT? A MOUNTED CAVALRY ASSAULT!

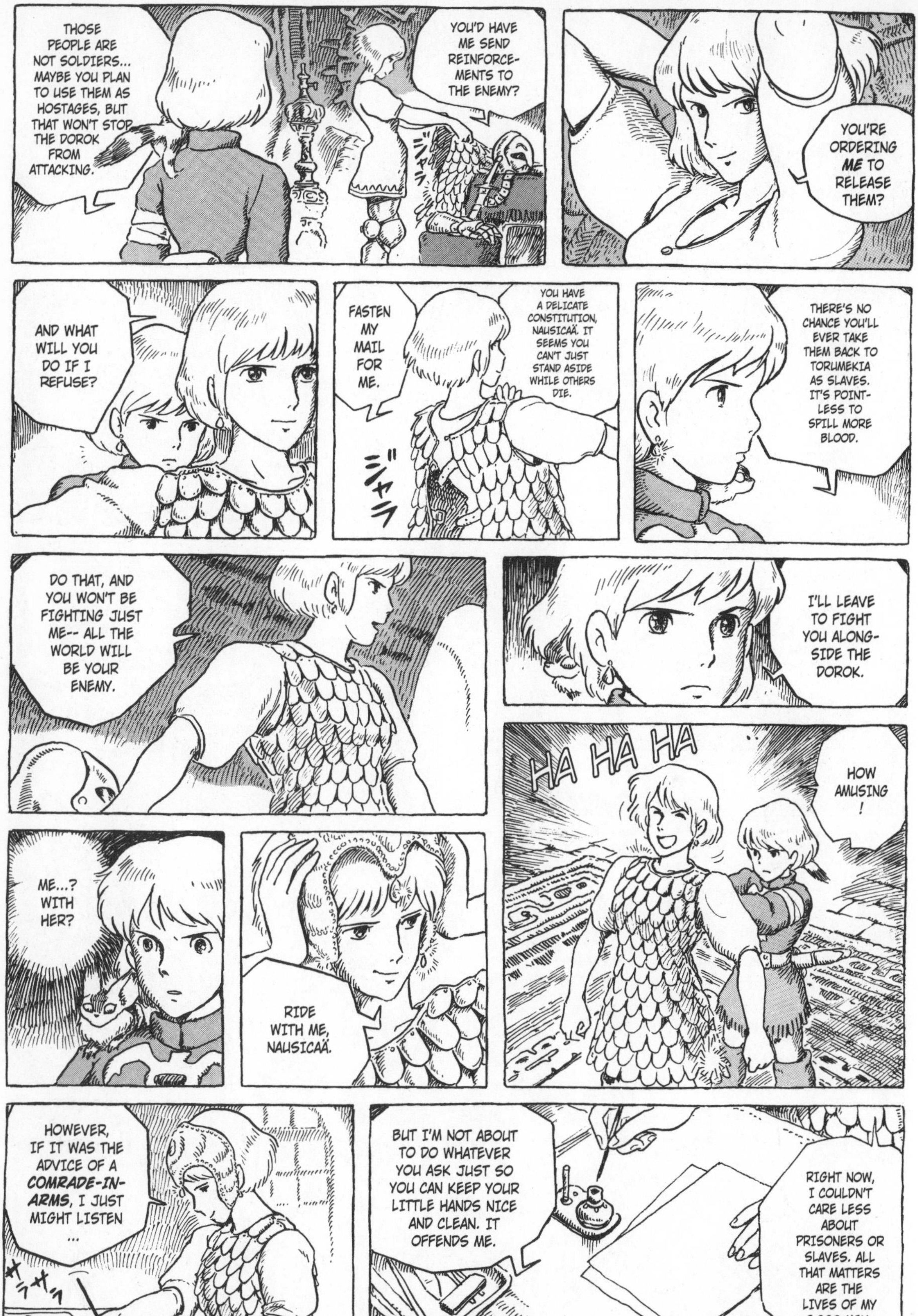
YOU'RE ORDERING *ME* TO RELEASE THEM?
YOU'D HAVE ME SEND REINFORCEMENTS TO THE ENEMY?
ジャラ
THOSE PEOPLE ARE NOT SOLDIERS... MAYBE YOU PLAN TO USE THEM AS HOSTAGES, BUT THAT WON'T STOP THE DOROK FROM ATTACKING.
THERE'S NO CHANCE YOU'LL EVER TAKE THEM BACK TO TORUMEKIA AS SLAVES. IT'S POINTLESS TO SPILL MORE BLOOD.
YOU HAVE A DELICATE CONSTITUTION, NAUSICAÄ. IT SEEMS YOU CAN'T JUST STAND ASIDE WHILE OTHERS DIE.
FASTEN MY MAIL FOR ME.
ジャラ
AND WHAT WILL YOU DO IF I REFUSE?
I'LL LEAVE TO FIGHT YOU ALONGSIDE THE DOROK.
DO THAT, AND YOU WON'T BE FIGHTING JUST ME-- ALL THE WORLD WILL BE YOUR ENEMY.
HOW AMUSING!
HA HA HA
RIDE WITH ME, NAUSICAÄ.
ME...? WITH HER?
RIGHT NOW, I COULDN'T CARE LESS ABOUT PRISONERS OR SLAVES. ALL THAT MATTERS ARE THE LIVES OF MY 2,000 MEN.
BUT I'M NOT ABOUT TO DO WHATEVER YOU ASK JUST SO YOU CAN KEEP YOUR LITTLE HANDS NICE AND CLEAN. IT OFFENDS ME.
HOWEVER, IF IT WAS THE ADVICE OF A *COMRADE-IN-ARMS*, I JUST MIGHT LISTEN ...

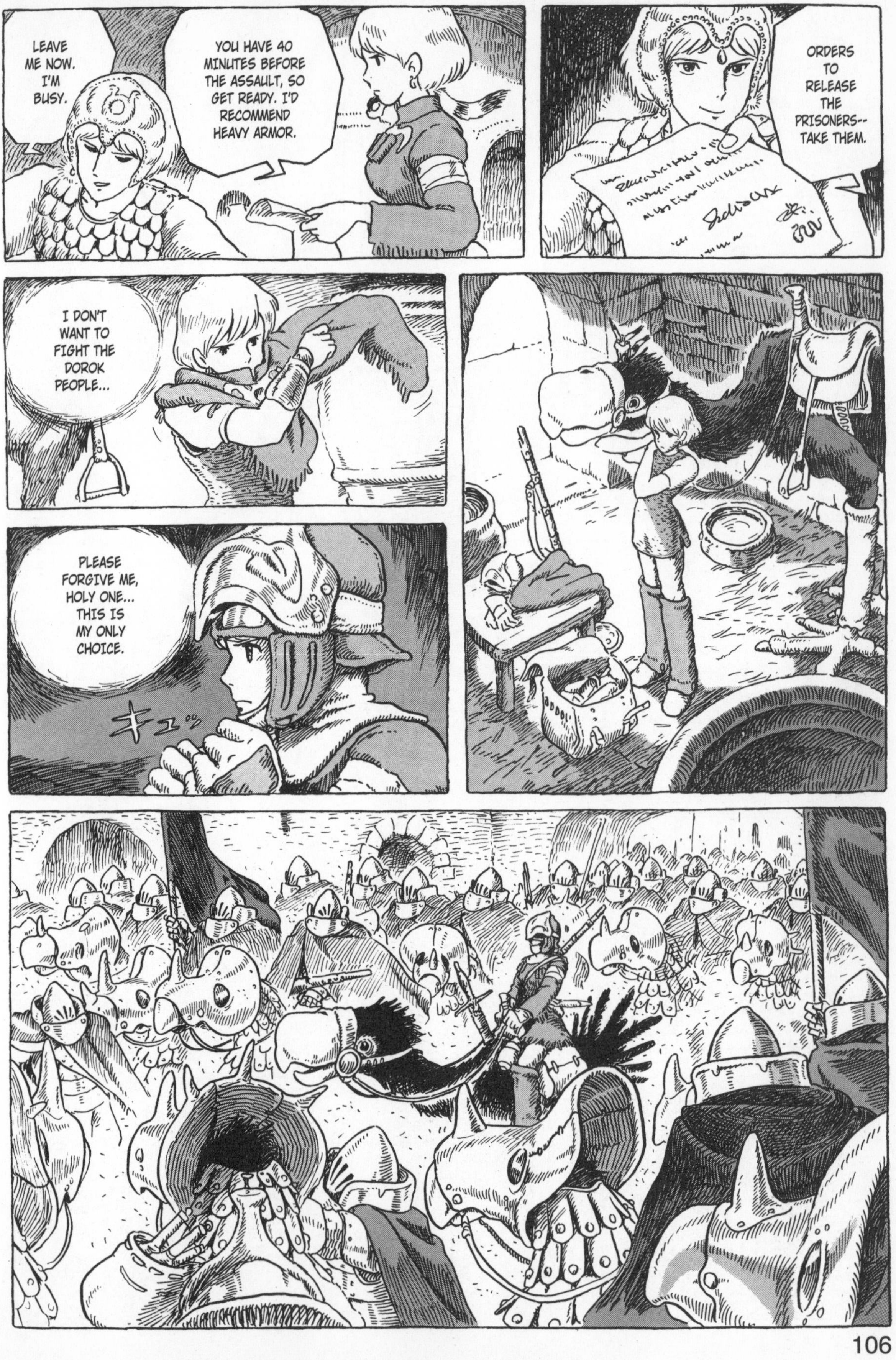
ORDERS TO RELEASE THE PRISONERS-- TAKE THEM.
YOU HAVE 40 MINUTES BEFORE THE ASSAULT, SO GET READY. I'D RECOMMEND HEAVY ARMOR.
LEAVE ME NOW. I'M BUSY.
I DON'T WANT TO FIGHT THE DOROK PEOPLE...
PLEASE FORGIVE ME, HOLY ONE... THIS IS MY ONLY CHOICE.
キュッ

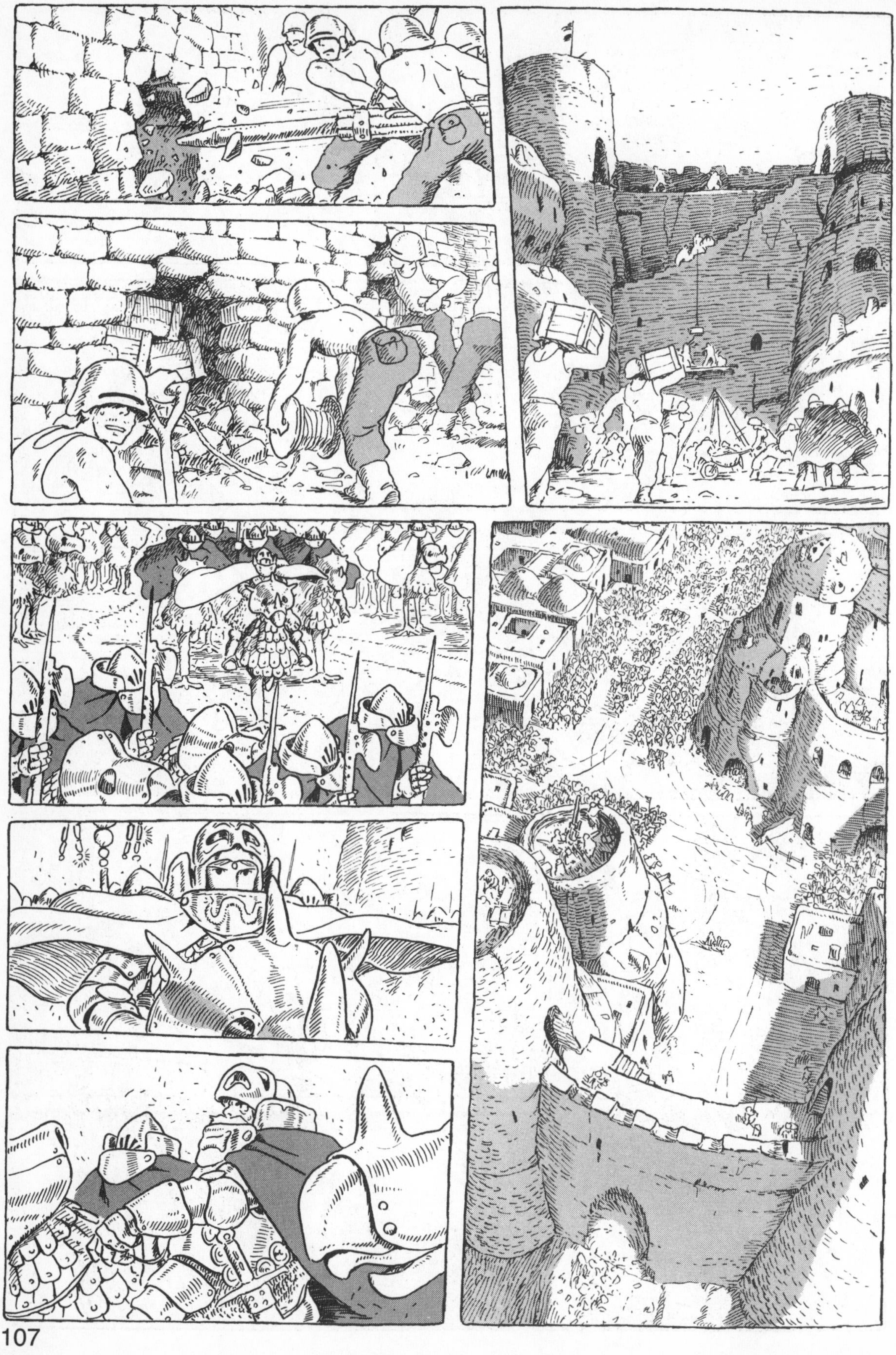

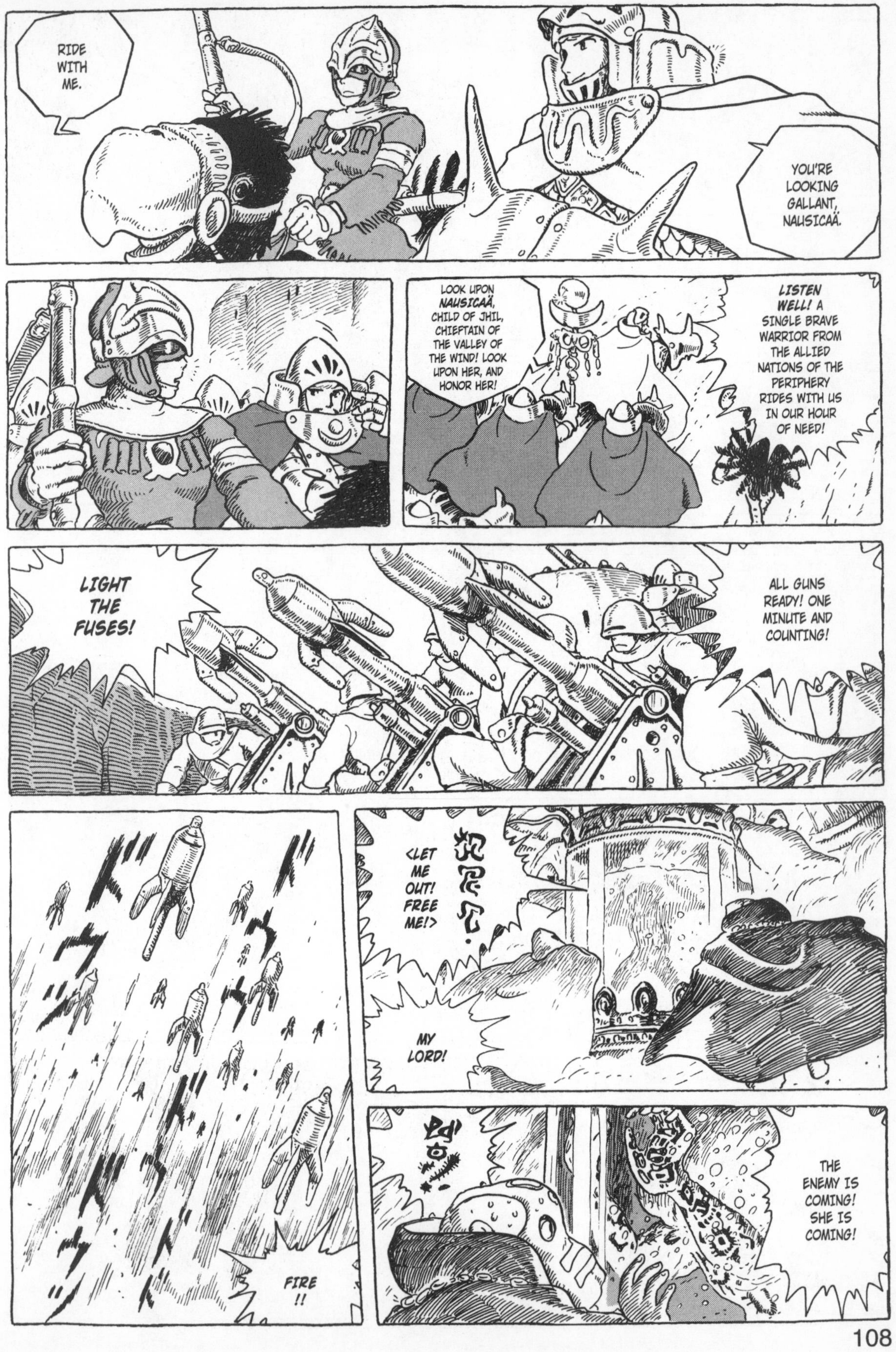
YOU'RE LOOKING GALLANT, NAUSICAÄ.
RIDE WITH ME.
LISTEN WELL! A SINGLE BRAVE WARRIOR FROM THE ALLIED NATIONS OF THE PERIPHERY RIDES WITH US IN OUR HOUR OF NEED!
LOOK UPON NAUSICAÄ, CHILD OF JHIL, CHIEFTAIN OF THE VALLEY OF THE WIND! LOOK UPON HER, AND HONOR HER!
ALL GUNS READY! ONE MINUTE AND COUNTING!
LIGHT THE FUSES!
<LET ME OUT! FREE ME!>
MY LORD!
THE ENEMY IS COMING! SHE IS COMING!
FIRE !!

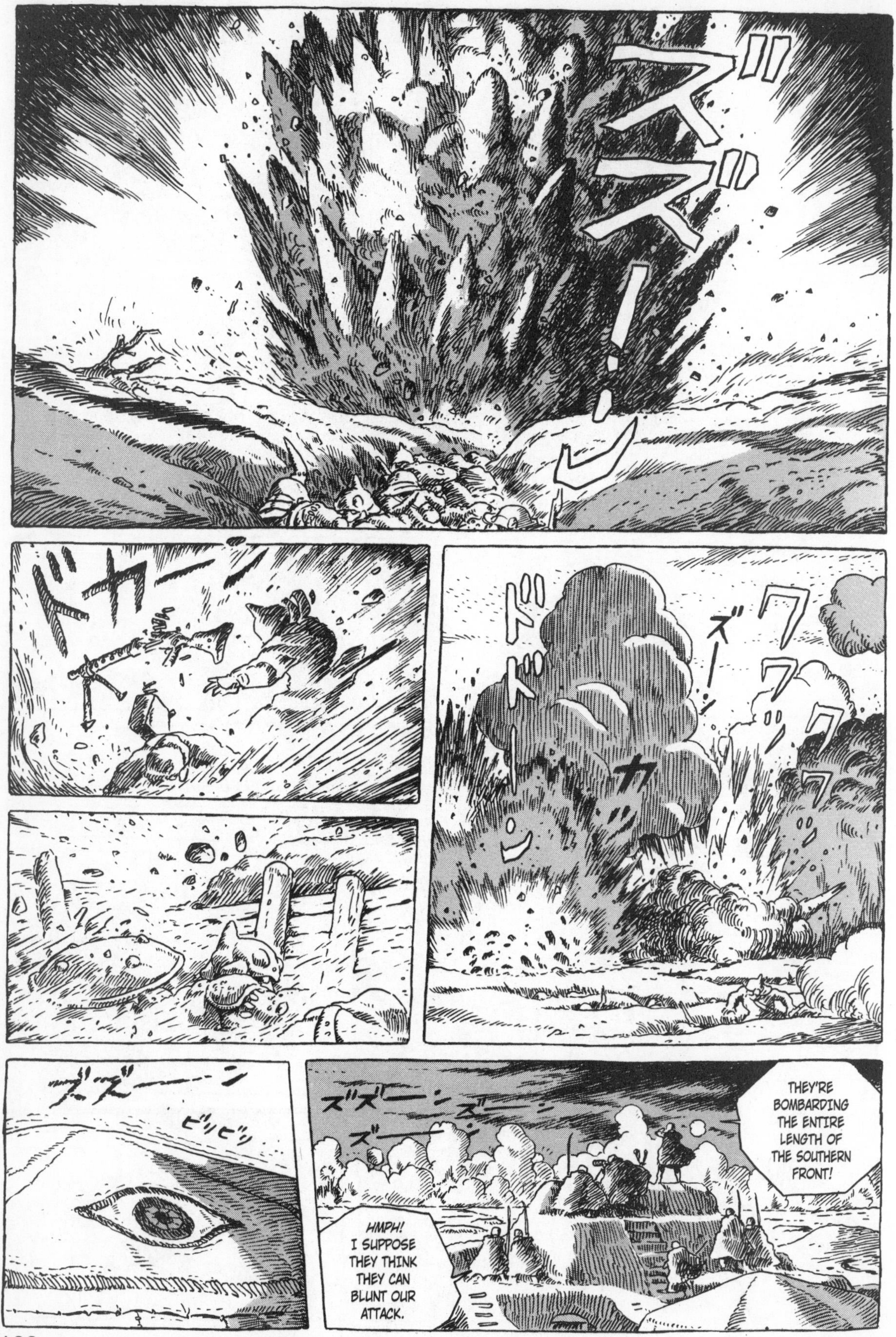
ズズーーン
ドカーン
ドドーン
ズーン
カッ
THEY'RE BOMBARDING THE ENTIRE LENGTH OF THE SOUTHERN FRONT!
HMPH! I SUPPOSE THEY THINK THEY CAN BLUNT OUR ATTACK.
ズズーーン
ビッビッ

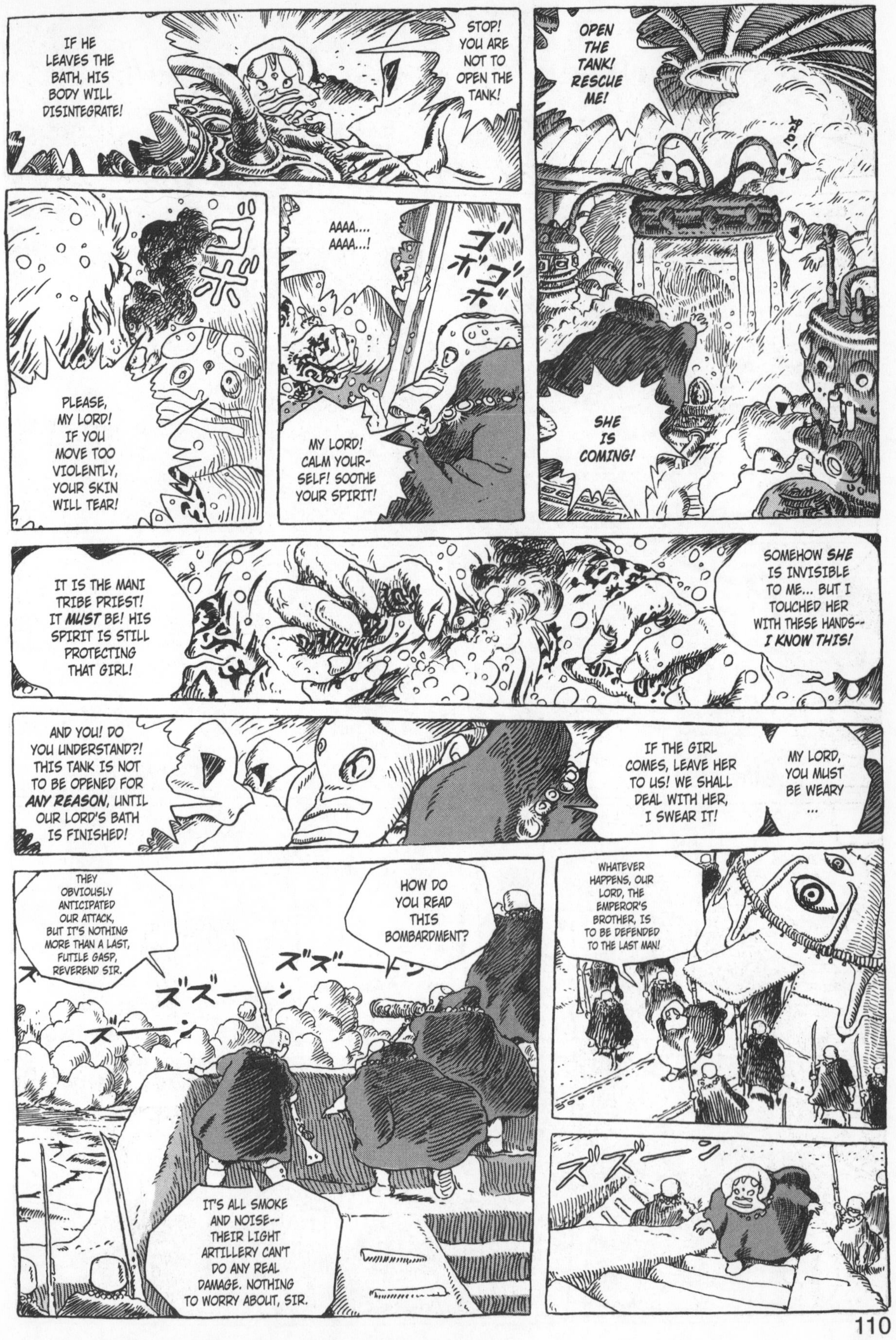
OPEN THE TANK! RESCUE ME!
SHE IS COMING!
STOP! YOU ARE NOT TO OPEN THE TANK!
IF HE LEAVES THE BATH, HIS BODY WILL DISINTEGRATE!
AAAA.... AAAA...!
ゴボゴボ
MY LORD! CALM YOUR-SELF! SOOTHE YOUR SPIRIT!
ゴボ
PLEASE, MY LORD! IF YOU MOVE TOO VIOLENTLY, YOUR SKIN WILL TEAR!
SOMEHOW SHE IS INVISIBLE TO ME... BUT I TOUCHED HER WITH THESE HANDS-- I KNOW THIS!
IT IS THE MANI TRIBE PRIEST! IT MUST BE! HIS SPIRIT IS STILL PROTECTING THAT GIRL!
MY LORD, YOU MUST BE WEARY ...
IF THE GIRL COMES, LEAVE HER TO US! WE SHALL DEAL WITH HER, I SWEAR IT!
AND YOU! DO YOU UNDERSTAND?! THIS TANK IS NOT TO BE OPENED FOR ANY REASON, UNTIL OUR LORD'S BATH IS FINISHED!
WHATEVER HAPPENS, OUR LORD, THE EMPEROR'S BROTHER, IS TO BE DEFENDED TO THE LAST MAN!
ズズーン
HOW DO YOU READ THIS BOMBARDMENT?
THEY OBVIOUSLY ANTICIPATED OUR ATTACK, BUT IT'S NOTHING MORE THAN A LAST, FUTILE GASP, REVEREND SIR.
ズズーーン
ズズーン
ズーン
IT'S ALL SMOKE AND NOISE-- THEIR LIGHT ARTILLERY CAN'T DO ANY REAL DAMAGE. NOTHING TO WORRY ABOUT, SIR.

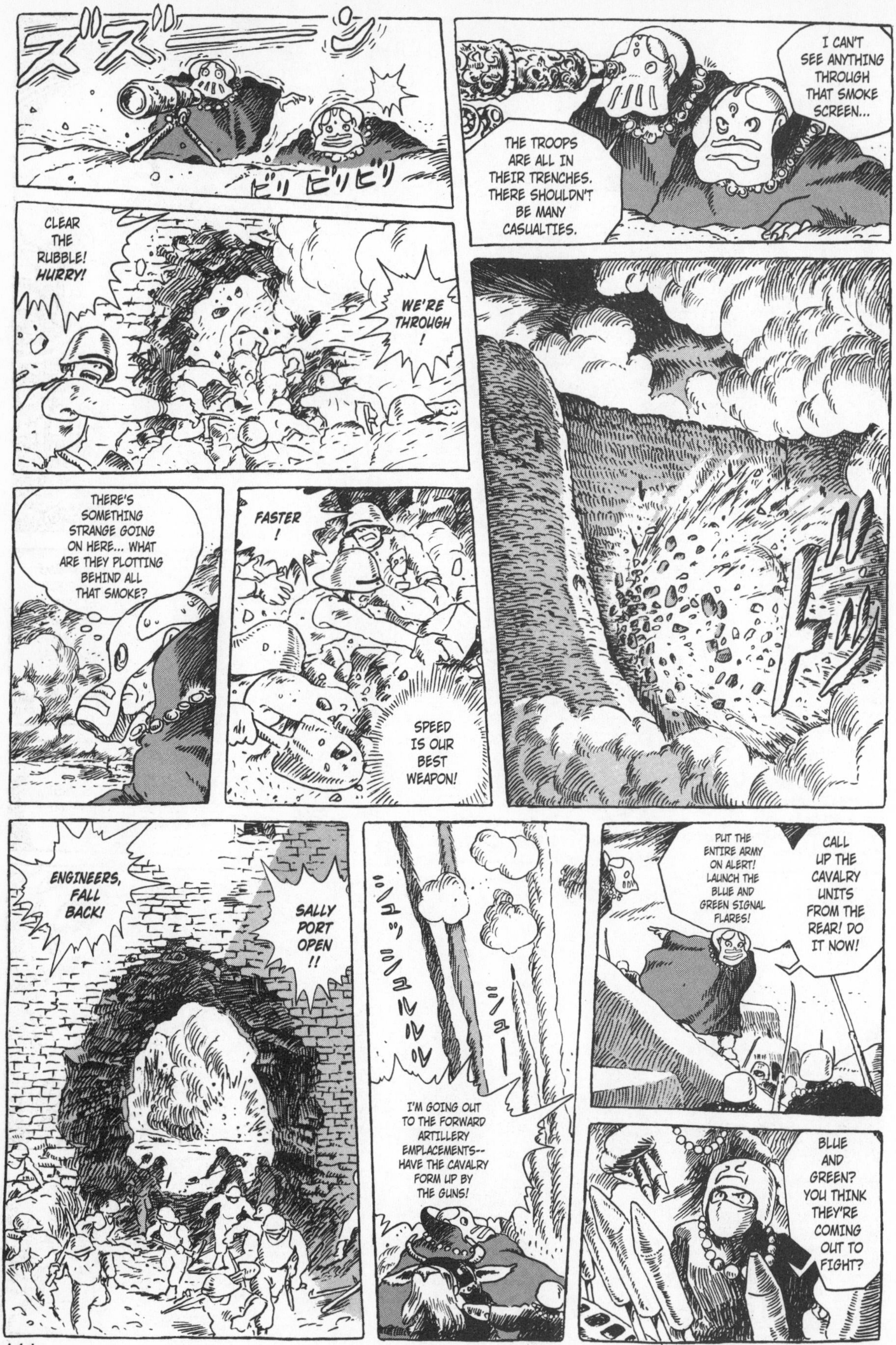
I CAN'T SEE ANYTHING THROUGH THAT SMOKE SCREEN...
THE TROOPS ARE ALL IN THEIR TRENCHES. THERE SHOULDN'T BE MANY CASUALTIES.
ズズーーン
ビリ ビリビリ
CLEAR THE RUBBLE! HURRY!
WE'RE THROUGH!
FASTER!
SPEED IS OUR BEST WEAPON!
THERE'S SOMETHING STRANGE GOING ON HERE... WHAT ARE THEY PLOTTING BEHIND ALL THAT SMOKE?
CALL UP THE CAVALRY UNITS FROM THE REAR! DO IT NOW!
PUT THE ENTIRE ARMY ON ALERT! LAUNCH THE BLUE AND GREEN SIGNAL FLARES!
BLUE AND GREEN? YOU THINK THEY'RE COMING OUT TO FIGHT?
シュー
I'M GOING OUT TO THE FORWARD ARTILLERY EMPLACEMENTS--HAVE THE CAVALRY FORM UP BY THE GUNS!
SALLY PORT OPEN!!
ENGINEERS, FALL BACK!

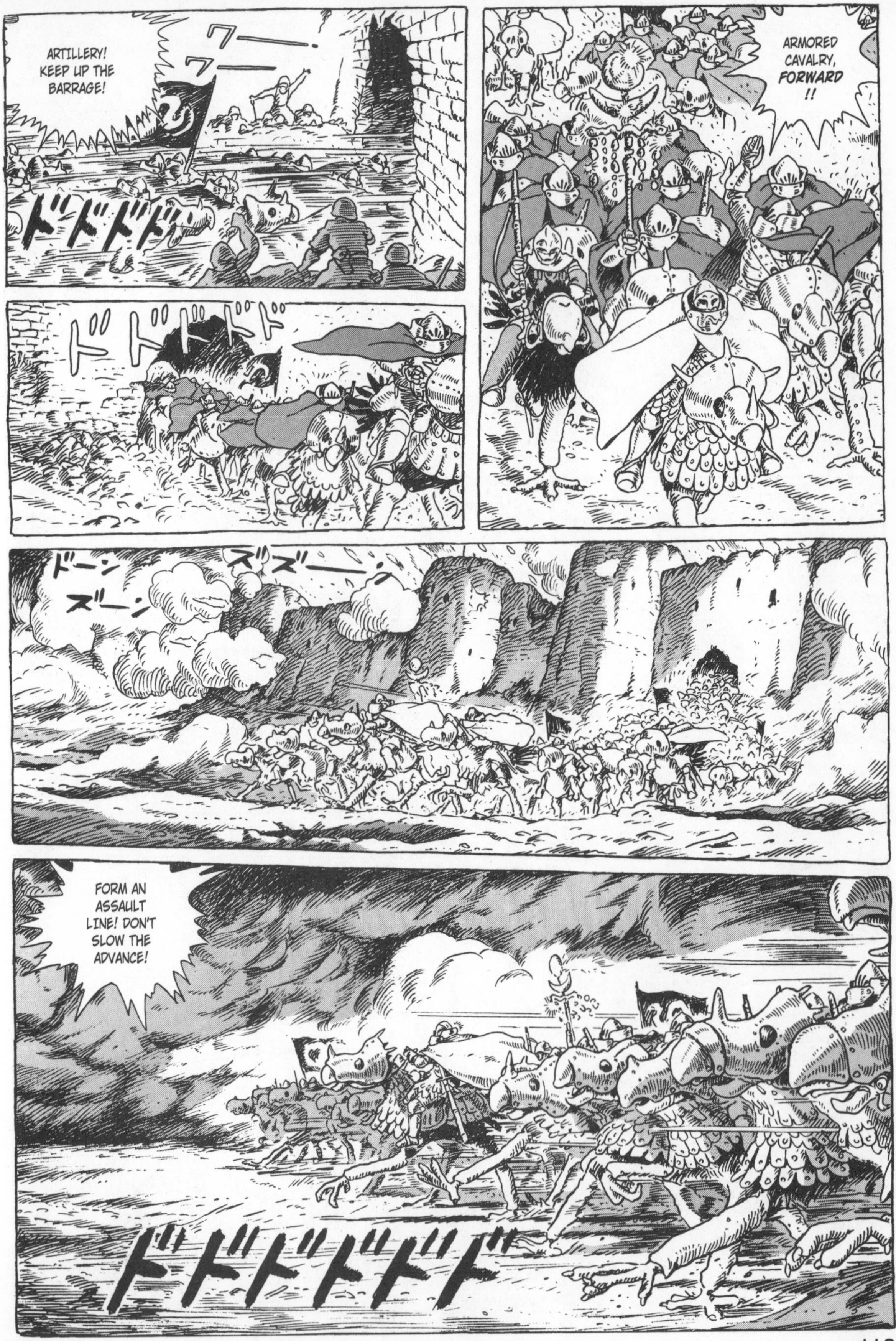
ARMORED CAVALRY, **FORWARD** !!
ARTILLERY! KEEP UP THE BARRAGE!
ワーー
ワーー
ドドドドド
ドドドドド
ズズーン
ドーン
ズーン
FORM AN ASSAULT LINE! DON'T SLOW THE ADVANCE!
ドドドドドドド

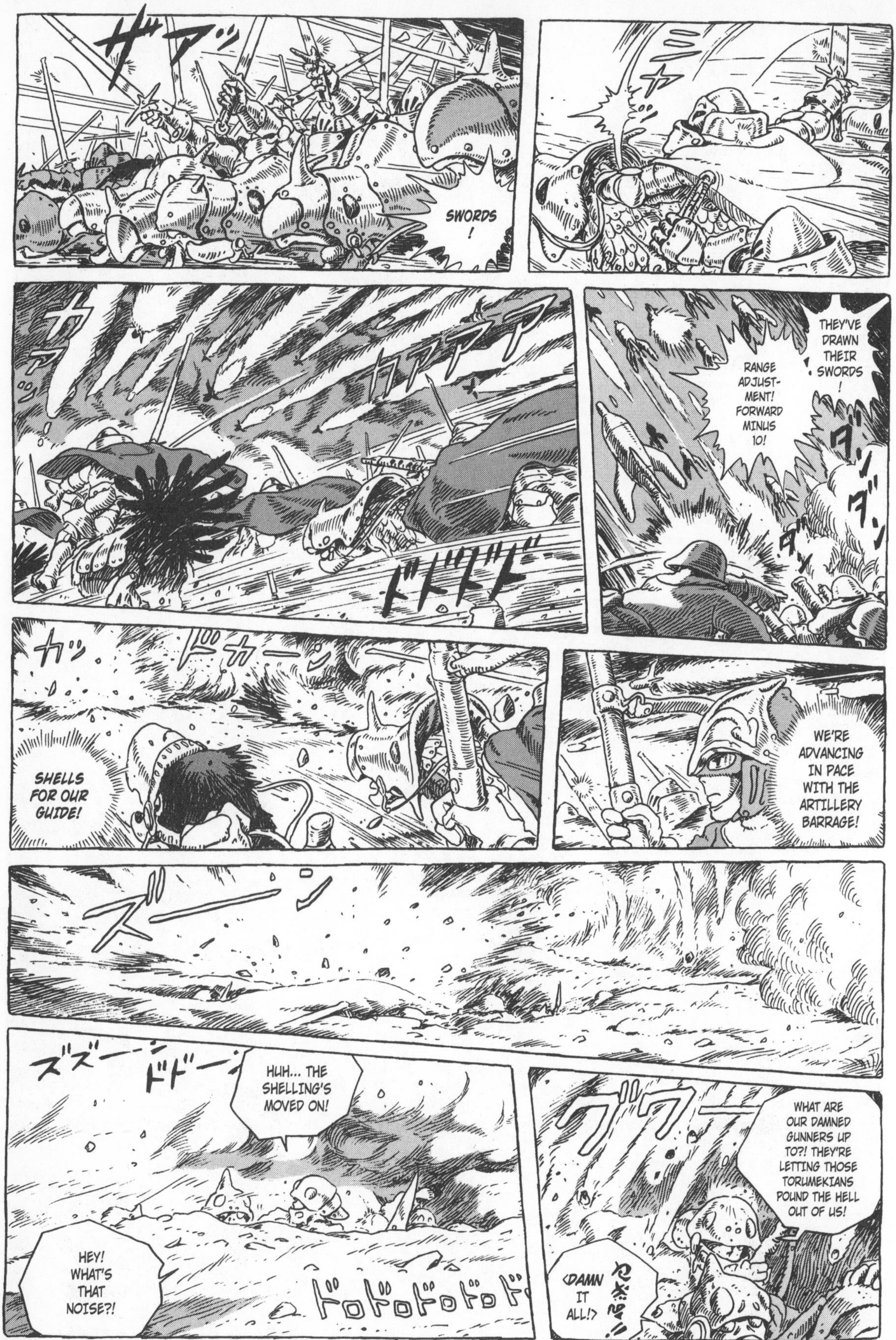
SWORDS!
THEY'VE DRAWN THEIR SWORDS!
RANGE ADJUSTMENT! FORWARD MINUS 10!
WE'RE ADVANCING IN PACE WITH THE ARTILLERY BARRAGE!
SHELLS FOR OUR GUIDE!
WHAT ARE OUR DAMNED GUNNERS UP TO?! THEY'RE LETTING THOSE TORUMEKIANS POUND THE HELL OUT OF US!
<DAMN IT ALL!>
HUH... THE SHELLING'S MOVED ON!
HEY! WHAT'S THAT NOISE?!

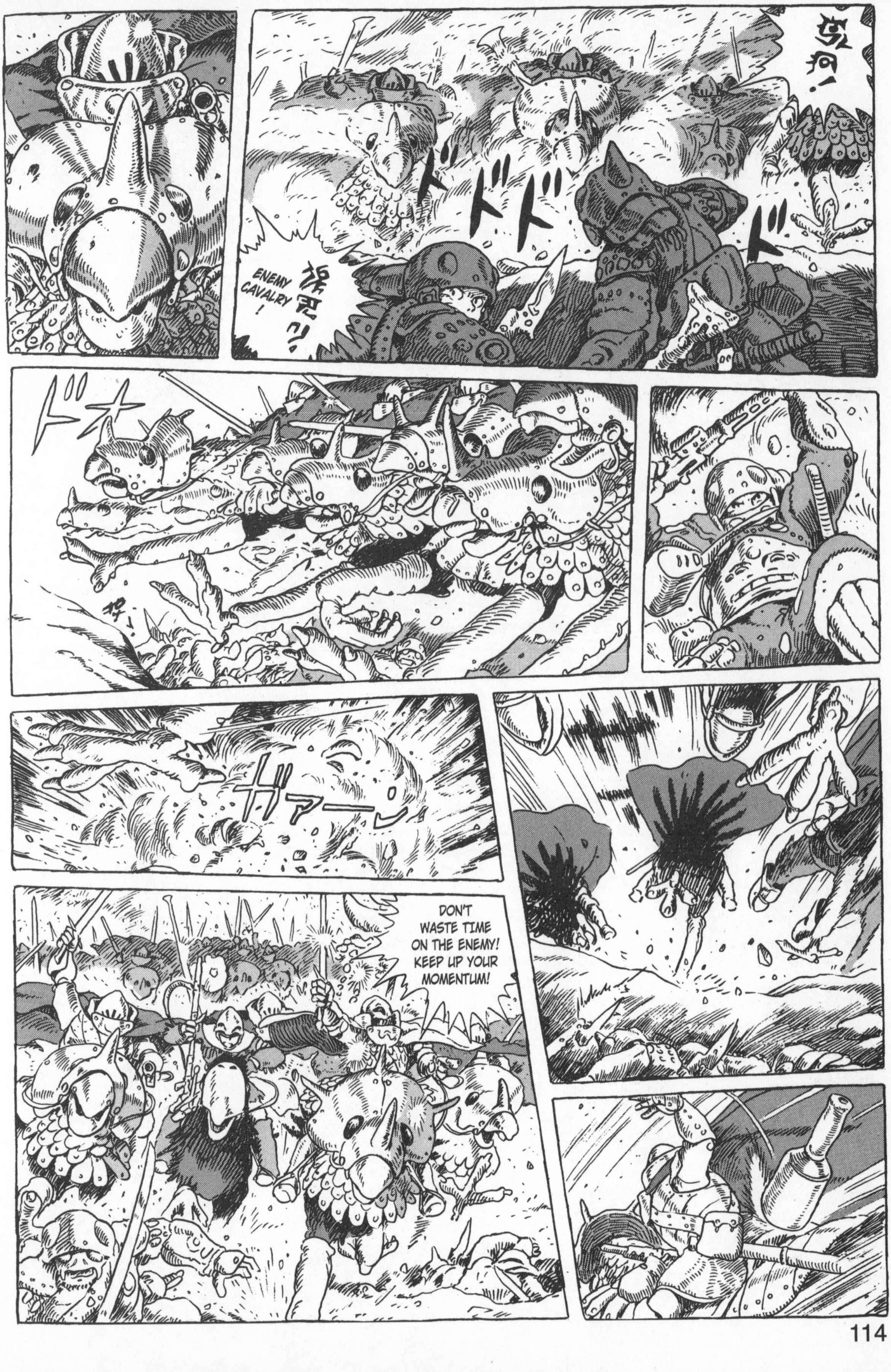
ENEMY CAVALRY!
DON'T WASTE TIME ON THE ENEMY! KEEP UP YOUR MOMENTUM!

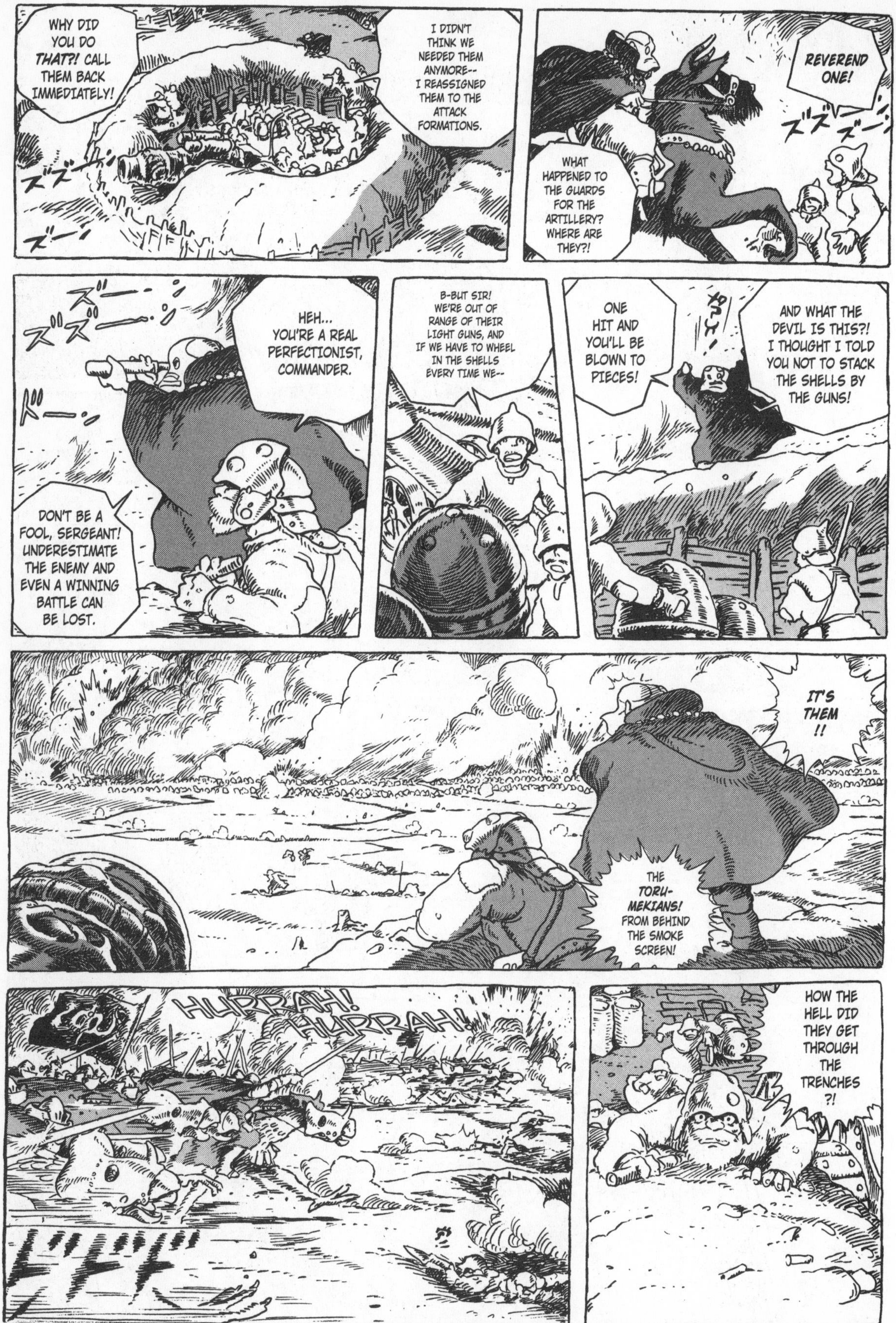

REVEREND ONE!
WHAT HAPPENED TO THE GUARDS FOR THE ARTILLERY? WHERE ARE THEY?!
I DIDN'T THINK WE NEEDED THEM ANYMORE-- I REASSIGNED THEM TO THE ATTACK FORMATIONS.
WHY DID YOU DO *THAT?!* CALL THEM BACK IMMEDIATELY!
AND WHAT THE DEVIL IS THIS?! I THOUGHT I TOLD YOU NOT TO STACK THE SHELLS BY THE GUNS!
ONE HIT AND YOU'LL BE BLOWN TO PIECES!
B-BUT SIR! WE'RE OUT OF RANGE OF THEIR LIGHT GUNS, AND IF WE HAVE TO WHEEL IN THE SHELLS EVERY TIME WE--
HEH... YOU'RE A REAL PERFECTIONIST, COMMANDER.
DON'T BE A FOOL, SERGEANT! UNDERESTIMATE THE ENEMY AND EVEN A WINNING BATTLE CAN BE LOST.
IT'S THEM !!
THE *TORU-MEKIANS!* FROM BEHIND THE SMOKE SCREEN!
HOW THE HELL DID THEY GET THROUGH THE TRENCHES ?!
HURRAH! HURRAH!

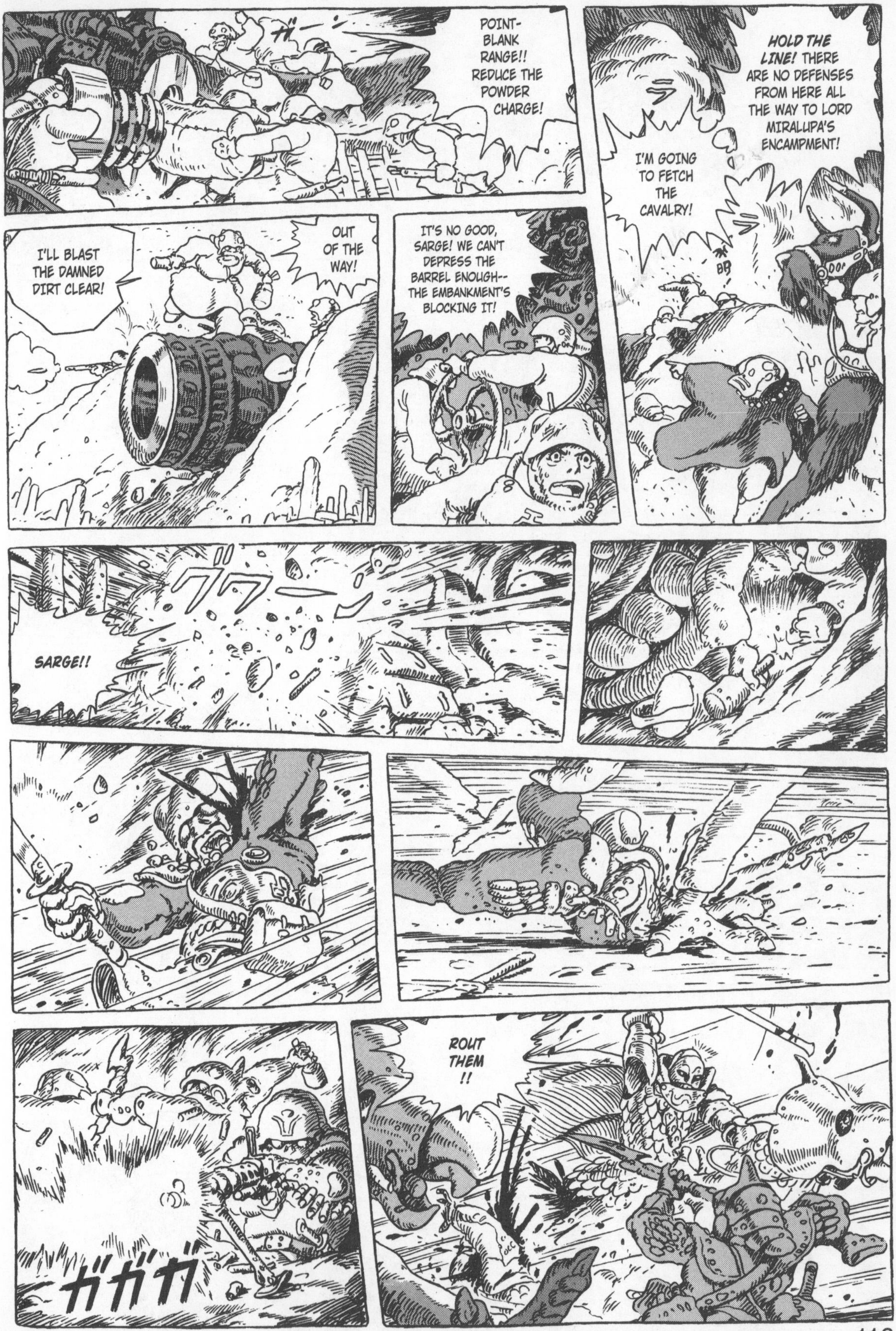
POINT-BLANK RANGE!! REDUCE THE POWDER CHARGE!
HOLD THE LINE! THERE ARE NO DEFENSES FROM HERE ALL THE WAY TO LORD MIRALUPA'S ENCAMPMENT!
I'M GOING TO FETCH THE CAVALRY!
I'LL BLAST THE DAMNED DIRT CLEAR!
OUT OF THE WAY!
IT'S NO GOOD, SARGE! WE CAN'T DEPRESS THE BARREL ENOUGH-- THE EMBANKMENT'S BLOCKING IT!
SARGE!!
ROUT THEM !!
ガガガ

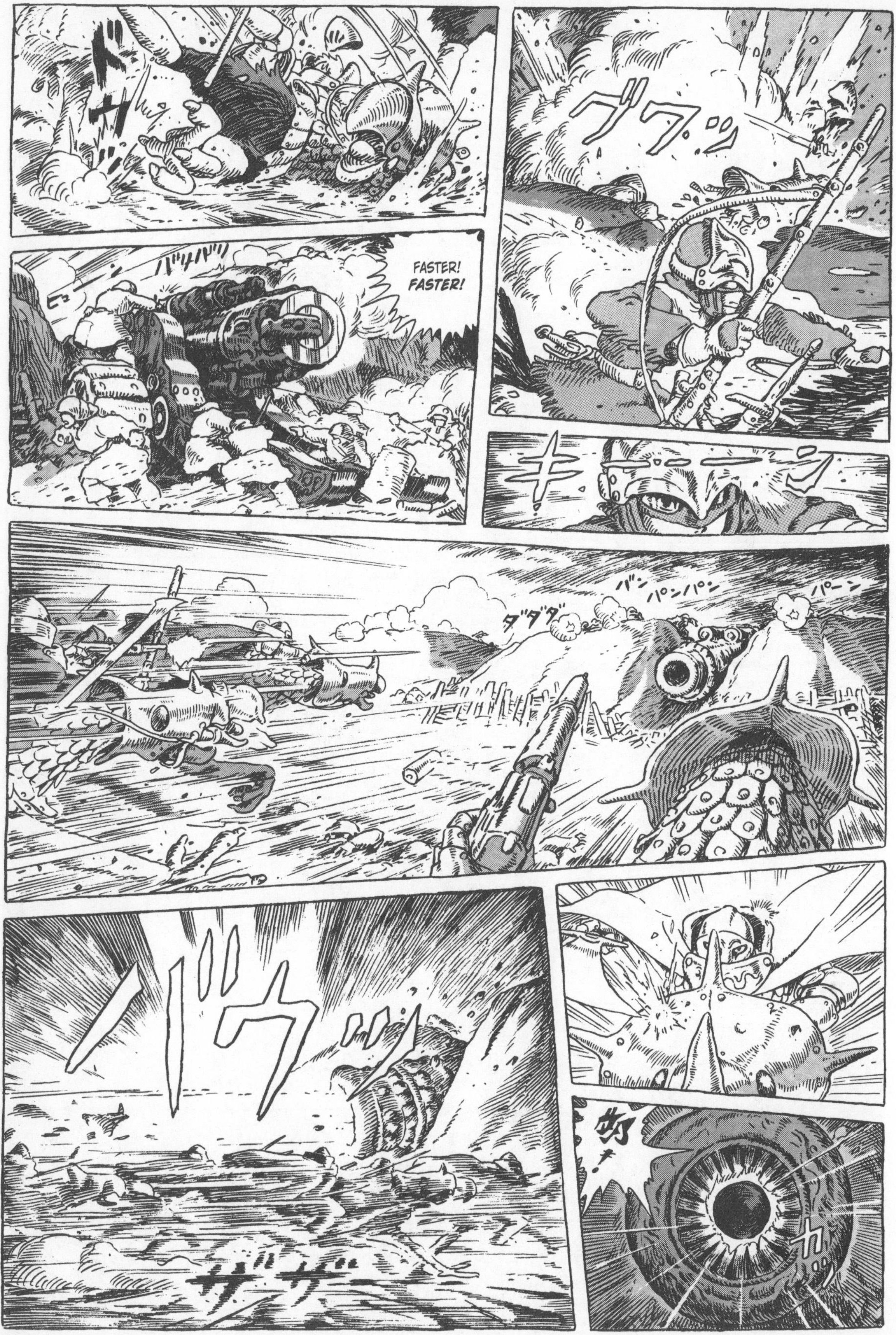
FASTER!
FASTER!

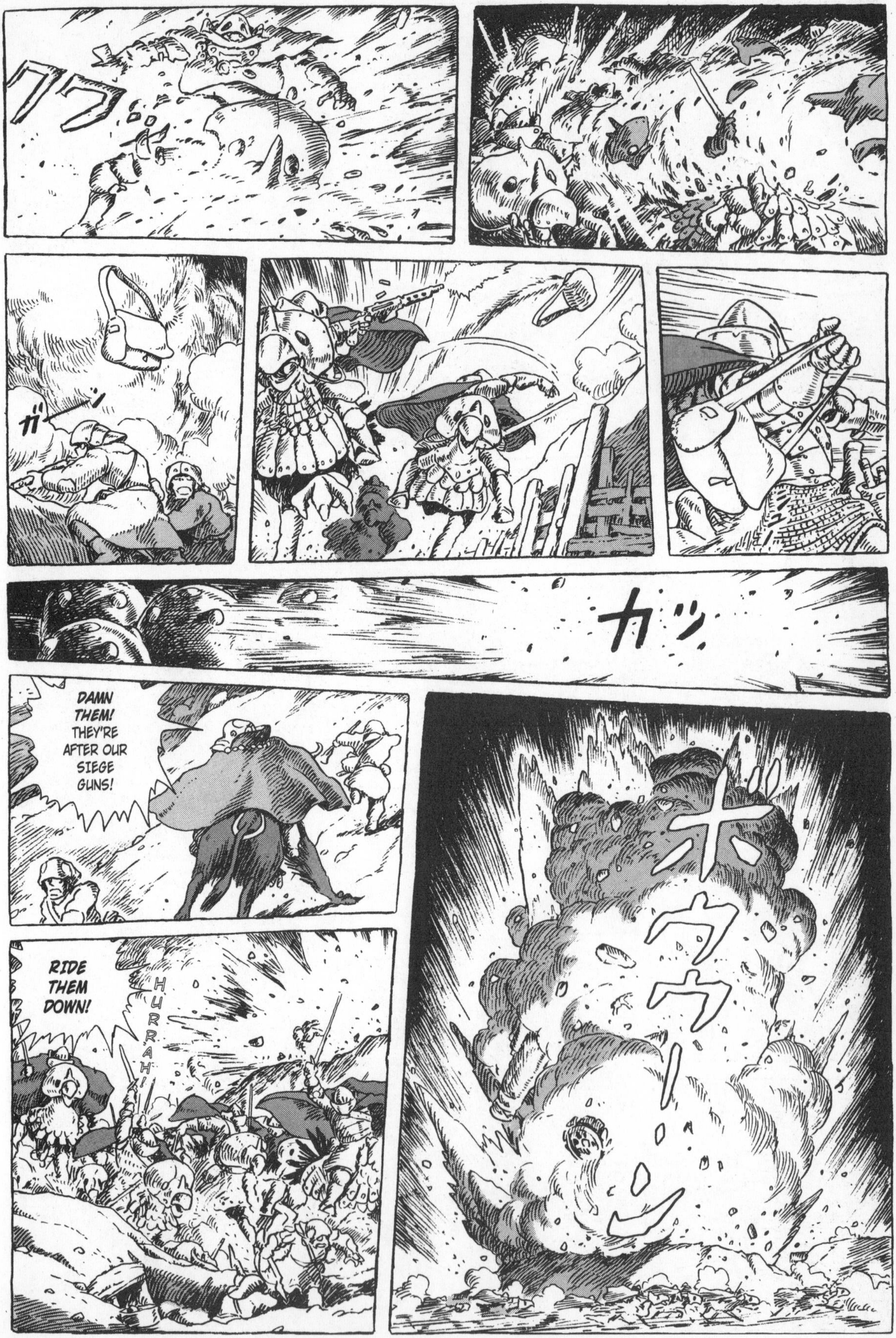

ワワ
ガーン
カッ
DAMN THEM! THEY'RE AFTER OUR SIEGE GUNS!
ホウウー
RIDE THEM DOWN!
HURRAH!

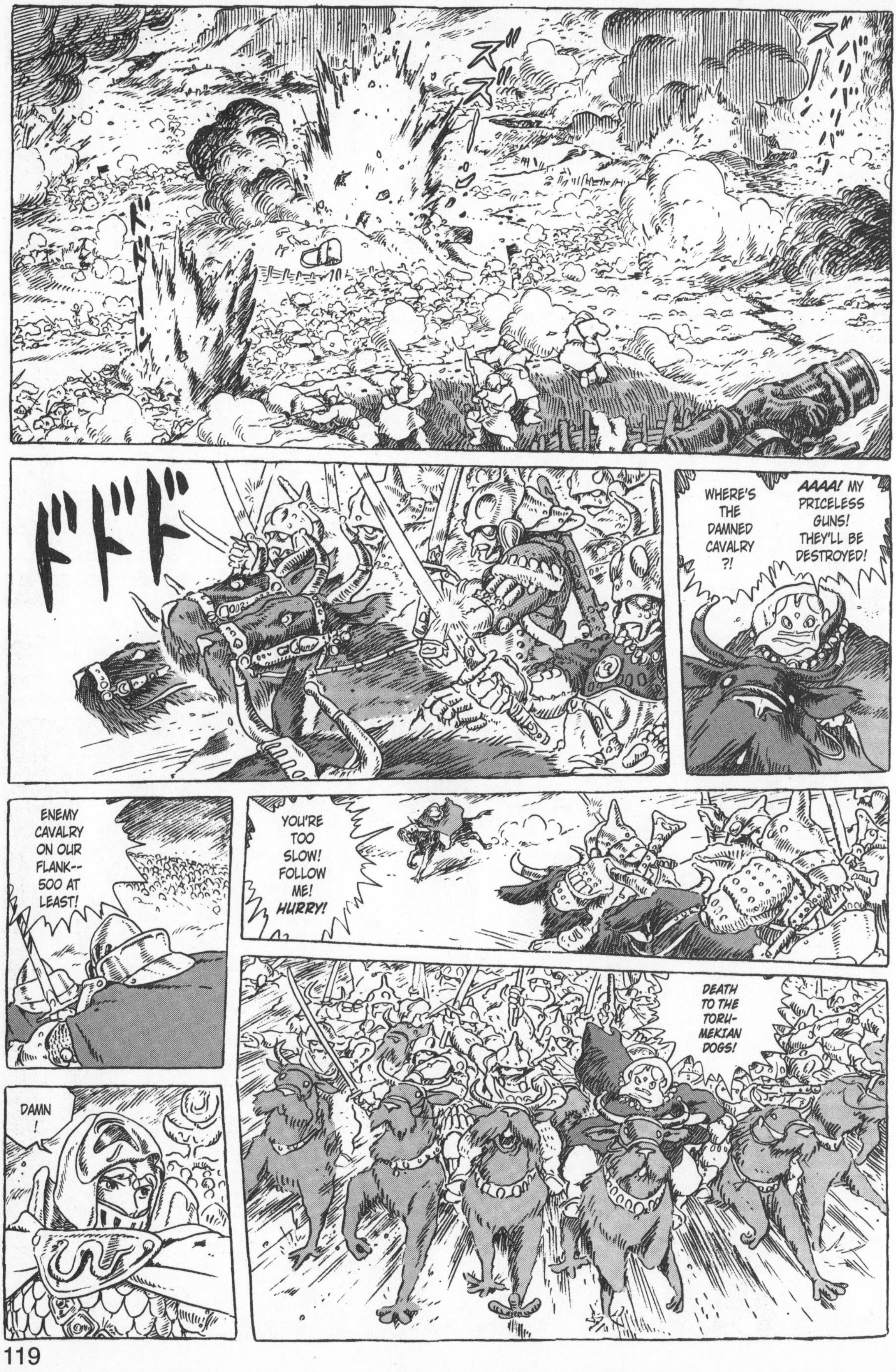
AAAA! MY PRICELESS GUNS! THEY'LL BE DESTROYED!
WHERE'S THE DAMNED CAVALRY ?!
ドドド
YOU'RE TOO SLOW! FOLLOW ME! HURRY!
DEATH TO THE TORU-MEKIAN DOGS!
ENEMY CAVALRY ON OUR FLANK-- 500 AT LEAST!
DAMN !

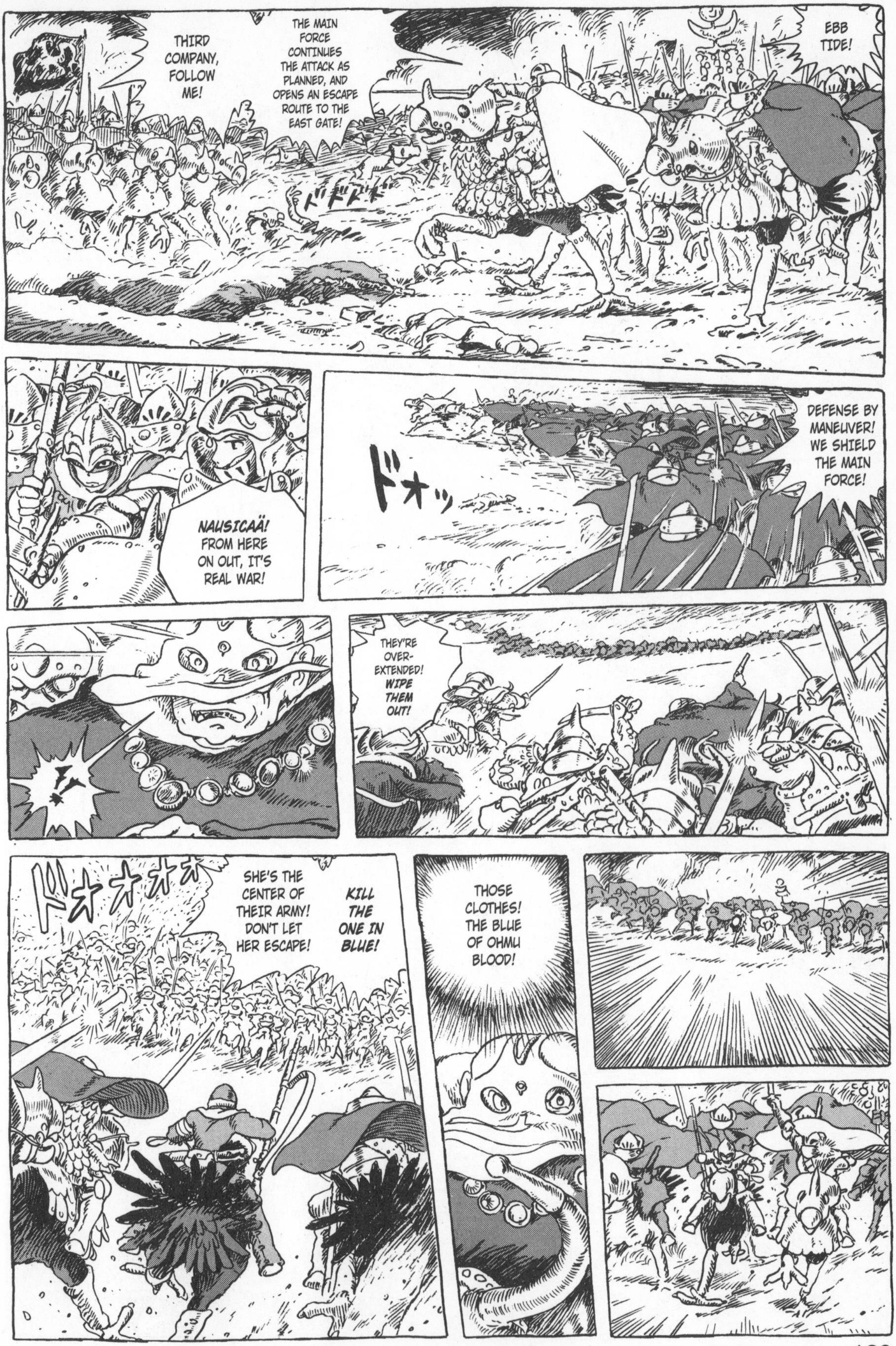
EBB TIDE!
THE MAIN FORCE CONTINUES THE ATTACK AS PLANNED, AND OPENS AN ESCAPE ROUTE TO THE EAST GATE!
THIRD COMPANY, FOLLOW ME!
ドドドド
DEFENSE BY MANEUVER! WE SHIELD THE MAIN FORCE!
ドオッ
NAUSICAÄ! FROM HERE ON OUT, IT'S REAL WAR!
THEY'RE OVER-EXTENDED! WIPE THEM OUT!
THOSE CLOTHES! THE BLUE OF OHMU BLOOD!
KILL THE ONE IN BLUE!
SHE'S THE CENTER OF THEIR ARMY! DON'T LET HER ESCAPE!
ドオオオオ

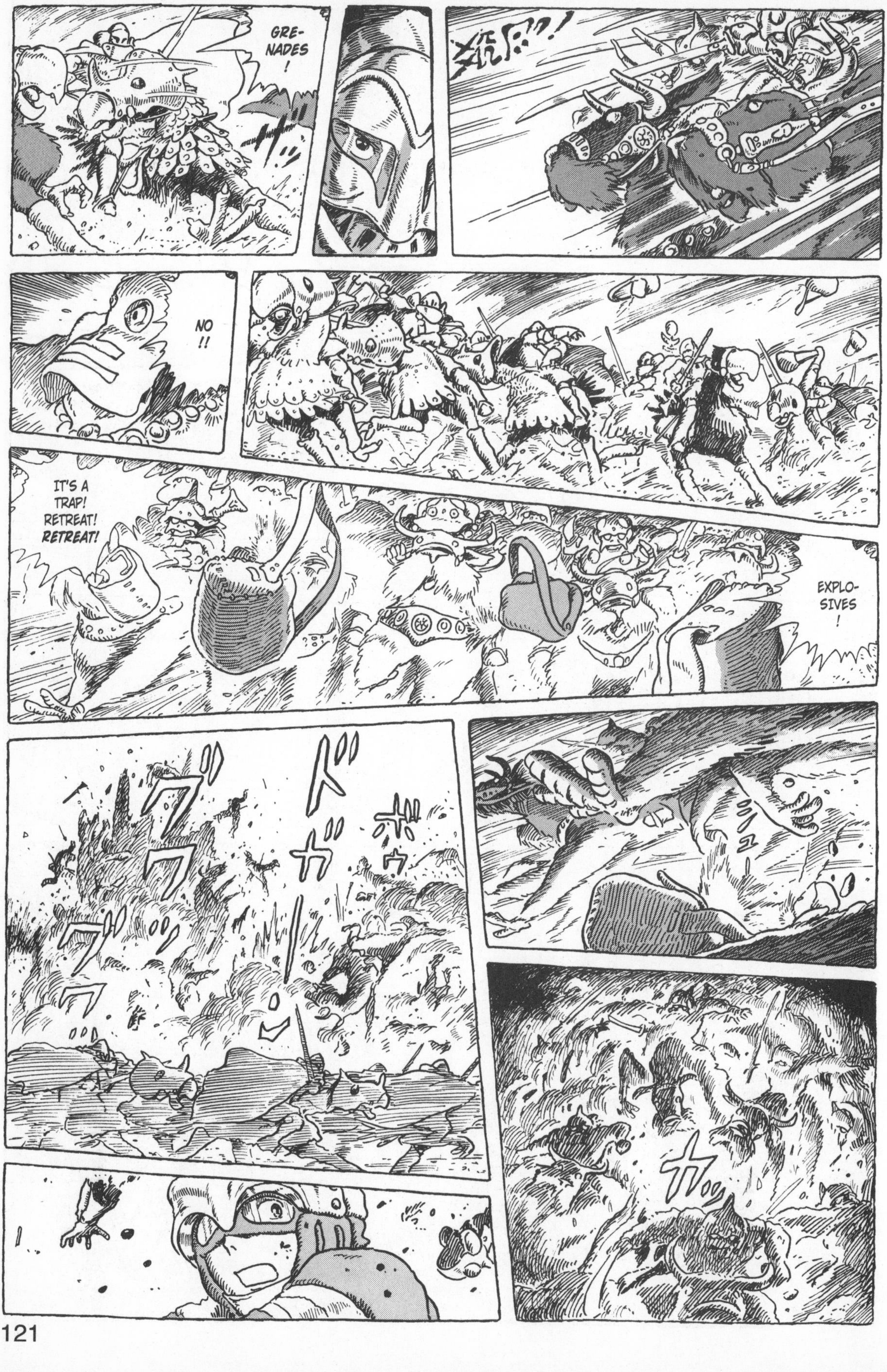
GRE-
NADES
!
NO
!!
EXPLO-
SIVES
!
IT'S A
TRAP!
RETREAT!
RETREAT!

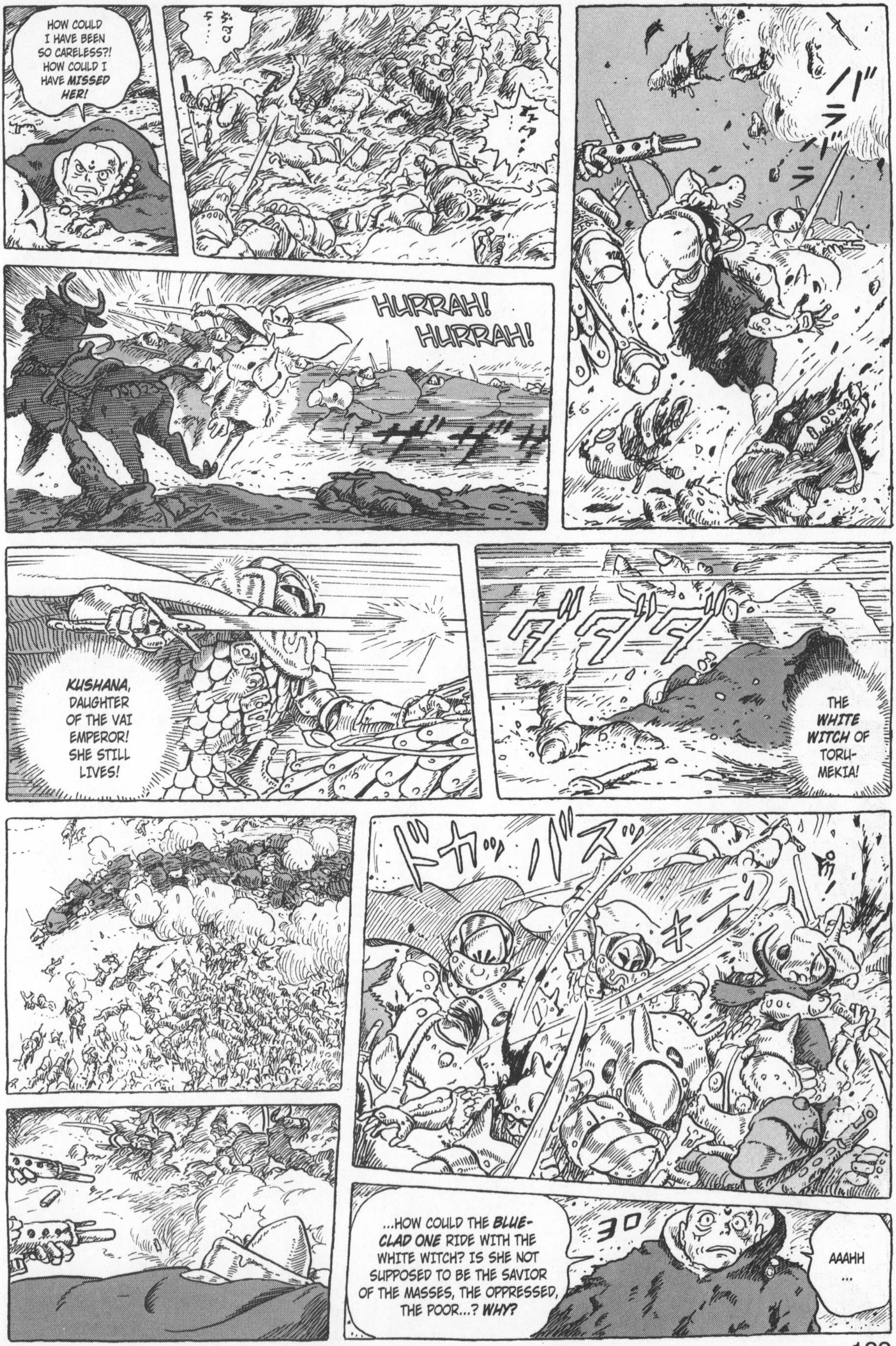
HOW COULD I HAVE BEEN SO CARELESS?! HOW COULD I HAVE MISSED HER!
HURRAH! HURRAH!
THE WHITE WITCH OF TORU-MEKIA!
KUSHANA, DAUGHTER OF THE VAI EMPEROR! SHE STILL LIVES!
AAAHH ...
...HOW COULD THE BLUE-CLAD ONE RIDE WITH THE WHITE WITCH? IS SHE NOT SUPPOSED TO BE THE SAVIOR OF THE MASSES, THE OPPRESSED, THE POOR...? WHY?

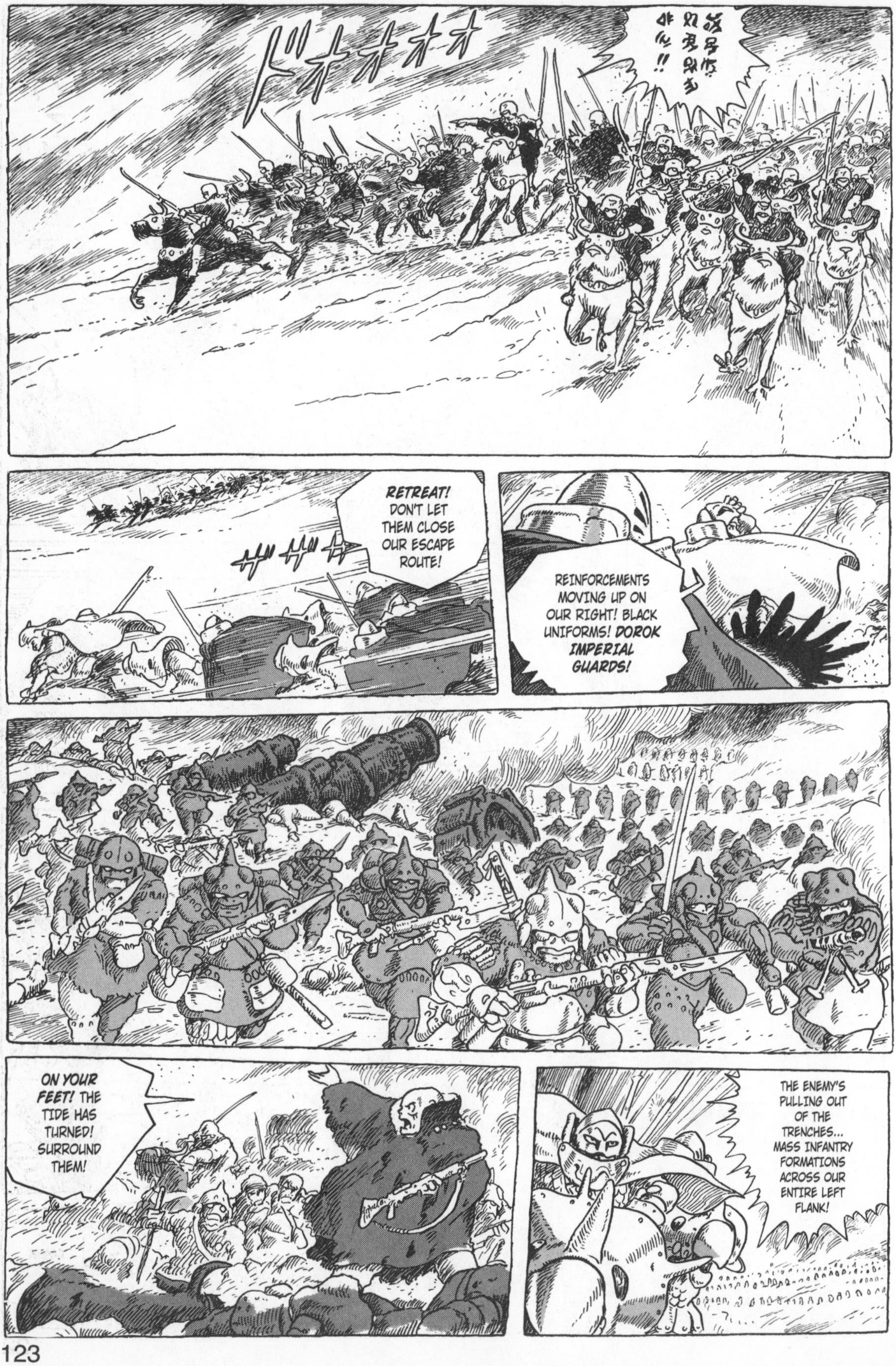
ドオオオオ
REINFORCEMENTS MOVING UP ON OUR RIGHT! BLACK UNIFORMS! DOROK IMPERIAL GUARDS!
RETREAT! DON'T LET THEM CLOSE OUR ESCAPE ROUTE!
ザザザ
THE ENEMY'S PULLING OUT OF THE TRENCHES... MASS INFANTRY FORMATIONS ACROSS OUR ENTIRE LEFT FLANK!
ON YOUR FEET! THE TIDE HAS TURNED! SURROUND THEM!

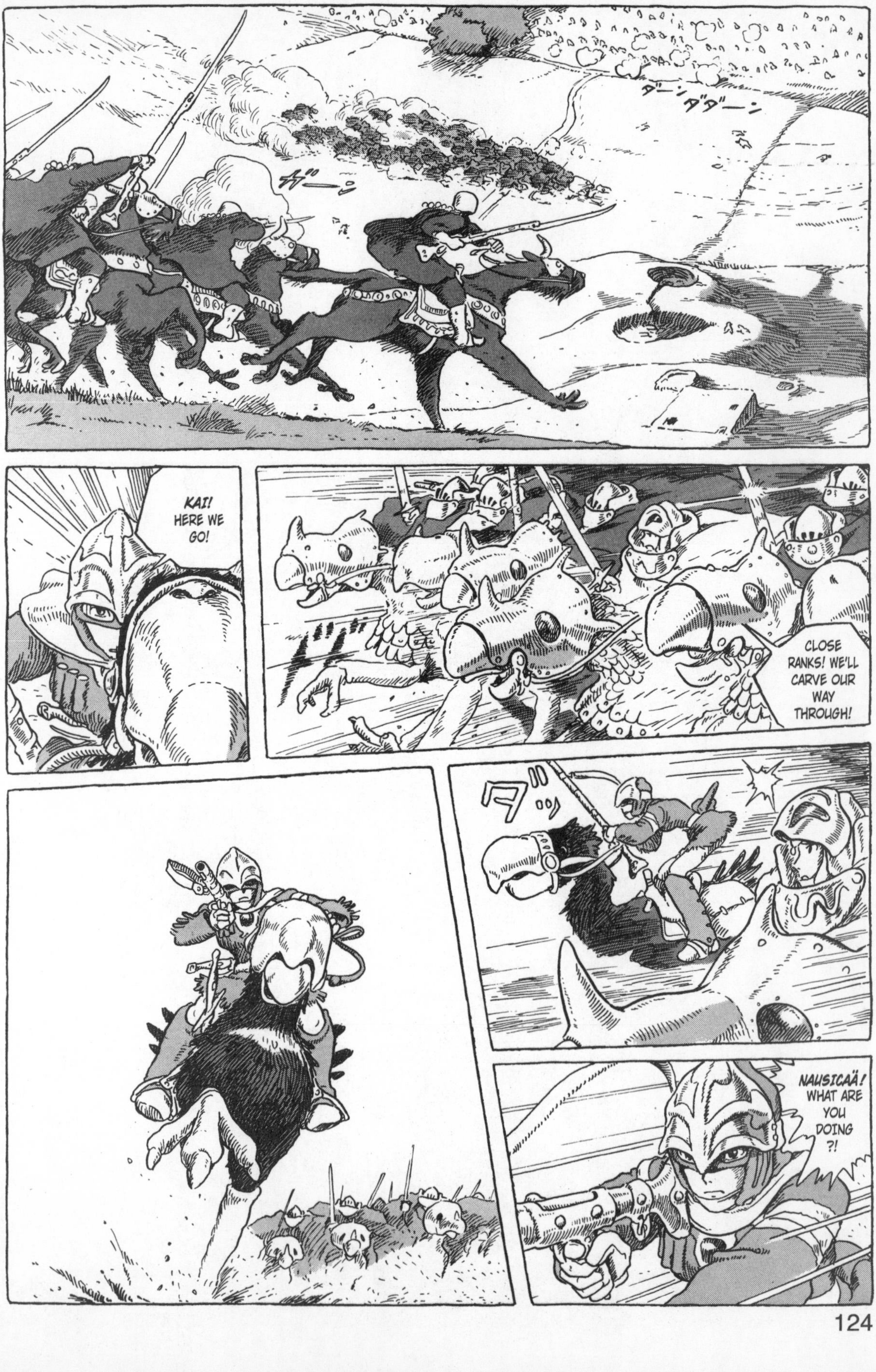
CLOSE RANKS! WE'LL CARVE OUR WAY THROUGH!
KAI! HERE WE GO!
NAUSICAÄ! WHAT ARE YOU DOING ?!

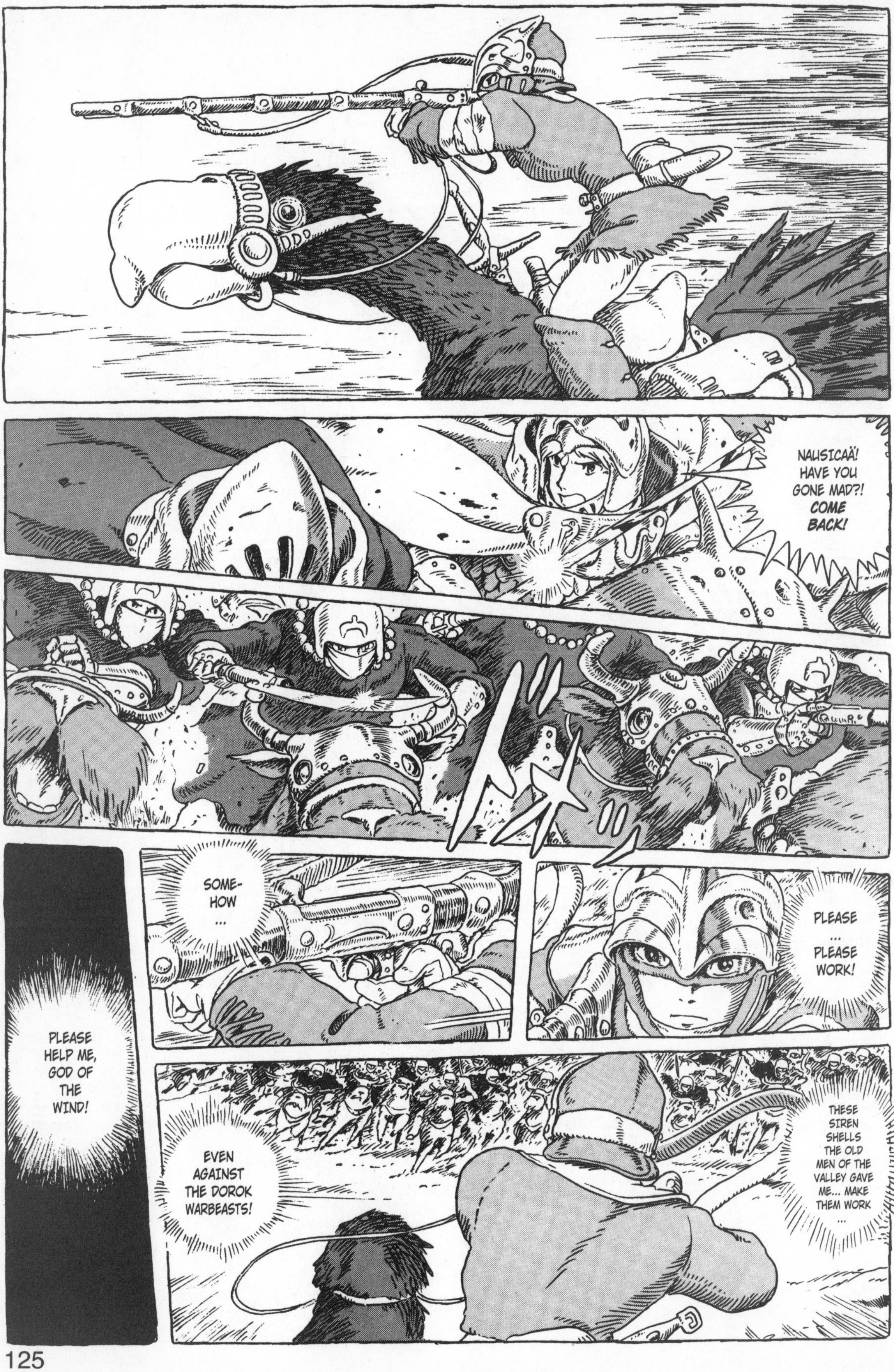
NAUSICAÄ! HAVE YOU GONE MAD?! COME BACK!
PLEASE ... PLEASE WORK!
SOME-HOW ...
THESE SIREN SHELLS THE OLD MEN OF THE VALLEY GAVE ME... MAKE THEM WORK ...
EVEN AGAINST THE DOROK WARBEASTS!
PLEASE HELP ME, GOD OF THE WIND!

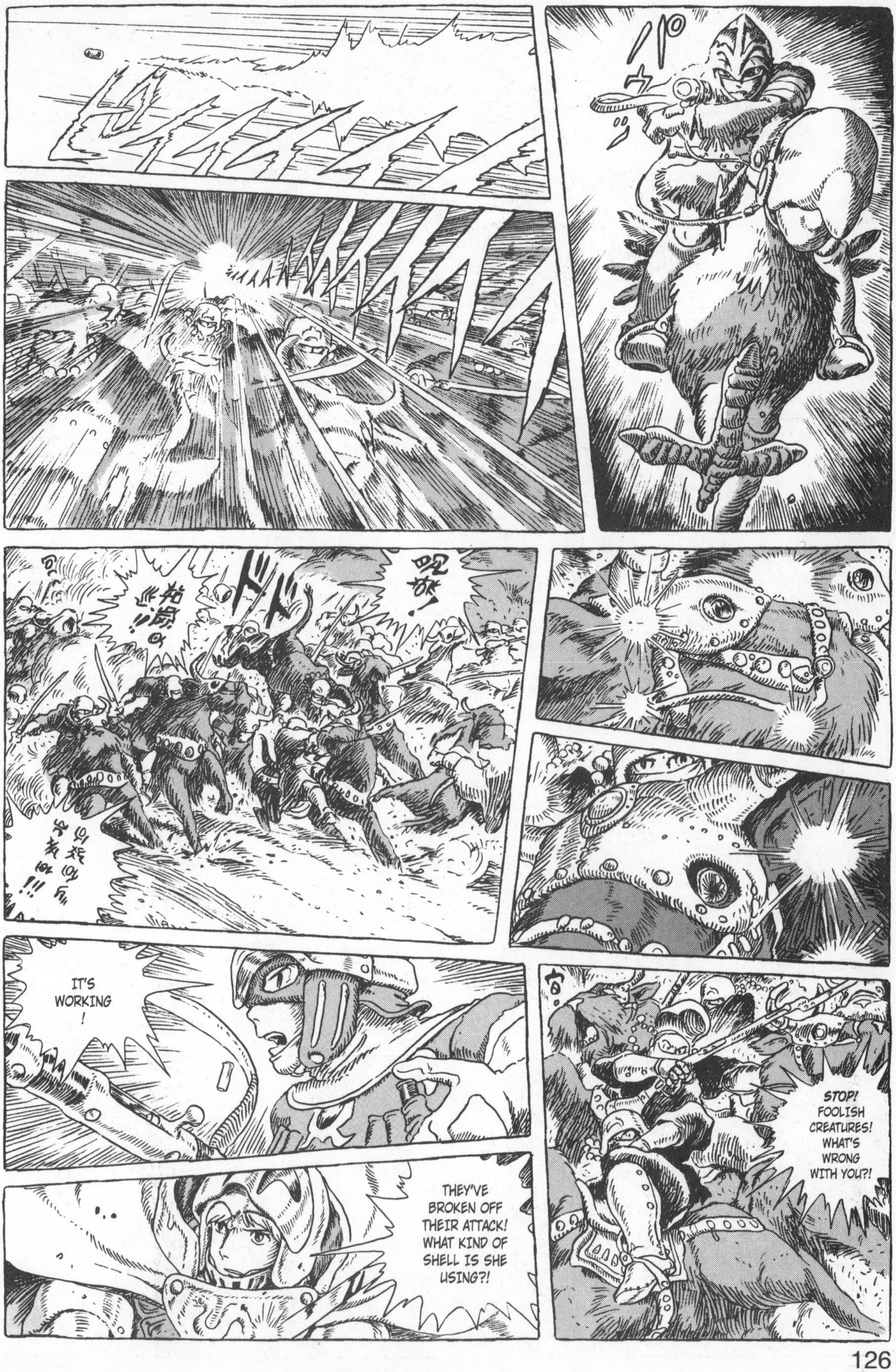
STOP! FOOLISH CREATURES! WHAT'S WRONG WITH YOU?!
IT'S WORKING!
THEY'VE BROKEN OFF THEIR ATTACK! WHAT KIND OF SHELL IS SHE USING?!

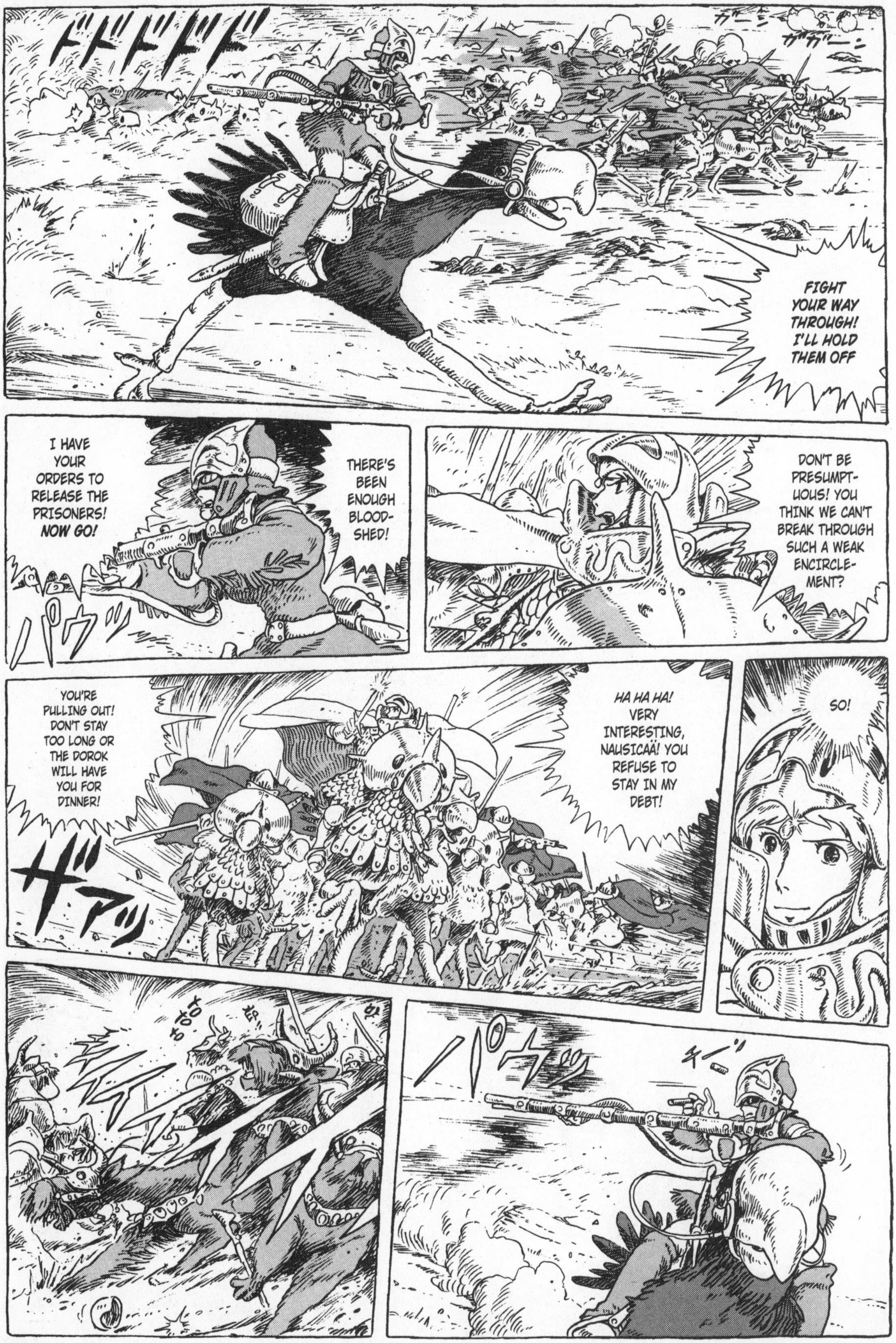
ドドドドド
FIGHT YOUR WAY THROUGH! I'LL HOLD THEM OFF
DON'T BE PRESUMPTUOUS! YOU THINK WE CAN'T BREAK THROUGH SUCH A WEAK ENCIRCLEMENT?
THERE'S BEEN ENOUGH BLOODSHED!
I HAVE YOUR ORDERS TO RELEASE THE PRISONERS! NOW GO!
パウッ
SO!
HA HA HA! VERY INTERESTING, NAUSICAÄ! YOU REFUSE TO STAY IN MY DEBT!
YOU'RE PULLING OUT! DON'T STAY TOO LONG OR THE DOROK WILL HAVE YOU FOR DINNER!
ザアッ
パウッ

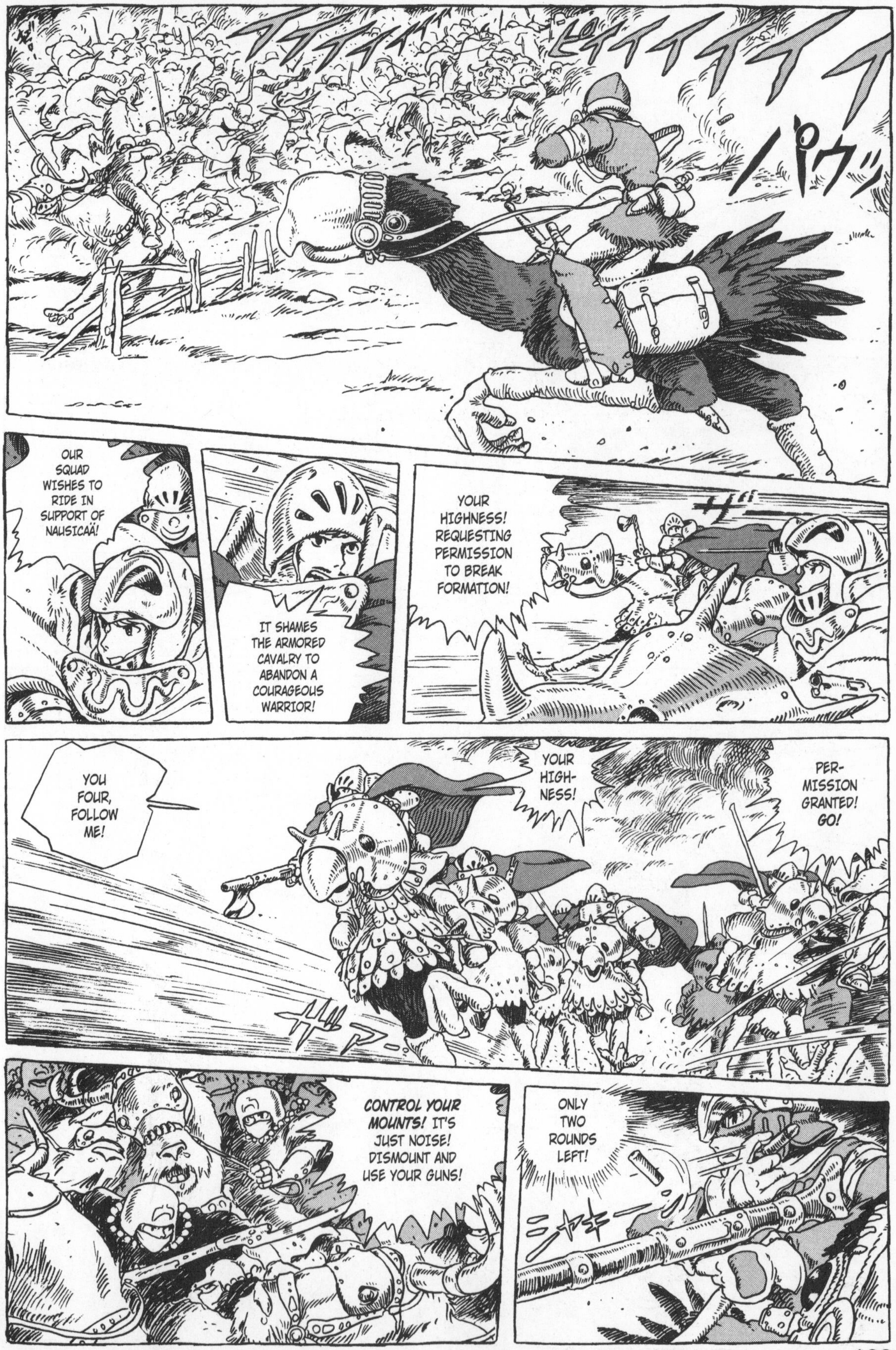

パウッ
YOUR HIGHNESS! REQUESTING PERMISSION TO BREAK FORMATION!
IT SHAMES THE ARMORED CAVALRY TO ABANDON A COURAGEOUS WARRIOR!
OUR SQUAD WISHES TO RIDE IN SUPPORT OF NAUSICAÄ!
PER-MISSION GRANTED! **GO!**
YOUR HIGH-NESS!
YOU FOUR, FOLLOW ME!
ONLY TWO ROUNDS LEFT!
CONTROL YOUR MOUNTS! IT'S JUST NOISE! DISMOUNT AND USE YOUR GUNS!

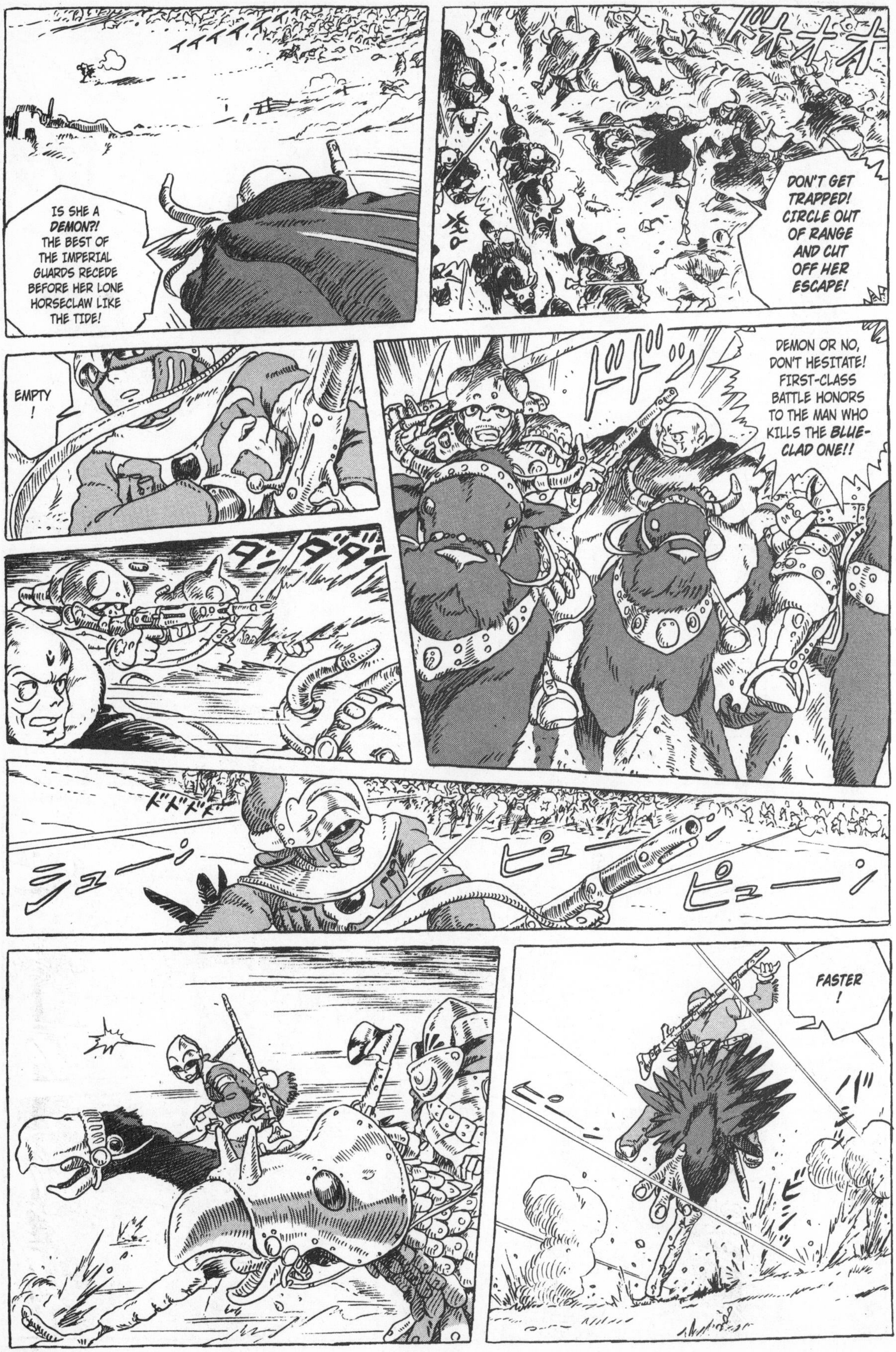
DON'T GET TRAPPED! CIRCLE OUT OF RANGE AND CUT OFF HER ESCAPE!
IS SHE A DEMON?! THE BEST OF THE IMPERIAL GUARDS RECEDE BEFORE HER LONE HORSECLAW LIKE THE TIDE!
DEMON OR NO, DON'T HESITATE! FIRST-CLASS BATTLE HONORS TO THE MAN WHO KILLS THE BLUE-CLAD ONE!!
EMPTY!
FASTER!

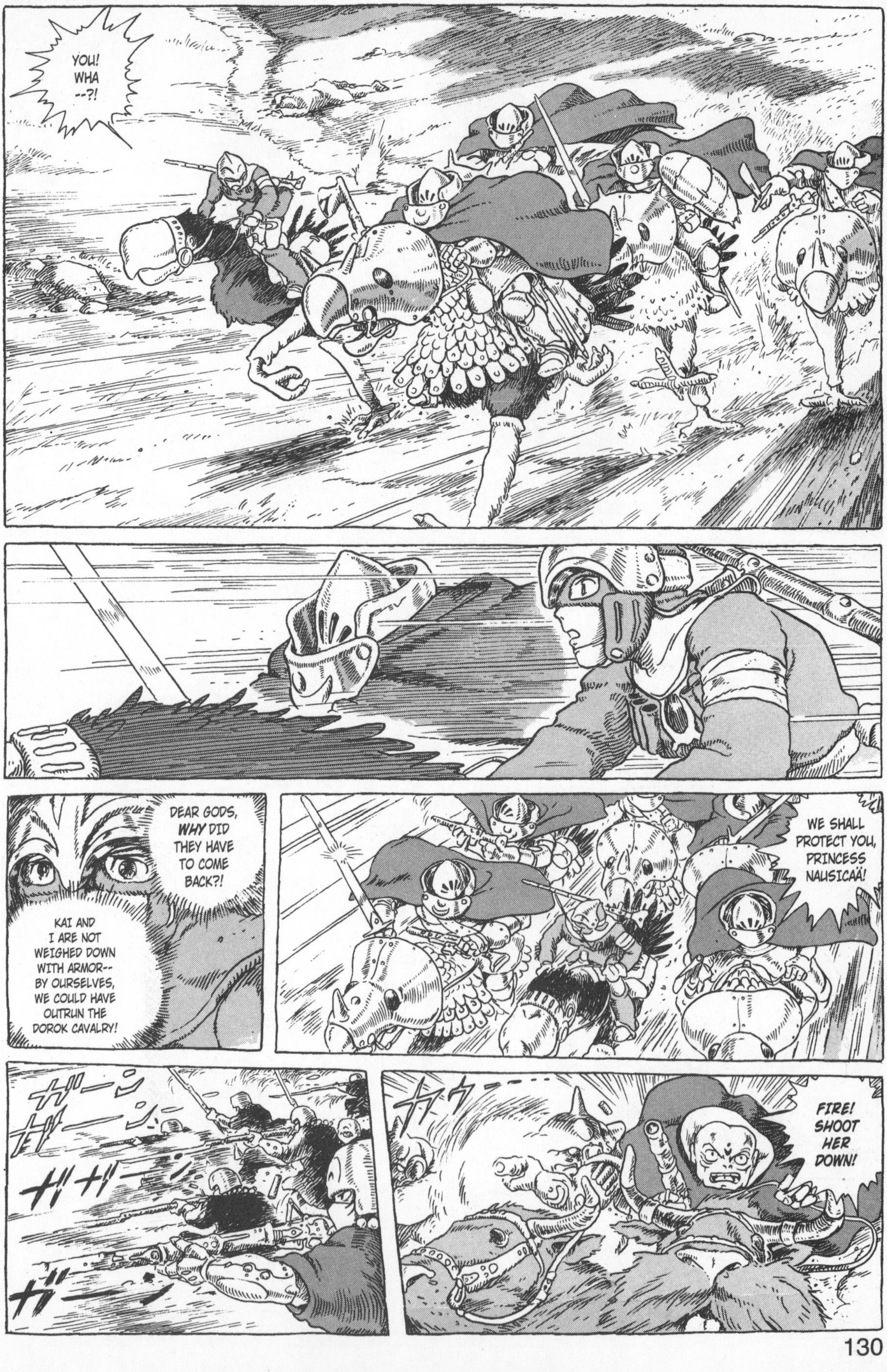
YOU! WHA --?!
WE SHALL PROTECT YOU, PRINCESS NAUSICAÄ!
DEAR GODS, **WHY** DID THEY HAVE TO COME BACK?!
KAI AND I ARE NOT WEIGHED DOWN WITH ARMOR-- BY OURSELVES, WE COULD HAVE OUTRUN THE DOROK CAVALRY!
カウーー
FIRE! SHOOT HER DOWN!
ガーン
ガーン
ガガー
ガー

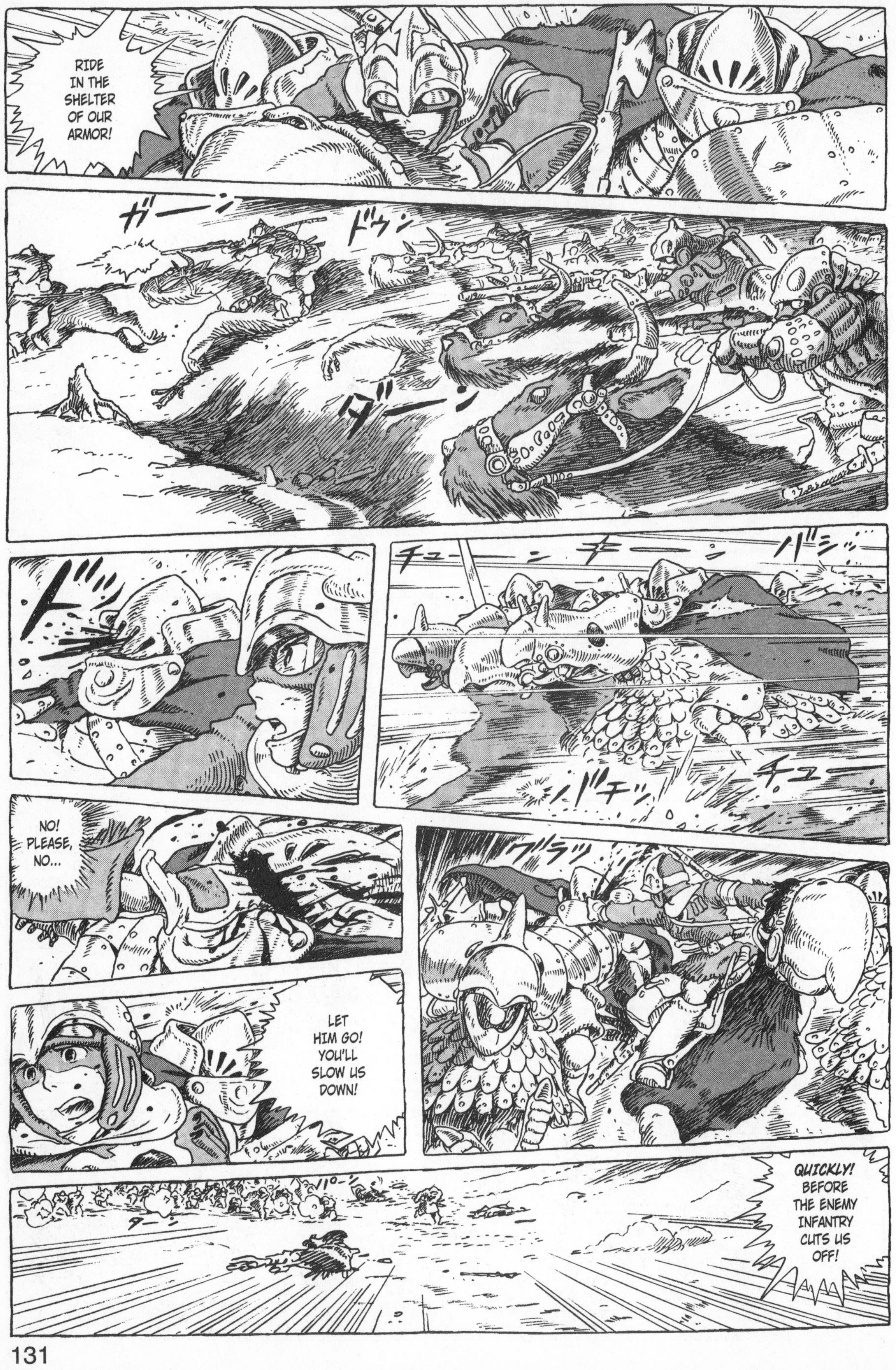
RIDE IN THE SHELTER OF OUR ARMOR!
ドウン
ガーン
ダーン
バシッ
チーン
チューン
チュ
バチッ
ドッ
グラッ
NO! PLEASE, NO...
LET HIM GO! YOU'LL SLOW US DOWN!
QUICKLY! BEFORE THE ENEMY INFANTRY CUTS US OFF!

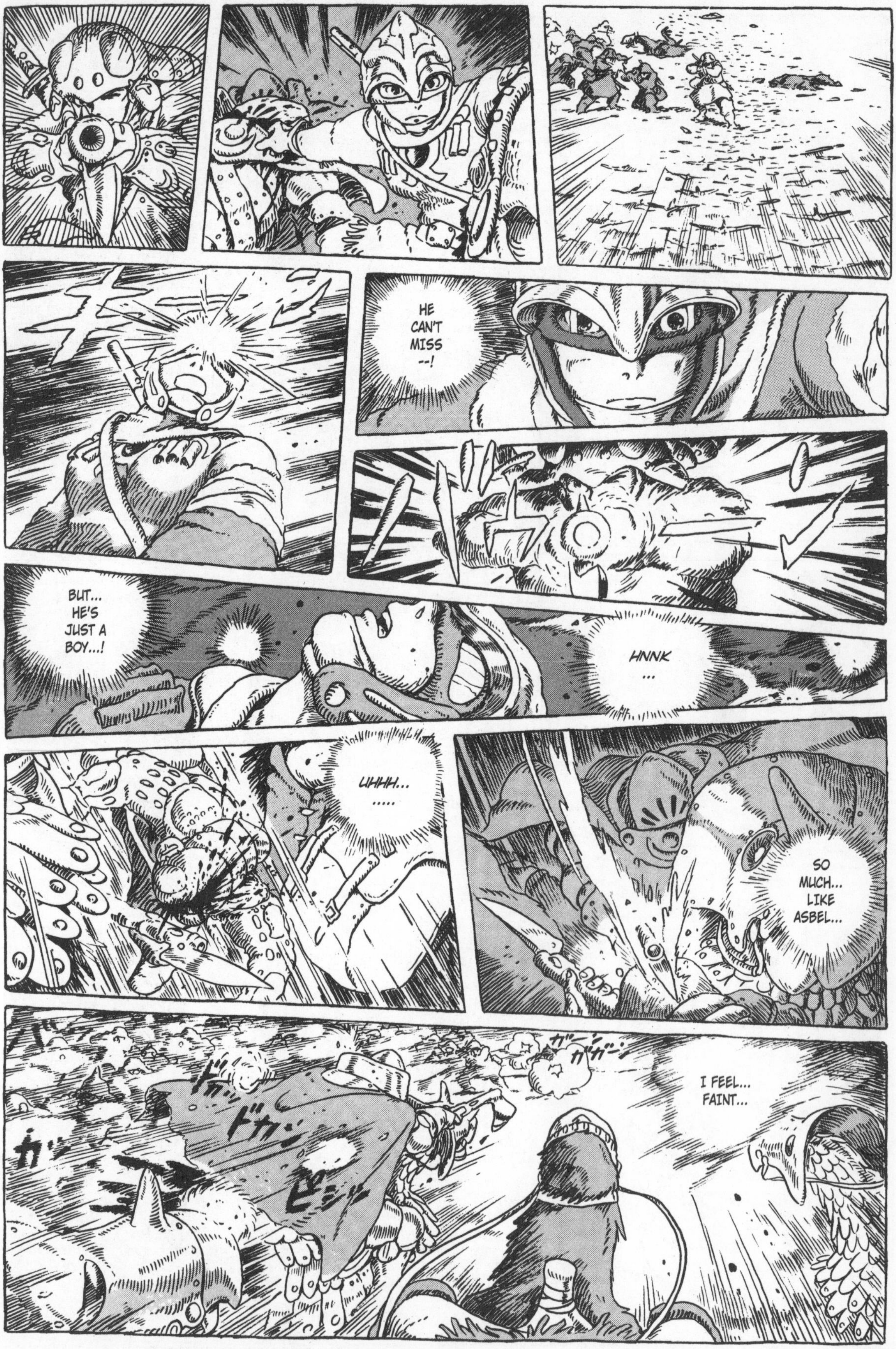
HE CAN'T MISS --!
HNNK ...
BUT... HE'S JUST A BOY...!
SO MUCH... LIKE ASBEL...
UHHH... .....
I FEEL... FAINT...

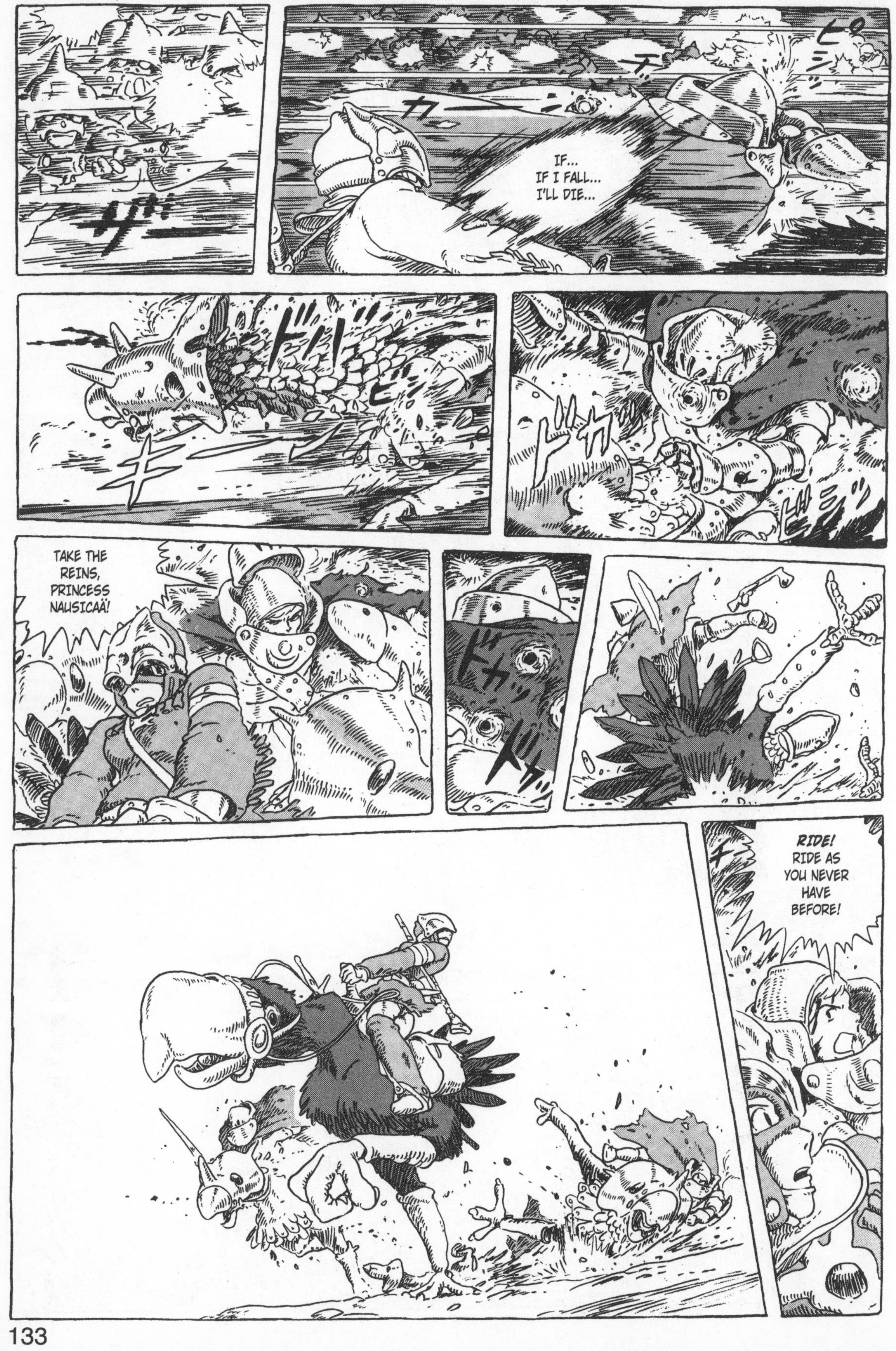
IF... IF I FALL... I'LL DIE...
TAKE THE REINS, PRINCESS NAUSICAÄ!
RIDE! RIDE AS YOU NEVER HAVE BEFORE!

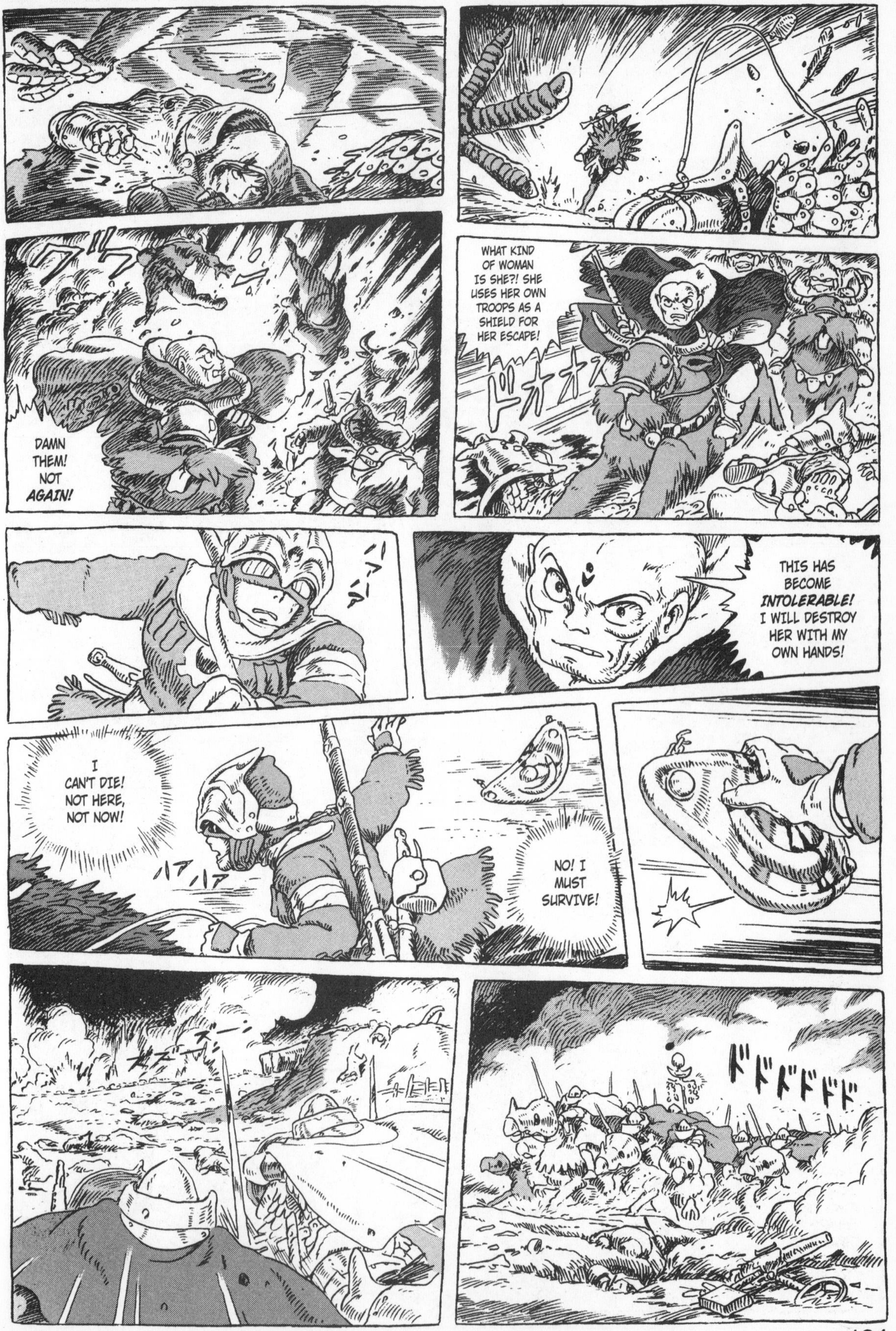
WHAT KIND OF WOMAN IS SHE?! SHE USES HER OWN TROOPS AS A SHIELD FOR HER ESCAPE!
DAMN THEM! NOT *AGAIN!*
THIS HAS BECOME *INTOLERABLE!* I WILL DESTROY HER WITH MY OWN HANDS!
I CAN'T DIE! NOT HERE, NOT NOW!
NO! I MUST SURVIVE!
ドドドドドド

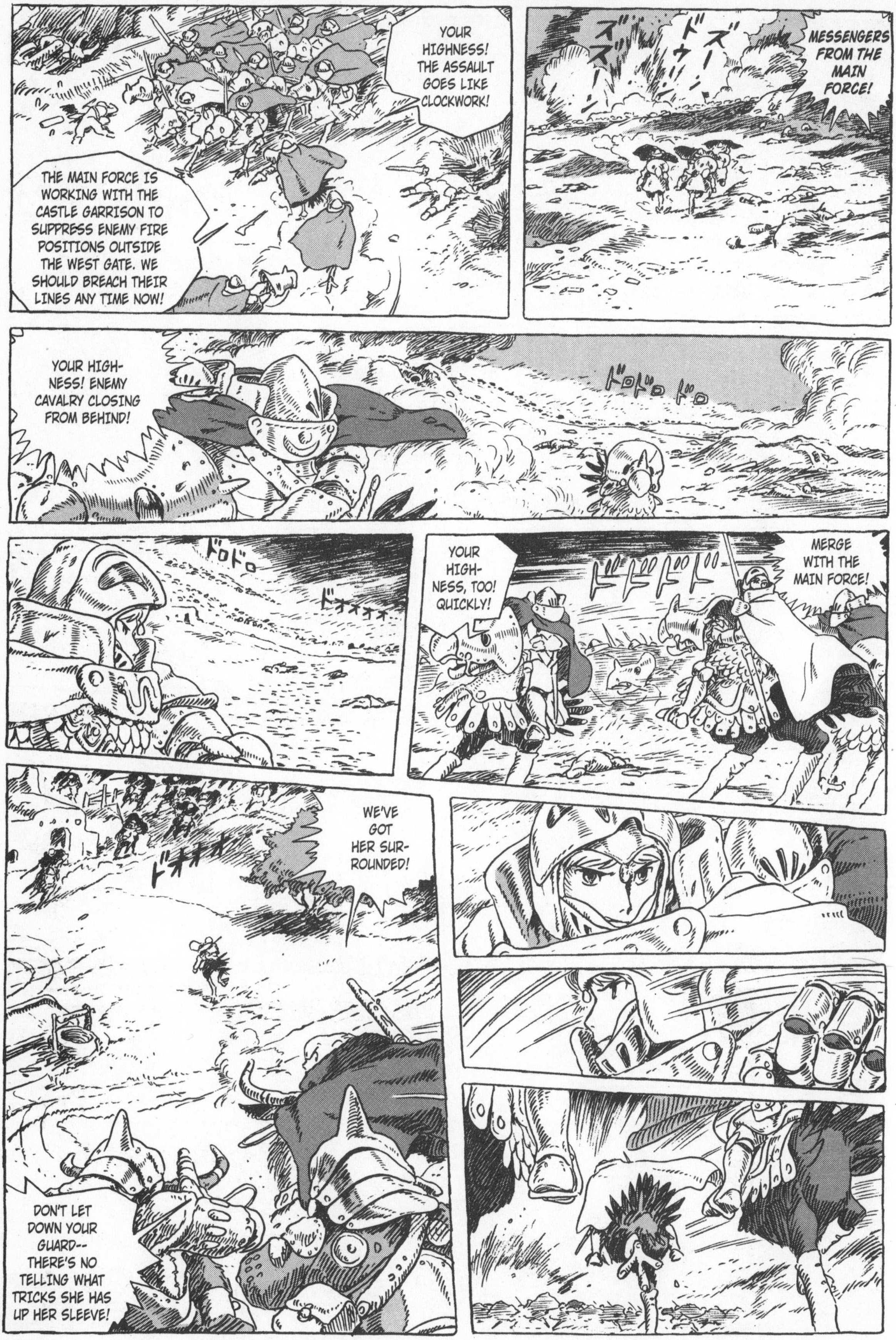
MESSENGERS FROM THE MAIN FORCE!
YOUR HIGHNESS! THE ASSAULT GOES LIKE CLOCKWORK!
THE MAIN FORCE IS WORKING WITH THE CASTLE GARRISON TO SUPPRESS ENEMY FIRE POSITIONS OUTSIDE THE WEST GATE. WE SHOULD BREACH THEIR LINES ANY TIME NOW!
YOUR HIGH-NESS! ENEMY CAVALRY CLOSING FROM BEHIND!
MERGE WITH THE MAIN FORCE!
YOUR HIGH-NESS, TOO! QUICKLY!
WE'VE GOT HER SUR-ROUNDED!
DON'T LET DOWN YOUR GUARD-- THERE'S NO TELLING WHAT TRICKS SHE HAS UP HER SLEEVE!

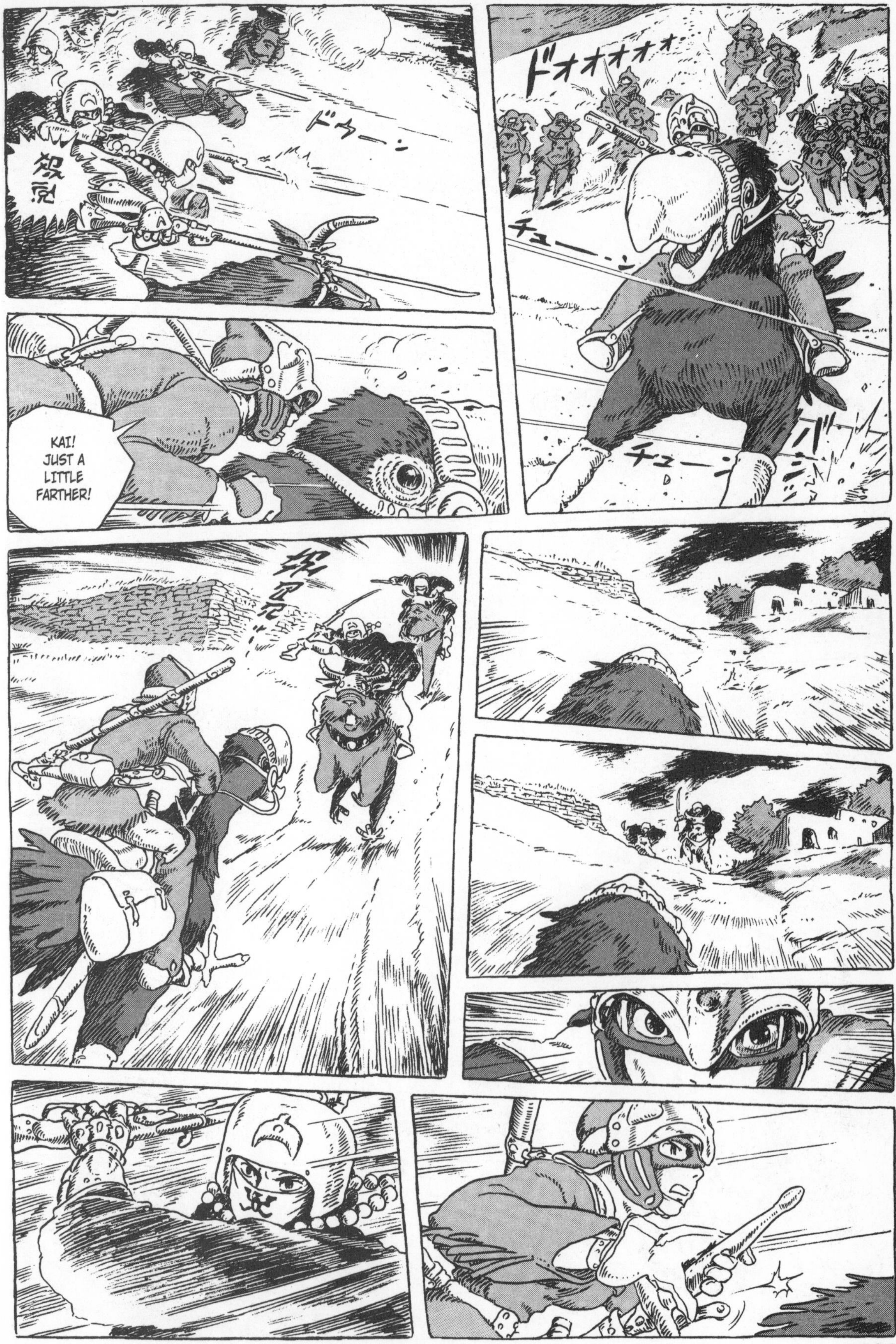
ドオオオオオ
チューーン
チューーン
ドゥーーン
KAI! JUST A LITTLE FARTHER!

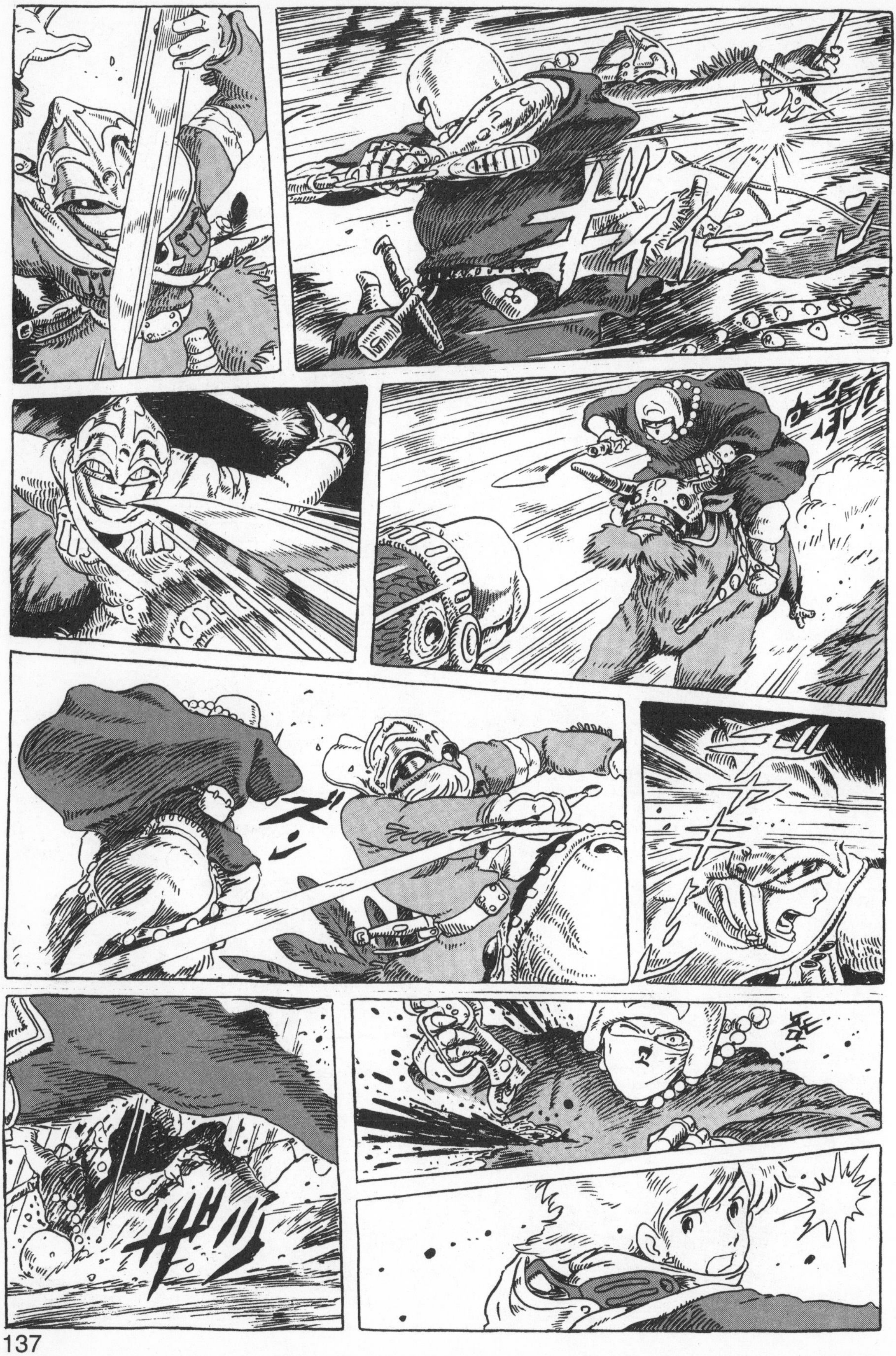
ギィィーン
ズッ
ザッ

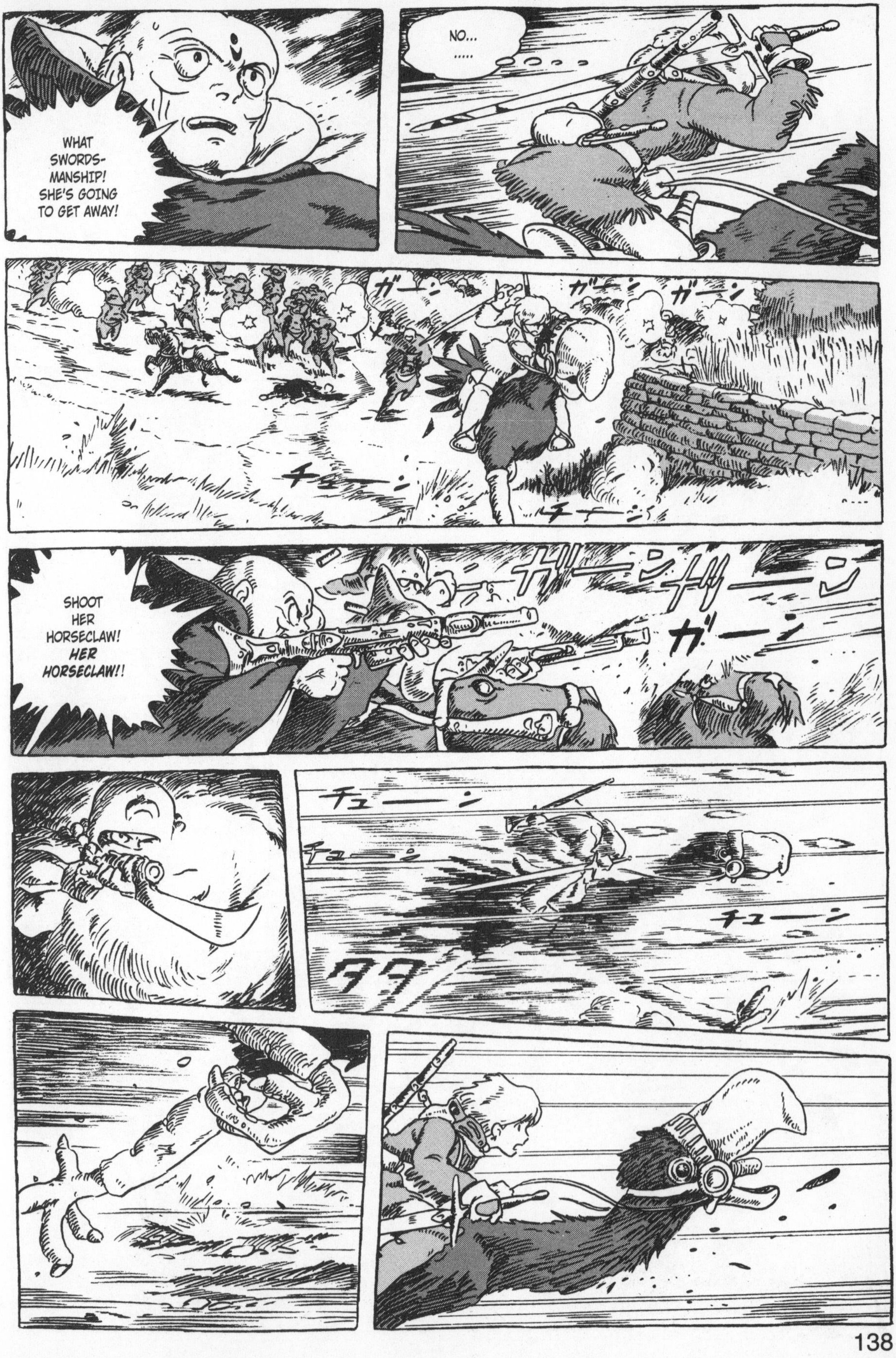
NO...
.....
WHAT SWORDS-MANSHIP! SHE'S GOING TO GET AWAY!
ガーン
ガーン
ガーン
チューン
ガーン
ガーン
ガーン
SHOOT HER HORSECLAW! **HER HORSECLAW!!**
チューン
チューン
チューン
タタ

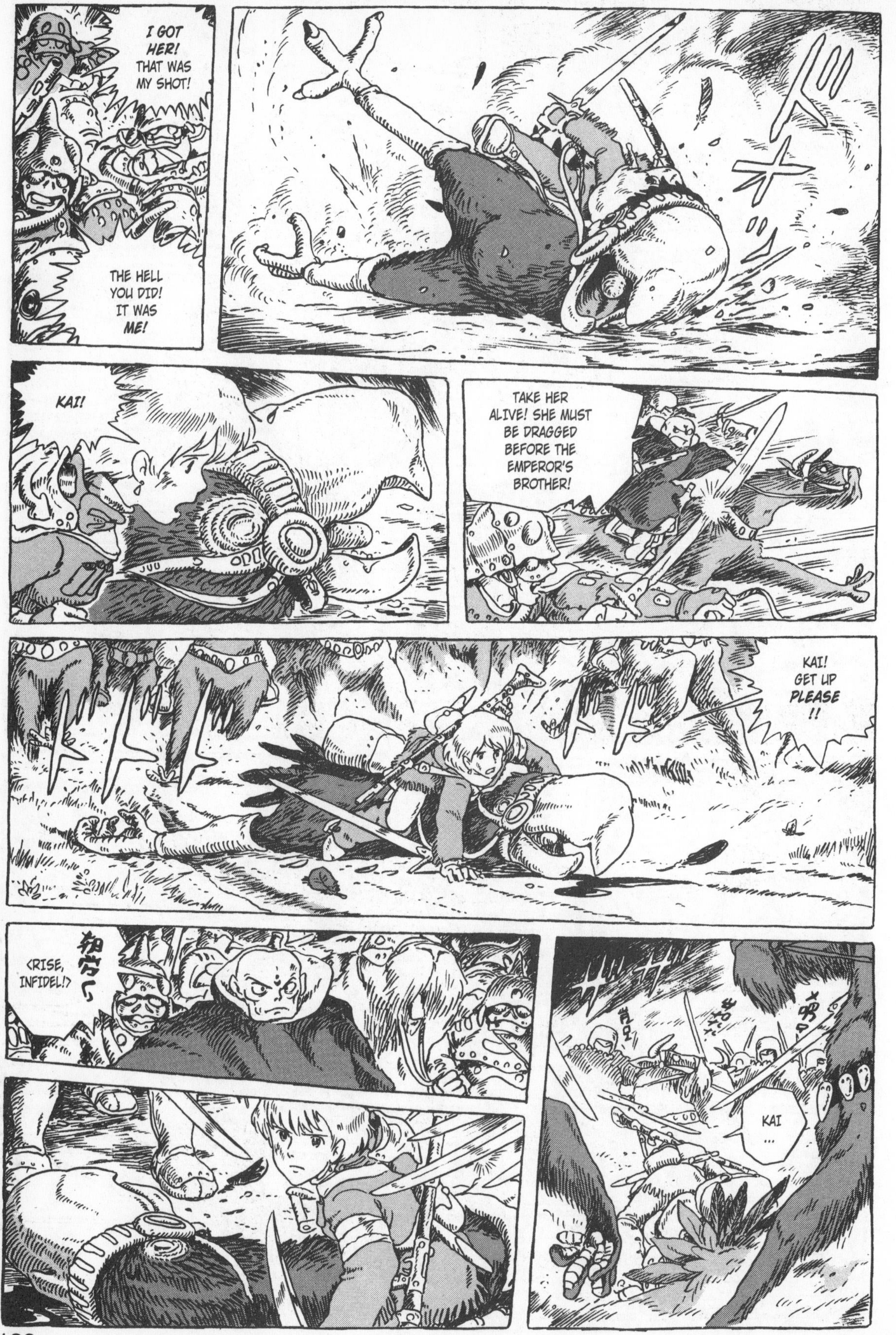
I GOT HER! THAT WAS MY SHOT!
THE HELL YOU DID! IT WAS ME!
TAKE HER ALIVE! SHE MUST BE DRAGGED BEFORE THE EMPEROR'S BROTHER!
KAI!
KAI! GET UP PLEASE !!
KAI ...
<RISE, INFIDEL!>

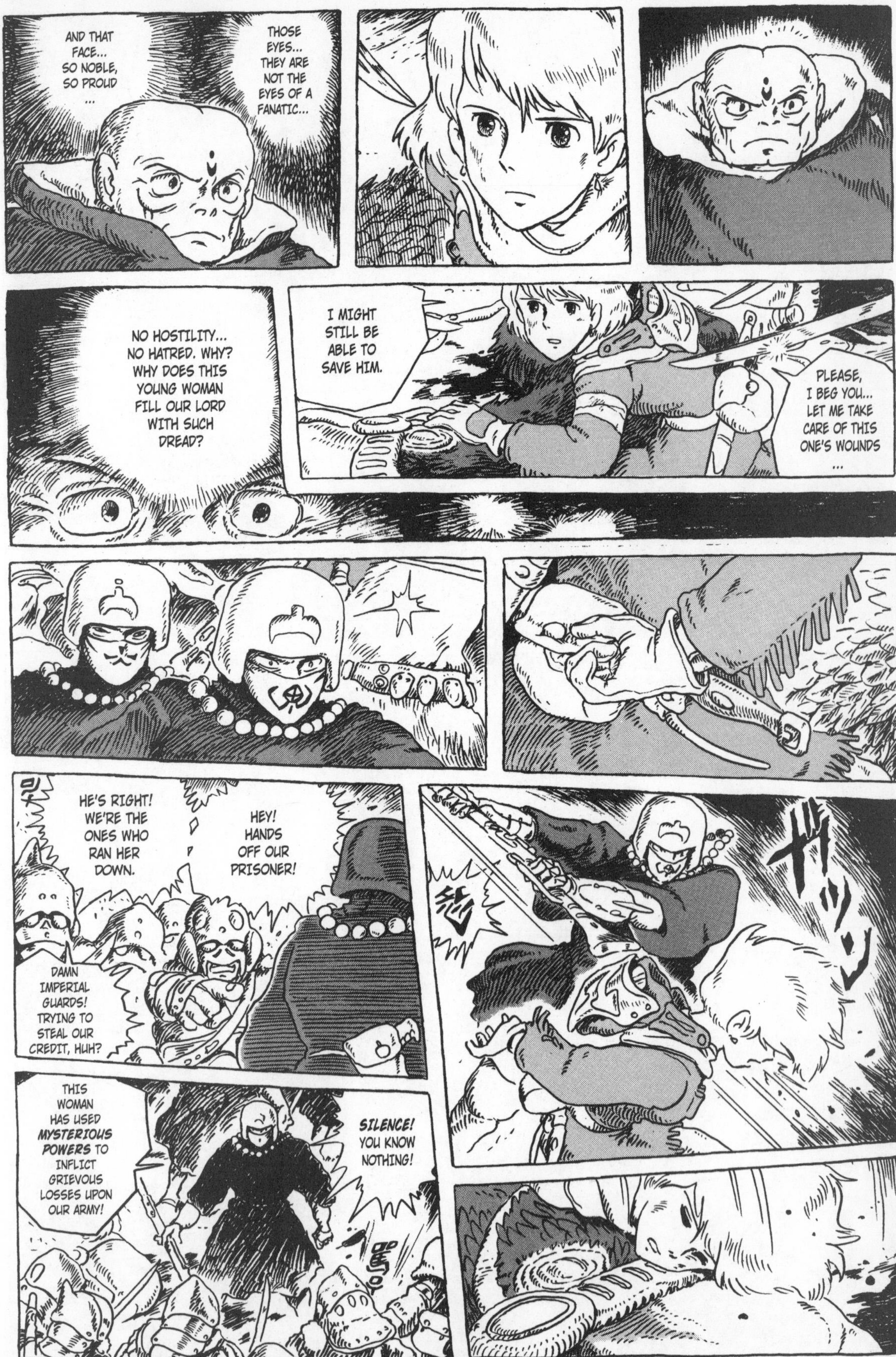
THOSE EYES... THEY ARE NOT THE EYES OF A FANATIC...
AND THAT FACE... SO NOBLE, SO PROUD ...
PLEASE, I BEG YOU... LET ME TAKE CARE OF THIS ONE'S WOUNDS ...
I MIGHT STILL BE ABLE TO SAVE HIM.
NO HOSTILITY... NO HATRED. WHY? WHY DOES THIS YOUNG WOMAN FILL OUR LORD WITH SUCH DREAD?
HEY! HANDS OFF OUR PRISONER!
HE'S RIGHT! WE'RE THE ONES WHO RAN HER DOWN.
DAMN IMPERIAL GUARDS! TRYING TO STEAL OUR CREDIT, HUH?
SILENCE! YOU KNOW NOTHING!
THIS WOMAN HAS USED MYSTERIOUS POWERS TO INFLICT GRIEVOUS LOSSES UPON OUR ARMY!

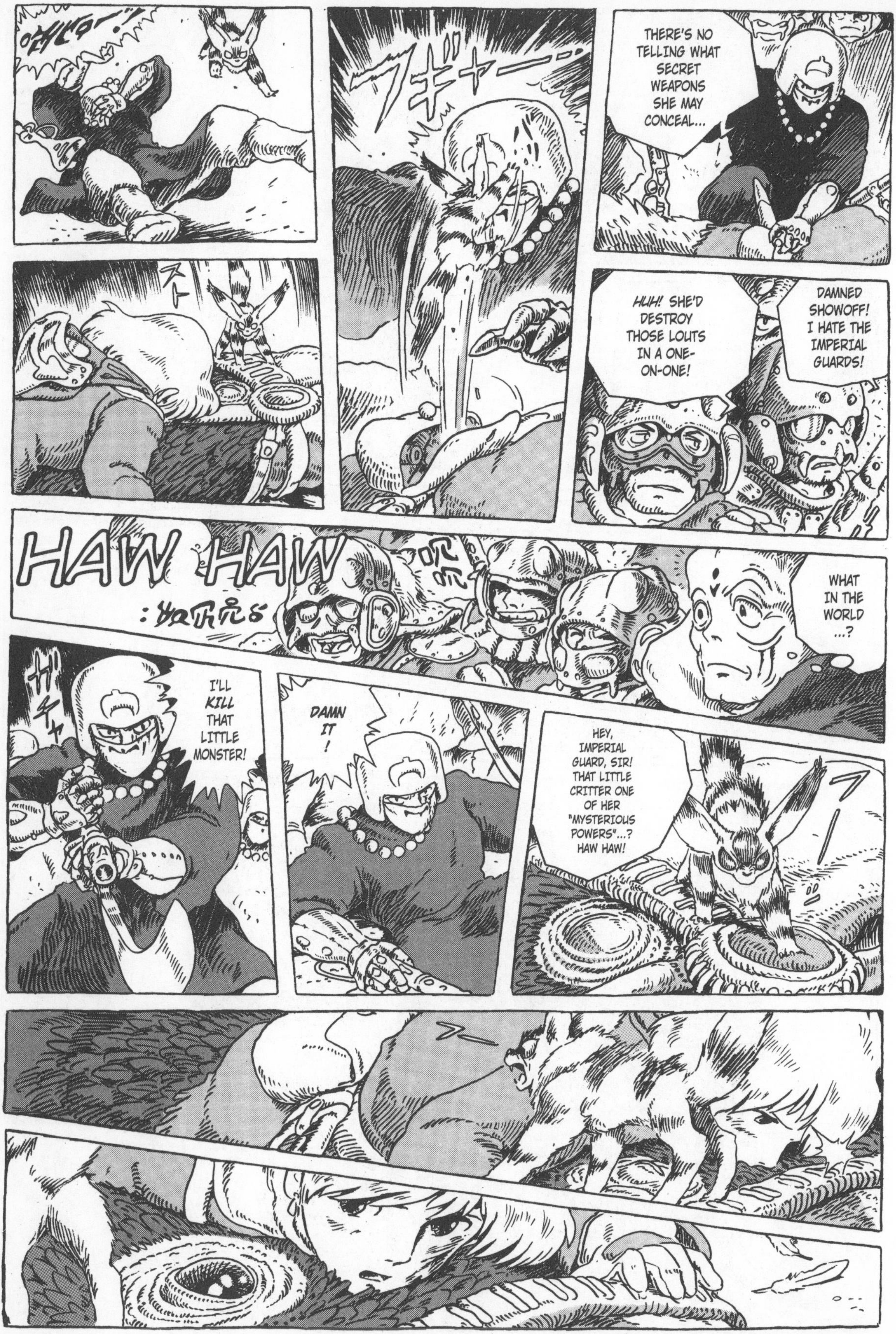
THERE'S NO TELLING WHAT SECRET WEAPONS SHE MAY CONCEAL...
フギャー
DAMNED SHOWOFF! I HATE THE IMPERIAL GUARDS!
HUH! SHE'D DESTROY THOSE LOUTS IN A ONE-ON-ONE!
WHAT IN THE WORLD ...?
HAW HAW
HEY, IMPERIAL GUARD, SIR! THAT LITTLE CRITTER ONE OF HER "MYSTERIOUS POWERS"...? HAW HAW!
DAMN IT!
I'LL *KILL* THAT LITTLE MONSTER!

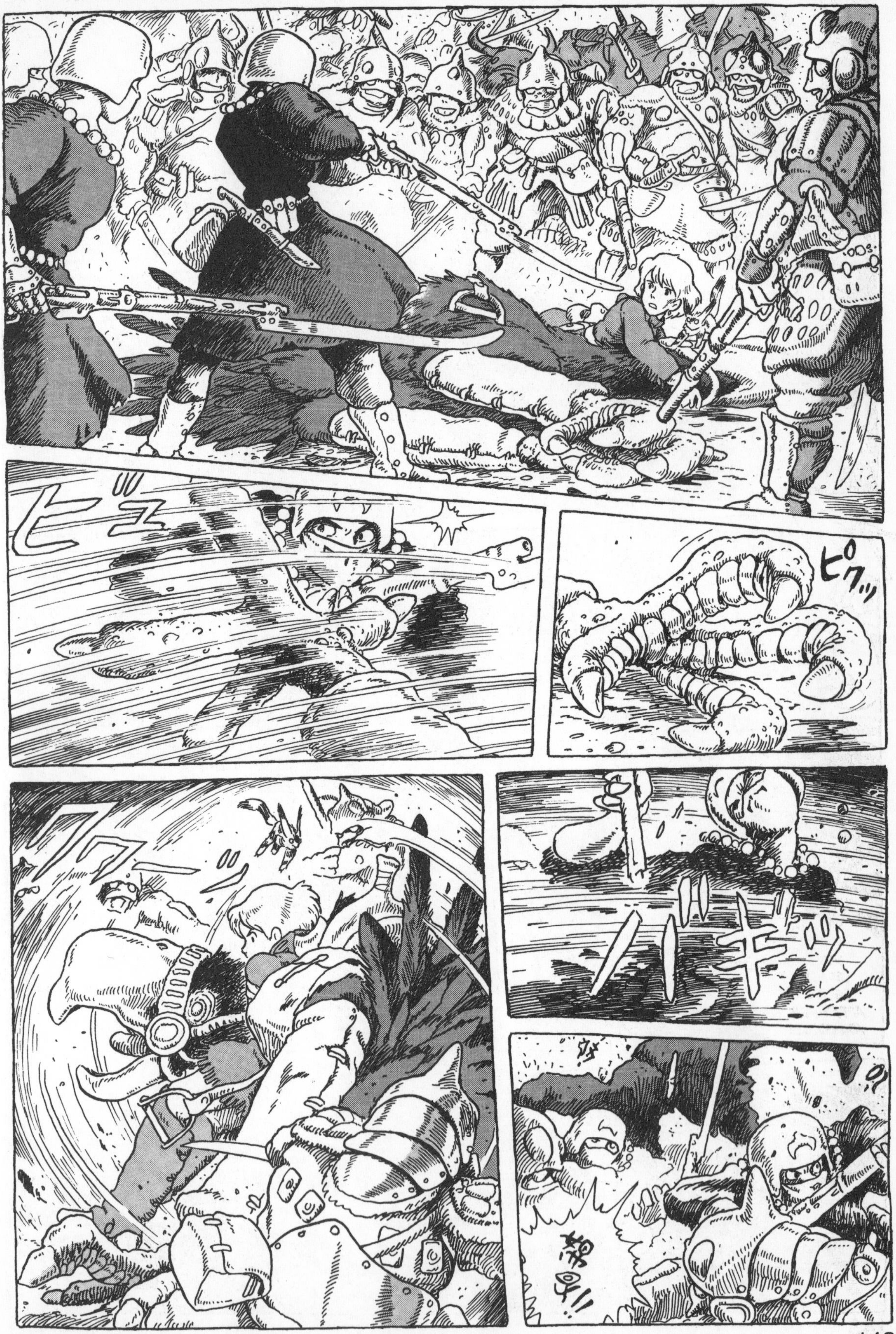
ピクッ
ビュ
バギッ
ワーッ

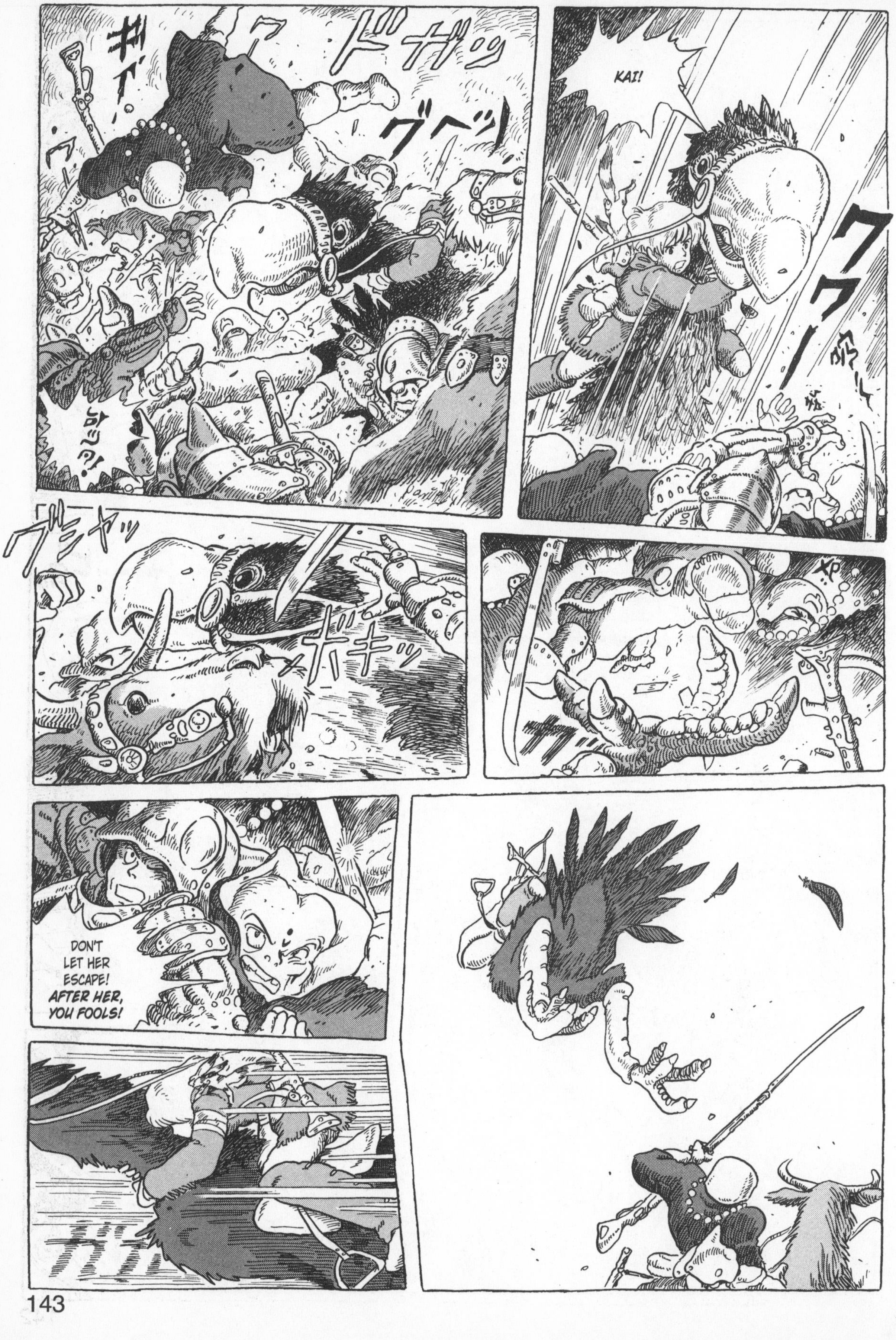
KAI!
ドガッ
グヘッ
グシャッ
ボキッ
DON'T LET HER ESCAPE! AFTER HER, YOU FOOLS!

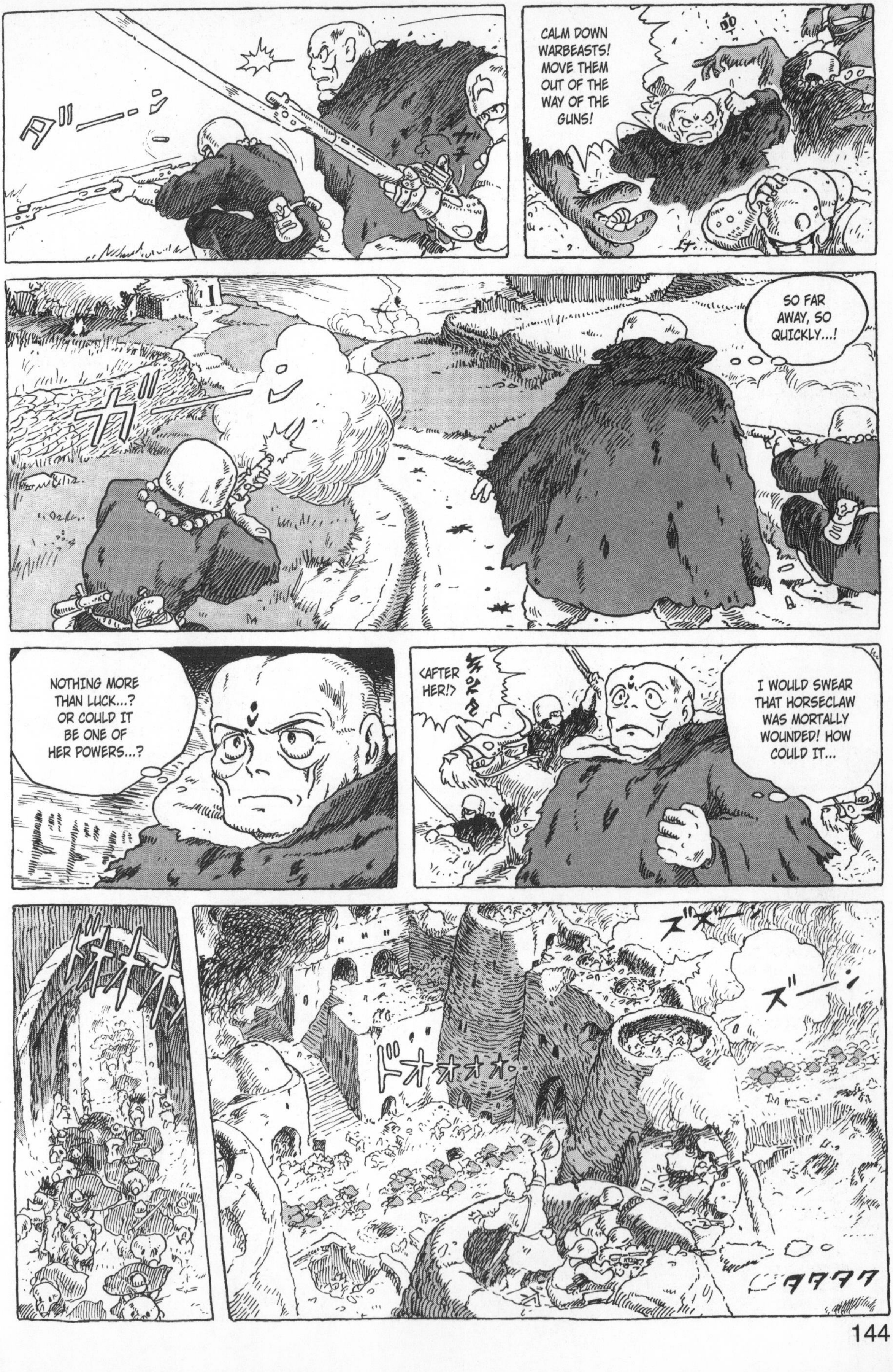
CALM DOWN WARBEASTS! MOVE THEM OUT OF THE WAY OF THE GUNS!
ダーーン
SO FAR AWAY, SO QUICKLY...!
ガーーン
<AFTER HER!>
I WOULD SWEAR THAT HORSECLAW WAS MORTALLY WOUNDED! HOW COULD IT...
NOTHING MORE THAN LUCK...? OR COULD IT BE ONE OF HER POWERS...?
ズズーン
ズーン
ドオオオオ
タタタタ

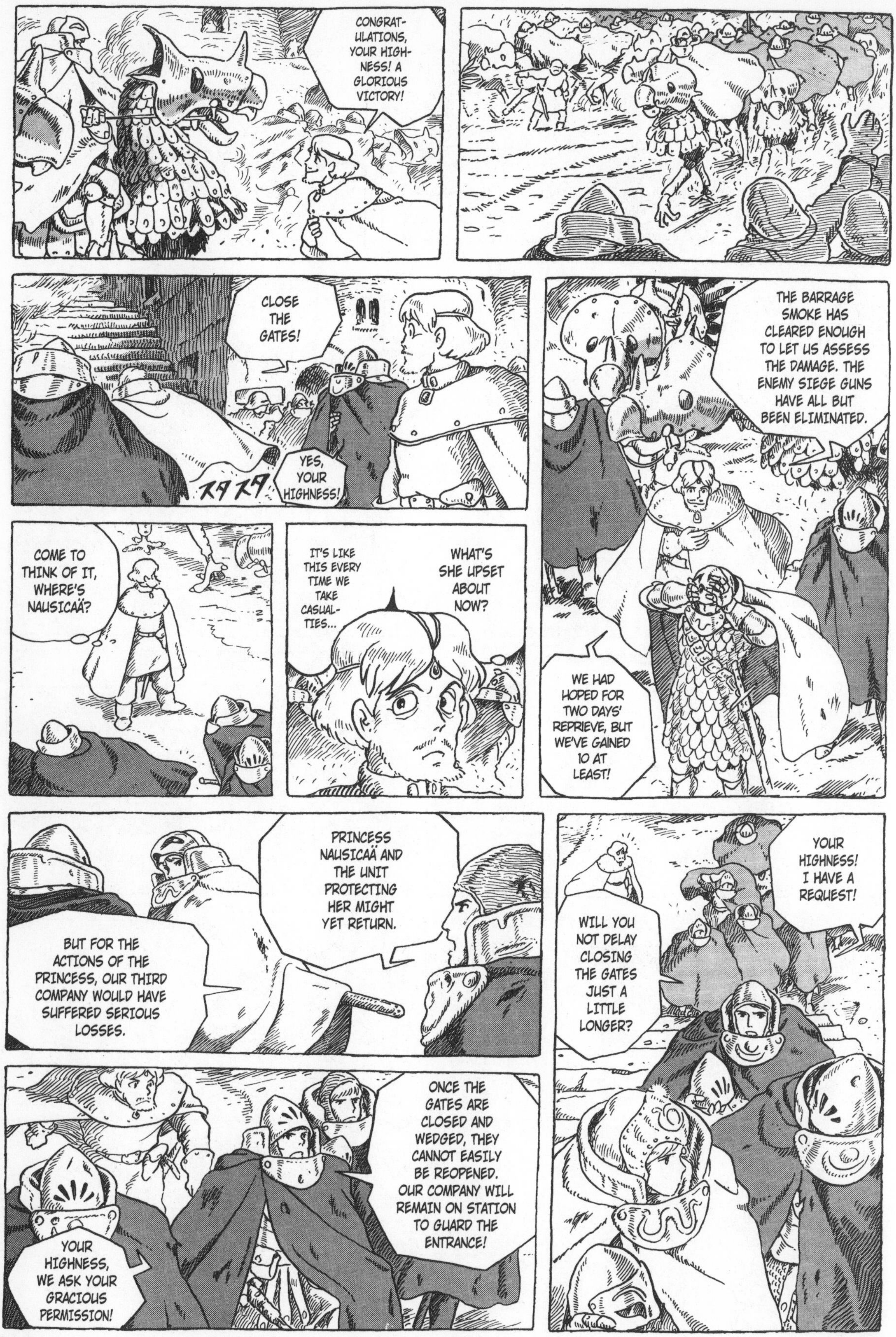
CONGRATULATIONS, YOUR HIGHNESS! A GLORIOUS VICTORY!
THE BARRAGE SMOKE HAS CLEARED ENOUGH TO LET US ASSESS THE DAMAGE. THE ENEMY SIEGE GUNS HAVE ALL BUT BEEN ELIMINATED.
WE HAD HOPED FOR TWO DAYS' REPRIEVE, BUT WE'VE GAINED 10 AT LEAST!
CLOSE THE GATES!
YES, YOUR HIGHNESS!
スタスタ
WHAT'S SHE UPSET ABOUT NOW?
IT'S LIKE THIS EVERY TIME WE TAKE CASUALTIES...
COME TO THINK OF IT, WHERE'S NAUSICAÄ?
YOUR HIGHNESS! I HAVE A REQUEST!
WILL YOU NOT DELAY CLOSING THE GATES JUST A LITTLE LONGER?
PRINCESS NAUSICAÄ AND THE UNIT PROTECTING HER MIGHT YET RETURN.
BUT FOR THE ACTIONS OF THE PRINCESS, OUR THIRD COMPANY WOULD HAVE SUFFERED SERIOUS LOSSES.
ONCE THE GATES ARE CLOSED AND WEDGED, THEY CANNOT EASILY BE REOPENED. OUR COMPANY WILL REMAIN ON STATION TO GUARD THE ENTRANCE!
YOUR HIGHNESS, WE ASK YOUR GRACIOUS PERMISSION!

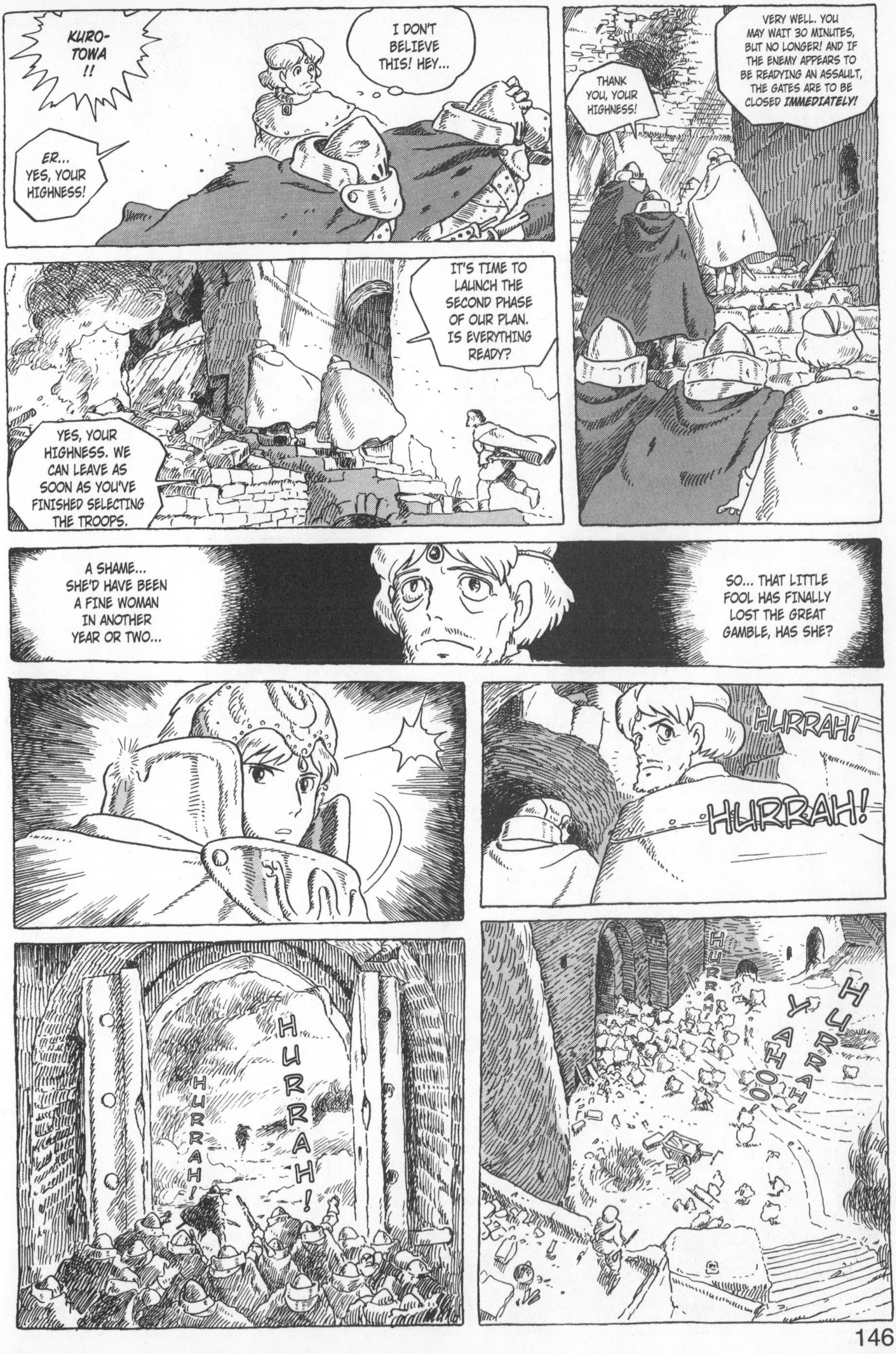
VERY WELL. YOU MAY WAIT 30 MINUTES, BUT NO LONGER! AND IF THE ENEMY APPEARS TO BE READYING AN ASSAULT, THE GATES ARE TO BE CLOSED **IMMEDIATELY!**
THANK YOU, YOUR HIGHNESS!
I DON'T BELIEVE THIS! HEY...
KURO-TOWA !!
ER... YES, YOUR HIGHNESS!
IT'S TIME TO LAUNCH THE SECOND PHASE OF OUR PLAN. IS EVERYTHING READY?
YES, YOUR HIGHNESS. WE CAN LEAVE AS SOON AS YOU'VE FINISHED SELECTING THE TROOPS.
SO... THAT LITTLE FOOL HAS FINALLY LOST THE GREAT GAMBLE, HAS SHE?
A SHAME... SHE'D HAVE BEEN A FINE WOMAN IN ANOTHER YEAR OR TWO...
HURRAH!
HURRAH!
HURRAH!
YAHOO!
HURRAH!
HURRAH!
HURRAH!
HURRAH!

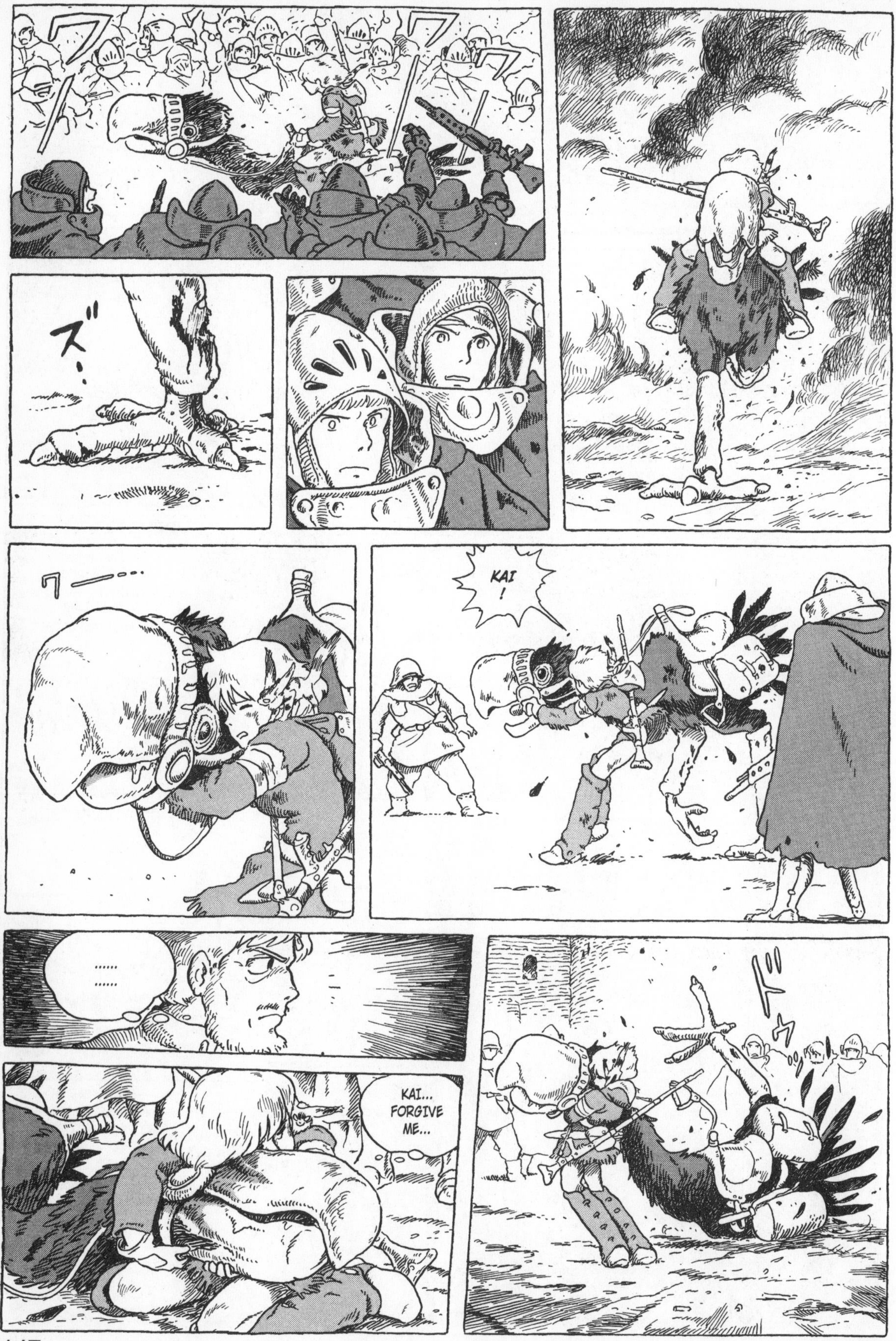
ワ
ワ
ワ
ズ…
KAI !
ワー……
ドウ
……
……
KAI... FORGIVE ME...

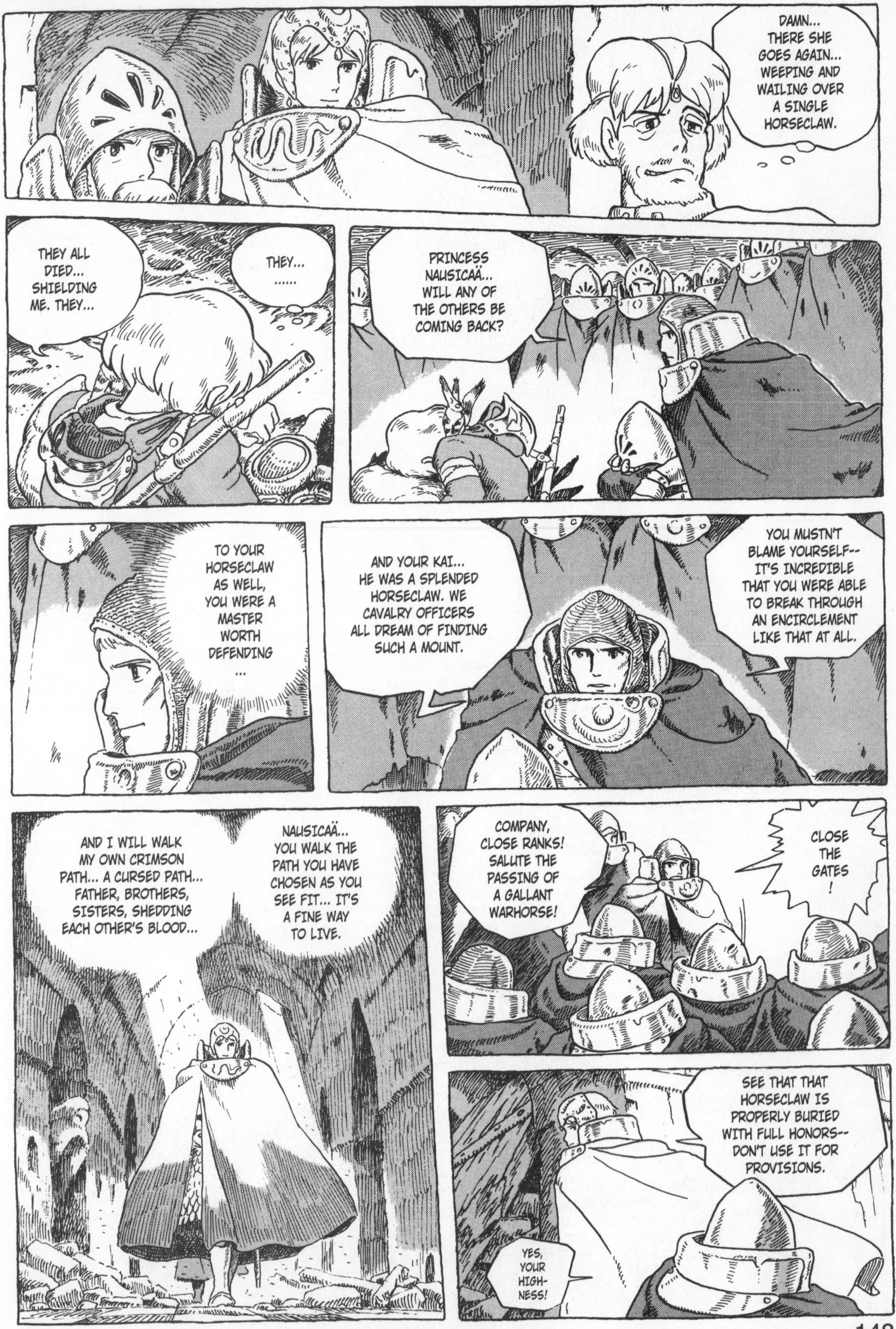
DAMN... THERE SHE GOES AGAIN... WEEPING AND WAILING OVER A SINGLE HORSECLAW.
PRINCESS NAUSICAÄ... WILL ANY OF THE OTHERS BE COMING BACK?
THEY ALL DIED... SHIELDING ME. THEY...
THEY... ......
YOU MUSTN'T BLAME YOURSELF-- IT'S INCREDIBLE THAT YOU WERE ABLE TO BREAK THROUGH AN ENCIRCLEMENT LIKE THAT AT ALL.
AND YOUR KAI... HE WAS A SPLENDED HORSECLAW. WE CAVALRY OFFICERS ALL DREAM OF FINDING SUCH A MOUNT.
TO YOUR HORSECLAW AS WELL, YOU WERE A MASTER WORTH DEFENDING ...
CLOSE THE GATES !
COMPANY, CLOSE RANKS! SALUTE THE PASSING OF A GALLANT WARHORSE!
SEE THAT THAT HORSECLAW IS PROPERLY BURIED WITH FULL HONORS-- DON'T USE IT FOR PROVISIONS.
YES, YOUR HIGH-NESS!
NAUSICAÄ... YOU WALK THE PATH YOU HAVE CHOSEN AS YOU SEE FIT... IT'S A FINE WAY TO LIVE.
AND I WILL WALK MY OWN CRIMSON PATH... A CURSED PATH... FATHER, BROTHERS, SISTERS, SHEDDING EACH OTHER'S BLOOD...

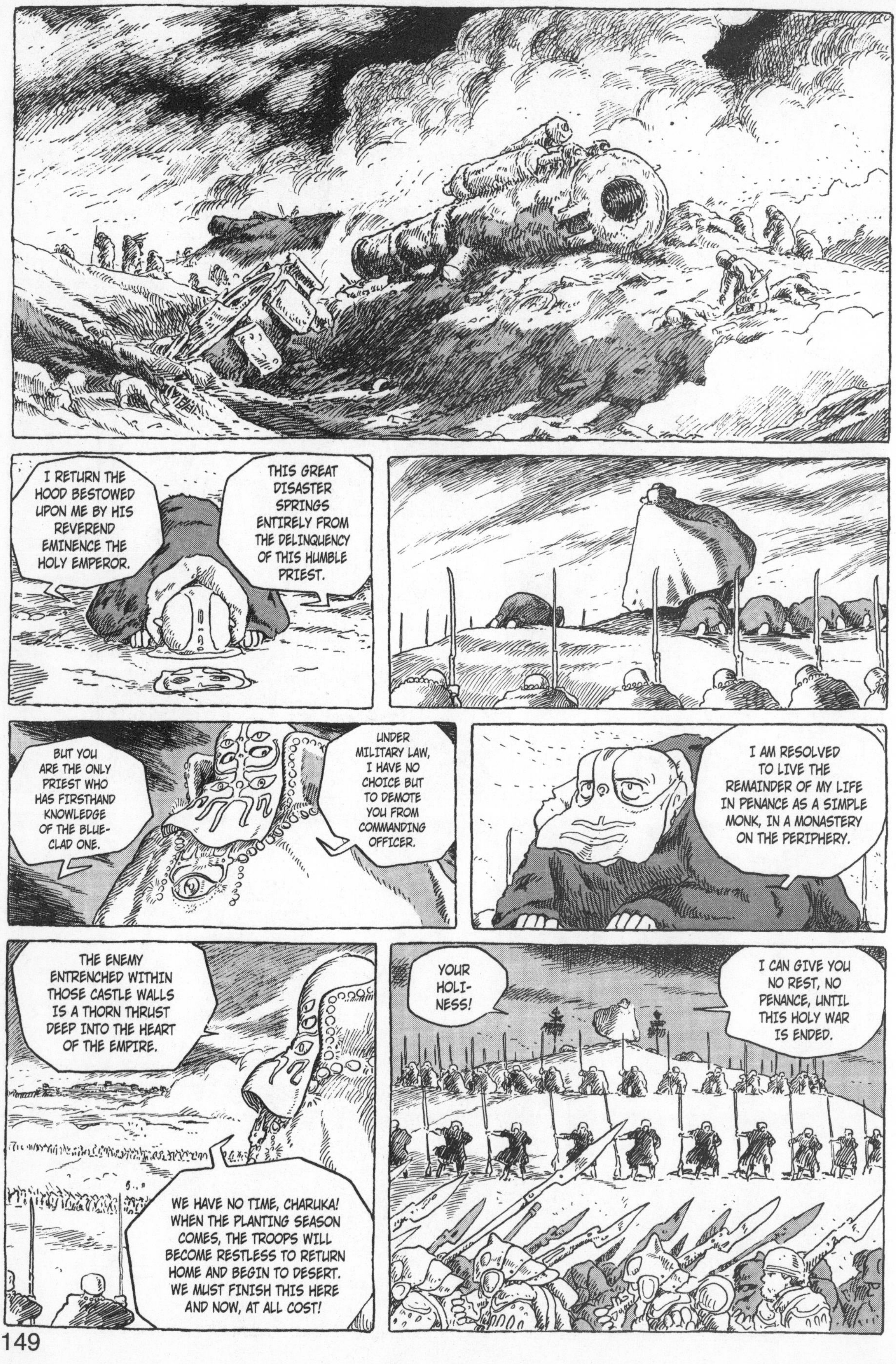
THIS GREAT DISASTER SPRINGS ENTIRELY FROM THE DELINQUENCY OF THIS HUMBLE PRIEST.
I RETURN THE HOOD BESTOWED UPON ME BY HIS REVEREND EMINENCE THE HOLY EMPEROR.
I AM RESOLVED TO LIVE THE REMAINDER OF MY LIFE IN PENANCE AS A SIMPLE MONK, IN A MONASTERY ON THE PERIPHERY.
UNDER MILITARY LAW, I HAVE NO CHOICE BUT TO DEMOTE YOU FROM COMMANDING OFFICER.
BUT YOU ARE THE ONLY PRIEST WHO HAS FIRSTHAND KNOWLEDGE OF THE BLUE-CLAD ONE.
I CAN GIVE YOU NO REST, NO PENANCE, UNTIL THIS HOLY WAR IS ENDED.
YOUR HOLINESS!
THE ENEMY ENTRENCHED WITHIN THOSE CASTLE WALLS IS A THORN THRUST DEEP INTO THE HEART OF THE EMPIRE.
WE HAVE NO TIME, CHARUKA! WHEN THE PLANTING SEASON COMES, THE TROOPS WILL BECOME RESTLESS TO RETURN HOME AND BEGIN TO DESERT. WE MUST FINISH THIS HERE AND NOW, AT ALL COST!

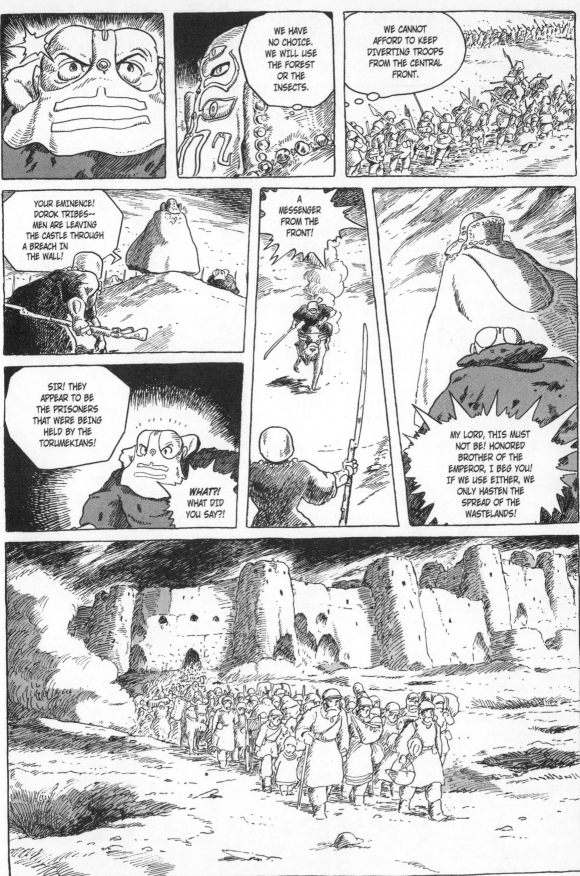

WE CANNOT AFFORD TO KEEP DIVERTING TROOPS FROM THE CENTRAL FRONT.
WE HAVE NO CHOICE. WE WILL USE THE FOREST OR THE INSECTS.
MY LORD, THIS MUST NOT BE! HONORED BROTHER OF THE EMPEROR, I BEG YOU! IF WE USE EITHER, WE ONLY HASTEN THE SPREAD OF THE WASTELANDS!
A MESSENGER FROM THE FRONT!
YOUR EMINENCE! DOROK TRIBES-- MEN ARE LEAVING THE CASTLE THROUGH A BREACH IN THE WALL!
SIR! THEY APPEAR TO BE THE PRISONERS THAT WERE BEING HELD BY THE TORUMEKIANS!
WHAT?! WHAT DID YOU SAY?!

Nausicaä of the Valley of the Wind Guide to Sound Effects

VIZ has left the sound effects in *Nausicaä of the Valley of the Wind* as Hayao Miyazaki originally created them — in Japanese. Use this glossary to decipher, page-by-page and panel-by-panel, what all those foreign words and background noises mean. The glossary lists the page number then panel. For example, 6.1 indicates page 6, panel 1.

Page.Panel		Effect
37.6	FX:	Mozo (shuffle)
38.1	FX:	Gushu gushu (gwosh slosh)
38.4	FX:	Zu (zwich)
38.6	FX:	Don (tump)
38.7	FX:	Zulu (zlifch)
38.8	FX:	Gigigi (geeeh)
39.1	FX:	Bibiin bibiin (bzzzz bzzzzz)
39.2	FX:	Viiii (bzzzzz)
39.3	FX:	Zawa zawa (rustle rustle)
39.3	FX:	Pita pita (pwip pwip)
39.4	FX:	Peta (stick)
39.8	FX:	Bibiiiiiin bibiiiiiin (bzzzz bzzzz)
40.2	FX:	Biiiiiiin (bzzzzz)
40.6	FX:	Gigi (gegeeh)
40.7	FX:	Ba (bwah)
40.8	FX:	Zaba (zwooosh)
41.1	FX:	Goso goso (shuffle shuffle)
42.2	FX:	Yoro (wobble)
42.4	FX:	Ba (rip)
42.6	FX:	Dou (dwooosh)
42.7	FX:	Shuuwa (shwooosh)
43.2	FX:	Ki (kree)
43.3	FX:	Ki (kree)
44.2	FX:	Uoooooon (wrooooom)
44.5	FX:	Ha (gasp)
44.7	FX:	Chi (tsk)
45.1	FX:	Ooooon (wroooom)
45.12	FX:	Suu suu (fshh fshh)
46.7	FX:	Gobo gobo (cough cough)
46.8	FX:	Wana wana (tremble tremble)
46.10	FX:	Ba (bwah)
46.11	FX:	Gobo gobo (cough cough)
47.1	FX:	Uiiiiin (wreeeeen)
47.4	FX:	Ooooo (wrooooo)
48.11	FX:	Kuku (choke)
49.2	FX:	Ki (kree)
49.4	FX:	Uooo (wrooooh)
49.5	FX:	Chuu chuu (shuch shuch)
49.8	FX:	Gubi (gulp)
49.9	FX:	Mogu (munch)
49.10	FX:	Vuvuvuvu (beep beep beep beep)
49.11	FX:	Uooooo (wroooh)
50.3	FX:	Gon gon gon (gwhum gwhum gwhum)
50.3	FX:	Goon goon goon (gwoon gwoon gwoon)
50.4	FX:	Golon golon golon (gwrom gwrom gwrom)
50.4	FX:	Goon goon goon (gwoon gwoon gwoon)
50.7	FX:	Oooon (wroooom)
51.1	FX:	Hiiii (hweeeeh)
51.2	FX:	Uoooon (wwoooom)
51.4	FX:	Goon goon goon goon goon (gwoon gwoon gwoon gwoon gwoon)
51.7	FX:	Zaaa (zshaaa)
52.3	FX:	Goooo (gwooh)
52.3	FX:	Za (zsh)
20.6	FX:	Baaaa (kaboom)
21.1	FX:	Uoooon (wrooooon)
21.2	FX:	Sa (swoosh)
21.4	FX:	Dododo (bwatata)
21.5	FX:	Gan bali gagaaan (gonk vwip gaboom)
21.6	FX:	Gyaaan (gywaaaan)
22.5	FX:	Ba (bwah)
22.7	FX:	Bau (bwooosh)
22.8	FX:	Shuuu (fwoooosh)
23.1	FX:	Goooo gooo (gwooh gwooh)
23.4	FX:	Bafu (bwof)
23.6	FX:	Pachi pachi (crackle crackle)
23.7	FX:	Goooo (gwooh)
23.7	FX:	Pachi pachi (crackle crackle)
24.1	FX:	Douuu (booom)
24.2	FX:	Baaaa (bwatata)
24.3	FX:	Dododo (bombombom)
24.4	FX:	Piku (twitch)
24.5	FX:	Tata (dash)
24.9	FX:	Ki (kree)
25.1	FX:	Goo goo (gwooh gwooh)
25.1	FX:	Buo (bwoosh)
25.2	FX:	Goho goho (cough cough)
25.4	FX:	Uooooon (vwrooom)
26.3	FX:	Fu (fwoh)
26.4	FX:	Goooo (gwooh)
26.5	FX:	Don don (bam bam)
26.10	FX:	Gali gali (grack grack)
27.1	FX:	Doka (crack)
27.2	FX:	Mowa (mwoof)
27.7	FX:	Po (boof)
28.5	FX:	Za (zash)
28.6	FX:	Gi (creak)
31.3	FX:	Mogu mogu (chew chew)
31.6	FX:	Chuu chuu (shuch shuch)
31.9	FX:	Tatata (dash)
32.1	FX:	Daan daan (bang bang)
32.11	FX:	Dou (dwom)
33.5	FX:	Saaa (shaaa)
33.6	FX:	Goho goho (cough cough)
33.7	FX:	Zei zei (wheeze rasp)
34.1	FX:	Ta (tump)
34.3	FX:	Gaaan (baaang)
34.4	FX:	Kachi kachi kachi (kachik kachik kachik)
34.6	FX:	Basu (bam)
34.7	FX:	Piiii (pweoooo)
34.8	FX:	Iiiin iiiin (eeeeeen eeeen)
35.1	FX:	Pita (freeze)
35.2	FX:	Ta (dash)
35.4	FX:	Solo solo (tiptoe tiptoe)
36.2	FX:	Gigigi (gggiiii)
36.5	FX:	Gili gili (gachh gachh)
37.3	FX:	Gyu gyu (ram ram)
37.4	FX:	Monyu monyu (mwunch mwunch)
3.1	FX:	Bolololo (bwrtttt)
3.3	FX:	Gan (gonk)
3.4	FX:	Doka (whack)
3.9	FX:	Kaaan (kooong)
4.2	FX:	Gasha (clang)
4.4	FX:	Oooo (wrrrmm)
4.7	FX:	Hyuuu (hwooosh)
5.2	FX:	Hyuuu (hwooosh)
5.4	FX:	Hyuuu (hwooosh)
5.10	FX:	Goooo (gwooh)
6.1	FX:	Hyuuu (hwooosh)
6.7	FX:	Mishi mishi (creak creak)
6.10	FX:	Goooo (gwooh)
7.4	FX:	Hyuuu (hwooosh)
7.5	FX:	Goooo (gwooh)
7.7	FX:	Bali bali (crackle crackle)
8.1	FX:	Gala gala (rumble rumble)
8.2	FX:	Ka (flash)
8.5	FX:	Baaaaaan (bwaaaaamm)
8.6	FX:	Gala gala (bam bam)
9.3	FX:	Paka (vzzt)
9.6	FX:	Katan (clink)
10.5	FX:	Dota dota (dum dum)
10.7	FX:	Shu shuu shuu (fshh fshh fshh)
10.7	FX:	Dokku dokku dokku doki dokku dokku dokku (ba-dump ba-dump ba-dump ba-dump ba-dump da-bump da-dump)
10.8	FX:	Dokku dokku (ba-dump ba-dump)
11.1	FX:	Goooo (gwooh)
11.6	FX:	Uoooooon (wrooooom)
11.8	FX:	Golon golon golon (gwrom gwrom gwrom)
12.1	FX:	Uooon (vwoooom)
12.2	FX:	Dou dou (boom boom)
12.5	FX:	Bau (bwak)
12.7	FX:	Guoooo (gwrooom)
13.1	FX:	Bo (boff)
13.3	FX:	Goon goon goon (gwum gwum gwum)
13.4	FX:	Uooon (vrooom)
15.4	FX:	Bata bata (fwap fwap)
15.10	FX:	Dosa (thud)
16.7	FX:	Piku (jolt)
17.5	FX:	Uoooo (wroooo)
17.6	FX:	Pon (plop)
17.7	FX:	Goooo (gwooh)
18.1	FX:	Uoooo (vwooooooo)
18.2	FX:	Saaa (sshhh)
18.3	FX:	Uoooo (vwooooh)
18.6	FX:	Ba (bwoosh)
19.1	FX:	Dododododo (bwatatata)
19.2	FX:	Goooo (gwooh)
19.4	FX:	Uoooo (wrooooh)
19.5	FX:	Chika chika (flash flash)
19.8	FX:	Giiiiin (gweeeeeen)
20.2	FX:	Bau (boom)
20.5	FX:	Dou (bawoom)

52.6——FX: Zazaa (zzshh)
53.4——FX: Ki (screech)
53.4——FX: Doka doka (thud thud)
53.5——FX: Datatata (dum dum dum)
53.7——FX: Batan (slam)
53.8——FX: Uoooo (bweeeep)
54.1——FX: Oooooo (fwoooooh)
54.3——FX: Ba (bwah)
54.4——FX: Buoooo (vwooooh)
54.6——FX: Doba (spew)
55.1——FX: Oooo (oooooom)
55.4——FX: Uoooon (wroooom)
55.7——FX: Da (dash)
56.1——FX: Shuu shuu shuu (fshh fshh fshh)
56.3——FX: Saaa (shaaaa)
56.5——FX: Saaa (shaaaa)
56.7——FX: Doo (dwom)
56.8——FX: Uoooon (wroooom)
57.3——FX: Ka (flash)
57.4——FX: Goon goon goon goon goon
(gwoom gwoom gwoom gwoom gwoom)
57.5——FX: Vueeee (vwooosh)
57.5——FX: Golon golon (rumble rumble)
57.7——FX: Zuzuuun zuuun (zzaboom zabooom)
58.1——FX: Dou (boom)
58.3——FX: Zugaaan (zagooom)
58.4——FX: Bishi doka bon (bwap crash booof)
58.5——FX: Zuzuun zuun zuzuun zuzuun
(zaboom zzzzboom zaboom zzzboom)
58.8——FX: Gyuuun (gweeen)
59.1——FX: Uoooooooon (vwroooooooom)
59.2——FX: Kiiii (vooshhh)
59.8——FX: Waaa waa waa waa waa (crowd yelling)
59.8——FX: Uoooo (wrooooon)
60.3——FX: Voooo (vwoooh)
60.5——FX: Chiin pishi ka (kachang piing konk)
60.6——FX: Oooo (wroooh)
61.6——FX: Dododo dodododo (dwatatata dwatatata)
61.7——FX: Bau (bwoosh)
61.7——FX: Goooo (gwooh)
62.2——FX: Zuun zuzuun zuzuun zuun zuzuun zuun
bababaaan (zaboom zzaboom zzaboom zabom
zabooom zaboom bwatatata)
62.3——FX: Uooo (wrooon)
62.3——FX: Zuzuuun (zabooom)
64.3——FX: Do (kaboom)
64.4——FX: Gaan gaan (bang bang)
64.5——FX: Uoooon (wrooon)
65.2——FX: Uooo (wroooh)
65.3——FX: Guuuun (gweeen)
65.4——FX: Ba (bwaft)
67.3——FX: Bi (vwip)
67.7——FX: Goon gooon (gwoom gwoom)
67.9——FX: Duooo (vwoooh)
68.1——FX: Zuzuuun (kaboom)
68.2——FX: Zuun zuuun (zaboom zzzaboom)
68.2——FX: Dooo (dwooosh)
68.3——FX: Bata bata (fwap fwap)
68.4——FX: Oooooooon (wroooooom)
68.5——FX: Uooooo (vwoooooosh)
69.2——FX: Dolodolodolodolo (dwam dwam dwam dwam)
69.2——FX: Zaaa (zshaa)
70.4——FX: Ba (bam)
70.8——FX: Gui (poke)
70.9——FX: Kiiin (claaang)

71.1——FX: Gan (gonk)
72.3——FX: Ki (kree)
72.3——FX: Een een (waaah waaah)
74.3——FX: Tsuuu (skritch)
75.1——FX: Gooon gooon (gwooom gwooom)
75.2——FX: Golon golon golon (gwrom gwrom gwrom)
76.9——FX: Hyulululu (hwoot tweeee)
77.1——FX: Hyulululululu (hwoootootle)
77.2——FX: Lululu hyuu (lulu hwoot)
77.5——FX: Tyuu (voosh)
77.6——FX: Suto (shtk)
79.1——FX: Suuu suuu (fshh fshh)
79.3——FX: Suu (fshh)
79.7——FX: Suu (fwash)
80.3——FX: Hita hita (hwut hwut)
80.4——FX: Yulaaa (wrooooh)
81.5——FX: Su (shaw)
82.4——FX: Nyuuu (nwoiiink)
83.9——FX: Vuoooo (vwoooooh)
83.10——FX: Uoooo (wroooh)
84.4——FX: Dolo dolo dolo dolo (dwam dwam dwam dwam)
85.4——FX: Dolodolodolo dolodolodolo
(dwamdwamdwam dwamdwamdwam)
85.4——FX: Dodon don (dom dom)
85.4——FX: Zuzuzun (dom dom)
85.5——FX: Dodon don dodon don
(do-dom dom do-dom dom)
85.5——FX: Kakakan kakakan (cl-cl-clack cl-cl-clack)
85.6——FX: Dodon don dodon don
(do-dom dom do-dom dom)
85.6——FX: Kakakan kakakan (kl-kl-klack kl-kl-klack)
85.7——FX: Dodon don (do-dom dom)
85.7——FX: Dolodolodolo dolo (dwamdwamdwam dwam)
85.7——FX: Kuwaan kuwawan kuwaaan
(gong gooong gooon)
86.2——FX: Dolodolodolodolo (dwamdwamdwamdwam)
86.2——FX: Dokodokodoko (domdomdomdom)
86.7——FX: Mogu mogu (munch munch)
86.8——FX: Ba (fling)
87.1——FX: Don don (dom dom)
87.2——FX: Don don (dom dom)
87.7——FX: Vuiiiiin (vweeeen)
88.1——FX: Vuiiii (vvweee)
88.1——FX: Vuilololo (vweerm brumble)
88.3——FX: Hyulululu (hwalsh)
88.10——FX: Shuuuu kobokobo (fshhhh glug glug)
88.11——FX: Shuuuu shuuu shuuu kobokobo
(fshhhh fshhh fshhh glug glug)
89.1——FX: Dokun dokun dokun (pump pump pump)
89.2——FX: Jyuuu (sizzle)
89.2——FX: Pichi (pop)
89.3——FX: Puchi puchi puchi (pwop pop pwop)
89.4——FX: Shuu shuu shuu (fshh fshh fshh)
89.10——FX: Gobogobogo (glug glug glug)
89.12——FX: Dododo (da-bo-booom)
89.13——FX: Zuuun gaan zuzuun (zaboom glank zaboom)
90.1——FX: Zuuun zuuun (zaboom zaboom)
90.2——FX: Uoooon (wwroooom)
90.3——FX: Gaaa (gshaaa)
90.4——FX: Ba (bwaf)
90.4——FX: Aaa (shaaa)
90.6——FX: Dadada (bwatata)
90.6——FX: Goooo (gwooh)
90.7——FX: Uoooo (wroooh)
90.8——FX: Oooooon (oooooohm)

91.2——FX: Zuzuun zuun (zaboom zaboom)
91.2——FX: Bali bali gaan dododo gaan
(bwatata gwoom boom boom boom)
91.3——FX: Wana wana (tremble tremble)
91.4——FX: Yoro yoro (wobble wobble)
91.7——FX: Zoon zozoon (zaboom zzaboom)
91.8——FX: Hyuuuun hyulululuuuuuu
(fwoooosh hwrrrrl rrrllllsh)
92.1——FX: Guwa (graboom)
92.2——FX: Daan zuuun ka zuzuun
(bang zuboom flash zuzboom)
92.5——FX: Zuuun (zaboom)
92.9——FX: Dobauu (dagshhh)
93.1——FX: Zuuuun (zagooom)
93.2——FX: Baki baki baki (bwak bwak crack)
93.3——FX: Douu (dagoom)
93.3——FX: Zuzuuu (zgggshh)
93.4——FX: Guwaan (graboom)
93.6——FX: Kaaan (claaank)
93.7——FX: Bou (bwooof)
93.7——FX: Hyulululu (hwrrrrl)
93.8——FX: Ba (splosh)
94.2——FX: Zuuun (zaboom)
94.5——FX: Dou (daboom)
94.6——FX: Goooo (gwooh)
94.9——FX: Gooo gooo (gwooh gwooh)
94.9——FX: Tata (dash)
95.2——FX: Kuwa (boom)
95.5——FX: Hyulululu (hwrrrl)
95.6——FX: Ka (flash)
95.7——FX: Guwa (graboom)
95.9——FX: Dolodolodolo (dwamdwamdwamdwam)
96.1——FX: Kila (glint)
96.4——FX: Gula (wobble)
96.5——FX: Hila hila (hwoosh hwoosh)
96.6——FX: Bala bala (rush rush)
96.6——FX: Waa (aah)
96.8——FX: Dada (dash)
96.9——FX: Ha (gasp)
96.9——FX: Zaza (zshha)
96.11——FX: Zuzuuun (zaboom)
98.2——FX: Zulu (drag)
98.3——FX: Gasha gashaan (crash craaash)
98.4——FX: Kalakalaan (clank clink)
99.1——FX: Solo (slink)
99.2——FX: Gu (grip)
99.3——FX: Tsu (prick)
100.6——FX: Yulaaa (waver)
101.1——FX: Zolo (zlurp)
101.9——FX: Kii (kreee)
101.11——FX: Kuuu (coooo)
104.8——FX: Za za za (zush zush zush)
105.2——FX: Jala (jlink)
105.4——FX: Jala (jlink)
105.12——FX: Sala sala (skritch skritch)
106.5——FX: Kyu (vwip)
108.7——FX: Douu dou dou dodo dou
(blam blam blam blam blam)
109.1——FX: Zuzuuun (zzzaboom)
109.2——FX: Kuwa kuwa zuuun ka dodoon
(kwah kwah zaboom flash kaboom)
109.3——FX: Dokaan (kaboom)
109.5——FX: Zuzuun zuun zuun
(zzzaboom zaboom zaboom)
109.6——FX: Zuzuun (zzaboom)

135.1 —FX: Zuuun douuun zuzuun
(zaboom boom zzzaboom)

135.3 —FX: Dolodolodolo (rumble rumble rumble)

135.4 —FX: Dododo (domdomdom)

135.5 —FX: Doo dolo dolo (dwam rumble rumble)

135.9 —FX: Dooo (dommm)

136.1 —FX: Doooo (dommm)

136.1 —FX: Chuun chuun (vwip vwip)

136.1 —FX: Bashi (blam)

136.2 —FX: Douuun (baaang)

137.1 —FX: Giiiin (ga-channng)

137.1 —FX: Zaa (zshaa)

137.5 —FX: Jakiiin (clang)

137.6 —FX: Zun (zash)

137.9 —FX: Za (thud)

138.3 —FX: Gaan gaan gaan (bang bang bang)

138.3 —FX: Chuun chiiin (ching chang)

138.4 —FX: Gaan gaan gaan (bang bang bang)

138.5 —FX: Chuun chuun chuun (chang chang chang)

138.5 —FX: Tataa (dash)

139.1 —FX: Do (thud)

139.5 —FX: Dododododo (domdomdom)

139.6 —FX: Zaza (zshha)

140.8 —FX: Gatsun (whack)

141.3 —FX: Fugyaaa (fwakeeeeaah)

141.3 —FX: Bali (scratch)

141.5 —FX: Suto (shtk)

141.9 —FX: Gacha (ga-chik)

141.10 —FX: Fuu (hiss)

142.2 —FX: Piku (twitch)

142.3 —FX: Byu (vwah)

142.4 —FX: Baki (bwack)

142.6 —FX: Kuwaa (kwaah)

143.1 —FX: Kuwaa (kwaah)

143.2 —FX: Doga (dwak)

143.2 —FX: Gueee (Gheeeh)

143.2 —FX: Waa waa (waah aaugh)

143.3 —FX: Ka (kick)

143.4 —FX: Boki gusha (crack crush)

143.7 —FX: Gaga (dash)

144.2 —FX: Daan (bang)

144.3 —FX: Gaan (bang)

144.5 —FX: Dododo (domdomdom)

144.6 —FX: Zuzuun zuun (zzzaboom zaboom)

144.6 —FX: Tatata (bwatata)

144.6 —FX: Dooo (dabooom)

144.7 —FX: Doooo (dommm)

145.4 —FX: Suta suta (stomp stomp)

147.2 —FX: Waa waa waa (yeaaah yeaah yeaaah)

147.4 —FX: Zu (zsh)

147.6 —FX: Kuu (coooo)

147.7 —FX: Dou (thud)

122.1 —FX: Bala bala (tunk tunk)

122.4 —FX: Zazaza (zshaaa)

122.5 —FX: Dadada (domdomdom)

122.7 —FX: Kiin basu doka (clang thwack dwuff)

122.8 —FX: Yoro (wobble)

123.1 —FX: Doooo (dwoooooh)

123.3 —FX: Zazsaza (zzshaa)

124.1 —FX: Daaan dadaan gaaan (bang ba-baang boom)

124.2 —FX: Dodo (domdom)

124.4 —FX: Da (dash)

125.3 —FX: Do (dom)

126.1 —FX: Pau (pow)

126.2 —FX: Piiii (pweeeee)

126.3 —FX: Iiiiiii (eeeeee)

126.6 —FX: Dodo (dwam dwam)

127.1 —FX: Gaaan gagaan (bang ba-bang)

127.1 —FX: Dodododo (domdomdom)

127.3 —FX: Pau (pow)

127.5 —FX: Za (zzshaa)

127.6 —FX: Chiin (kachak)

127.6 —FX: Pau (pow)

127.7 —FX: Iiii (eeee)

128.1 —FX: Pau (pow)

128.1 —FX: Piiii (pweeeeeh)

128.1 —FX: Iiiiiii (eeeeee)

128.2 —FX: Zaa (zzshaa)

128.5 —FX: Za (zshaa)

128.6 —FX: Shakiiin (sshklaang)

129.1 —FX: Dooo (dwammmm)

129.2 —FX: Iiiiiii (eeeeee)

129.3 —FX: Dodo (domdom)

129.5 —FX: Tan dadan (bang bang bang)

129.6 —FX: Pyuun pyuun shuun (pyiiing piing fwshh)

129.6 —FX: Dododo (domdomdom)

129.7 —FX: Bashi bishi piiin (vwip vwip piiing)

130.5 —FX: Kauu (glow)

130.6 —FX: Gaan gan gagann gaan (bang bang bang bang)

131.2 —FX: Doun gaan daan (boom bang bang)

131.3 —FX: Bashi bachi (bwap crack)

131.3 —FX: Chuu kiin chuun (kween vwoosh)

131.4 —FX: Do (dwup)

131.5 —FX: Gula (wobble)

131.8 —FX: Paan daan (baaang bang)

132.5 —FX: Bauuun (bwoom)

132.6 —FX: Kiin (kaang)

132.10 —FX: Gaaan gagaan (bang bang)

132.10 —FX: Doka dokan pishi (dagoom kaboom vwip)

132.10 —FX: Ba (vwah)

132.10 —FX: Ka (clank)

133.1 —FX: Pishi chi (chang clang)

133.2 —FX: Zaa (zshaa)

133.3 —FX: Doka bishi (dwak vwip)

133.4 —FX: Doba bishi (dwak vwak)

133.4 —FX: Kiiin (keeen)

133.6 —FX: Doka doka (dnk dnk)

133.8 —FX: Chii (chang)

134.2 —FX: Dooo (dommmm)

134.3 —FX: Shu (voosh)

134.4 —FX: Guwaan (kaboom)

134.6 —FX: Ha ha (huff huff)

134.8 —FX: Ha ha (huff huff)

134.9 —FX: Dododododo (domdomdomdomdom)

134.10 —FX: Zuun zuzuun (zaboom zaboom)

109.6 —FX: Bili bili (shudder shudder)

110.3 —FX: Gobo gobo (glub glub)

110.4 —FX: Gobo (glub)

110.8 —FX: Zuzuun (zzzaboom)

110.9 —FX: Zuzuun zuzuun zuun (zzaboom zaboom zaboo)

111.2 —FX: Do (booom)

111.3 —FX: Zuzuun (rrrrumble)

111.3 —FX: Bili bili bili (shudder shudder)

111.9 —FX: Shuu shu shulululu (fshhh fsh shwrrrrrlsh)

112.2 —FX: Waa waa (yaaay yeaaah)

112.2 —FX: Dodododo (domdomdom)

112.3 —FX: Dodododo (domdomdom)

112.4 —FX: Zuzuun doon zuun (zzaboom boom zaboom)

112.5 —FX: Dododododododo (domdomdomdomdom)

113.1 —FX: Sha (shwa)

113.2 —FX: Zaa (zshaaa)

113.3 —FX: Dan dan dan (boom boom boom)

113.4 —FX: Kaaaa kaa (kashooom kashoom)

113.4 —FX: Dodododo (domdomdom)

113.6 —FX: Dokaan (kaboom)

113.6 —FX: Ka (flash)

113.7 —FX: Zuuun (zaboom)

113.8 —FX: Guwaaaa (gaboommm)

113.9 —FX: Zuzuun dodoon (zzzaboom kaboom)

113.9 —FX: Dolodolodolodolo (rumble rumble rumble rumble)

114.1 —FX: Dodododo (domdomdom)

114.4 —FX: Dooo (dwoooh)

114.5 —FX: Za (zsha)

114.7 —FX: Gaaan (bang)

115.1 —FX: Zuzuun zuuun (zzaboom zaboom)

115.2 —FX: Zuzuun zuun (zzaboom zaboom)

115.5 —FX: Zuzuun zuun doon (zzaboom zaboom daboom)

115.8 —FX: Laaa laa (wraaaaagh yeaaaagh)

115.8 —FX: Dodododo (domdomdom)

116.1 —FX: Laaa laa (wraaaaagh yeaaaagh)

116.2 —FX: Gaaan (boom)

116.6 —FX: Guwaaan (gaboom)

116.10 —FX: Gagaga (gwipipip)

117.1 —FX: Guwa (gaboom)

117.2 —FX: Kiiin (shweee)

117.3 —FX: Dou (thud)

117.4 —FX: Bali bali (bwatata)

117.4 —FX: Hyuuun (hwooosh)

117.5 —FX: Paan pan pan ban pda
(pow pow pow bang bwatata)

117.7 —FX: Ka (flash)

117.8 —FX: Bau (boom)

117.8 —FX: Zazaa (zshaaa)

118.2 —FX: Kuwa (vwoosh)

118.3 —FX: Shuu (fshh)

118.5 —FX: Gaaan (bang)

118.6 —FX: Ka (flash)

118.7 —FX: Bouuun (kaboom)

119.1 —FX: Bali bali bali zuuun zuzuun dodoon
(bwatatata zaboom zzzaboom kaboom)

119.3 —FX: Dododo (domdomdom)

120.1 —FX: Dododo (domdomdom)

120.2 —FX: Do (dom)

120.9 —FX: Doooo (dommm)

121.3 —FX: Za (zash)

121.7 —FX: Shuu (fshhh)

121.8 —FX: Ka (flash)

121.9 —FX: Bou dogaan guwa guwa
(bwoof kaboom boom boom)